# THE
# BITTER PEACE

# THE
# BITTER PEACE

## CONFLICT IN CHINA 1928-37

### PHILIP S. JOWETT

AMBERLEY

To my family

First published 2017

Amberley Publishing
The Hill, Stroud,
Gloucestershire, GL5 4EP

www.amberley-books.com

ISBN 978 1 4456 5192 7 (hardback)
ISBN 978 1 4456 5193 4 (ebook)

British Library Cataloguing in Publication Data.
A catalogue record for this book is available from the British Library.

Maps by User Design.
Typesetting and Origination by Amberley Publishing.
Printed in Great Britain.

# CONTENTS

# ACKNOWLEDGEMENTS

This book would not have been possible without the support of many people over the years who have helped me with information and advice.

In particular I would like to thank Lennart Andersson, James Boyd, John Cloake and Paul. V. Walsh.

# Map 1, 1929–1931

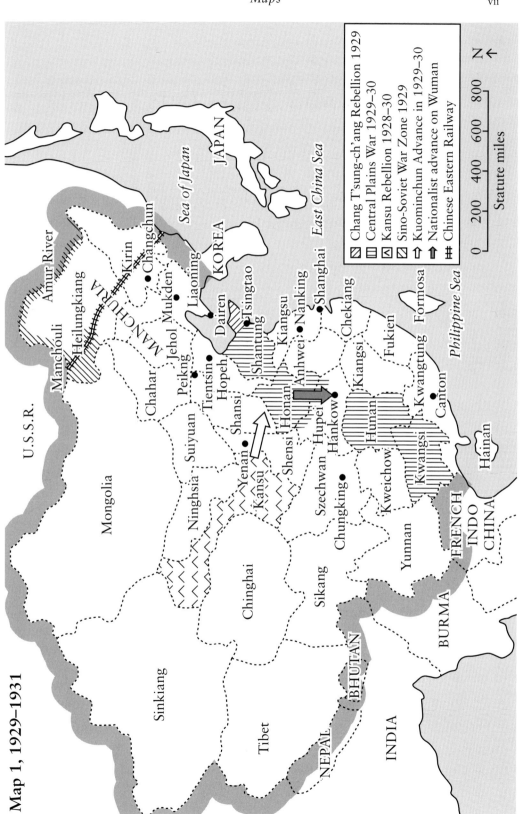

Chang T'sung-ch'ang Rebellion 1929
Central Plains War 1929–30
Kansu Rebellion 1928–30
Sino-Soviet War Zone 1929
Kuominchun Advance in 1929–30
Nationalist advance on Wuman
Chinese Eastern Railway

N

0   200   400   600   800
Statute miles

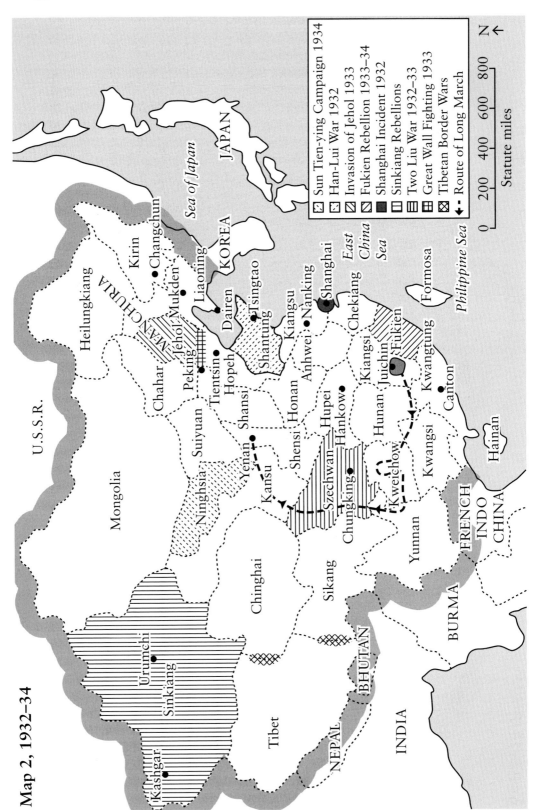

Map 2, 1932–34

Legend:
- Sun Tien-ying Campaign 1934
- Han-Lui War 1932
- Invasion of Jehol 1933
- Fukien Rebellion 1933–34
- Shanghai Incident 1932
- Sinkiang Rebellions
- Two Liu War 1932–33
- Great Wall Fighting 1933
- Tibetan Border Wars
- Route of Long March

0 200 400 600 800
Statute miles

# Map 3, 1935–37

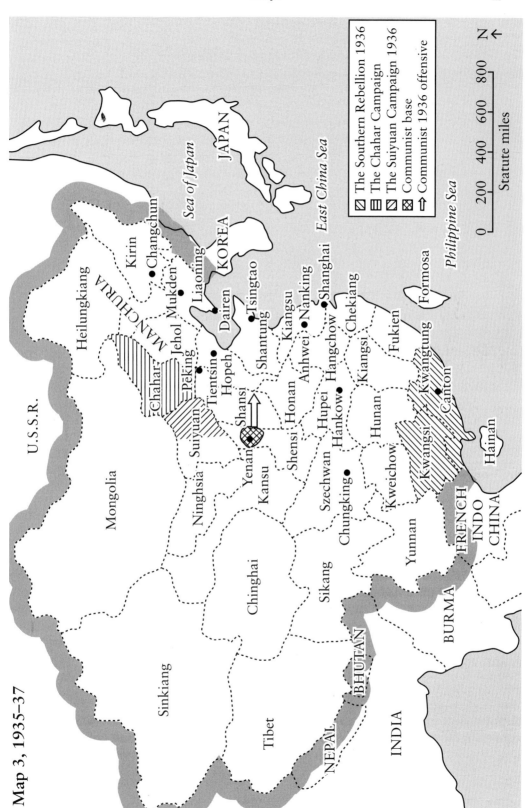

Legend:
- The Southern Rebellion 1936
- The Chahar Campaign
- The Suiyuan Campaign 1936
- Communist base
- Communist 1936 offensive

Statute miles
0 200 400 600 800

U.S.S.R.

MANCHURIA

Sea of Japan

JAPAN

KOREA

East China Sea

Philippine Sea

Mongolia

Sinkiang

Chinghai

Tibet

Sikang

Szechwan

Kansu

Shensi

Ninghsia

Suiyuan

Chahar

Jehol

Heilungkiang

Kirin

Changchun

Mukden

Liaoning

Peking

Tientsin

Hopeh

Shansi

Shantung

Honan

Anhwei

Hupei

Hunan

Kweichow

Yunnan

Kwangsi

Kwangtung

Kiangsi

Fukien

Chekiang

Kiangsu

Nanking

Hangchow

Shanghai

Tsingtao

Dairen

Hankow

Chungking

Canton

Hainan

Formosa

Yenan

BURMA

FRENCH INDO CHINA

INDIA

NEPAL

BHUTAN

# INTRODUCTION

China in 1928 had only recently emerged from a long period during which its people believed they were superior to their Asian neighbours. This institutionalised arrogance had locked Imperial China into a mindset that allowed European powers to exploit its real weaknesses. A series of foreign incursions into Chinese territory which began in 1840 and continued into the 20th Century left China at the mercy of Imperial Japan in 1894. The defeat of Imperial China in the Sino-Japanese War of 1894–95 and its humiliation during the Boxer Rebellion in 1900 showed the Qing Government's fatal weaknesses. The overthrow of the Qing Dynasty in 1911 gave the Chinese people the hope that they would see an improvement in their daily lives after centuries of corrupt Imperial rule. Under the rule of the Qing emperors from the 17th Century the ordinary people of China had suffered from neglect by uncaring Imperial officials. Any sign of dissent was met with imprisonment or execution, as Imperial rule depended largely on fear to control the people. This did not stop the numerous anti-Imperial rebellions that disturbed China throughout the 18th and 19th centuries. By the mid-1800s the level of rebellion had increased and the Qing Dynasty held on to power on several occasions by the narrowest of margins. The Taiping Rebellion in the 1860s cost several million lives as large areas of China were fought over by armies which were hundreds of thousands strong. Other rebellions sometimes only affected a single province but in a country as large and populous as China this often meant that it affected millions of people every time. Any conflict usually involved looting of property and the stealing of crops, which would then lead to widespread starvation. Most Chinese peasants anyway had a hand-to-mouth existence with survival from one harvest to another their main obsession. China had always suffered from droughts, floods and other natural disasters that made the day to day life of its people even more difficult. The consequent famines cost the lives of millions of people with little notice taken by the outside world. When the new Chinese Republic was born in 1912 it was not surprising that the people of China hoped that their lives would improve. Within a few months the leader of the new republic Sun Yat-sen – having found the task of ruling China beyond him – had been forced to resign. His place was taken by the last Commander-in-Chief of the Qing Army who was installed as President and then briefly in 1916 as Emperor.

Yuan Shi-kai's death in 1916 saw a period of even worse misrule in China with the start of the Warlord Era. This involved a series of weak governments in Peking which were totally ignored by the country's provincial military governors. Officially, these military governors were supposed to be the representatives of the

Peking Government in their province. Within a short time it emerged that the vast majority of them were going to rule their provinces as their own personal fiefdoms. They taxed the people of their provinces ruthlessly to pay the wages of their troops and to buy arms for their expanding armies. In their search for greater power these warlords often joined with others to form cliques which then went to war with other similar groups. This meant that warlord conflicts could involve armies approaching half a million men on each side. In 1920, 1922 and 1924, major conflicts took place between warring cliques whose aim was to install their own Peking Government. Important warlords like Wu Pei-fu, Chang Tso-lin and Feng Yu-hsiang formed alliances with each other. They then frequently betrayed each other and then formed new alliances with generals they had fought in the previous war.

China in the mid-1920s was split up into regional powers that controlled several provinces; with the Fengtien clique in the North, the Chihli clique in Central China and the Kuominchun in the north-west. Meanwhile in the South a new political force was developing which had ambitions to end the continuing chaos in China. The revolutionary Sun Yat-sen, after leaving office in 1912, had spent time in exile but by 1920 came back to China to try and defeat the warlords. Before his death in 1925 Sun had laid the foundations for a revolution which was to be led by a national revolutionary army. He realised that the ballot box was never going to bring more progressive politics to China and the warlords would continue to rule the country regardless of their people's wishes.

When Sun Yat-sen died he was replaced by a young officer called Chiang Kai-shek, who, although a loyal follower of the dead leader, had a more aggressive approach to China's problems. He would expand the recently formed National Revolutionary Army and turn it into a military force capable of defeating the warlords on the battlefield. It was obvious to Chiang that the only way to end the rule of the warlords was by force, not by reason. With a strong army behind him Chiang would advance from his base in southern China and march northwards into warlord territory. This so-called Northern Expedition would be an anti-warlord crusade which he hoped would gain the support of the long-suffering Chinese people. In 1926 he had built his National Revolutionary Army into a 100,000-strong force which would be capable of defeating one warlord army at a time. The northern warlords of China had on paper about 700,000 men under arms. Undaunted, Chiang's army advanced through the southern and central Chinese provinces defeating some warlords in detail. At the same time he used the age-old Chinese tactic of 'silver bullets', using monetary bribes and offers of command to get individual armies and commanders to change sides. In this he was helped by the fact that in China in the 1920s, troops' loyalty was to their commander. They did not really care who ran the government, they just cared who commanded them, fed them and paid them. So when Chiang bribed a general he was not just gaining his services, he was gaining the services of thousands of troops. In this way Chiang was able to expand his army over the two years of his campaign to almost a million men! By 1927 he had gained the support of Feng Yu-hsiang and Yen Hsi-shan, two of the most powerful northern warlords. He now had only to defeat the Armies of the

Ankuochun group, which was an alliance of all the remaining northern warlords. By mid-1928 the last of the major warlords, Chiang Tso-lin, had withdrawn with his army to Peking. There he was joined by the remaining warlord armies ready to fight the final battle for the 'Soul of China'. When Chang Tso-lin, the 'Manchurian Warlord', decided to withdraw into his Manchurian stronghold he was assassinated. In an ominous move, the Japanese Kwangtung Army leaders who had supported Chang in his war with Chiang had decided he was now 'surplus to requirements'. He had outlived his usefulness and the Japanese decided to get rid of him and try and take over the Manchurian provinces he had controlled. The death of Chang accelerated the demise of the Ankuochun and Chiang's allies entered Peking in June 1928.

Chiang Kai-shek was now acknowledged by the Chinese people and his army as the ruler of a new Nationalist China. With a new capital at Nanking in central China, the days of firm but corrupt Imperial and chaotic warlord rule were now thought to be over. However, the long hoped-for peace which Chiang's rule could have brought to China was fated to be short-lived. The China that Chiang now attempted to rule was blighted by poverty, banditry, famine and underdevelopment. Being poor and sick in China in 1928 was a death sentence with any medical care reserved for the rich and a very few working people. In 1930 there were 30,000 official hospital beds for 400,000,000 people; that's 15,000 people per hospital bed. Millions of Chinese peasants were forced out of their homes by poverty and hunger, going to work in the country's big cities.

Famines had periodically hit China throughout the 1920s with one bad harvest causing widespread starvation. People were reduced to eating sawdust, flour made from leaves and ground stones, thistles, tree bark and roots. Sometimes famines were caused by a plague of locusts or other natural phenomena like heavy frosts or hailstorms. It was rare that these famines made the world news and they had to be on a large scale to get anywhere near the front page. One famine that did get some notice was the 1928–1930 Kansu famine, which covered that province and parts of Henan and Shansi provinces. A total of 3 million people died, 2 million in Kansu province alone. Some turned to cannibalism in desperation. In 1929 there were over 57,000,000 people affected in some way by famine throughout China. Unless people decided to lay down and die where they were, the only solution to a local famine was to leave. This meant moving to one of the big cities and trying to get work, usually hard labour, while already malnourished. In 1933 there were an estimated 65,000,000 homeless people in China and this was after five years of Nationalist rule.

Banditry plagued China into the 1930s with ex-soldiers making up the majority of the outlaws. When a Chinese soldier left the army he was usually cut off from his family who had often given him up as dead. If his commander had taken him out of his home province during a campaign it was often impossible for him to return home anyway. It was hardly surprising then that many former soldiers turned to banditry; which was itself often a way back into the army. When a Chinese commander was looking to expand his arm, local bandit groups were often a ready-made source of recruits. Although this recruitment policy had been banned with the victory of Chiang, like other instructions by the

Nationalist leader it was largely ignored. Although at times during Nationalist rule the army did recruit, it was not until 1937 that this soaked up any significant number of redundant soldiers. Most provinces had endemic banditry; there were for instance 100,000 bandits active in Henan province in 1931. By 1930 owing to the continuous fighting in China in the previous decade the number of bandits in China had reached an astounding 500,000 men. They were organised into bands of from 100 up to 10,000 people, with women joining as well. Large bandit armies even laid siege to Nationalist-held towns in the early 1930s as the countryside in some parts of China became uncontrollable. Although not a political threat to Chiang, the large numbers of bandits just made fighting his real enemies like the Communists much harder.

Opium was another blight on early 20th century China with millions of its people addicted to the drug. As well as civilans, thousands of China's troops were opium addicts in the 1920s. In some southern provinces like Yunnan and Kweichow the vast majority of soldiers were addicts and often received the drug instead of, or as part of, their pay. Some with untreated wounds took opium as a pain killer when no other medicine was available. The drug was often a warlord's main source of income and they sold it directly or taxed those who transported it through their provinces. In the 1920s many warlords had organised opium suppression campaigns which made great play of ending the trade. No one was fooled by piles of burning opium when the drug was being traded with the tacit permission of the provincial governors. Numerous wars in the 1920s and continuing into the early 1930s were fought over territory where opium was transported. The Kwangsi clique in the early 1930s was caught bringing huge amounts of the drug into Shanghai. They were no more than annoyed when this was discovered and the drugs were whisked away into the city before the authorities could react. Money from his particular deal had been earmarked to pay for the Kwangsi Army's latest arms shipment. In 1933 the 10th Nationalist Army was sent to Changsha, the capital of Hunan province, to fight the Communists. Its commander General Hsu Yuan-ch'uan spent most of the time his army was stationed there trying to buy opium from Western Hunan to sell in Changsha and in the city of Hankow. In reality, the importance of opium to the Chinese economy meant that even under Chiang's strict rules there was no way to control the trade in the 1930s. It was not surprising when some Nationalist generals turned to opium to raise money when they received no money from the central government.

The other main source of income for the warlords of the 1920s and the Nationalist militarists of the 1930s was of course taxation. Even in times of famine or while a province was involved in a conflict the generals collected taxes. Apart from standard types of taxes on land ownership there was a whole host of inventive taxes. These could be imposed for the birth of a child, getting married, owning a pig and going to a brothel. Taxes were even imposed on peasants who didn't grow opium, which was described at the 'laziness tax'. Land taxes were the most lucrative and would often be collected years in advance when a general was short of funds. The claiming of taxes years in advance had been a feature of China during the 1920s and this abuse was to continue into the 1930s. In 1932

General Liu Wen-hui of Szechwan was collecting taxes 25 years in advance in an effort to pay for his war. The commander of the 29th Army, General Tien Sung-yao was collecting his taxes 28 years in advance while General Teng Hsi-hou the commander of the 28th Army collected them 40 years in advance; but he doesn't win the laurels in the tax race. By 1934 the 29th Army was claiming taxes 66 years in advance and the 28th Army a staggering 74 years ahead of their due date.

The depredations suffered by the ordinary Chinese are illustrated by the story of the city of Changteh in Hunan province in the year 1929. Author Hallett Abend tells the sorry tale:

Today most of the people of Changteh are nearly destitute and the surrounding countryside is overrun with bandit gangs. Five successive generals held successive sway in Changteh during 1929, and each of them levied his own 'annual taxes' and blandly ignored the tax receipts given by his predecessors. Early in 1929 General Tan Tao-yuan, who had been well liked by the people, moved up the river to fight General Li Tsung-jen. Before he evacuated the city, however he levied the customary tribute, in order to pay arrears to troops.

During his absence General Chao Tuh-pien, formerly a highly successful bandit leader but now become respectable, moved in and took over the 'protection' of Changteh. He at once demanded $250,000 in silver coin, declaring that his troops had not been paid for many months, and that if this sum were not forthcoming he would be unable to control his men and they might loot the city. Soon after the money was paid over General Chao's army marched out, but at once General Li Yuen-chieh's army marched in. This angered the two preceding ruling generals, Tan and Chao, so they combined forces and laid siege to Changteh. After a fortnight's siege, General Chao's men made a breach in the walls, captured the city, and 'looted every home and shop' according to Chinese reports. They made off to the mountains taking with them hundreds of tons of merchandise, more than $1,000,000 in cash, about 80 women and girls who have never been heard of since, and 30 wealthy men who were held for ransom. Early in July of 1929 General Wu Shang's army took over the city without bloodshed. The troops were clean, orderly, well uniformed, and seemed well disciplined. But soon dissension broke out amongst the junior officers of this army. A mutiny seemed likely, so General Wu fled secretly, taking with him his new concubine and considerable treasure which had been wrung from the citizens as taxes'. Next in succession was General Wang Pei, and there seemed promise of quiet and security, but within a fortnight he was murdered by his own mutinous troops, and Changteh seemed to face the uncertainty of a new looting. At this critical juncture General Tai Tao-yun arrived with his army, and since then order has been well maintained. But of course General Tai's men must be paid, so new taxes have been levied to appease the city's new defenders. (Hallet Abend, *Tortured China*, pp. 75–77)

Despite all the problems that Chiang and China faced in 1928 and 1929 he and his supporters really did have a vision of how a modern China should be. They wanted the country to be strong and able to defend itself against foreign aggressors and to have a modern infrastructure. The idealism that the new rulers of China had in the late 1920s was soon to be frustrated by the reality. The Northern Expedition had cost the country and its Nationalist Government millions and they now had an oversized army of 1,700,000 troops on their hands. It was common sense that now China was at peace its large army should be reduced drastically. Unfortunately the National Revolutionary Army was a composite force which, although officially a single army, in reality was made up of the armies of several ex-warlords who had little loyalty to Chiang. They had no intention of losing troops from their armies and Chiang's insistence that they do so would lead to the first conflict of the post-warlord era. The dreams of ordinary Chinese for a new beginning would have to wait while the old problems of disunity tore the country apart for the next nine years.

# 1

# 'CHIANG'S SWORD', 1928–1937

When Chiang Kai-shek and his National Revolutionary Army won its final victories against the northern warlords in 1928 he immediately faced a new challenge. He had to try and wield a new National Army for China out of the disunited and disorganised NRA. This new Nationalist Army would have to face a myriad of rebellions, civil war and invasions over the next turbulent decade. From a numerically large army backed up by a few aircraft and a handful of ships he had to try and create modern armed forces. The challenge was not made any easier by the fact that China after 17 years of continuous wars was bankrupt. Rebellions broke out almost immediately after he took power. His obsession with the growing threat of Communism only served to push him harder to build a powerful sword to smite them with.

If the Nationalist Party which he led was to unite all the diverse provinces of China into a modern state, he knew it would have to be done by force. Only when all his enemies were defeated could he hope to lead a truly united China as a power in Asia in the 20th Century.

## The National Revolutionary Army, 1926–1929

Formed in the early 1920s the National Revolutionary Army was originally the military wing of the Nationalist Kuomintang Party. The Kuomintang had been formed by revolutionary Sun Yat-sen to try and overthrow the Qing Dynasty. This was achieved in 1911 but within a few years, as described, the new Republic was a shambles with the country controlled by regional warlords. After Sun's death in 1925 his less revolutionary protégé Chiang Kai-shek took charge of the Kuomintang and the NRA. He soon decided that the only way to unify China and defeat the regional warlords was by military force. The opening of a military academy at Whampoa at Canton in Kwangtung province in the early 1920s meant that a new class of highly politicised officers was now trained. At the start of the Northern Expedition in 1926 the National Revolutionary Army had a strength of 100,000 men. The men who made up this early NRA were mainly from the southern provinces of China with a hard core having been trained by Soviet Advisors at Whampoa. As they advanced northwards the NRA was joined by new volunteers and by the defeated soldiers of warlord armies Within five months this force had grown to a strong army of 264,000 troops formed into 200 regiments. Unfortunately, the rapid grown of the NRA had been achieved by taking in individual soldiers and whole armies formerly under the command of

Chiang Kai-shek, the Generalissimo of Nationalist China, dominated the country from his elevation to Commander of the National Revolutionary Army in 1925 until 1949. Chiang spent all of his political and military career fighting rebellions against his rule and was a great survivor. Even when finally defeated by the Communists in the Chinese Civil War in 1946–49 he did not give in. He could have gone into a comfortable exile but instead he established an anti-Communist base on the island of Taiwan.

warlords. In February 1928 the National Revolutionary Army was reorganised into four Group Armies after the absorption of large warlord armies. These included the Kuominchun or People's Army of General Feng Yu-hsiang and the Army of Shansi under General Yen Hsi-shan. The 1st Group Army was made up of the original National Revolutionary Army formed in 1924. A 2nd Group Army had been formed out of the divisions of Feng Yu-hsiang and the 3rd Group Army was organised from the Shansi Army. The 4th Group Army was made up exclusively of divisions of the Kwangsi Army from south-west China.

At the end of the Northern Expedition the National Revolutionary Army had reached a strength of 1,620,000 men. This was made up in 1929 of the 1st Group Army under Chiang Kai-shek's direct command with 240,000 men. Feng Yu-hsiang's Kuominchun made up the 2nd Group Army with 220,000 men and Yen Hsi-shan's 200,000 men made up the 3rd Group Army. The 4th Group Army was made up of Kwangsi troops with a strength of 230,000 men and Chang Hsueh-liang's former Fengtien army which had a strength of between 190,000–250,000 men. Some estimates of Chang's Army reached almost 400,000 men but this is almost certainly an over-estimation based on Fengtien propaganda. Troops from Yunnan province totalled 30,000 men and the rest of the southern provinces contributed 540,000 to this total. Out of the southern total about 300,000 are supposed to have belonged to the various warlords of Szechwan province. This huge and unwieldy army was really a loose grouping of armies with varying degrees of loyalty to Chiang and the Nationalist Government. Even if every single soldier and commander had been loyal to him, Chiang knew that the NRA was simply unaffordable. In order to modernise, the NRA would have to be made much smaller and this would mean the demobilisation of hundreds of thousands of troops.

## National Army Demobilisation, 1929

China simply could not maintain a united army totalling several million troops. The new Nationalist Army had to be drastically reduced to make it a viable force for the country to finance. The main problem in any reduction plan for the NRA was that many Nationalist commanders were 'unreformed' warlords. To retain power a warlord needed his own army loyal to him and his officers and any reduction in numbers weakened their hold on their province or district. On the 1st of January 1929 the Demobilisation Conference met in Nanking to try and iron out a fair reduction in the size of the National Army. It was attended by a large number of military and political leaders from all over China. These included Chiang Kai-shek, General Yen Hsi-shan, the 'Shansi Warlord', General Feng Yu-hsiang, 'The Christian Warlord', and General Li Tsung-jen, one of the Kwangsi leaders. Chiang Kai-shek was appointed the chairman of the conference and each of the most prominent generals was given a specific task to perform. Lasting for three weeks the conference did officially iron out some of the problems but the main item on the agenda was not resolved. Another meeting was held in August to finalise the arrangements for demobilisation of most of the Nationalist Army. This meeting was not well attended by the military leaders; not a good omen for any lasting agreement. It was decided nevertheless that China should be divided into six regions, with five of them incorporating the territory of one of the pre-1928 major warlords. The sixth region covered the territories of minor warlords and included the provinces of Szechwan, Kweichow and Yunnan. It also specified that the new National Army would be limited to 65 divisions of 11,000 men each. According to the 'National Military Re-organisation and Disbandment Committee' the total strength of the main Chinese armies in 1929 was 1,502,000. The armies were divided into the 1st Army Group with 224,000 men, 2nd Army Group with 269,000 men, 3rd Army Group with 206,000 men, 4th Army Group with 287,000. In the various Szechwan Armies there was a reported 200,000 men and the Yunnan Army had 70,000 while the Kweichow provincial forces had 60,000. Total Manchurian armies were officially 186,000 men with 109,000 in Fengtien, 53,000 in Kirin province and 24,000 in Heilungkiang province.

Not without some justification, Chiang's rivals like Feng Yu-hsiang and Yen Hsi-yen argued that this planned demobilisation was an opportunity for Chiang to emasculate their armies. There was opposition to the demobilisation from within Chiang Kai-shek's inner circle as it was going to be extremely expensive. Chiang's Finance Minister, T.V. Soong resigned his post as he said he could not find the finances to pay for it. In reality the demobilisation was never going to take place voluntarily and it was to take several conflicts in 1929 and 1930 to bring it about. Even after almost two years of civil conflict there were still many generals who refused to comply with Chiang's instructions. The lack of unity in the Chinese military was never going to be solved simply by reducing the size of the generals' armies. Only the final victory of the Communists at the end of the Chinese Civil War in 1949 was to end the provincial mentality of the Nationalist Army.

## The Chinese Soldier, 1928–1937

There was no such thing as an average Nationalist soldier during the 1928 to 1937 period. Some were nothing better than uniformed bandits. Others were highly disciplined and patriotic men who were willing to sacrifice their lives for China. Just as it is impossible to describe the average Chinese army of the period it is also impossible to say what the average soldier was like. The Chinese system did not exactly help create the right type of soldier. They were so often mistreated by the state and their commander. Soldiers were often unfed, badly clothed, seldom paid and when ill went untreated, so it is not surprising that many turned into 'Bad Iron'. This was the term used by most of the long-suffering Chinese population, who quoted the proverb, 'Good iron does not make nails, good men do not make soldiers.' Besides their own countrymen's poor opinion of them, soldiers also faced the patronising attitude of foreign commentators.

Ragged troops of the National Revolutionary Army march into another northern city taken from the northern warlords in 1928. Although they do not look particularly martial, these men had defeated by bravery and with rare discipline better armed enemies. Officers of this army would go on to spend all their careers fighting in a large number of conflicts. Some of these soldiers had not seen their homes for several years and many would never return to them as they continued to fight in the 1930s.

One 1933 article by an American, Mr O.D. Rasmursen, sums up the racist attitude of many westerners to the Chinese Army and in particular to its poor other ranks.

The Chinese soldier is of inferior material to the Japanese, although as a result of the state of civil war which prevailed in China from 1915 until 1927 a large number of Chinese have seen active service. The qualities of a Chinese soldier are inherent in himself as a representative of the class from which he is drawn. He still views war as not so much as a science but as a noisy device to overawe his enemies. He believes that a fierce manifestation of prowess, wrath and loud explosions should 'put the wind up' his adversaries, and if they do not at once flee the neighbourhood he suspects his own talents as a showman and redoubles his demonstration.

Mr Rasmursen does at least express some grudging admiration for the steadfastness of the Chinese soldier: 'He is fearless to a degree of recklessness, stubborn when cornered, and amazingly indifferent to hardship and pain.' The praise doesn't last long:

In open fighting he thinks too much. He is apt to consider discretion the better part of valour, regardless of orders. His retreat is not necessarily a panic or a mutiny, unless taken so by his superior officers ... If on the winning side, he is not anxious to follow up a beaten foe, unless driven, one victory a day fulfils his obligations.

He ends the article with a passage which shows how little he actually knew about the Chinese soldier: 'Before Chiang Kai-shek whipped his men into some kind of semblance of a fighting machine, Chinese soldiers would not fight in the rain. They might be induced to march in it, but only if provided with umbrellas. The pack of each man contained an oil paper gingham and it was a common sight at one time to see regiments on the road with every man holding an umbrella over his head.'

In 1932 a report on the Chinese Army emphasised the continuing warlord system operating within the Nationalist framework. As O.D. Green says, many Chinese soldiers in the late 1920s early 1930s were 'mere uniformed coolies – peasants attracted by the prospects of £1.00 a month, usually months in arrears, food and lodgings at least and possibility of loot. These men drift from side to side with the varying fortunes of their leaders. When a Chinese general collapses and retires abroad it is etiquette for him to write asking his opponent to take charge of his troops.'

An interview with a soldier in 1938, in this case a woman soldier called Miss Yao Jui-fang, does not fit this sorry description. Miss Yao had been fighting the Japanese since 1931. As a 14-year-old she joined the volunteer army of Ma Chan-shan in Manchuria. She took part in the Battle for the Nonnni River in November 1931 before being sent to fight in the defence of Jehol in 1933. Most of her time in Manchuria and Jehol was spent going backwards and forwards along the Great Wall carrying messages between the various Chinese armies. While acting as courier she had training as an officer and fought in Chahar in 1934 in the secret war there. Her last major battle was in Shanghai in 1937 where she was in the support role and a year later she was still fighting the invader as a veteran 20-year-old.

## Nationalist Army Strength and the 1928–1932 Nationalist Army Division

Despite the attempts to reduce the size and increase the quality of Nationalist Army units it was still too large for purpose in the early 1930s. According to the 1933–34 League of Nations report, the strength of the Chinese Army in December 1933 was 1,316,580 men. The Army was made up of 134 infantry divisions, 33 independent infantry brigades, 6 independent infantry regiments, 8 cavalry divisions and 14 independent cavalry brigades. Other units included 4 brigades, 19 regiments and 9 companies of artillery and 9,000 Military Police in 5 regiments. This large army was basically an infantry force with little artillery and few up-to-date weapons. The cavalry divisions in the order of battle had 48,000 men and the 14 Brigades 28,000 men. On the eve of the war with Japan the Nationalist Army stood at 1,700,000 regulars and 518,400 reserves (see chapter 15).

In the aftermath of the Northern Expedition Chiang Kai-shek decided to try and standardise his National Revolutionary Army into regular divisions. The plan was to have two types of division, 'A' and 'B', with the first having 12,525 men and the second 8,943. Type A divisions had two brigades with three regiments each and Type B divisions had three brigades with two regiments each. Chiang was not happy with this new arrangement and decided in the midst of civil conflict to complicate matters by converting all Type A divisions into B divisions. The Type C division was now introduced, which was almost identical to the Type B to add to the complexity. By 1930, 100 dvisions had been converted to the B or C divisional organisation. The armies outside the control of Chiang's government in Nanking not surprisingly did not comply with his plans. The included the armies of Szechwan, Kweichow, as well as those in Kansu and other north-western provinces. In addition the North-Eastern Army of Chang Hsueh-liang had yet to change any of its organisation and it was unlikely that it would. With the turmoil that was going on in China at the time it is amazing that *any* divisions were adjusted, especially when it meant some officers losing troops. Another change came in officially in 1932 with the introduction of yet another type of division. Although it kept the same two-brigade system as before, each brigade was now 4,949 strong. Each 1932 type division now had 13,502 men and its artillery element had increased from a 642-strong battalion to a 1,667-strong regiment. Again, it would be interesting to know how many divisions were actually converted from B or C structure to the new 1932 version. It was probably only the armies under the closest control of Chiang that even attempted to alter their organisation.

Nationalist troops march towards the front during the build-up to the Jehol Campaign of early 1933. This photograph shows typical soldiers of northern China in the late 1920s and early 1930s. They wear various styles of peaked cap, which would soon be phased out of service with the Nationalist Army. The men carry all their kit and one soldier at the front of the column has an umbrella strapped to his back.

After the failure of the first Extermination Campaigns against the Communists it was decided to reorganise some aspects of the Nationalist Army in 1933. It was intended that this new divisional structure should only be used for units that were fighting the Communists in Kiangsi. Divisions were found to be too top heavy with too many headquarters staff. To try and address this the headquarters staff at the brigade level were got rid of so that regiments were now responsible to divisional level staff officers. At the same time, the frontline units were brought up to strength and the number of regiments per division was now flexible. This meant that some divisions had three regiments while others when necessary had five. Regiments had three battalions with each battalion having three companies as well as a machine gun company. Infantry companies had three platoons made up of three squads with each squad have thirteen privates and a squad leader. Every attempt was made to make sure that these 'Chaio-Fei' divisions received up to date rifles and machine guns. It was also stipulated that 'every combatant had a rifle and every officer had a pistol and the machine gun company had four Maxim machine guns. All divisions whenever possible had the correct number of support units with artillery, engineers, signals and transportation companies. Despite these improvements the new divisions still had many inbuilt weaknesses. It was noted that artillery often had to be left behind at HQ during operations due to lack of draft animals. The divisions which were named as being reorganised along the 'Chaio-Fei' line were the 3rd to 6th, 8th, 10th, 11th, 14th, 24th, 27th, 43rd, 46th, 59th, 67th, 79th, 83rd, 87th to 90th, 92nd to 94th and the 97th to 99th Division.

The last reorganisation of the Nationalist division took place in the year leading up to the outbreak of the Sino-Japanese War. This 1937 division was really introduced in 1936 as the reorganised division was to be the model for all of the Nationalist Army during the first years of the war with Japan. It had 10,923 officers and men made up of two Brigades of 4,949 each and had 247 light machine guns, 54 heavy machine guns and 30 81mm mortars. The Artillery Battalion had 16 howitzers or field guns crewed by 502 with 23 officers. Only 10 divisions had been organised to this standard by July when the war with Japan started. It was also doubtful if many divisions reached the official strengths when it came to mortars and the 243 grenade launchers per division was sheer fantasy. If there were any grenade launchers in service with the Chinese in 1937 they were a locally produced type. These were similar to the famous knee mortar used by the Imperial Japanese Army.

## The Chinese Nationalist Militia, 1928–1937

In the early years of the Nationalist Government there were attempts to improve the corrupt militia system that had been in place for many years in China. Before 1928 any militia in China were recruited on a local basis usually by magistrates or the local landlord. They were basically private armies of the ruling class and were used by them to keep the peasants in line, often with brutality. The first attempt to reform the militia system began in 1928 with an edict calling for the establishment of stronger official control over the existing 'Household Conscription Militia'. They were to be controlled by a unified 'bureau' led by the local magistrate who was assisted by so-called Vice Heads. These Vice Heads were selected from amongst the local elite, which led to the usual nepotism that had dogged the earlier militia. All existing full-time militias were to be reorganised into a two-tier system with the first tier known as the 'Standing Companies' or 'Changbeidui'. At the same time 1 in every 3 males under the age of 40 was to be recruited into the second tier – unpaid militia known as the 'Watch Patrols' or 'Shouwangdui'.

To keep a close connection between the two tiers of the militia select men from the Watch Patrols were to serve for three years in Standing Companies. The first problem with the new system was that not enough magistrates were coming forward to raise militia units. Their duty was more often than not performed by their Vice Heads, who were in many cases the same men who had abused their positions under the old system. The fact that too few Watch Patrols were being raised meant that in turn the Standing Companies were short of volunteers. They were supposed to rely on the better candidates from the Watch Patrols transferring to the first tier militia after showing promise in the second tier. so the new militia units were as bad as the old ones but with a different title.

The Standing Companies that were raised were found to be operating on their own without any co-operation with neighbouring units. This meant that they were often outnumbered when they came up against bandits or Communists. In

Nationalist amphibious tanks line up while on exercise in the mid-1930s with the white sun insignia of the Kuomintang on their turrets. These are Carden-Loyd M1931 light tanks with wooden floats which were purchased by the Nationalist Army in the mid-1930s. Modern weaponry like these tanks was never bought in enough numbers to make a difference and was lost amongst the millions of infantrymen.

1930 another reform was introduced to answer this problem. Firstly all Standing Companies in one county were to be consolidated into a single so-called 'Peace Preservation' unit of a battalion – Bao'an-tuan – or regiment – Bao'an-dadui. These new types of militia were to be professionalised by receiving proper military training and by instilling regular army discipline and esprit-de-corps. Magistrates would no longer be in charge and the Peace Preservation units would from now on be commanded by ex-officers or by civilians with a military education. The officers were to be appointed by a 'Rural Pacification' Commander who had no local loyalties. In 1933 the Peace Preservation Corps was further professionalised by the amalgamation of county units into approximately 24 regiments. These large units were attached to multi-county Peace Preservation Districts which meant that much larger forces could be put into the field. At the same time the second tier Watch Patrols were reorganised with every male between the ages of 18 and 45 liable for service. This on paper created a force three times stronger than under the 1 man in 3 system previously used. As this force was reformed at the height of the anti-communist campaigns these new units were re-designated as 'Communist Extermination Volunteer Corps'. All members of the CEVC units were to attend three half-day training sessions a month, which usually entailed a lot of drill and little practical military tuition.

## Nationalist Army Officer Training

The Whampoa Military Academy at Canton was staffed by a few Soviet military advisors who worked alongside chosen Chinese officers to give the training to officer cadets. Its first class in 1924 had 645 students selected from 3,000 applicants who came from higher class backgrounds. By January 1926, 5,540 cadets had graduated from the Academy and these formed the officer corps of the National Revolutionary Army. Heavy casualties suffered by the cadet officers during the Northern Expedition from 1926 to 1928 were hard to replace. 2,600 of the cadets had died during the campaign, often leading their men from the front. When the NRA took Nanking, which had been chosen as the new capital of China by Chiang Kai-shek, he ordered the Whampoa Academy to be moved there. The Whampoa was to become the Central Military Academy and although the Soviet training methods were to be retained, all Russian instructors were dismissed. Bearing in mind Chiang's wish for a strong Central Chinese Army to emerge from the National Revolutionary Army, his Central Executive Committee declared: 'Military Education should be unified and all military schools in the country shall be placed under the direct control of the government.' Any individual commander who established his own military academy would be punished. The new Central Military Academy began to take on foreign instructors who were nearly all Germans (see below). The old Army Staff College in Peking was reorganised and was renamed the 'Army Staff College of China' and its Chinese name was abbreviated to 'Lu-ta'. Instruction at the 'Lu-ta' was divided into two courses, the regular staff course and the command course. It took in younger officers above the rank of Captain who had three years of service in the army at least. The aim of the college was to turn out the higher-ranking Nationalist Army officers of the future. There were attempts to get long-established higher ranking officers to take a 'refresher' course. This was intended to improve their command skills but it failed owing to the arrogance of the officers (or perhaps their well-founded scepticism?) and it was cancelled after a year.

When Chiang Kai-shek fell out with the Soviet Union in 1927 one consequence was the removal of those Russian military advisors. Chiang was quick to try and replace them with other foreign experts and his natural choice was to turn to Germany. He had an affinity with Germany and had considered attending a military academy there before going to Japan. Chiang first approached General Erich Ludendorff, the ex-German commander, but he decided that his fame might be counterproductive. Instead Lundendorff recommended his ex-Chief of Staff, Colonel Max Bauer, to lead the proposed advisory group. Bauer eventually brought to China a hand-picked team of 25 in November 1928 who immediately began training selected Nationalist units. The Germans proved not only to be adept military trainers but sensitive to the Chinese mentality. Instead of criticising Chinese officers in public they realised that the oriental fear of losing face meant a private talk was more productive. They also rewrote the German army manuals to accommodate Chinese needs and even adapted imported equipment. The Germans soon developed a good relationship with the young Chinese officer cadets who were open to their instructors' new ideas.

Chinese trainee pilots in front of their US-supplied Fleet trainer with their American instructor in the mid-1930s. The Jouett Mission, which came to China in 1932, managed to train a reasonable number of pilots despite adverse conditions. They also had to face competition from an Italian training mission, which meant scrabbling for scarce resources.

Bauer's death in 1929 was a blow to the Military Mission. He was succeeded by Lieutenant-Colonel Hermann Kriebel. Kriebel proved unpopular as he wanted to concentrate on tactics rather than the organisation of the Nationalist Army. He was replaced in May 1930 by General Georg Wetzell who proved to more suited to the Chinese way of doing things. Wetzell got Chiang's permission to expand the Military Mission from the then 40 to 90 advisors. In addition, he was allowed to increase the number of specialist training schools and to concentrate them in the Nanking area. By 1937 there were separate schools which specialised in Infantry, Cavalry, Artillery and Engineering training. There were other schools which specialised in everything from Anti-Aircraft Defence to Chemical Warfare.

The mission trained a 1st Model Division starting in 1929, which was given a minimum of six months training in the classroom and on exercise. This division, as the name suggests, was to be a blueprint for every Nationalist division. It had selected officers and soldiers who were politically reliable with loyalty to Chiang Kai-shek. Its troops were issued with the smartest uniforms and had all the up-to-date weaponry that the government could provide. In 1930 a 2nd model division was formed, which was to be renamed the 88th Division and was to be one of the elite units of the Army. The reliable 4th Nationalist Division was then introduced into the training programme increasing the number of troops under instruction in late 1931 to 30,000. The 88th Division and the 1st Division (renamed the 87th) were to see service in the battle for Shanghai in 1932 (see chapter 6).

In 1934 Wetzell was succeeded by General Hans von Seeckt, the chief architect of the post-1918 German Army. Von Seeckt had proved to be an able organiser who managed to create a superbly trained 100,000-strong German army. This was achieved despite the restrictions on the size, equipment and weaponry of the German military imposed by the Versailles Treaty. The General had visited China in 1933 to hold discussions with Chiang, so when he arrived the next year he immediately put his plans into action. He halved the number of advisors down to 45 having selected the best of the original staff to improve the quality. His main concern was to streamline a lot of the Nationalist Army's support services and urged the introduction of a modern supply system. Chinese officers were to be selected more carefully to avoid political appointments of cadets chosen for their loyalty rather than their ability. Von Seeckt used his contacts in the German arms industry to begin supplying the Chinese with modern weaponry. The idea was to standardise the weapons used by the Nationalist Army rather than relying on local arsenals. These arsenals produced a wide variety of rifles, machine guns and artillery with types chosen on the whim of the local military governor. This standardisation meant, for instance, that an artillery regiment received its Krupp field guns as well as maintenance and communication equipment. They also received ammunition and spare parts and even the steel helmets that the crews would use.

The Military Mission's aims were ambitious and in many ways outreached the capability of the Nationalist Army. Weaknesses in the organisation of the Army were to effect the progress of the training and equipping of the new divisions. Rivalries among its commanders meant that they fell out over the allocation of any new weaponry. Some generals who Chiang deemed to be of doubtful loyalty did not receive any of the new weapons. This caused further resentment, which further undermined the loyalty of the generals to their leader.

When General von Seeckt returned to Germany due to poor health in March 1935 he was replaced by another capable officer, General Alexander von Falkenhausen. He inherited a programme which between 1934 and 1936 trained and organised 20 divisions. Not all of these new divisions would receive the same level of equipment and weaponry. They would, however, be more capable of handling any new weaponry that the Chinese could buy. In 1936 a new three-year plan was introduced by von Falkenhausen, which – if the outbreak of full-scale war had not intervened – would have led to a truly modern Chinese army.

The work of the military mission was eventually curtailed by events taking place outside of China. On the 25th of November 1936 Nazi Germany and Imperial Japan signed the Anti-Comintern Pact. This military pact was to lead to closer military ties between two fascist states opposed to the Soviet Union and world Communism. Germany's military aid to Japan's enemy, Nationalist China, now became something of an embarrassment to Hitler. The outbreak of full-scale war between China and Japan in July 1937 meant it was now a matter of urgency to remove the German Military Mission. It took a year before the mission finally left in July 1938 and in that time its influence had been seen on the battlefield. During the titanic struggle for the city of Shanghai in autumn 1937 over 80,000 German-trained troops fought the Japanese almost to a standstill. Unfortunately for the Nationalists, most of of their elite German-trained and equipped divisions were sacrificed in the battle.

## Military Spending and New Weaponry for the Nationalist Army

Nationalist Military expenditure from 1928–29 compared to 1936–37 grew by over 50% but decreased as a percentage of total government expenditure. In 1928–29 they were spending 210 million Chinese Dollars, which was just over 50% of the country's total. By 1932–33 military spending had risen to 321 million Dollars and was still just under 50% of total spending. In the fiscal year 1936–37 military spending had risen to 322 million but the improvement in the Chinese economy meant this was only 32.5% of the country's total spend. These figures show a few things of note including the fact that their spending in 1936–37 reveals they were not buying the modern weaponry other nations were. The spending was of course a considerable amount for a relatively underdeveloped country; but they were not buying the bigger ticket items like battleships and large amounts of modern heavy weaponry.

The Nationalist Army was still desperately short of modern weaponry, especially heavy artillery and armoured vehicles. In 1928 it was estimated that the various armies in China had a total of 2,500 field guns between them, along with 700 mountain guns. These were mostly late-19th-century guns and the mix of types and calibres made it difficult to keep them supplied with shells. Armoured vehicles consisted of a few FT-17 tanks and a number of locally made armoured cars, which had little combat value. Small arms were the usual mish-mash of types with the Gew-88 rifle the most common. Many Chinese troops in the early 1930s were still armed with the C-96 semi-automatic pistols with an added wooden stock. These had been imported in huge numbers from Germany and Spain and acted as a substitute rifle for the Chinese. A modern army needs modern weaponry and Chiang was keen to equip at least his best and most loyal divisions with new equipment. New rifles purchased for the Nationalist Army were usually 7.62mm Mausers, which were also made in several arsenals. They bought large numbers of the Belgian FN24 and the Czech VZ24, licensed copies of the Mauser. Machine guns were bought from every small arms producer in Europe, the greatest number from Czechoslovakia. These were the ZB26 light machine gun and the ZB53 heavy machine gun, the latest types available. As part of its modernisation programme the Nationalist Army imported more modern artillery and other heavy weaponry in the mid-1930s. The German Training Mission unsurpisingly recommended artillery from their country's main manufacturers like Krupp. Types of artillery bought included the PAK 35/36 37mm anti-tank gun and the 7.5 cm Leichte Gebirgs Infantriegeshutz 18 and 7.5cm Infantriegeschutz L/13 infantry guns. Heavier guns included

Nationalist troops take part in parade ground bayonet drill in the summer of 1936. The stiff kepi type caps worn by these men were usually worn by select northern troops. These men probably belong to the North-East Army of Chang Hsueh-liang, which at this time was fighting Communists in Shensi. They are armed with the shortened version of the Mauser 98k produced in Belgium and Czechoslovakia.

48 105mm and 44 150mm German field guns along with 72 Swedish 75mm Mountain guns. Anti-tank guns imported in the 1930s included every type of 20mm gun on the market, such as the Breda 20/65 and the Swiss Solothurn S5/106 2cm. In the 1935–36 period the Nationalist Army also took delivery of a number of armoured vehicles but the Chinese policy of ordering from different sources continued. They bought 29 Carden-Loyd M1931 light amphibious tanks in 1935 and 4 M1936 light tanks in 1936. From Italy they bought 20 CV33/35 tankettes in 1936 and from Germany they bought between 10 and 15 PzKpfw I light tanks in the same year. In an attempt to build a larger armoured force they bought 20 Vickers 6-ton tanks, 16 were the Mark E 'Type B' version, which had a single turret with a 47mm gun. The other four were the command version of the tank with Marconi radios but still armed with the 47mm. China's most powerful generals still acted as independent warlords buying weaponry from whoever would sell it to them. This was understandable when only the divisions whose loyalty was not in doubt received heavy weapons from Chiang Kai-shek. New artillery and armoured vehicles were supplied to the core divisions in Central China that Chiang could rely upon. This policy of keeping the better weaponry in trusted hands extended to the individual armies. A general would keep any artillery he had at his headquarters so as to stop any rebellious subordinates from overthrowing him. Similarly, a lower ranking officer would keep the unit's machine gun close by in case his men mutinied. If a general had his own funds he

would try and import his own weapons from abroad. Alternatively, he would try and set up a substantial arsenal to produce rifles, machine guns and even artillery for his own army. In the South of China the independently minded governor of Yunnan, General Lung Yun, ordered 10 French Renault UE carriers in 1936. He also ordered four French AMR ZT light tanks armed with the 13mm Hotchkiss heavy machine gun; but these were not delivered until 1940.

## The Nationalist Air Force, 1928–1937

The air arm of the National Revolutionary Army during the Northern Expedition was largely made up of old planes captured from the northern warlords. Several of the warlords had created their own air arms with the latest types of planes imported into China from 1920. The Manchurian warlord Chang Tso-lin had at least 100 aircraft, mainly light bombers flown by White Russian pilots. Other major warlords including Feng Yu-hsiang, leader of the Kuominchun, had smaller air forces with a couple of dozen aircraft. Most warlords had to be content with air forces of up to a dozen planes usually flown by expensive foreign pilots from France, Germany and Russia. During the Northern Expedition the National Revolutionary Army's air arm received a few Russian R-1s to join the ones they captured. Their improvised and cobbled together air force was just about adequate for its role in the 1926–28 fighting. It was never going to be substantial enough to serve as the air force of the new state. Chiang placed orders for new aircraft as soon as he could from several countries, with the first purchases coming from the USA. A total of 34 Vought Corsairs multi-purpose aircraft in two types were bought in 1930 and these were followed by 10 Douglas O-2MC light bombers. A number of German Junkers aircraft were also purchased about this time including 10 K-47 fighters and several light transports. These were joined under the influence of the US and Italian Air Missions (see below) by large numbers of Italian and more US aircraft. In 1933 100 Italian and 275 US aircraft were ordered with 154 Curtiss Hawk II and III fighters arriving over a three-year period. Other US aircraft included 36 Northrop 2E Gamma light bombers, 31 more Vought Corsairs and 36 Douglas O-2MCs. Twenty-four Italian Fiat 32 fighters, 18 Breda 27 fighters, 20 Savoia S72 transport / bombers and 14 Caproni 101 bombers were imported. In addition 40 German aircraft of various types arrived including Heinkel 66 dive bombers and 6 Heinkel 111A medium bombers. Even with a high attrition rate, the Nationalist air force now had a large number of aircraft. During the early and mid-1930s the new air force began to play an important role in putting down several rebellions. It had competition from a few independent provincial air arms, especially in Kwangsi and Kwangtung provinces.

Nationalist aircraft were particularly important during the five Nationalist Extermination Campaigns from 1930 until 1934. On the eve of the Sino-Japanese War in July 1937 the Nationalist Air Force had 10 fighter Squadrons, 8 Light Bomber Squadrons, 9 Reconnaissance Squadrons, 2 Heavy Bomber Squadrons and 2 Attack Squadrons. This carefully husbanded force was to be devastated in the early months of the war with Japan. With foreign support having been withdrawn the Chinese put up a brave fight against the Imperial Army and Naval Air forces but were outclassed in most encounters.

## The US Air Mission, 1932–1935 and Italian Training Mission, 1933–1937

The defeat at Shanghai in 1932 after a brave fight by the Nationalist Army was largely down to the total air superiority of the Japanese Navy and Army's Air Forces. Almost immediately after the battle, Soong, the Chinese Finance Minister, with Chiang Kai-shek's approval sought help from the USA to establish a modern air force. Although no official US mission could be sent, private individuals with air force experience could go to China. This mission would establish a training school to train new and re-train existing Nationalist pilots. They would order the US trainers and other equipment needed to run the school and this would be run through the American Commerce Department. Official US opposition to the mission continued but in July 1932, a Colonel John. H. Jouett and nine pilots, four mechanics and one secretary arrived in Shanghai. They were given a three-year contract and established their school at Hangchow, which had few of the facilities needed. Despite the lack of basic facilities such as water supply, electricity and no repair workshops the mission soon managed to re-train a number of pilots. By September 1932 they had set up a course to train new pilots and had soon trained several hundred Chinese to fly. They also trained a few Chinese flying instructors and set up most of the facilities lacking when they arrived. Although the school performed miracles there was always friction amongst the Americans themselves and between them and their Chinese pupils. Without official support from the US and with sometimes half-hearted support from the Chinese, the mission was bound to struggle. The Nationalist officer in overall charge of the mission was changed several times over the three years of the contract. Every officer who succeeded to the job was said by Jouett to have had less understanding than his predecessor about the role and needs of the mission. The arrival of a rival official Italian Air Mission in 1933 caused further problems as it was seen to be favoured by the Chinese. Nevertheless, Colonel Jouett and his US volunteers continued to fulfil their contract and brought in a five-year programme to improve the air force further. Jouett's mission ended in June 1935 when thr contract ended and the staff returned to the USA. When another US advisor, Claire L Chennault, arrived in China in 1937 he was impressed by the standard of the Chinese pilots who had been through Jouett's Flying School.

When a Nationalist official called H.H. Kung visited the Italian dictator Benito Mussolini in 1933 he was highly impressed by the charismatic leader. They discussed the establishment of an Italian Flying Mission to China which would be 'paid for' by funds from the Boxer Indemnity owed to Italy by the Chinese since 1900. The mission would provide instructors and aircraft and would be led by Colonel Roberto Lordi who brought 20 staff with him. A flying school was established at Nanchang, close to Chiang Kai-shek's anti-Communist headquarters. The mission started with two instructors in 1933 but by October 1934 there were eight at the school. They specialised in training bomber crews and had an initial intake of 60 Chinese pupils. In addition to the school, funds for the opening of an aviation factory to produce Italian fighters was also part of the deal. The big advantage that the Italians had over their American rivals was that they had official backing from their government. Lordi was replaced in 1935 by General Scaroni, who flew to China in a Savoia-Marchetti SM72 transport given as a present to Chiang Kai-shek. By the time Scaroni arrived the Italian mission was beginning to lose favour with the Chinese, however. It was criticised for turning out sub-standard pilots, which was blamed on the corrupt selection policy of the school. Instead of selecting pilots purely on their merits the Italians were accused of favouring the sons of Nationalist officials regardless of their talent for flying. The school had training courses for fighter pilots, bomber crews and observers. As mentioned earlier, in 1933 the Chinese ordered a number of Italian aircraft and some of these aircraft were used in the later encirclement campaigns fought by the Nationalists against the Red Army. Although the Italians continued their work in China for the next few years there was no expansion of its organisation from the original set-up. The Italian mission left China abruptly when the full-scale war with Japan began in July 1937. Mussolini was growing closer to Japan politically and did not want to upset his future ally by supporting their enemy.

## The Chinese Nationalist Navy, 1928–1937

The Nationalist navy was in 1928 an amalgamation of the various regional fleets which served the warlords in the 1920s. Certain provinces had built up their own small fleets of smaller ships and gunboats with the Kwangtung and Kwangsi navies two of the strongest. The three main fleets in 1920s China had largely kept out of civil conflicts since the 1911 Revolution and waited until 1927 to give their allegiance to Chiang Kai-shek. In 1928 in the coastal province of Fukien the powerful naval clique there submitted plans for the expansion of the navy. Chiang knew he could not afford to keep the navy at its present strength and ignored the three admirals' proposal. To try and neutralise any possible naval rebellions Chiang moved the main Fukien Admiral, Chen Shao-k'uan, to Nanking to organise the navy. This was a ruse to remove him from direct command of the navy and bury him in an office job.

Chiang Kai-shek inherited the Central Fleet of the 1920s, made up of the 1st and 2nd Squadrons and a training Squadron. In addition, the nominally loyal 4th Squadron in Canton was part of the Nationalist navy although in reality it stayed largely independent. The priority for Chiang was his army and air force with the navy coming a very poor third when it came to government finances. In the late 1920s and early 1930s a number of river gunboats had been ordered from Hong Kong to improve the anti-piracy work of the Fleet. In 1929 a new gunboat, the *Hsien Ning* was completed to be joined by two others, the *Yung*

*Sui* and the *Ming Chuen*. Further attempts to improve the Fleet were frustrated by the lack of funds.

New vessels that were purchased in the late 1920s and early 1930s tended to be the smaller patrol craft which were more affordable than the large ships. Ships were involved in a number of operations including the defence of Manchuria in 1931, the Shanghai Incident in 1932 and the suppression of the Fukien Revolt in 1933–34. In 1933 the Central Fleet was made up of the 1st Squadron with the cruisers, *Ning Hai*, *Hai Yung* and *Hai Chou* and the gunboats *Yat Sen*, *Yung Chien*, *Yung Chi* and *Chung Shan*. It also had three transports, the *Pu An*, *Hwa An* and *Ting An* as well as new patrol boats *Kiang Ning* and *Nai Ning* and a number of older patrol boats. The 2nd Squadron that was based on the Yangtze River had 11 gunboats, the *Yung Sui*, *Hsien Ning*, *Chu Ting*, *Chu Yu*, *Chu Chien*, *Chu Tai*, *Chu Kuan*, *Kiang Chen*, *Kiang Tuan*, *Ta Tung* and *Tze Chion*. There were also two seaplane carriers, the *Wei Sheng* and *Teh Sheng* and river gunboats, *Chiang Hsi* and *Chiang Kun* and four patrol vessels. In the same year the Nationalist navy was contemplating the buying of a number of destroyers from Great Britain. This enormous outlay on enough of these larger vessels to form a flotilla was soon stopped by Chiang Kai-shek. Instead the funds which had been earmarked for the expansion and modernisation of the navy were transferred to the air force.

In 1933 the Navy's three cruisers, *Hai Chi*, *Hai Chen* and *Chao Hao* defected to the semi-autonomous Kwangtung navy. They spent two years in Canton with their crews underpaid and unappreciated with nothing in particular to do. On the 15th of June 1935 the crews had had enough and left the port and moved out to sea while harassed by Kwangtung air force light bombers. By the end of 1936 the Nationalist navy was preparing for further aggression by the Japanese with a war plan in place. As the Nationalist Army was supposed to withdraw inland in front of the Japanese Imperial Army, the navy's role was to be limited. All the fleets were given the task of delaying any naval attack on the Nationalist capital Nanking and on Shanghai. Older ships and boats were designated to move into any of the main rivers to be used as block ships.

## 2

# 'CRUSH THEM ALL WITH A SINGLE BLOW': THE CENTRAL PLAINS WAR, 1929

The Central Plains War, which lasted from March 1929 until November 1930, was in reality not just one conflict. It was a series of campaigns, rebellions and conflicts between the newly formed Nationalist Government of Chiang Kai-shek and a group of rebel generals and their armies. At various times over the two years of the war Chiang's armies were fighting the armies of the Kwangsi clique from southern China and the two northern warlords Feng Yu-hsiang and Yen Hsi-shan. His army also faced a number of rebellions – some related others not, to the main conflict – which was fought as its name suggests in the Central Plains of China. All the combatants in 1929–30 had fought within the framework of the National Revolutionary Army during its 1926–28 campaign against the northern warlords. Although united in their dislike of the reactionary northern warlords like Wu Pei-fu, Chang Tsung-ch'ang and Chang Tso-lin this hatred for their common enemy was the only uniting factor. The disbandment of large parts of the Nationalist Army was never going to be accepted by many of its commanders. These men may have fought under the Nationalist flag but their armies were usually loyal to them first. Any reduction in an army's numbers was seen as a direct threat to its leader and would not be tolerated. At the same time there were power struggles taking place in many provinces as the old warlord cliques tried to maintain their pre-1928 power bases.

The main protagonists in the 1929 fighting all had large armies available to them with Feng Yu-hsiang's Kuominchun having close to 300,000 men. southern armies that were a potential threat to Chiang totalled 350,000 and these were made up of Kwangsi and Kwangtung armies. Kwangsi had 60,000 troops in its northern-controlled provinces and these were known as the Wuhan Army. Chiang Kai-shek's armies at the start of the conflict in 1929 were about 240,000 strong but this figure was to fluctuate during the war. Chang Hsueh-liang and his 200,000 strong Manchurian Army was going to stay out of the fighting in 1929. He did mobilise 50,000 of his troops during the conflict but had no intention of sending them into battle.

Chiang Kai-shek faced two major problems in northern China in early 1929 with the first concerning General Feng Yu-hsiang the leader of the Kuominchun or 'Peoples Army'. Feng controlled three provinces, Kansu, Shensi and Honan but was finding it difficult to raise taxes in all three provinces, which were all relatively poor. The western province of Kansu was also experiencing a major famine which had killed millions and a brutal Muslim rebellion. Feng's only saving grace was his partial control of the much richer province of Shantung in North-Eastern China. During the Northern Expedition his Kuominchun had fought for control of the province on behalf of Chiang Kai-shek. The

Junior officers of the National Revolutionary Army celebrate a victory in the summer of 1929. The casualty rate amongst young officers in the Northern Expedition of 1926–28 was horrendous. These officers are fortunate to have survived the war but would soon be called upon to fight in a series of campaigns.

Kuominchun still had control of the western third of the province and Feng asked Chiang if he could take the rest of it. It was now vital, said Feng, for him to gain full control of the province and to be allowed to begin raising taxes there.

Meanwhile in Hunan province the powerful Kwangsi clique from the south-west of China were unhappy with the situation there. During the Northern Expedition the Kwangsi clique had gained control of several provinces in the North of China including Hunan. Chiang was unhappy with the amount of territory and taxes that the Kwangsi clique controlled and he appointed his own protégé General Lu Ti-ping as governor. Chiang was now able to make sure all tax revenues from Hunan now went into the Nanking coffers. Not surprisingly the Kwangsi leaders argued that as their troops were still stationed in Hunan they should receive funds to pay for their upkeep. Although the Kwangsi Armies still controlled the province the presence of Chiang's appointee as governor could not be tolerated. Besides the tax issue they were also angry that Lu's control of Hunan compromised their supply lines to the Kwangsi Army further North.

Kwangsi forces now acted and drove General Lu out of Hunan having attacked his headquarters at Changsha. With a challenge to his leadership from Kwangsi, Chiang Kai-shek now needed to secure his position before going to war with the rebels. Chiang bribed Feng Yu-hsiang with the offer of large amounts of territory in Shantung province. In reality, the continued presence of large numbers of Japanese troops there prevented him from taking control of the province anyway.

He also bribed other military leaders in North and Central China to keep them out of the war while he dealt with the Wuhan Armies. Chiang now attempted an admirable *ruse de guerre*; he sent General Tang Sheng-chih northwards to Peking. Tang had been in command of several Hunan Armies when he had been defeated by the Kwangsi Armies and had been sent into exile. His formerly loyal Hunanese troops had been incorporated into the Kwangsi Army and had been sent to garrison Peking. These Hunanese soldiers were now under the command of Kwangsi General Pai Ch'ung-hsi but had little love for their new commander. Pai was absent when Tang arrived in Peking, which allowed the Hunan General to contact his former unit commanders.When their old commander turned up the Hunanese troops gladly changed sides and Peking fell to Tang's re-won army. Tang's coup was a major blow for the Kwangsi leadership as they lost the power struggle with Chiang.

## The Wuhan Army *vs* the Nationalist Army, March–April 1929

The Kwangsi clique army advanced northwards as part of the National Revolutionary Army between 1926 and 1928. During their advance they gained control of large amounts of territory in the northern provinces. The ambitions of its leaders had now expanded from their own fiefdom in the far South. They had no intention of giving up this new influence over Central and North China without a fight. The fighting which would take place in the spring of 1929 was between the Kwangsi Armies based in the North, commonly known as the Wuhan Army, and Chiang's Nationalist Army. An armed confrontation between the two powerful armies became inevitable and both began to prepare for it. The Wuhan Army was under the command of two of the three most powerful Kwangsi Generals, Li Tsung-jen and Pai Chung-tsi, 'The Muslim General'. Their army established defences in the Wuhan region. They adopted the title for their forces of 'Protect the Party Save the Country Army' and claimed they were saving the 'soul of China'. Chiang pragmatically tried to make peace with the rebellious generals but all attempts had failed by the end of March. In the meantime Chiang had not been idle and by the 30th of March the 9th Division of the National Army was nearing Hangchow, 35 miles to the east of Hankow, one of the Kwangsi-held cities. In early March Kiukiang became the centre of the military build-up of both the Nationalist 1st Army and the Wuhan forces. The Wuhan Army had stationed 10,000 men and 40 field guns at the town of Wusueh opposite Kiukiang. They claimed that this disposition was purely precautionary and was a totally defensive move. Wuhan Army dispositions in early March saw 80,000 men in the vicinity of Wuhan and on the North Bank of the Yangtze River. Another 30,000 troops were stationed in Hunan province and 20,000 in Hupei province. Fighting began at the end of the month with the Nationalists moving about 150,000 troops towards Wuhan. This offensive was largely planned by Chiang's German Military advisor Colonel Max Bauer, a World War 1 veteran. At the same time another 30,000 Kwangsi troops had been mobilised and were advancing rapidly to the support of the Wuhan forces.

The crew of one of Chiang Kai-shek's artillery pieces prepare to fire towards rebel positions during the Central Plains War. Their field gun is a German 75mm M03 supplied to one of the warlord armies defeated by Chiang Kai-shek's National Revolutionary Army in 1928. After their victory in 1928 the NRA placed orders with European arms dealers for modern weaponry to equip their army, air force and navy.

The Nationalists now massed even more troops for their offensive against the rebel stronghold. Chiang Kai-shek took personal command of the right flank of his army on the Kiukiang Front. The Kwangsi Army received offers of support from the ever rebellious Cantonese in Kwangtung province. The Kwangtung leaders were furious at the detention of their popular General Li Chai-sum, the southern delegate to the Nanking Congress. When Chiang Kai-shek heard about the Cantonese offer of support to his enemy and the mobilisation of its army he reacted. As a sign of his intent to fight all rebels Chiang Kai-shek immediately ordered the execution of General Li in revenge. The General sent a message to his men before his death saying 'The moment an outstanding expedition starts out from Canton it may be the hour for me to pay the death penalty.' The furious Wuhan forces now tried to launch two simultaneous offensives towards Anhui and Kiangsi provinces. Chiang now faced a possible declaration of war by the Kwangsi clique with the possibility of Kwangtung province also joining Wuhan. In early April the Wuhan forces were, however, undone by the switch of General Li Ming-jui with his men to the Nationalist Army. This was followed by the desertion of General Hsia-wei's Army who had lost faith in the cause of the Wuhan forces. These reverses were blamed on the failure of the Wuhan Government to get support from the Kwangtung Armies, who were still undecided. These reverses for the Wuhan forces led General Feng Yu-hsing, the 'Kuominchun' or people's army leader, to jump off the fence and bring his forces into action against the Wuhan rebels. On the 2nd of April Feng sent some of his Kuominchun down from the North to complete an encircling of the Wuhan defences. With Nationalist forces moving towards them and now with the Kuominchun joining the attack, the Wuhan Army's war was lost. During the Nationalist-Kuominchun advance towards Hankow the Wuhan Army did put up some stiff resistance in several rearguard battles. Reports said that large numbers of casualties were returning to hospitals in Nanking indicating the fierceness of the fighting. Nationalist gunboats on the Yangtze River bombarded Wuhan positions 10 miles east of Hankow while their armies were 20 miles away from the city. Feng was in a position to outflank either warring faction and his attitude was still in doubt at that time.

On the 4th of April the vanguard of the Nationalist Army advanced up to the Wuhan defence system, 20 miles east of Hankow but keeping out of rifle shot. Wuhan defences were described as the most elaborate seen in China with 'miles and miles of barbed wire, spiked palisades, trenches and artillery emplacements'. The defence of these fortifications indicated that the 60,000 strong Wuhan Army still had fight in it. This was despite the fact that it had been deserted by its Kwangsi masters and had not received support from Kwangtung province as hoped. Chiang had ordered his 105,000 Nationalist troops made up of the 1st, 2nd and 3rd Armies against the Wuhan defences on the 1st of April. Just before the attack began, in a typical Chiang tactic he bribed 5,000 of the Wuhan garrison to change sides at that moment. The Nationalist Army prepared for an all-out attack on Wuhan on the 5th of April, which was described by a correspondent as an 'infantry, cavalry and artillery attack supported by gunboats'. With the Wuhan Army bottled up in the city it was expected that their troops would fight to the death. With this in mind Nationalist ships had mined the Yangtze River to stop the Wuhan forces from escaping by boat from the city. They had warned all the Yangtze shipping companies about the mines, so forewarning the Wuhan command. Two days later the situation on the Yangtze River took a dramatic turn as the Wuhan Army's defences collapsed and the troops retreated towards Hankow. The appearance of thousands of fleeing Wuhan troops in the city caused widespread panic amongst the citizens. About 5,000 Wuhan troops decided the game was up and went over to the Nationalist Army. Thousands of civilians tried to enter the foreign concessions in the city to escape the chaos. The defeat of the Wuhan Army was blamed on the Kwangsi General deciding to surrender to Chiang Kai-shek. Panic soon subsided when it was seen that most of the defeated Army was not entering the city but retreated northwards towards Hunan province. All the Wuhan generals had left the city ahead of their troops leaving the administration in chaos. There was still some remnants of the Wuhan Army in the city and some looting did take place. Later reports said that retreating army had being hemmed in and had to fight to escape across the border into Hunan. This defeat led swiftly to the Kwangsi clique losing all of its territory in the North of China and retreating back to their home province. The first threat of the year to Chiang Kai-shek's rule was over but more were to come over the next few months.

## A Political Rival; and Feng *vs* Chiang, May 1929, 1st Round

As well as the military threats that his Nationalist Government faced Chiang also had to deal with political rivals within the Kuomintang Party in the 1920s and 1930s. Chiang's main rival in the 1920s was Wang Ching-wei who had joined the Kuomintang after being imprisoned for an attempt on a Qing official's life. He emerged after the death of Sun Yat-sen in 1925 to be a sometime political ally, sometime rival to Chiang Kai-shek.

Wang Ching-wei and Chiang Kai-shek were in bitter competition for much of the 1920s and 1930s over the leadership of the Kuomintang Party. Wang represented the left wing of the party while Chiang was very much on the right wing. The Kuomintang after the death of Sun Yat-sen in 1925 was dominated by Chiang and his clique of generals and politicians. It was Wang Ching-wei's struggle to pull the party to the left that was the catalyst for much of the infighting. On several occasions it appeared that Wang had gained the upper hand having drawn support from many of the Nationalist generals. In 1929 he emerged as the main political leader of the rebellion trying to overthrow Chiang by military means. A few years earlier he had been one of the leaders of the alternative Nationalist Government in Wuhan during the Northern Expedition of 1926–28. In March 1929 Wang tried to garner support for his plan to defeat Chiang by sending a long telegram denouncing the Third National Congress of the Kuomintang Party being held in Nanking. This telegram was sent by Wang from his exile in Paris but was intended to pave the way for his return to China to lead an anti-Chiang campaign.

Feng Yu-hsiang had been allowed by Chiang Kai-shek to control much of Shantung province since 1928 after his Kuominchun had battled for it during the Northern Expedition. To Feng the province was so important because the other three provinces he controlled – Kansu, Shensi and Honan – provided him with so little revenue. In January 1929 however Shantung province was divided between 6 armies, with the Kuominchun controlling only the western quarter. The rest of the province was divided between the armies of three officially pro-Nationalist Generals. General Liu Chen-nien in the North-East, General Liu Hei-ch'i in the South-East and General Ku Chen in a small area in the East. The Japanese Army was also stationed along the Tsinan-Tsingtao Railway with the remainder of the province controlled by bandits and remnants of other armies. With Feng now facing a new revolt in Kansu province in February, his reasons for securing control of Shantung were even more pressing. When Chiang Kai-shek took control of Shantung province in April 1929 there was little that Feng Yu-hsiang and his commander, Sun Liang-ch'eng, could do. Feng did not have enough troops in the province and the Japanese garrison there would never have withdrawn from the territory they held.

The defeat of the Wuhan Army had ended the temporary alliance between Chiang and Feng and both men prepared their forces for a new campaign. Feng had reluctantly accepted the role of War Minister in Nanking but life in the capital did not suit his simple country ways. He spent all of his brief time in Nanking criticising the newly installed Nationalist establishment. It was obvious

Immaculately turned out Nationalist troops march past their leader Chiang Kai-shek in 1929. It was the elite troops like these sub-machine-toting bodyguards that held the Nationalist Army together during the severe trials it faced in 1929–30. In this photograph you can see the contrast between the grey cotton uniforms of the soldiers and the woollen khaki worn by the officers.

to Feng that the post of War Minister was purely honorary and he had ambitions to hold real power in China. After leaving Nanking he returned to his base in the north-west to plan for a rebellion against Chiang.

After defeating the Wuhan Army Chiang Kai-shek now felt confident to take on his erstwhile ally. He began planning a campaign against Feng Yu-hsiang after he had thwarted the Kuominchun commander's plans in Hankow and Shantung province. Matters between Chiang and Feng had been brought to a head by the withdrawal of Feng's protégé from his office of Governor of Shantung. He had been earmarked for a role in the takeover of Tsinan when the Japanese withdrew their forces from the city. Under the threat of large Nationalist armies from Hopei and Kiangsu provinces the governor had been forced to leave Tsinan. The Nationalist armies were threatening to totally envelop Kuominchun forces in Western Shantung province. Feng was in a weak position at this time as he was running short of arms, ammunition and food for his troops. This shortage was made worse by the famine taking place in his army's base provinces of Honan and Kansu. Feng's attack on Shansi province was largely to try to commandeer the supplies he needed for further campaigning. On the 16th of May his commanders were prompted by Feng to appoint him as 'Commander of Chief of the North-Western Armies charged with the saving of the Country'. Feng then ordered his Generals to move their armies to the front to prepare for the coming war. He also instructed them to blow bridges on the approaches to his fiefdom knowing that the railways were going to be vital in the coming fighting.

Chiang was still determined if possible to keep Feng out of any war and began to send what became a long exchange of telegraphs between the two leaders. While Chiang sent a number of polite, measured and calm messages to Feng the replies he received were more to the point. Feng's messages were short, angry and defiant and left Chiang in no doubt that war between them was inevitable. In mid-May 30,000 of Feng's troops moved east from Honan province to take over the garrisoning of the city of Tsinan. The city had been evacuated by the Japanese Army after a delay at the request of Chiang Kai-shek, who was trying to stop Feng from taking it. By the 20th of May Feng's Kuominchun troops had retreated from Hsinying and those north of the Yellow River had fallen back on the city of Changteh. Chiang Kai-shek had telegraphed the Kuominchun General Han Fu-chu, one of Feng's main commanders, to accuse his troops of dynamiting bridges along the Peking–Hankow Railway. This sabotage had stopped trains from travelling further westwards than the town of Kweiteh. The Nationalists were surprised to find out that Kuominchun divisions stationed on the Lunghai and Peking–Hankow Railway had withdrawn into Honan and Shensi provinces. This retreat by the Kuominchun was not the result of any offensive action by the Nationalist Army. Chiang told Han that if he did not receive a satisfactory answer to his question then the Nationalists would attack his forces. Successes by

Soldiers of Feng Yu-hsiang's Kuominchun in a machine gun position during the first years of fighting in the Central Plains War in 1929. At first sight, the men could belong to any of the combatants during the many-sided war in Central China, 1929–30. The Soviet-made Maxim M1910 heavy machine gun was, however, mainly used by Feng's Kuominchun. In addition, the straw hat seen at the feet of one of the soldiers was an item of quasi-military clothing usually worn by his troops.

Nationalist forces along the Southern Yangtze had emboldened Chiang to begin a serious effort to defeat Feng and his Kuominchun. Chiang Kai-shek had cancelled the despatch of 70,000 troops to North Hupeh province and had instead reinforced his forces on the Lunghai Railway. A total of 100,000 Nationalist troops were concentrating at Hsuchow, the important junction of Tientsin, Pukow and Lunghai Railways. On the 21st of May Feng suffered a blow when a large number of troops under the command of General Liu Chin-hua defected to the Nationalists. Liu's soldiers were from the Kuominchun's 2nd Group Army and his defection was rewarded with a high command in Chiang's Army. Another problem for Feng in late May was the shortage of ammunition, with only enough for another month's campaigning. He decided to attack Shansi province. Feng evacuated to the North Bank of the Yellow River and began withdrawing his troops to his stronghold at Chengchow. The Kuominchun was being moved along the Peking–Hankow Railway and as they went they created havoc in the Lunghai region blowing up bridges. Feng's retreat from the war zone was mystifying – if he had continued fighting he could have relieved pressure on his Kwangsi Allies. On the political front, on the 23rd of May the Kuomintang Central Executive Committee removed Feng from its organisation. At the same time Chiang Kai-shek bribed two of Feng's subordinates, General Shih Yu-san and General Han Fu-chu, to change sides leaving the Kuominchun in disarray. Although Nationalist forces followed close behind the Kuominchun, they did not engage them at all. To emphasise their intention to keep fighting, 28 of Feng's generals issued a denunciation of Chiang Kai-shek. Feng was obviously the author of this document and it was seen as a declaration of war against Chiang. Chiang Kai-shek was furious that he could not attend the commemoration of his mentor Sun Yat-sen's funeral in Peking. The two divisions which were considered necessary to guard Chiang were tied up in fighting elsewhere.

## The Kwangsi–Kwangtung Campaign

The defeat of the Kwangsi clique in the North now put their forces in direct conflict with the forces of neighbouring Kwangtung province. Chiang was busy fighting Feng and the Kuominchun in the North so assigned the defeat of Kwangsi to Kwangtung, Hunan and Yunnan Armies. On the 5th of May Kwangsi forces that had begun to advance into Kwangtung clashed with their army. Two days later the Kwangtung Expeditionary Corps led by the 3rd Division moved westwards to meet the Kwangsi Army. An official declaration of war was issued on the 9th of May by both the Nationalist Government in Nanking and the Kwangtung provincial government. The Kwangsi Army had reached within 100 miles of Canton with heavy fighting taking place along the Canton-Kowloon Railway. Command of the southern forces was shared amongst various Cantonese generals while the Kwangsi force was under the command of General Hsu King-tong. The Railway authorities had been advised to stop all trains going to Kowloon while the fighting was ongoing. Kwangsi forces were advancing rapidly on Canton and had captured the town of Shiuhing, pushing the enemy in front of them.

On the 11th of May the Kwangsi clique suffered a terrible blow when the whole of their Navy was captured by the ships of the Kwangtung Navy. Its ships had been caught in the open by aircraft from the Kwangtung Air Force, which had machine-gunned them until they surrendered. Meanwhile the Kwangsi Armies continued their advance southwards towards the Kwangtung capital, Canton. They had split into three columns and these were preparing to envelop the city. On the 13th, just as they were to begin their last 30-mile advance into Canton they received a last minute offer from the Kwangtung authorities. Their commanders were offered a reported $285,000 a month payment for an indefinite period if they agreed to turn back. Kwangtung authorities also agreed that the Kwangsi Army would be allowed to continue to move their lucrative opium crop through their territory. As a final bribe the Kwangtung authorities agreed to supply the Kwangsi Army with weapons and some volunteers to bolster their forces. The fact that Kwangsi province was also being threatened by other forces meant that the offer was too good to refuse. On the 24th of May 5,000 Kwangsi troops surrendered under the command of General Pai Chung-hai in the vicinity of Lupa on the North River. They gave up the fight having made a last desperate effort to capture Canton, which saw their forces break through the Kwangtung defences 20 miles from the city. Just as they appeared to be on the brink of victory some of their units ran out of ammunition. The Kwangtung reinforcements rushed from Canton hurled them back and a two-day battle then ensued. As many as 50% of the Kwangsi troops, having no bullets left, surrendered. Morale in the Kwangsi Army was broken according to reports by the very accurate bombing of the Cantonese bombers of the beleaguered troops. Both sides had suffered heavy casualties with the hospitals of Canton filling up with those lucky enough to get back from the fighting.

## Air Warfare in 1929

At the start of the fighting in the Central Plains War in the spring of 1929 the use of air power was not high on the belligerents' priorities. The fledgling air arm of the Nationalist Government at Nanking did have 4 Squadrons but each had only 2 or 4 aircraft. All the combat aircraft were old, worn-out types like the French Breguet 14A and the Russian R-1. Modern aircraft in the National Air Force were restricted to a few trainers and German Junkers light transports. Chiang Kai-shek realised the importance of military aircraft and had established a reasonably sized air arm for his National Revolutionary Army from 1926 to 1928. He wanted to bring in new modern combat aircraft but this would not be possible until later in the conflict.

Yen Hsi-shan's Shansi air arm was not much smaller than the National air force and had 6 British Gypsy Moth and 5 French Morane-Saulnier trainers. Its only combat aircraft were a couple of old Breguet 14 light bombers and it also had a modern Junkers F13 light transport. The Kwangsi clique had no aircraft in 1929 and the disadvantage they faced because of this led them to establish one in 1931. Feng Yu-Hsiang's Kuominchun had negotiated with the

Kuominchun soldiers move through a railway station in this undated photograph from the late 1920s or early 1930s. Feng Yu-hsiang's troops had been at war almost constantly since 1920, mostly against the northern warlords and many were hardened veterans. These men may be wearing unkempt uniforms with their distinctive soft cotton hats but they were good fighters. Their German Gew-88 rifles were the most common type in use with Chinese armies at the time and were copied in a number of local arsenals.

German firm Junkers to buy three W33 light transports which could be used as light bombers He also ordered four DH-60 trainers and asked Junkers to train 12 Chinese pilots to fly the planes. Although some planes were delivered before the end of the fighting they did not see much service in support of the Kuominchun. The scarcity of aircraft and the huge size of the area of the war meant air to air combat was rare in 1929. Most air combat involved one or two aircraft on either side and often resulted from a bombing raid on a city or town. In late October a raid by a lone Kuominchun light bomber did take place over the city of Chengchow. After dropping a few bombs the bomber was pursued by a National Army plane, which forced it to land. The pilot and observer of the Kuominchun plane were taken prisoner and offered to change sides and fly for the Government.

## Feng *vs* Chiang, 2nd Round

If Feng thought he was going to get the support of Yen and his Shansi Army he was to be disappointed. The Shansi leader was to spend 1929 claiming he

General Feng Yu-hsiang, the 'Christian Warlord', poses in front of his headquarters during the first year of the Central Plains War. In 1929 Feng still had his powerful Kuominchun army behind him but was now officially part of the Nationalist Army command. Feng was at war with Chiang Kai-shek and the Nationalists from early 1929 until the last month of 1930. He was never going to be happy to live in Chiang's shadow and a clash between the two military giants was inevitable.

supported bopth Chiang *and* Feng as the two battled it out for North China. He accepted the offer of the post of Deputy Commander-in-Chief of the National Land, Sea and Air Forces from Chiang. At the same time he did not fight Feng as he sympathised with him on most things but was worried about the consequences of rebelling. He thought that Chiang would prevail in the end and then he would lose his control of Shansi province if he fought him. Yen, if nothing else, had proved to be a survivor and was never a great risk taker so this stance was in character. Yen's role within the Nationalist military was always going to be purely honorary and he sat out the war throughout 1929.

War between the Nationalist Government and Feng's Kuominchun appeared to be inevitable. On the 12th of October the Government ordered the arrest of the War Minister, General Lu Chung-lin and General Liu Chi, two of the ablest of the Kuominchun Generals. These arrests were on the pretext that both Generals were plotting against the Nanking Government. The Kuominchun was reported to be on the move with its objective the city of Hankow.

During the last two months of 1929 the fighting in Central China had been undecided with heavy fighting taking place in Western Hupeh province. In an effort to stop the advance of Kuominchun into West Hupeh, fresh Nationalist Army troops were sent to the front. Some of the Nationalist units which made up these reinforcements had too many raw troops in them with poor morale. General Sen Yin-ji's 5th Nationalist Division was particularly unreliable and mutinied soon after arriving at the front. The men killed some of their officers and promptly marched towards Kuominchun lines to join their forces. Any arms and ammunition brought over by this division would have been gratefully received as Feng's soldiers were now desperately short of both. In a number of engagements Feng's troops began to run out of ammunition and had to withdraw from the battlefield. At the battle of Loyang desperate measures were called for and the local Kuominchun commander ordered several suicidal charges. These were led by 'da-dao' sword-wielding troops who charged screaming at well dug-in National Army positions suffering horrendous casualties. Feng Yu-hsiang was now looking to boost his forces and announced on the 7th of November that he was going to be fighting 'hand in hand' with Yen Hsi-shan. This was a total fabrication as Yen had no intention of joining Feng and stayed strictly neutral during 1929. The Nationalist forces had their own problems and were hard pressed in the Tengfeng and Yungyang sector. They were facing well dug-in Kuominchun at Siangyang along the vital Lunghai Railway. A large Kuominchun force was also advancing along the Han River towards the city of Hankow. If all the Kuominchun armies in the vicinity of Hankow had attacked in a co-ordinated way they could have defeated the Nationalists in the tri-city region of Wuhan. Unfortunately for Feng, his army now failed to act and it was time for Chiang Kai-shek to take decisive action.

## The Siege of Tengfeng

On the 9th of November the Nationalists launched a large-scale general offensive all along the front with their main objective being the Kuominchun fortified city of Tengfeng. Their positions around the city of Tengfeng were particularly strong with as many as 100,000 troops entrenched there. Kuominchun engineers had done a great job in building the entrenchments to complement the natural terrain around the city. Trenches were dug along the lines of hills above the city and its rivers were incorporated into its defence system. No matter how strong the Kuominchun positions were, they were soon enveloped by superior numbers of Nationalist troops. There were other well fortified cities held by the Kuominchun at Linju, Heishihkuan and Sungliang. With strong garrisons, these cities should have been able to come to Tengfeng's aid but they left the city's defenders to fend for themselves. The total Nationalist force available for the attacks on the fortified cities under Kuominchun control was 160,000 men. This huge force included 60,000 troops under the direct command of Chiang Kai-shek and his advisors. Chiang liked to look after his own troops and when it was noticed that his men were shivering he ordered wadded winter coats for them all. Nationalist troops were sent against Tengfeng's defences in futile frontal assaults but these failed. In response the Kuominchun sent their special 'dare to die' corps on night attacks against the Nationalist defences but both sides stood firm. According to reliable reports much of the fighting at Tengfeng was done by sword-wielding soldiers on both sides. At times the siege of Tengfeng became a brutal 'battle without rifle fire'. As fierce as the fighting around the city was, the siege ended abruptly on the 15th of November as the defenders surrendered. This sudden capitulation was probaby a result of the troops running out of food and water.

After the fall of Tengfeng the Nationalists moved immediately on to the city of Linju, which they soon besieged on three sides. When the city fell Chiang Kai-shek himself gave his opinion on how the battles for Tengfeng and Linju had gone: 'Sparing our beloved soldiers I avoided frontal attacks, but besieged the rebels in their strongholds. I gave orders for a general offensive to begin on November 15th. Tengfeng was occupied and on the afternoon of November 16th the rebels counterattacked but were badly beaten. Four tanks were captured and the rebels retreated in disorder the same night. Linju was occupied the following morning and 20,000 rebels were taken prisoner.'


## The Kuominchun Defeat

By mid November Kuominchun Armies held several of the largest cities in Honan with strong garrisons. Chiang Kai-shek had established his headquarters at Hsuchong and was directing his armies' operations personally. Since the fighting had begun in the autumn his forces had suffered 30,000 casualties and he had to bring in two of his 'elite' armies to the battle. These were under the command of two of his most trusted Generals, Liu Chih and Kou Su-t'ung. Chiang ordered them to take the city of Tungkwan within two weeks. Even as the Kuominchun was having several local successes against the Nationalists in November, it was showing signs of breaking. Feng's war effort began to unravel in mid-November as the Nationalists reinforced in the centre of the front. At the same time, more and more Kuominchun troops began to surrender; 4,000 surrendered at Mihsien and 1,000 prisoners arrived at Hankow. On the 18th of November two of Feng's Generals, Sung Liang-chen and Pang Ping-hsun, surrendered to Chiang taking their armies with them. In typical Chinese fashion Sung demanded command of the Nationalist 6th Army with Pang as his vice-commander.

Nationalist Armies were also struggling – several of the best were defeated and others deserted to the Kuominchun. Chiang had even called a meeting of his staff and his German military advisors to try and control this crisis. Just as the war seemed to be heading for a stalemate, the Kuominchun suddenly and without warning withdrew all forces from Honan province in the second half of November. This shock move was said by Feng to be purely for military reasons as his armies were short of arms and ammunition. Rumours circulated that Feng had been bought off with 'Silver Bullets' by Chiang, which may have some truth to it. Some said that as the campaigning season was over anyway, he took the money and withdrew to prepare for another year's fighting. By the first week in December the war in Honan province had largely petered out, with Feng now isolated and fighting alone. His morale was also affected by Chiang Kai-shek's adeptness at bribing rival commanders. As the fighting calmed down Nationalist forces were still pushing some Kuominchun divisions further into Shensi province. This quiet period at the front allowed some unhappy troops to show their indiscipline with a mutiny taking place at Pukow. Two divisions of these mutinous troops refused to go as ordered southwards to fight in Canton. Instead, they advanced northwards after disarming any loyal soldiers, looting shops and stealing railway rolling stock as they went. Until the mutineers could be brought back into line more troops had to be sent in their place as the Nationalists built up their forces for an attack against the rebel 'Ironsides'.

## Two More Rebellions

### The 'Autumn War', Chang Fa-k'uei's Rebellion

Throughout the main conflict in the Central Yangtze region a number of local rebellions complicated the bigger issues. One rebellion which severely tested Chiang Kai shek was the revolt of his former commander General Chang Fa-k'uei. Chang was a popular general during the Northern Expedition leading his famous 'Ironsides'. He became a well known and popular officer amongst the public and earned the title 'Hero of the Iron Army'. Chang wanted to support Wang Ching-wei, whom he identified with politically and began a pro-Wang rebellion on the 17th of September at Ichang. His intention was to take his army southwards to conquer Canton in Kwangtung province, which would then become a base for Anti-Chiang armies. The move to the South was in direct defiance of Chiang Kai-shek's orders to take the 'Ironsides' to the Lunghai Front to fight Feng Yu-hsiang. Chang's troops had moved into Hunan province by the end of September but were defeated by Hunanese Armies. He also suffered the loss of his HQ at Ichang meaning he had to return to try and defeat the Nationalist Army there. In early October the Nationalist Army operating around Ichang suffered a heavy loss on the Upper Yangtze River. Three steamers full of Nationalist troops were moving up the Upper Yangtze River in the vicinity of Ichang. When travelling through a gorge the steamers came under artillery fire from both banks with 50 soldiers being killed and 200 wounded. One badly damaged vessel did manage to escape the ambush but the other two were captured by the 'Ironsides'. In total 5,000 Nationalist troops were taken prisoner by Chang's men. Regardless of this success Chang and his 'Ironsides' had still not managed to get to Kwangtung and Canton. By the end of the year he had managed to move his army through Hunan province again and reached the Hunan-Kwangsi border. His army was joined now by a number of volunteers and he had a 20,000-strong cavalry force and 200 bandit volunteers amongst its ranks. Chang's popularity was evident when the 24th Nationalist Division of 15,000 was ordered to move against his army. The troops refused to obey the order and mutinied hoping to join Chang; but they were too far away to reach him. Meanwhile, from his new base on the Kwangsi border he made contact with the province's generals and agreed a joint offensive against Kwangtung. Their joint offensive never really got off the ground and was described at the time as a 'disaster'. Chang did not give up and even though his army was diminishing he continued to fight. Another joint operation with Kwangsi troops in the summer of 1930 was also a failure and he disappeared from the military scene. He later spent time living in the USA where his fame and his politics attracted attention, especially from the Chinese population. In 1936 Chang reconciled with Chiang Kai-shek and served with distinction during the Sino-Japanese War.

## The Tang Sheng-chih Rebellion

In March 1929 50,000 Kwangsi troops formerly under the command of General Pai Chung-hsi had gone over to the Nationalist Army. They were placed under the command of General Tang Sheng-chih, who had recently professed his loyalty to Chiang Kai-shek. Tang had a longstanding dispute with the Kwangsi faction after they had forced him out of Hankow in 1927. General Tang was never fully committed to Chiang and rumours of his disloyalty began to surface just as the Nationalists were consolidating their victory in the 1929 fighting. On the 6th of December a bodyguard of the Honan General Tang Sheng-chih, stationed in Nanking, was disarmed on Chiang Kai-shek's orders. This was the first indication to many in the capital that the General had begun a revolt in Honan. Just a few weeks before he revolted Teng had been instrumental in defeating Feng Yu-hsiang's Kuominchun. In the tangled politics of China at this time an ally could become an enemy in an instant, often as a result of some perceived slight. Tang was reported to have taken great offence at having his permission to re-occupy the city of Hankow in Hupei province withdrawn. His local rival General Liu Chi was supposed to leave Hupeh with his army and return to his own province of Kiangsi. This would allow Tang to take control of Hankow, which would be a major and reliable source of finance for his large army. When Liu Chi refused to leave the province Tang decided that he was capable of taking Hankow by force. Tang's two-division army was described as being 'formidable in both numbers of equipment' but so was Liu's Army. Liu had large numbers of troops in northern Hupeh and southern Honan and was not willing to give up his control of the region. Although Tang and Liu had just fought alongside each other against Feng they were still prepared to go to war. The fighting took place at the height of winter with both armies suffering terribly; Tang's troops fared worst. They were fighting in the more exposed positions with no winter uniforms and many were found frozen to death at their posts. So heavy were Tang's losses from the fighting in the arctic conditions that his drive on Hankow had ground to a halt by early January. As his army broke up around him, Tang was now just another rebellious general who had failed in his attempt to gain more power. A price of $50,000 was placed on his capture alive, $30,000 was offered for his head.

# 3

# 'SEND AS MANY DIVISIONS AS YOU LIKE':
# THE CENTRAL PLAINS WAR, 1930

During the 1929 fighting between the Kuominchun and the Nationalists Feng Yu-hsiang claimed on several occasions that he had the support of the Shansi leader Yen Hsi-shan. In reality, Yen, although sympathising with Feng, remained neutral and kept out of the fighting. However in February 1930 Yen cast the die and demanded the resignation of Chiang Kai-shek. Yen Hsi-shan had telegraphed Chiang deploring the failure of the Nationalist Government to 'unify the country'. He also rather haughtily blamed Chiang and his government for not upholding the principles of Sun Yat-sen. His last accusation was that Chiang had reneged on his promise to resign from the Presidency. This telegram was basically a declaration of war on Yen's part and a rallying call to all who opposed Chiang. Chiang immediately issued a denunciation of Yen, who then began building an anti-Chiang alliance of northern and southern military leaders. He was not surprisingly chosen to be the Commander of Chief of the anti-Chiang coalition he was building.

In March Yen invited all of Chiang's political and military opponents to his provincial capital at Taiyuan to discuss 'National Affairs'. All the main rebel generals attended and agreed to begin a military campaign against Chiang Kai-shek as soon as possible. In the same month an important meeting took place in Mukden as Chang Hsueh-liang mulled over which side to back. He took advice from three of his prominent generals, Chang Tso-hsiang, military governor of Kirin province, Wang Fu-lin of Heilungkiang province, and General Tang Yu-lin from Jehol. The consensus was that Manchuria and its powerful North-Eastern Armies should remain neutral for the time being.

## The Feng-Yen Alliance's Plan and Nationalist War Preparations

The Nationalist Army at the start of the 1930 fighting were estimated at 295,000 men, who in general were well trained, equipped and armed. They also more or less united behind Chiang Kai-shek while their opponents were an alliance with varying objectives. The only thing that really united the Feng-Yen-Kwangsi Alliance was their opposition to Chiang and his government, which is not the same as allegiance to a single leader. On paper the Alliance had an overwhelming advantage with 700,000 men available. They were however a mixed bag of some well trained regulars together with poorly armed militia raised at the outbreak of the war. For instance, it was estimated that out of Feng Yu-hsiang's 250,000 troops only 140,000 could be described as reliable.

Young soldiers of General Feng Yu-hsiang's Kuominchun pose outside their barracks armed with German Bergman guns during the Central Plains War. All of the men wear the straw hat, which often replaced conventional headgear in the 'Christian Marshal's' army. Feng had difficulty acquiring modern weaponry because his forces were isolated in north-west China. In the 1920s he had to rely on the Soviet Union for rifles and other small arms and heavier weaponry was harder to get hold of.

The Shansi Army of Yen Hsi-shan had 181,000 troops in February and these were all fairly well trained and armed. In the South the Kwangsi Army, despite its defeat in 1929, still had 60,000 troops which were well trained by Chinese standards. The 700,000 total of anti-Chiang troops which is always quoted included 219,000 men in miscellaneous smaller armies. These were only available to the Feng-Yen-Kwangsi Alliance on paper and would not fight in 1930. southern armies which were at least officially loyal to Chiang totalled several hundred thousand, but similarly, many were unreliable. As usual, there were a large number of troops in various armies in China who owed allegiance to their commander only. The other unknown in 1930 was the presence in Manchuria of Chang Hsueh-liang's 409,000 troops in his North-Eastern Frontier Defence Force. Whichever side Chang decided to join would de facto win the war – but at the start of the conflict he was firmly neutral.

The strategy of the Feng-Yen Alliance was to take the offensive in Honan province to contain the Nationalists along the Lunghai and Peking–Hankow Railways. At the same time an offensive into the rich province of Shantung would establish the alliance there. Their forces would then advance towards Suchow and Wuhan by attacking along the Lunghai Railway and southwards along the Peking–Hankow and Tiajin–Pukow railway. Although Chang Hsueh-liang would not commit any troops to the alliance he was reported to have promised munitions. In the South the Kwangsi clique would hopefully attack Hunan province and the city of Wuhan to link up with Feng-Yen forces in the North. These offensives would put the alliance in charge of most of Central China and rob Chiang of his loyal provinces. Without the control of these provinces Chiang would have to come to some accommodation with Feng and Yen or withdraw from Chinese politics completely.

In preparation for the coming fighting Chiang Kai-shek had been busy along with his German military advisors training troops in his Lower Yangtze stronghold. This so-called 'Basic Army' would form the core of the future Nationalist Army, which he hoped to build up to 20 divisions. Chiang realised that ideally he needed another year to get the number of trained troops he needed. While the rank and file were receiving training thousands of young officers were passing through war school. As at Whampoa the officer cadets were given political indoctrination alongside military training. Chiang received a limited amount of German and Czechoslovakian arms for this new army. He also bought artillery from Japan; one of his last purchases before the war in January included 15 field guns at $40,000 each. Chiang knew that he had to conserve as many of his reliable troops as possible for the battles ahead. He decided to use his less loyal troops in the first attacks as they were basically expendable. As far as he was concerned, the cannon fodder would change their allegiance if captured. They would then need feeding and would prove just as unreliable in the service of Feng or Yen and would 'embarrass the rebels without materially depleting Nanking's real fighting strength'. As well as building his own army, Chiang was busy trying to bribe the lesser commanders on the Alliance side to change sides or disband their armies. His German Military Advisors now insisted on building powerful trench systems on the northern bank of the Yangtze River. This was so that as the war developed his trained and half trained troops could fall back on prepared positions at any time. These well prepared defences included several lines of entrenchments with barbed wire, some of which was electrified. As preparations were going on for the spring hostilities the Nationalists commandeered all the available merchant ships to transport their troops to the Northern Front.

## Early Fighting in the North

In early March the first serious fighting took place between Shansi troops under the command of General Wang Sun-jui and Nationalist forces under General Han Fu-chu. The fighting was in central Honan province, half-way between Chengchow and Hankow. Kuominchun reinforcements were sent from their stronghold at Chengchow to help while Han was sent assistance by Chiang. General Shih Yu-san's Army also moved against Han Fu-chu's beleagured force. Another war front was developing in March 200 miles north-west of Hankow at the town of Siangyang in north-west Hupeh. A 5,000-strong Kuominchun Army attacked the recently prepared Nationalist defences there. This force was joined by further Kuominchun reinforcements but they were facing a 70,000-strong Nationalist Army under General Ho Chen-chun. Further south at Shihchiaachuang, four Shansi divisions were in readiness and large supplies of ammunition and food stuffs were being brought up. Meanwhile Feng's Cavalry had reached Chengchow. The Feng-Yen Alliance plan was for 40,000 Kuominchun troops to be sent down the Peking–Hankow Railway towards the major cities of Hankow and Wuchang. Eighty thousand Shansi troops were to be sent along the Lunghai Railway with their targets the city of Hsuchow first and then, if this was successful, an attack on Nanking. The Kuominchun were concentrated in the Loyang-Chengchow region while in Northern Honan the Kuominchun-Shansi forces were occupying the Lunghai Railway. The main battle front extended for 70 miles from Tangshan to Kuoyang, with both armies having received substantial reinforcements including aircraft.

Chang Hsueh-liang courted both sides during the early months of the 1930 fighting and tantalised them with offers of help. In early May he was reported by well informed sources to have offered Feng and Yen the services of 80,000 of his men. In addition he offered them valuable artillery and the use of products from the huge Mukden Arsenal. Although these claims were not officially denied by Chang, it suited him to appear to be mulling over which side he would back. As both the Nationalists and the anti-Chiang alliance were desperate that he should join them, they put up with his prevarication. With a powerful army behind him he could risk annoying the warring parties while he decided.

Soldiers of Yen Hsi-shan's Shansi army gather around a US-made Colt 95 medium machine gun at their barracks during the Central Plains War in 1930. Yen could not rely on being able to bring in weaponry from outside China during the 1920s and so built up a large arsenal at his capital, Taiyuan. This produced a number of rifles, artillery and machine guns, although the Colt 95 was not made in the arsenal and was one of the few Yen imported.

## War in Shantung Province

The vanguard of Yen Hsi-shan's Shansi Army, which was initially 15,000 strong, was able in May to advance into Shantung province as the Nationalists were otherwise occupied in Honan province. In late May the Shansi Army launched its offensive north-eastwards into the province under the command of General Shi Yu-sen. The Shansi troops made good progress taking the provincial capital Tsinan on the 25th of June. They then occupied the nearby cities of Taian and Tsining with the defending Nationalist Army retreating in disorder. Under the command of General Han Fu-chu, who had defended Tsinan, the Nanking Army withdrew along the Kiaochow-Tsinan Railway. They withdrew in good order and Han established a new headquarters at Weihsien to await Chiang's orders. Considering his position and probably shamed by his defeat, General Han threatened to retire from the army. His 30,000 men were vital to the Nanking war effort and his retirement would affect their capability. Chiang tried to dissuade the sulking Han to change his mind by sending him some additional equipment and 20,000 reinforcements to bolster his army. This present from Chiang did the trick and General Han changed his mind and prepared to go back to war. The General had formerly served in the Kuominchun but fell out with Feng when Peking was taken in 1928. In Eastern Shantung, General Liu Chen-nien regarded his 35,000 as 'up for sale' to the highest bidder and was taking offers of munitions from both sides in the civil war. Although he was officially on the side of Chiang Kai-shek, he, like many other Chinese Generals, was open to offers. The presence of the Shansi Army could not be tolerated by Chiang and his Nationalist Army. Their control of the railway links to Honan province put the whole of the Nationalist effort there in jeopardy. In July Chiang launched his offensives north into Shansi and west into Honan province along the railway system.

Shansi forces suffered a heavy defeat in the 15th of August on the South bank of the Yellow River during their retreat from Tsinan. Nationalist General Chang Kwan-n'gai's division took the city of Tsinan capturing a large haul of Shansi weaponry. This included over 30,000 rifles, 230 pieces of artillery and 3 of the small Shansi aircraft. The General and his men were well rewarded for their victory and for capturing Tsinan with $200,000 in gold. The Shansi Army was devastated with large numbers of them retreating in panic having abandoned their well-prepared entrenchments. They disobeyed Yen's orders to protect the railway and it was every man for himself. Large numbers fell into enemy hands. Thirty thousand of them did manage to regroup and begin digging new trenches south of the town of Tehchow. Estimates of the number of soldiers killed, wounded or deserted reached 40,000. As the Shansi Army began to withdraw from Tientsin, on the 11th of September Yen Hsi-shan was aboard his armoured train and was being hunted down by aircraft as he travelled along the Tientsin-Pukow Railway. When the train was eventually located by the planes they did drop several bombs but Yen was able to escape on this occasion. Other Shansi adherents were not that lucky and a body of troops was captured with their equipment near Tsinan. The war booty taken from the troops included 9 precious field guns, 5 machine guns and 18,000 rifles. Most of the rifles were immediately sent to Nanking for refurbishing by the city's arsenal. These losses were costly in every way for the beleaguered Yen, who was already spending $6,000,000 a month on the war. The $1 million he was spending on non-military matters in his province pales in comparison. Yen's Army continued to suffer further defeats and by mid-September Shantung province was firmly in the hands of the Nationalist Army.

## The North-Eastern Front

The Lunghai or North-Eastern Front was the most vital during the Central Plains War and was fought along the length of the Lunghai Railway. This railway ran from the coast in Kiangsu province to the border of Kansu but its most important section ran through Northern Honan province. In March hostilities were developing along the railway and 17 Kuominchun generals requested that Feng Yu-hsiang should move to Chenchow. They wanted him to establish his headquarters there as the city was positioned at the junction of two vital railways. Chengchow was where the Lunghai Railway running east to west crossed the Peking–Hankow Railway running North to South. At the end of March Shansi troops began advancing southwards into North-East Honan province and soon captured the provincial capital, Kaifeng. Yen tried to keep his troops happy by sending money to all those involved in the victory. Kuominchun troops also entered the province in support and they took over most of the fighting in Honan. By April there were six Kuominchun divisions holding Chengchow, which was to become the bulwark of Feng's army in Northern Honan. To show his support for his Kuominchun allies the Shansi leader stationed five divisions in the region of Chengchow. He also moved another three divisions to the Hopei-Shantung border ready for an advance into Shantung when the time was right. Yen was committing all his army to the coming

Nationalist General Fang Chen-wu leaves a meeting with officers of the Japanese Imperial Army in Shantung province in June 1930 during the Central Plains War. He is shaking the hand of General Saito at the Imperial Army HQ in Tsinan, where he has been reassuring the Japanese. In what must have been a humiliating meeting, he has had to tell Saito that the fighting going on around the city against Yen His-shan's army would not threaten the Japanese garrisons in the eastern Chinese province.

campaign and by placing a large part of it in Northern Honan he was showing this to Feng Yu-hsiang. Feng began moving large numbers of Kuominchun units along the length of the railway and into the Han River Valley. In early March the first serious fighting on the North-East Front took place between Shansi troops under the command of General Wang Sun-jui fought Nationalist forces under General Han Fu-chu. The fighting was taking place in Central Honan province half-way between Chengchow and Hankow. Kuominchun reinforcements were sent from their stronghold at Chengchow to help while Han was sent assistance by Chiang. General Shih Yu-san's Army also moved against Han Fu-chu's beleaguered force. During the same month a large Kuominchun cavalry force arrived at Chengchow to further strengthen the garrison there.

The Kuominchun was now concentrated in the Loyang-Chengchow region while in Northern Honan the joint Kuominchun-Shansi forces were occupying the Lunghai Railway. At the end of April Feng Yu-hsiang held a parade of his best troops on the Northern Front including his elite 'Big Sword' units. Feng had even issued the da-dao fighting swords to some of his cavalry creating a new type of heavy cavalry. At the same time Yen Hsi-shan was leaving his headquarters at Taiyuan on his special armoured train with his bodyguard. Accompanying him were 7 trains full of his best troops headed for the Lunghai Front. Both leaders of the Feng-Yen Alliance were now ready to commit as many troops as needed to defeat Chiang. Their alliance was based on their mutual enmity to Chiang and if victorious they would probably fall out amongst themselves. According to reports this was the reason that Chiang Kai-shek was relatively relaxed about his long-term prospects. He was convinced that Yen and Feng would sooner or later let their own ambitions get in the way of victory. An interesting conversation was recorded between the two leaders, which showed how deep their mutual respect really went. Feng started the conversation by asking Yen, 'What do you think of your soldiers?' Yen replied, 'I don't know, what do you think?' Feng then turned the conversation around by saying; 'I'm happy with mine, why, I could hold four divisions of the Manchurians with one of mine.' Yen: 'And what about Chiang Kai-shek's?' Feng: 'They're better but one division of mine could hold three of his.' Yen: 'What do you think of mine?' Feng: 'Oh you could send as many of your divisions as you like against mine!'

As the war began to develop on the Northern Front rumours spread about defeats and victories that had not yet taken place. On the 15th of May the Feng-Yen Alliance had claimed to have destroyed a Nationalist division in the Lunghai Sector. This was denied by Chiang's spokesman, who said the two armies on that front had not even clashed yet. Within a few days the Nationalists contradicted themselves when they said they had won several engagements with the Kuominchun in the same sector. In mid May Nationalist forces were reported to be advancing northwards into Honan province to fight the Feng-Yen Armies. On the 17th of May the Nationalist 1st, 3rd and 11th Divisions were ordered to capture the city of Kweiteh in North-Eastern Honan with Chiang Kai-shek setting up his field HQ at the station outside the city. Feng Yu-hsiang had established his field headquarters in a cave to try and escape the attentions of Nationalist aircraft. The 3rd Nationalist Division chased the Kuominchun troops of General

Wan Hsuian-tsai to the Liu Ho River. In mid-May a battle broke out between a force of retreating Kuominchun troops and their comrades defending Kweiteh. The defending troops under the command of General Sun Tien-ying mistakenly fired at the men moving towards their positions. There was reported to be a great loss on life on both sides and the two commanders almost went to war again over the mistake. Meanwhile Shansi troops from Laifeng had been sent to reinforce the Kuominchun at Kweiteh and on the banks of the Liu Ho River. The Shansi Army at Kweiteh was reported to be as strong as five infantry divisions but their stay was to be short-lived. Two days later the Feng-Yen Alliance Army had evacuated Kweiteh and concentrated their forces at the nearby city of Lanfeng. This defence force was made up of five Kuominchun divisions and one cavalry division, which should have been strong enough to defend the city. In preparation for the attack on Lanfeng the 3rd Nationalist Division had captured the town of Ningling. They then linked up with the 1st Nationalist Division and moved up to Lanfeng for an assault on the town. The Nationalist Armies were under the command of General Liu Chi, General Koo Tso-tong and General Chen Chi-cheng. These were some of Chiang's most dependable generals and he expected them to deliver him a much needed victory. On the 22nd of May after an 18-hour battle superior Nationalist forces delivered a crushing defeat to the Kuominchun and captured Lanfeng. The city was 20 miles east of Kaifeng and its loss left the next Kuominchun-held stronghold exposed. The titanic battle for Lanfeng resulted in very heavy casualties on both sides and 20,000 Kuominchun were reported to have been captured. The Nationalist victory was facilitated by the defection of one of the Kuominchun generals. In another blow for the Kuominchun their Commander-in-Chief on the Lunghai Railway, General Wan Hsuan-t'sai was captured and was thrown in a dank cell in the city of Hsuchow. Chiang now stated that he would soon capture Kaifeng and then would move on to take Chengchow Feng Yu-hsiang's main stronghold in the North. Later in the month the Nationalists suffered a number of setbacks in battles along the railway when forces under Chen Cheng, one of Chiang's most trusted generals, was defeated. Chiang was only able to stabilise the front by moving large numbers of troops into the fighting. At the end of May it was decided that the Shansi forces on the Lunghai Front would stay on the defensive. Chiang now took personal command of the Nationalist Army and decided to give his troops a few weeks rest before their next offensive. This rest was disturbed by a large-scale raid by Feng's 'Big Sword' cavalry whose successes included, according to *Time* magazine, the capture of an airfield. The Nationalist airfield had 12 planes on the ground and in addition a reported 50 ground crew and pilots were captured. Claims by Feng Yu-hsiang that his troops also captured 30,000 Nationalist troops were denied by Chiang Kai-shek and were probably false.

In the middle of June the Nationalists advanced towards Kaifeng, the strategically important city to the east of Chengchow. Feng Yu-hsiang had now established his field headquarters at Kaifeng from where he would direct his war in North China. For the time being Feng had decided to adopt a defensive position and let the Nationalists try and break his forces down. The advance on Kaifeng was led by one of Chiang's elite cavalry corps who got as far as 15 miles from the city. Nationalist infantry of the 2nd Army Corps penetrated

Soldiers of the Young Marshal's North-Eastern Army march past him at a parade in Mukden in Manchuria. This parade took place about the time that their leader had committed himself to Chiang Kai-shek and the Nationalists. Chang Hsueh-liang's troops were some of the most disciplined and better trained in China. When they moved against the forces of Yen Hsii-shan and Feng Yu-hsiang during the Central Plains War in 1930, the rebels' defeat was inevitable.

the Kuominchun first defence line at Lanfeng. A Nationalist offensive westwards along the Lunghai Railway was started with large reinforcements added to the initial force. Meanwhile on the Peking–Hankow Railway Nationalist Forces were continuing to advance northwards. Kuominchun counter-attacks on the railway were a failure with the climax being an eight-hour battle after which 5,000 of their troops were taken prisoner. Fighting around Kaifeng continued into late June with a mammoth week-long battle taking place along a 50-mile front. Chiang threw up to 150,000 men into this battle but even this force was insufficient to defeat the resilient Kuominchun. When the attack petered out the Nationalist cause in the North seemed to be waning, although Chiang was as determined as usual. The Nationalists almost lost his leadership however in June when he and his headquarters were nearly overrun by Kuominchun cavalry.

To counter his frustration about Kaifeng, Chiang ordered his troops to put heavy pressure on the Lunghai Front. By the end of June two Shansi divisions on the Lanfeng-Lunghai front were forced to withdraw into Hopei province. This left only Kuominchun troops to defend the Lunghai Front and several formations of Feng's Army tried to gain the initiative by pushing the Nationalist Army back. According to the commander of the National Army's 2nd Army Corps, these divisions tried desperately to break through his left wing on the 27th and 28th of June. The repeated and increasingly desperate attacks failed under heavy artillery fire from the National Army lines. It was in battles like this that the Nationalists newly won superiority in artillery came into play. The Kuominchun, regardless of the performance of their infantry and cavalry, could not compete when it came to heavy weaponry. Once they had pushed the Kuominchun back the

Nationalists went on the counter-offensive. The offensive was successful and sent the Kuominchun in retreat back to their base at Kaifeng leaving 2,000 prisoners and large amounts of munitions behind them. In early July Feng tried to improve his situation by ordering his 20,000 Kansu reserves to join the fighting. On the 6th of July Feng suffered another reverse when a large Kuominchun force tried to cross the Liu Ho River in Anhui province. Six Kuominchun divisions under the command of General Chang Wei-si were attempting the river crossing in the early hours of the morning. When they were half-way across they were shelled by Nationalist artillery under the command of General Hsu Yuan-chan. In the ensuing panic the Kuominchun troops were sitting ducks and suffered at least 2,000 dead and thousands wounded. Hsu's troops took a further 1,000 prisoner and also captured 3 field guns, 7,000 rifles, 5 machine guns and a large amount of ammunition. This was a particularly grievous loss for the Kuominchun, who were already desperately short of ammunition. The offensive against Kaifeng had continued through late June into mid-July with the Kuominchun suffering a heavy defeat on the 18th. For three weeks there had been continuous heavy fighting around the city, which had turned into a bloody stalemate. Both sides had suffered at least 40,000 casualties in the battle and Chiang realised he was wasting his troops. On the 19th of July Chiang decided to call off the offensive against Kaifeng and concentrate his forces instead on Chengchow to the west. This pragmatic decision released a large number of Nationalist troops for service on the more important fronts including the fighting around Chengchow.


## War in the South

The Kwangsi clique's contribution to the Feng-Yen Alliance in 1930 was limited by the losses they had suffered in 1929. After their defeat the four joint leaders of Kwangsi, Generals Li Tsung-jen, Pai Ch'ung-hsi, Li Chi-shen and Huang Shao-hsiung fell out. They were persuaded to ally themselves with the northern generals but their theatre of operations was this time to be strictly in their southern stronghold. The furthest North they would be realistically prepared to fight was in Hunan, the province to the North of Kwangsi. A Southern Alliance was struck with the rebel General Chang Fa-kwei who had regrouped after his defeats in 1929. Chang had brought his army to Kwangsi at the end of 1929 and had common cause with the Kwangsi Generals. He still had 95,000 of his loyal 'Ironsides' troops under his command and these well trained troops could swing the balance. They were opposed in the South by the large Kwangtung Army as well as the Yunnan and Kweichow provincial armies, which were loyal to Chiang Kai-shek. Feng and Yen hoped that the Kwangsi Armies would advance through Hunan into Hupeh province to threaten Hankow. With their armies attacking from the South the Kuominchun was going to attack the vital city from the east. In late May the Kwangsi Army of General Chang Fat-fui was ordered to advance against Hankow. At the same time another joint Kwangsi-Ironsides Army was to advance on the Hupeh provincial capital. As they advanced northwards Chang Fa-kwei's Army captured the Hunan capital Changsha on the 5th of June. The capture of

Changsha caused a great deal of panic in Hankow as there were few Nationalist troops to oppose the southerners' further advance. However, the advance of Chang's 'Ironsides' was stopped when their rear was cut off with the Nationalist recapture of Changsha on the 17th of June. The city was taken by the Hunanese Commander-in-Chief, General Ho Chien, who had been chased out of Changsha by the 'Ironsides'. Most of the Kwangsi Army now moved eastwards leaving Chang and his 'Ironsides' along with a few Kwangsi divisions to fight the Nationalist Armies that were gathering in Hunan. These were made up of Kwangtung and Yunnanese troops as well as the 'elite' 3rd Model Nationalist Regiment under General Tan Tao-yuan. General Tan had been successful against the Kwangsi Army in 1929 and his presence gave the Nationalists an edge. As the main Kwangsi army moved back to its provincial capital at Nanning, Chiang Kai-shek ordered his southern armies to pursue them. In early July 1930 Chang Fa-kwei's men were finally cornered and heavily defeated in Southern Hunan province losing 15,000 men. They were part of a larger force made up of Chang's troops, three Kwangsi divisions and one rebel Hunanese division. A number of Hunanese troops had gone over to the invaders in April and some were still fighting with them. A well dug-in Kwangtung army of three divisions broke the allied force and slaughtered them by the thousand. This victory allowed the transfer of seven veteran Nationalist divisions for service in Honan and Shantung. For the rest of the war the remaining Kwangsi armies were besieged in their strongholds, with large forces defending Nanning. By mid-September the northern part of Kwangsi was occupied by Hunnanese armies while the south-eastern part was held by Kwangtung armies. In the central belt of the province the garrisons at Nanning and other big cities which were besieged by Yunnanese armies held out. By the end of the month Yunnanese troops had occupied the suburbs of Nanning and it was only the end of the war in the North which saved them. They now only had enough strength to control Kwangsi and for the next six years were content to try to consolidate their hold.

## Other Fronts

Away from the main fighting in Northern Honan and Shantung provinces there were a number of 'sideshow' fronts. Although the fighting on these fronts was just as bloody as the main theatres of the war, it was not as decisive. From March Feng Yu-hsiang had threatened to attack the important city of Hankow in Hupeh province. In late March he opened a general offensive in Western Hupeh with Hankow as his objective. The advance reached as far as the town of Siangyang 200 miles north-west of Hankow but came up against Nationalist defences. A 5,000-strong Kuominchun Army tried to attack the recently prepared Nationalist defences at the town. This force was joined by further Kuominchun reinforcements but they were facing a 70,000-strong Nationalist Army under General Ho Chen-chun. At the same time on the other side of the Central Plains fighting was taking place in North Anhwei province. This was between large Kuominchun and Nationalist forces for the control of the city of Pukow. In mid-May in fighting for Pukow the Nationalist General Liu Chi announced that he had defeated a large Kuominchun

Light artillery of the Nationalist Army fire their 19th-century mountain guns during the Central Plains War in 1930. There was a shortage of medium and heavy pieces suffered by all the military cliques in the 1920s. Chiang Kai-shek had placed orders with European arms dealers as soon as he came to power in 1928. Most of these new field guns were still undelivered when the wars with Feng and Yen began in 1929.

force capturing 10,000 prisoners along with 5,000 rifles and 6 field guns. At the same time another Nationalist General, Koo Tso-tong, claimed to have routed the Kuominchun and to have taken 10,000 rifles and 19 field guns at Pukow. These losses were a terrible blow to the Kuominchun war effort, particularly the 25 field guns which were in short supply in Feng's army. At the end of July Feng Yu-hsiang again made preparations for an attack on Hankow saying that the Nationalist generals there were willing to join him. In reality though, Feng's threat to attack Hankow had depended on the support of the Kwangsi army from the South. Their defeat now made it impossible for the Kuominchun to attack the well defended city unless he was victorious in the North.

## Chiang's Political Opposition and the Nationalist Offensive

Wang Ching-wei once again led the political opposition to Chiang Kai-shek in 1930, after being expelled from the Kuomintang in December 1929. In February 1930 he accused the Nationalist Government of 'bribery, corruption and dictatorship' and having silenced all political opposition with terror tactics. An 'Enlarged Conference of the Kuomintang 'was held in Peking which incorporated every viewpoint of the Anti-Chiang alliance. On the 3rd of September an alternative Chinese Government was formed in Peking but was of little concern to Chiang. The Nationalist leader knew that rival governments were not a threat and it was on the battlefield that the future of China would be decided. With this in mind he ordered the launch of a large offensive in northern China to finally crush his opponents.

A huge Nationalist offensive was in preparation in the first days of September with an estimated 300,000 men in 27 divisions to be used to finally crush the rebels. They were to take part in a two-pronged offensive against the city of Chengchow with the first advance going westwards along the Lunghai Railway and the second northwards up the Hankow–Chengchow Railway. This large army was under the joint command of Generals Chou Ting-kwai, Chang Kwang-ng'ai and Koo Tso-tong. In addition, the 1st Training Division under General Fang Yi-pei was to join the army for the offensive.

The heaviest fighting took place between the 7th and 16th of September with the well trained Kuominchun troops putting up stiff resistance. It was estimated that Feng still had 200,000 'disciplined and well-equipped troops in strongly entrenched positions' on the Lunghai Front. On the 17th Feng's divisions launched a counter-offensive which gained some ground for the Kuominchun and inflicted heavy losses on the Nationalist Army. The main aim of this successful Kuominchun offensive however was to cover Feng's retreat to his base in Shensi province. On the 25th Feng was forced to surrender Lanfeng, one of the strongest Kuominchun positions on the Lunghai Railway. The Nationalist offensive launched on the Lunghai–Hankow–Chengchow Railway Front was making great progress by the 1st of October. Its troops had crossed the Lo Ho River and were continuing their advance on the vital city of Chengchow. Two divisions of the Nationalist Army under the command of General's Chiang Kwang-ngai and Cho Ting-kai from Canton had attacked the city of Haishihkuan. The Shansi army was also under pressure from North-Eastern Army divisions advancing southwards down the Peking–Chengchow Railway. Instead of retreating in front of the larger Manchurian force, the Shansi Army began to prepare defences in and around the cities of Nankow and Chengting. Their intention was to defend these cities and the vital rail junction at the city of Shichiachuan. Shichiachuan was the key to any National Army advance on the Shansi capital at Taiyuan and had to be well defended.

## Chang Hsueh-liang Takes Sides

On the 18th of September Chang Hsueh-liang finally chose sides in the civil war and brought his powerful North-Eastern Army into battle. He sent an open telegram to the combatants saying that the Government of Chiang Kai-shek should now resolve any problems. This was code for 'Chiang Kai-shek is the legitimate leader of China and I will support him.' He then ordered his troops to go through the vital Shanhaikwan Pass from Manchuria into northern China to occupy North Hopei province. This audacious move gave Chang control of two of the most important northern railways, the Peking–Wuhan and Tienstin–Pukow. It also diverted the rich Tientsin customs revenues into his bank instead of Chiang's. Chiang was so relieved to finally get the support of the North-Eastern Army that he had to swallow his pride regarding Chang's extension of power. Chang was also confirmed as in command of the North-Eastern Border Defence Army, a huge force estimated at 409,000.

On the 22nd of September Chang's troops entered Hopei province, swiftly taking Peking, Tientsin and other important cities in northern China. After pledging his support to Chiang Kai-shek, Chang Hsueh-liang was beginning a partial mobilisation of his North-Eastern Army. He mobilised the 3rd and 5th Infantry Divisions, the 1st Cavalry Division and the 6th and 27th Artillery Brigades. At the end of the month, Chang's General Pei Fang-hsien occupied Paoting on the Chengchow-Peking Railway. He negotiated with Yen Hsi-shan for the transfer of the railway system around Peking to his forces. To emphasise the point he moved two armoured trains and a brigade of troops into the area to begin an advance, combined with troops from Paoting, on the strategic city of Shihchiachuan. Large numbers of North-Eastern Army troops moved into Honan province and cleared it of the last remnants of the Kuominchun by October. In early November Chang set up his HQ in Peking and was joined by his wife, who travelled by train to join him, as a sign of his commitment to Chiang. His ground forces meanwhile were advancing into Kalgan with a 3,000-strong force taking over from the retiring Shansi Army. In a show of force, the occupiers brought heavy artillery and tanks to emphasise Chang's superiority over Yen Hsi-shan.

## The Battle for Chengchow

The fighting around Chengchow and along the Peking–Hankow Railway was particularly ferocious at the end of September. Two Nationalist divisions under Generals Liu Mao-an and Ha Meng-yang outflanked the Kuominchun at Yunyang. These divisions then joined the assault on Chengchow, despite continued resistance by General Sun Lien-chung's troops. Kuominchun forces were digging defensive positions around the city but were under bombardment by Nationalist heavy artillery. Feng Yu-hsiang had ordered two divisions to be

Soldiers of Chiang Kai-shek's Nationalist Army clamber aboard a goods train during the Central Plains War. The troops are from one of the NRA's better units and are well armed with sub-machine guns and well equipped. China's railways were vital to all the warring factions in the fighting of 1929–30; with no motor transport they were the only way to move troops around the vast country.

sent to reinforce the defenders of Chengchow. On the 30th of September Chiang Kai-shek inspected large numbers of Nationalist troops at Fukow, which were to be used to attack Chengchow. Meanwhile, the battle for Chengchow had reached its climax with 80,000 Nationalist Army troops crossing the river. They were within a few miles of the city when they were met by an overwhelming Kuominchun force which had been positioned skilfully by Feng. He had been able to build new entrenchments in just the right place having had inside information on Chiang's plans. A Nationalist plane had been forced to land behind Kuominchun lines and it was carrying despatches that included Chiang's orders. The Kuominchun had an advantage at Chengchow in that its forces were operating on inner lines. This meant reinforcements could be quickly rushed to any threatened section of the defences. Nationalist lines had to stretch in a long semi-circle around Chengchow, which meant they needed more troops to man them. As Chiang moved more and more troops towards Chengchow this advantage waned and Feng was ready to strike his final blow. On the 6th of October a large Kuominchun army was defeated close to Chengchow. Chiang received a message from their commander General Li Chin-lin to say they wished to surrender. Their retreat along the Peking–Hankow Railway had been cut off after the line had been destroyed by Nationalist engineers.

The Nationalist Army continued their advance towards Chengchow and on the 8th of October the Army's 11th Division entered the outskirts of the city at 9.00 am. Twelve hours later the whole of the city was in Nationalist hands, along with Feng's HQ and large amounts of heavy weaponry and equipment. During the assault the Nationalists lost one of their best-loved commanders, General Chang K'uang-lo. A 30,000-strong Kuominchun force now retreated to a new position 40 miles north of the city. Some of these defeated troops moved towards the Shansi border but were met by a strong Shansi army there to stop them crossing it. Yen Hsi-shan made a strong protest about Kuominchun threats to southern Shansi and sent two artillery regiments to reinforce his forces on the border. Meanwhile the North-Eastern Army continued to advance southwards down the Peking–Chengchow Railway. Chang Hsueh-liang avoided direct clashes with the Shansi army as he did not want to fight the disciplined troops of Yen. In fact, it was reported that Shansi and Manchurian troops fraternised with each other when they came into contact. Feng Yu-hsiang and 30,000 men crossed the Yellow River to establish a new headquarters at Chiaotso. It was estimated that the total number of troops available to fight for the Kuominchun in October was as low as 50,000. With Feng's withdrawal from the main theatre, the war was lost by the Feng-Yen Alliance.

## The Defeated Shansi & Kuominchun Armies

In late October the North-East Army of Chang Hsueh-liang moved into Inner Mongolia and there was a threat of war there with the Shansi army. Inner Mongolia included the newly created provinces of Suiyuan and Chahar. Yen's troops massed on the northern Shansi border. Yen Hsi-shan concentrated 50–70,000 troops at strategic positions in north, east and south Shansi province. He also ordered the building of a number of fortifications to guard against the advance of the North-Eastern Army into his province. In preparation for any offensive by the Nationalist Army an additional 50,000 new recruits were being trained at two centres in North and Eastern Shansi. Yen's arsenals were also working overtime to try and supply these new troops and Taiyuan was reported to be full of new munitions. By the 29th of October North-Eastern troops and Shansi troops were facing each other on the Northern front. The Manchurian air force bombed Taiyuan from their base at Chengchow. The raid did not do too much material damaged and only four people were killed with several others injured. The Kuominchun meanwhile was disintegrating with wholesale desertions amongst units in North-West Honan, and in South-Western and Eastern Shansi provinces. Many isolated units deserted to General Shih Yu-san, the former Kuominchun commander who had defected back to the Nationalist Army, his former employer. Shih had immediately been given his old command back and was expected to attract other Kuominchun officers and men to change sides. Thousands of 'elite' Kuominchun cavalry under the command of General Chen Ta-chang had crossed the Yellow River into Honan province to surrender. At the same time, several other large Kuominchun forces to the west of the city of Chengchow had gone over to General Shih. In an effort to compensate for this loss of troops to the National Army General Sun Tien-ying was desperately trying to recruit soldiers. He had launched recruitment drives in North Honan and Southern Hopei provinces.

Feng Yu-hsiang had other problems. General Liu Yu-feng was marching his army towards Kansu province and away from the fighting. Strong Shansi formations had managed to return to their own province largely intact by the end of October. They were still well armed with a total of 60,000 rifles and more importantly 100 field guns. Remnants of the Kuominchun had also retreated into southern Shansi province from North Honan with 30,000 rifles and 50 or so field guns. By December Yen Hsi-shan was desperate for funds to pay his remaining soldiers or failing that, to feed them. The total revenue of Shansi province was $1 million – his paymasters were handing over $7 million in Shansi bank notes to his troops.

## The Air War, 1930

By the time the serious fighting took place in the summer of 1930 the air force of the Nationalist Government had grown substantially. The hodge-podge of different trainers, transports and elderly light bombers used in 1929 had been reinforced by modern military aircraft. In the summer of 1929 6 Potez-25 light bombers and 2 Potez-33 bomber / transports had arrived from France. These were joined by 12 up-to-date US Vought Corsair light bombers in January 1930 and a further 20 by September. With these new types of combat plane the National Government had a superiority over the air arms of any other province and was considered to be the National Air Force of China. When Chang Hsueh-liang joined Chiang in September 1930, he brought with him 36 aircraft. These were all light bombers which were based at Peking and were formed into bombing squadrons. In May Chiang got 16 new planes, which arrived with

12 French pilots to fly them. Because of the shortage of Chinese pilots he was forced to pay the mercenaries $1,200 each per month.

In opposition to the Nationalist air arm were the weak air arms of Yen Hsi-shan and Feng Yu-hsiang. The 12-strong Shansi air force was sent to the Northern Front in April under the command of it chief pilot Teng Chien-chun. It was made up mainly of modern light Junkers transports that could act as bombers when necessary. Feng's Air Force was even weaker so he tried to increase the number of aircraft by ordering 20 SVA light bombers from Italy in early 1930. It is not known if all of them arrived in China before the end of the war but half did arrive in June. In May the Nationalists had started using large squadrons of bombers to attack Feng's stronghold at Chengchow. One raid in May involved eight light bombers, which attacked Kaifeng, Kweiteh and Chengchow. The raid was a success but one Nationalist plane was shot down. Yen Hsi-shan offered a $1,000 reward to whoever was responsible. He was furious that Nationalist planes had also dropped leaflets over Chengchow offering $100,000 rewards for the heads of both Feng and Yen Hsi-shan. Yen tried to aid his ally Feng by sending some of his few improvised bombers to North Honan. On the 28th of August two Nationalist planes made a daring raid on Peking specifically to disrupt a session of the Anti-Chiang enlarged Kuomintang conference. They dropped a few bombs and then proceeded to fly over the city machine gunning any troops they saw while avoiding the fire of three anti-aircraft guns.

## The Railway War

Much of the fighting in the northern theatre in 1930 took place along the railways of Northern Honan province. Battles took place between several of the Nationalist Government's armoured trains and the trains of Feng's Kuominchun. Both armies had used these armoured monsters in the 1926–28 fighting and some had been captured from the defeated northern warlords during the earlier campaign. The railways were to play a vital role in the 1930 fighting to transport the large armies from one front to another. Chiang Kai-shek used the railways to great effect, moving large numbers of troops in Shantung in August to capture Tsinan. These had become available after the defeat of the Kwangsi Armies in southern China so had to be moved a great distance. Trains also transported thousands of troops into Kansu province against Feng's Army and to Shansi province to attack Yen's forces. The railways were vital to all sides and logistically they often made the difference between victory and defeat. Chiang Kai-shek was fortunate in having a logistics genius, General Yu Fei-peng on his staff who earned a reputation for moving troops quickly from one battle to another. When the fighting on the Lunghai Front was at a stalemate Chiang urgently needed troops moving to Shantung province to attack the Shansi Army. General Yu cleared the lines and moved a large number of men along the Tientsin-Pukow Railway, who duly defeated Yen Hsi-shan's troops. All the time the troops were on the trains they were under threat from Kuominchun forces but within a week they were back on the Lunhai Front ready to fight Feng's

Army. In China in the early 1930s this was nothing short of a logistics miracle. The war had a devastating effect on the Chinese railway system with a 1930 report on the Tientsin-Pukow Railway summing up the situation. It said that out of 1,988 wagons owned by the Railway 1,522 had been stolen or destroyed. At least 30% of the sleepers on the various lines were rotten and needed replacing.

## Aftermath of the War and the Cost

Chiang Kai-shek had proved himself an astute military commander during the Central Plains War. He had used political and military manoeuvring to equal effect, fighting his enemies when he could not buy them off. On the battlefield his organisational skills had proved to be superior to most of his adversaries who had seen long service during the warlord period. As one commentator said he 'successfully manoeuvred multiple army corps over fronts that could stretch as long as a thousand miles'. His victory, however, had been won at a high cost to his army and he had lost some of his best young officers in the war. All sides argued over the total number of military casualties suffered but an overall figure of 300,000 dead was broadly accepted. The National Army of Chiang Kai-shek claimed to have inflicted 150,000 losses on the various rebel armies. They gave their losses at a probably deflated figure of 30,000 dead and 60,000 wounded. Civilian casualties were not discussed by the military who had little interest in the suffering of the general population. Although the fighting had been restricted to one region of the country, hundreds of thousands of troops marching across northern China devastated the countryside.

On Christmas Day Marshal Chang Hsueh-liang consulted with Yen and Feng regarding the reorganisation of the Kuominchun and Shansi armies. The two defeated Generals agreed to his demands but asked for funds to pay for the demobilisation of large numbers of troops. In early January 1931 the defeated Kuominchun and Shansi armies were waiting to be disbanded by the victorious Nationalists. A total of 80,000 Kuominchun and 160,000 Shansi troops were reported to be content with their fate after the brutality of the 1929–30 fighting. In former days the defeated soldiers would have been quickly absorbed into the victor's armies but this was not the case on this occasion. Most soldiers were indifferent as to what role they were given by the Nationalists. They would be happy to remain as soldiers, work in labour battalions, or be disbanded. Their only concern was if they did get disbanded, whether they could retain their uniforms and receive some compensation, or be given alternative employment.

The Central Plains War fought between 1929 and 1930 was immensely costly to China on every level not only with the number of killed and wounded but in financial terms. As mentioned above, estimates of the number of military dead and wounded were about 150,000 on each side but this is almost certainly an underestimate. It was thought that Chinese military officials were usually ordered to reduce any casualties by 50%, so the actual figures were probably much higher. Civilian dead were not recorded at the time but with the amount of devastation caused all over China by the war, decease and famine would have taken a heavy toll. It was estimated at the time that civilian deaths would have been three times that of military deaths. The main cause of death in areas affected by the war was starvation due to the stealing of crops and stores by the various armies. In peacetime it was difficult enough for the peasants to survive and any conflict in China always resulted in many thousands of deaths. The devastation caused to villages, towns and cities by bombing raids was considerable. Although the amount of damage done by the combatants' aircraft cannot be compared to later conflicts it was still a major issue. Large parts of cities like Taian in Shantung province were destroyed by air attack with little hope for any reconstruction. Other towns like Nanning in Kwangsi province suffered sieges, which led to large numbers of deaths and damage to buildings. Over the course of the war it cost Chiang Kai-shek $10 million monthly to run his war machine. His main opponents also paid heavily for their war effort, with Yen Hsi-shan spending $7 million a month while Feng Yu-hsiang spent $3.5 million. Besides the pay for the vast armies the other main expense was on ammunition. Chiang Kai-shek bought 5,000 boxes of bullets during the war. Yen Hsii-shan and Feng Yu-hsiang between them bought 7,000 boxes of ammunition from foreign countries. Nearly all the money spent did not come out of the generals' pockets but was extracted in taxes from the population. Taxation was as usual in war raised to high levels and armies travelling through a village or town would extort more money from the people. Some armies may have paid for goods and food but this was usually with the armies' own issued paper money, which was of no real value.

When the peasants tried to rebuild their lives and begin to plant crops they were working land devastated by the fighting. The number of cultivated fields destroyed during the war by the digging of trenches and fortifications was said to be bigger than Belgium. In Honan province alone the frontline extended to over 60 districts and the trenches dug during the conflict covered about 4 million acres. In any case many of the males of working age had been forced to act as porters by all the armies. Others were forced to perform others tasks such as digging the miles of trenches, as soldiers would refuse to dig them themselves. Others were press-ganged into joining the army. Often it was the only means of feeding their families. In Chengchow in Honan province every male between the age of 15 and 60 were forced to perform these various military services. Another 8,000 were recruited into the army as itpassed through the city, further depleting the men available to do the farming.

The damage done to the already fragile infrastructure of China was terrible. This was especially the case regarding the railways, with bridges being blown up on most of the major routes. Yen Hsi-shan's army had destroyed bridges on the Tientsin-Pukow Railway that crossed the Yellow River. Wooden sleepers had been torn up along large stretches of the Lunghai Railway, which would take months to replace. Even when the railways were intact there were few wagons or trains available to run along them. On the river network, a vital part of the Chinese transport system, 90% of steamers had been commandeered by the military. Skilled railwaymen and river workers did not receive any wages because of the damage done to their tracks, bridges and other infrastructure. One thing was for sure: the financial cost of the war would be met on all sides by an increase in taxation for the long-suffering people of China.

# 4

# 'Illegal, Provocative Action':
# The Sino-Soviet War, 1929

When Chang Hsueh-liang came to power in Manchuria and North China he adopted the same strongly anti-Communist attitude and policies as his father Chang Tso-lin. His father had actively persecuted Chinese Communists and arrested and executed a large number of them in the 1920s. In April 1927 Chang Tso-lin's men had raided the Soviet Embassy in Peking, which was under his control at the time. They discovered a large stock of propaganda documents during the raid, which confirmed Chang's suspicions. He had long thought that the Embassy was being used as a base to subvert his government and to promote Communism in China. Other documents were found which showed that funds from the Chinese Eastern Railway were being used for the same purpose. Built during the pre-revolution era the jointly Russian-Chinese owned railway ran from Siberia through Manchurian territory. At the end of the line was the vital Russian port of Vladivostok and the railway formed the main line of communication to Moscow. Under agreements between the Chinese and Russia there could be no interference with any movements of goods and passengers along the strategic railway.

There was a cosy arrangement between the Soviet Union and Imperial Japan over control of the two main railways in the Manchurian region. This had always been at Manchuria's expense and hurt the pride of Chang Tso-lin and his successor, his son Chang Hsueh-liang. In 1925 the Japanese had tacitly acknowledged Soviet joint control over the Chinese Eastern Railway. At the same time the Soviet Union recognised Japan's control over the South Manchurian Railway. Both railways ran through Manchurian territory and the Nationalist Government would dearly have loved to seize both of them after 1928.

In March 1929 the Nationalists tried to open negotiations to alter the ownership of the Chinese Eastern Railway to make it more equal. When it became obvious that this was not going to happen rumours of Chang Hsueh-liang's intentions began to circulate during the spring. It appeared that Chang Hsueh-liang was determined to provoke a conflict with the Soviet Union. Talks between Chang and the Soviet Government were aborted when the 'Young Marshal' insisted on Chiang Kai-shek's inclusion in them. The Soviet Foreign Minister, Maxim Lituinov, thought that Chang Hsueh-liang was becoming a problem. He said that he would need a 'sharp wrap over the knuckles' to keep him in line or 'military action would become unavoidable'. In May Chang tried to put more pressure on the Soviets by demanding that they fulfil their promise made in 1924 to sell them the railway. Both sides escalated the propaganda battle with Chiang Kai-shek claiming that the Soviet position was 'imperialism, a red imperialism more dangerous than

The crew of a Red Army MS-1 light tank check out its tracks and armament before taking it into action. Several companies of this modification of the French Renault FT-17 were used during the 1929 fighting in Manchuria. In the late 1920s the Soviet Union was only just beginning to manufacture its own weaponry, usually copies of British and French types.

white imperialism'. Chang's anger regarding the railway grew when he found out that the Communist International had called a secret meeting on the 27th of May 1929 in the city of Harbin. Harbin was a large city in the North of Manchuria and Chang was angry that the Communists should have the effrontery to call their meeting there. The meeting was raided by Chang's police force and 40 Russians and about the same number of Manchurian Communists were arrested. Documents found at the meeting proved that the Russian staff who worked on the Chinese Eastern Railway were secretly using their positions to promote Communism. This information was enough for Chang to decide to seize control of the CER and put it under Manchurian control. If he succeeded it would also allow him to charge the Russians heavy tariffs to move their goods from Siberia to Vladivostok. Chang met with Chiang Kai-shek in Nanking in early July and asked for permission to take military action to seize the CER. On the 10th of July Chang's troops struck, seizing the railway and arresting some 1,200 Russian workers, officials and union leaders. The Russians were interned in a makeshift prison in abandoned railway buildings a few miles from Harbin. At the same time they were taking control of the CER, Chang's troops also seized the railway telegraph system and took control of the offices of the Soviet Far Eastern Trading Corporation, or Naptha Trust. They requisitioned a number of large paddle steamers from the Soviet Mercantile Fleet that belonged to the CER. These boats ran up and down the main rivers of Manchuria, the Amur and the Sungari.

The Russians were not surprisingly furious at Chang's seizure of the railway and pledged if necessary to take military action to regain control of it. They demanded the end of this 'illegal, provocative action' but at the same time offered Chang a 'peaceful route' out of the crisis. Chang was fixed on his policy and did not appear to be afraid of the actions of the Red Army. When the Soviet government gave him three days to reply to their demands, he ignored them. During the war of words the Soviet command insisted that they were fighting a war against the 'Chinese White Generals', not against the ordinary Chinese. They put out propaganda which proclaimed, 'The Red Army is the Friend of the Workers of China.' On the 17th of July all diplomatic contacs between Chang and Moscow was broken off. Fervour in Manchuria was strong with a number of Chang's generals demanding he immediately declare war on the Soviet Union. They claimed that they would be willing to personally lead their men into action against the hated Russians. A group of US pressmen were surprised when they interviewed Manchurian soldiers in the early stages of the war. The soldiers were in high spirits and said that they were unafraid of the Russians and that they were confident they could win.

## The Chinese North-Eastern Army

The Manchurian troops of the North-Eastern Army under the command of Chang Hsueh-liang were a mixed bunch. Some were veterans of his father Chang Tso-lin's Fengtien Army, while others were raw recruits raised by the Young Marshal since 1928. It is difficult to get an accurate figure on the total number of Manchurian troops but 200,000 is a likely estimate. Soviet claims of 300,000 regulars in the North-Eastern Army were high and the additional 200,000 they claimed were in the para-military and territorial forces was a lie. Much of the fighting in the war with the Soviet Union seems to have been done by irregular cavalry. It is obvious from reports that Chang Hsueh-liang did not sacrifice his best troops in the fighting with the Red Army. Some Manchurian units were well armed with modern rifles, sub-machine guns, machine guns and artillery. Others however were not, with photographic evidence showing that some north-eastern troops were armed only with broadswords and spears! Most of the heavy equipment and weaponry were leftovers from the pre-1928 army, even though Chang Hsueh-liang tried to order new weapons. The North-Eastern Army did have some medium and heavy artillery, as before 1928 Chang Tso-lin had purchased some modern guns. The Soviet estimate of the number of artillery pieces in the North-Eastern Army was an exaggerated 450. Most of these would have been the locally made heavy trench mortars of up to 120mm calibre. Chang also bought a number of FT-17 light tanks and some of these were reported to have been used. Chang Hsueh-liang probably hoped that the sheer weight of numbers could overwhelm the Red Army in 1929. The North-Eastern Army did have a strong air arm and 11 modern Potez 25 light bombers were moved to the frontline. After two of the planes were lost on the way to the battlefront the rest appear to have been kept out of the fighting for the duration.

## The White Guards

Throughout the fighting in Manchuria the Soviet press and the Red Army made constant references to 'White Guard' involvement on the Manchurian side. Nearly every Soviet report blamed attacks by armed groups on these White Russian émigrés who had settled in Manchuria after 1922. It would of course have made sense for Chang Hsueh-liang to employ these veterans of almost constant warfare from 1914 to 1922 in his army. There were definitely White Guard Detachments active in northern Manchuria with at least 3,000 guardsmen near the border. They were of all strengths from a band of a few dozen to some several hundred strong with heavier weaponry. A press report of July 1929 goes into some detail but its estimation of 20,000 White Guardsmen with their own modern air arm is almost certainly pure fantasy. Soviet claims of 70,000 White Russians ready to fight against them was pure speculation, although there were numerous anti-Soviet groups in Manchuria. Another report did say that 30,000 White Russians had applied to Chinese military authorities in Harbin to fight against the Soviets. The White Guards commanders in 1929 were listed as General Nichaeff and General Makarenko with political support from the infamous Ataman Gregoriv Semenov. Other leaders mentioned in Soviet propaganda were Khorvatov and Arestoulov and the famous civil war

Poorly dressed soldiers of the Red Army stand on parade, according to the original caption at the time of the Sino-Soviet War of 1929. The Red Army was still recovering from the catastrophic civil war and was in the process of reorganising its huge forces. Some of these soldiers would have been veterans of the fighting against the White Russians and were battle-hardened. Stacked in front of them are the Moisin-Nagant rifles which were the standard rifles of the Red Army, having been in service with the Czarist Army before 1917.

leader Ataman Dutov. Many of the volunteers came from amongst the veterans of Semenov and his fellow Ataman Kalymkov who had terrorised Siberia in the early 1920s. (Their troops in Siberia had murdered and raped with impunity after the fall of Kolchak's government.) According to reports the Guardsmen were armed with artillery supplied by Krupp and plenty of Maxim machine guns. When the war was over, one stipulation made to Chang Hsueh-liang was that he must clamp down on the guards and dismiss any he had serving in his army.

## The Outbreak of War and the Formation of the Special Far Eastern Army

When the first fighting broke out in Manchuria in July 1929 Chang Hsueh-liang showed his confidence to his staff by going on a brief holiday. He was seen on the beach in his bathing suit surrounded by his staff 'similarly attired' at the resort of Pei Tai Ho. Press reports said that instead of 'fiddling while Rome burned' like Nero, he 'bathed while his armies clashed'. In his absence his High Command had ordered 60,000 men to take up positions along the Chinese Eastern Railway. By the 24th of July it was reported that there were 50,000 troops under General Chang Tso-hsiang on the Kirin-Soviet border. Another 40,000 troops under General Fang Fu-lung were stationed at the northern border town of Manchouli. At the same time the Soviet Union was preparing its plans for the campaign in Manchuria, beginning with the creation of a new army.

A unit of Chang Hsueh-liang's North-Eastern Army pose outside their barracks during the war with the Soviet Union. This unit illustrates well the variation in weaponry carried by the Manchurian troops in 1929. The soldiers have rifles slung over their shoulders but are also armed with spears, while their NCOs have fighting swords. Chinese soldiers had carried fighting swords as well as firearms for many years but the spear-rifle combination is unusual.

The Soviet government knew that if they were to achieve their objectives in Manchuria, sending ad hoc military forces over the border was not going to be sufficient. On the 6th of August Moscow authorised funds to organise a 'Special Far Eastern Army' to be commanded by Russian Civil War hero General Vasili K Blyuker. Blyuker had just been given the role of Soviet Military Attaché in Berlin but his new position in Manchuria was temporary. He was a Far Eastern specialist who understood the Oriental ways of making war and was a past expert on the swift kinds of operations required in Manchuria. The Special Far Eastern Army, or ODVA, was recruited exclusively in the Siberian Military District whose resources were limited, with only 20 tanks and 20 armoured cars available. The armoured cars were sent on immediate patrol duty along the borders between the Soviet Union and Manchuria. The 18th Rifle Corps was activated in the Trans-Baikal sector while the 19th Rifle Corps was activated in the Nikolsk-Ussurisk sector of the Maritime province. The 21st Territorial and 12th Perm Rifle Divisions were moved to Chita and a company of MS-1 light tanks were attached to the Trans-Baikal force. Starting the build-up to the war with 30,000 men, the ODVA was soon expanded to 60,000 and eventually to between 100 and 113,000 men. East Army Corps had 3 Rifle Divisions and 1 Cavalry Brigade. The only troops that were not from Siberia were the 7,000 OGPU Secret Police responsible for internal security in Manchuria. Many of the ODVA were hardened veterans of the 1918–1922 Civil War with some having fought the remnants of the White

Typical cavalry of the North-Eastern Army ride through a Manchuria border town during the Sino-Soviet War. Chang Hsueh-liang's army was a mixture of immaculately turned out regular troops and scruffy irregulars like these. His forces were still in the process of reorganising when the fighting with the Red Army broke out. Much of the fighting in 1929 was done by troops like these, many of whom were little better than bandits.

Russian Armies in the east until 1922 and beyond. Air support for the ODVA was made up of 70 aircraft, which was a huge commitment for the still developing Red air force. Aircraft types included the R1 light bomber, Fokker DXI fighters and MR1 floatplanes attached to the River Fleet.

## August Fighting

Most of August was spent by the Red Army and the North-Eastern Army in a series of small and large-scale skirmishes and battles. Although most of the attacks were done by the Russians this tit for tat warfare also involved raids by the Chinese into Soviet territory. In an attempt to forestall any cross-border raids, the Manchurian 10th Brigade was ordered to the northern border area on the 11th. At the same time one division of Manchurian troops stationed at Hailar was sent to the border town of Manchouli. In Manchouli the hard-pressed garrison had desperately called for reinforcements of cavalry and artillery. Five days later the Red Army launched a fierce attack on Manchouli and Hailar which lasted from 15.30 until 19.30. Although there was a lot of exchange of fire between the two forces, the attackers claimed to have not lost a single casualty. On the Manchurian side losses were relatively light with 25 soldiers and their Platoon Commander killed. Next day on the 17th two Chinese Battalions, 1,000 men, attacked a Soviet border post manned by only 17 border guards armed with machine guns. Soviet propaganda said at the time that this tiny force managed to withstand numerous Chinese attacks. Part of the defence force was made up of the wives of the guards, who helped their husbands feed the machine guns.

In a battle on the night of 17th–18th August at Tungning, South of Suifenho, a Soviet mixed force of 1,400 infantry and cavalry backed by machine guns and artillery fought the Manchurian garrison. When large numbers of Chinese reinforcements turned up in the vicinity the Soviet force withdrew. It appeared that the Russians were only interested in acquiring food stuffs and other supplies and did not want to control territory. On the 17th the Manchurian Government had been informed of the threat of a large 10,000-strong Red Army force with 30 guns. This force attacked Manchurian positions between Manchouli and Chalainor, with the main threat against the latter town. The attack on Chalainor saw a rare local success for the Manchurians when the defenders withdrew to well-prepared defences. These trenches, 400 yards to the rear of the first trench, had been armed with machine guns. When the Red Army troops attacked they were slaughtered in large numbers by the Manchurians who, for once, stood their ground.

Two days after this Russian setback Red Army scouts aided by local Korean guides raided the village of Szetaohotze just across the border in the Manchurian province of Kirin. They looted and burned the village as a warning to the Manchurian authorities to stop any more raids. This attack was followed up by 3,000 Soviet troops with several field guns, which fired against the Chinese lines at Tungninghsien in Kirin province. As was usually the case, the Red Army withdrew as they did not want to take territory at this point. The same day

Soldiers of Chang Hsueh-liang's North-Eastern Army gather at a railway station in the winter of 1929. The troops are dressed for winter campaigning with padded cotton uniforms and fur hats. These soldiers had fought with the Soviet Army in the summer and autumn of that year and had been roundly beaten. Although these men are all well-armed with rifles, some of their less fortunate comrades were seen with nothing but spears during the 1929 war.

Soviet troops bombarded the Chinese defensive lines at Meiyachou village near Dalainor, 13 miles inside the Siberian-Manchurian border. A Red Army cavalry force then rushed the village and heavy fighting ensued. An attack by the Red Army at the town of Hsilingho had been repulsed as had another raid on Dalainor, which was well defended. The Manchurian garrison, well supplied with machine guns, repelled the raiders while suffering 27 killed and 31 wounded. The medical services of the Manchurian Army were primitive and few of the wounded would have survived. These low-level attacks by the Red Army were just the beginning and appeared to be a test for further escalation of the war. As one commentator at the time said, 'It is obvious that Russia was feeling her way, by these incursions into Chinese territory, to learn what the actual resistance would be and whether or not it would be wise for her to undertake a large scale operation.' (*Conflict in the Far East*, pg 114.)

As the fighting intensified during August Chang tried to reinforce and re-organise his army. He appointed the capable General Chang Tso-hsiang as commander of his cavalry and brought in reinforcements. During mid-August Manchurian reinforcements had been sent from different parts of the province. A large 24,000-strong Manchurian army had arrived at Tsitsihar and 10,000 men had reinforced Manchouli. 50,000 troops were also reported to heading for the war from Taonanfu on the 21st of August.

The border town of Manchouli was threatened on the 24th when the Chinese commander reported the advance of a Soviet armoured train. This 'monster' advanced to within 10 metres of the Manchurian entrenchments and then stopped. Two hundred troops charged from the train and began firing at the defenders in a fire fight which lasted for an hour. It appears that the gun crews of the train did not join in the battle for some inexplicable reason. On the same day a 500-strong Red Army raiding party crossed well inside Manchuria's eastern border near Lake Hanka. They fired at Manchurian troops at the town of Mishanhsien with their two machine guns and a single field gun. The Manchurian defenders were made up of two companies who exchanged fire with the Russians for three hours. When the Red Army unit withdrew they left behind a large number of Chinese casualties. This attack was closely followed up by a Red Army force that crossed the western Siberian-Manchurian border. Several armoured cars were involved in this attack but they withdrew across the border after an hour's fighting. These series of cross border raids had left many Manchurian units isolated and demoralised. They did not know where the next attack was coming from and whether aircraft, tanks, armoured cars or artillery would be involved. One 3,000-strong Manchurian force, for instance, was supposed to guard a 1,000-mile front with its headquarters at the town of Teheiho. Their position was precarious as they were far from their supply base at Tsitihar and were not getting fresh supplies. They were responsible for guarding the Chinese bank of the Amur River and were under constant threat of attack by the Red Army on the other side.

The Manchurian war effort was supported generally by the Chinese population, although many did not know what was happening there. In late August the merchants of Manchuria were asked to support their military by supplying troops with new uniforms. The appeal put out by Chang Hsueh-liang himself appealed for warm clothing from 'patriotic' businessmen for the soldiers, who 'sat in wet trenches'. Chang meanwhile was sending 60,000 more troops to the border areas at each end of the Chinese Eastern Railway. Thirrty thousand were assigned to the Western Manchurian Headquarters under Field Marshal Wang Shih-chen. The other 30,000 under General Ho Yu-kwang were to go to the Eastern Headquarters at Suifenho.

## Soviet Air Operations

The Red Army had complete air superiority. Much of the early Soviet air operations were reconnaissance flights with their aircraft flying low over Manchurian lines. They used red and green searchlights during night missions to highlight the enemy positions from only 1,000 ft. In August it was reported that something like 40, or over half of their air strength, weres operating constantly on these reconnaissance missions. As a show of strength on the 9th of September Soviet light bombers attacked the city of Suifenho on the Eastern Border destroying its railway station and killing 100 civilians. Another raid took place on the 4th of October when six aircraft bombed and machine gunned the border town of Manchouli killing 40 enemy troops. During the November offensive the Soviet Air Force came into its own using every aircraft to bomb the demoralised Manchurians. One raid on the 20th of November on the town of Chailonor by 27 aircraft dropped 300 bombs and killed an estimated 2,000 Chinese. There were also reports of Soviet planes mocking their Manchurian targets by dropping bags of soot and dirt on them, or just stones. The panicking Manchurian troops thought that these sacks contained chemical weapons. Other fake 'chemical bombs' used by the Soviet air force were rotten cabbages, which fooled the Manchurians. The lack of any air opposition to the Red Air Force meant that they had free rein over Manchuria. Only one or two reports even mention Manchurian aircraft and these appear to have been reconnaissance missions only.

## September–October Fighting and the River War

The months of September and October saw the war on land continue in a series of small battles, skirmishes and raids across the border. Manchurian cavalry was brought into the border region in large numbers and these were to play a major role in skirmishes. 'White Guardist' bands as they were described were reported to have made a series of small-scale raids on Siberian villages. How many of these raids were genuinely undertaken by White Russians is not known as their presence was good for Soviet propaganda. There were raids along the Sungari and Amur Rivers. Soviet Commando groups would be landed on the banks from frontier boats to attack Manchurian outposts. Several artillery duels took place during September but these were sporadic and usually lasted for a few hours before both sides broke off. Although this two-month period saw little major fighting on land, the war along the Rivers of Manchuria intensified.

The Sino-Soviet conflict was fought mainly along the northern and eastern borders of Manchuria and the Soviet Union. Although most of the fighting was between ground forces, the large and strategic rivers of Manchuria were also going to see much fighting. The Amur River formed the north-eastern border between the two countries while the junction of the Amur and Sungari Rivers was in the east. Forming the eastern Manchurian-Soviet border was the Ussuri River but this did not see any fighting during the war. Both sides had substantial river forces to patrol these border rivers so it was inevitable that clashes were to occur at strategic points. On the 21st of July two Chinese merchant ships, the *Ilan* and the *Haicheng*, were captured by the Soviet fleet on the Amur River. In early August another Chinese steamer was attacked with several of her crew killed and wounded. At the same time 150 more Chinese crewmen were captured in other skirmishes and these joined another 450 sailors already in Soviet prisons. These included 86 White Russians whose fate is not known; although they were regarded as traitors by their fellow Russians in the Red Navy. In mid-August another two Manchurian river steamers were captured when seven Soviet gunboats entered the Sungari River on the 17th.

At the start of the conflict the Soviet's sent in a large river fleet with 12 ships which were made up of monitors, gunboats and even an aircraft carrier. There were four Tayfun Class monitors, which were flat-bottomed gun platforms, name the *Lenin, Sverdlov, Krasnyi Vostok* and the *Sun Yat-sen*. The *Sun Yat-sen* was of course named after the veteran Chinese revolutionary who had died four years before. All were heavily armed with the *Lenin* and *Sun Yat-sen* having four turrets, each with a 120mm gun mounted. The other two monitors were more heavily armed – four turrets with a 152mm mounted in each. In support of the monitors were four smaller modern gunboats named the *Krasnoye Znamya, Bednota, Proletarii* and the *Buryat*. *Krasnoye Znamya* had two 120mm guns and 1 76mm while the *Bednota* and the Proletarii had two 102mms and a single 76mm; finally the *Buryat* had two 75mm guns. Smaller craft were made up of three patrol boats, and a single minelayer, the *Silnyi*. There were also two small minesweepers, the *TZ-1* with a 37mm gun and *TZ-2* with a 40mm. Of particular importance to the Soviet war effort was the presence of a seaplane carrier, the *Amur*, which was a converted Tayfun class monitor. This improvised carrier had been stripped of its guns and had a wooden hangar fitted in their place. It carried four MR-1 reconnaissance seaplanes, which were a modification of the British DH-9. Although the *Amur* was a makeshift carrier, it was to perform well during the war and its planes were to prove vital to the Soviet war effort.

The 'Chinese Amur River Flotilla' which faced the Soviet river fleet had the gunboat the *Kian Hyn* with a 120mm gun, an 88mm and four 52mm guns.

Volunteers from the military academy of a University in Manchuria prepare to go to the front from Mukden Railway Station. They are wearing their smart black kepi and tunic worn with khaki shorts and white socks and have their rifles stacked on the platform. Several patriotic groups like this were pictured on the way to the war but is unlikely that many got too near to the frontline.

Three older boats were the *Lee Ju* with two 52mm guns, *Lee Sui* with one 88mm, two 76mms and two 47mms and the *Chang Ping* with four 76mm guns. Three smaller vessels in the Chinese river fleet had two 47mm guns. Two other smaller boats were the *Kian Nai* and the *Kian Tun* with a single 52mm gun. They also had an armed transport boat called the *Lee Chuan* of 250 tons with a single 76mm and a floating battery named the *Tung-I*, which had two 120mms and two 76mms. The one advantage that the Manchurian boats had over their Soviet counterparts was that they could operate in shallow waters.

## The Battle of Lahasusu

The fighting along the rivers on the Manchurian-Soviet border was by October mainly concentrated around the mouth of the Sungari River at the town of Lahasusu. This Manchurian town had been turned into a fortified position with large numbers of troops sent to reinforce its defences. Up to nine infantry brigades were sent to bolster its defences and these were built up with new trenches and fortified positions. Most of the troops were stationed in new

This rare photograph according to its original caption shows a White Guard on the Siberian-Manchurian border during the 1920s. The number of White Russians who fought during the Sino-Soviet War is not certain but there were at least several thousand of them. He is dressed for his irregular role in the border region with warm quilted clothing and fur hat, and with bandoliers for his Moisin-Nagant M1891 rifle draped over him.

entrenchments built in the woods to the north-east of the town. Supposedly the garrison also received new artillery but this probably consisted of the larger trench mortars in common use in Manchuria. Further reinforcements were sent from the Manchurian River Fleet made up of armed sailors seconded from the steamer crews. The town's defences were augmented by the naval batteries of the Tsindao coastal defences. The Manchurian Admiral Shen Hung-lieh moved up to the frontline to take personal command of the fleet. River approaches to the town were protected by a system of mines set in barriers and above them wooden booms. A number of barges were loaded with rocks and were left ready to be sunk to block the channel when the Soviets attacked. The Soviet attack on the town was to involve their Amur Flotilla. On the night of the 12th of October, the Soviet fleet moved into position below Lahasusu and the fighting began at 06.12 am the next morning. Just before the attack began 21 Soviet aircraft made an attack on the Sungari River Fleet. The *Lenin*, the monitors, *Sverdlov*, *Sun Yat-sen*, the *Krasnyi Vostok* and gunboats faced the Chinese fleet of 11, mostly made up of gunboats including the most powerful, the *Kian Hyn*, armed with a 120mm gun. The Soviet fleet was full of inexperienced crew, most of whom were seeing action for the first time. As the Soviet ships moved towards Lahasusu they came under accurate fire from the Sungari River Fleet. The Soviets scored a direct hit on the steamer *Kiang Tai*, which began to burn. The *Krasnyi Vostok* then hit the magazine of the Chinese gunboat *Kiang Ping* and she went up in flames. As the battle went against them, some of the Chinese fleet limped further up the Sungari River out of range. The Manchurian gunboat *Lee Ju* showed some determination and managed to score several hits on the Soviet gunboat *Proletarii* and the monitor *Sun Yat-sen*. After putting up a good fight the *Lee Ju* was hit by the monitor *Krasnyi Vostok* and had to be grounded by her crew.

While the river battle was still going on the Soviet ships moved up to their designated disembarkation points for the infantry they were carrying. The Soviet 2nd Infantry Division landed on the bank near to Lahasusu, their objective the fortifications around the city, while the 2nd Division began frontal attacks on the forts.

A Light Infantry Regiment was landed to the rear of the Chinese defences. They launched an attack from the south-east forcing the defenders to move troops to that side of the fortifications. Street fighting took place until 15.00 when both the fortifications and Lahasusu itself fell. As the Soviet troops entered the city they opened its grain stores and let the people fill their sacks. This was a typical piece of Soviet psy-ops, which had the effect of turning the populace against their own troops. Some of the Chinese men in the city were hired by the Soviet Political officers to act as coolies to carry supplies for their advancing army. By the next day the last Manchurian troops had left the city and were in retreat to the town of Fuchin. Some of the fleeing troops were cornered by a mixed Soviet infantry and cavalry force and a large number of them were killed. The Soviet troops surrounded them with light artillery pieces and blasted them to pieces. In the Battle of Lahasusu the Chinese lost 1,000 men including 400 soldiers, 300 marines and 60 sailors, the Russians reported losing 275 killed during the battle. Other reports put the Russian losses at nearer to 400 killed, in what turned out to be of the heaviest losses for them during the war.

## The Battle of Fushin

Despite their heavy defeat at Lahahasu the Manchurian Army did not accept the Soviet peace proposal and prepared a counter-attack. It was expected that they would take advantage of the freezing of the Amur River and the forced withdrawal of the Soviet fleets to their winter base at Khararovisk. The Manchurians had decided to fortify the city of Fushin, which was reinforced by units from the surrounding garrisons. On the eve of the battle for the city the Manchurians could field 7th and 9th Kirin Infantry Brigades and part of the 43rd Cavalry Regiment. The garrison was strengthened by the arming of the city's militia and its police force while two more cavalry regiments and a large number of smaller units arrived from the nearby city of Sansin. In preparation for the battle the Manchurians had destroyed all the bridges on the road between Lahahasu and Fushin. They had also prepared 13 km of trenches 14 km from the city, were armed with field artillery. In the city barricades were built for what the Chinese claimed would be a determined defence. The Manchurians were left with the cruiser *Kiang Chin* and three steamers, the *Kiang Hai, Kiang Yung* and the *Kiang Un*. They also had the armed transport *Li Chuan* which had also escaped up the Sungari River after the defeat at Lahasusu. The Soviet force assigned to the attack on Fushin was made up of the Amur River Flotilla with co-operation from the 2nd Light Infantry Division and the 5th Amur and 4th Volochaevka Regiments.

The Soviet vessels that had been allotted to the Fushin Operation were divided into two groups with the 1st Group given the task of sailing into the town's harbour. This force included the monitors *Krasnyi Vostok*and the *Sun Yat-sen*, gunboats, two minesweepers, the minelayer *Silyni* and the armoured boat *Bars*. This 1st Group was to be under the command of the Admiral of the Fleet.

The 2nd Group were to land troops near to Fushin for the land attack on the city and the ships involved were the monitor *Sverdlov*, the gunboat *Bednota* and several steamers of the transport detachment. Aboard these ships of the 2nd Group were the 5th Amur Regiment, two Battalions of the 4th Volochaevka Regiment and a squadron of Red cavalry.

The land forces were under the command of the general who led the 2nd Light Infantry Division. The monitor *Lenin* was to stay behind the two Groups securing Lahahsusu and the Soviet Navy's escape route if necessary. On the eve of the battle the weather was beginning to grow colder, freezing sections of the Sungari River. The water level began to fall endangering the Soviet ships. Ice covered the decks of the ships and gathered on their rigging and on the clothing of their crews.

The two groups began their move up river on the night of the 30th of October with the 1st Group moving forward at 0.500. The minesweepers went ahead taking depth soundings and conducting sweeps. At 0.845 the 2nd Group left their moorings and moved after the 1st with each ship pulling two barges full of troops each. By 15.00 both Groups were approaching the Chinese barrage put across the river with the minelayers and gunboats in the vanguard. They were fired on by the Chinese cruiser *Kiang Chin* but her shells fell short and she had to withdraw. She suffered damage and was not to see action again. The barrage was found to include seven sunken barges with girders fastened to their decks making a formidable barrier. There were also two steamers, still afloat but damaged, anchored across the river. As it was getting dark the Soviet fleet chose to wait at anchor and renew their attack on the 31st.

In the morning the 2nd Group began disembarking its troops while the 1st Group engaged any Chinese ships that got too close. The 5th Light Infantry Regiment and the Squadron of Cavalry were landed with the task of outflanking the city. By 18.00 the Soviet Army units had taken the eastern suburbs of Fushin while other units took the western part of the city. As in Lahahasusu the Manchurians retreated into the city centre and the Soviet troops had to fight street by street. It had been taken by 02.00 the next morning. The Battle for Fushin was far more difficult than Lahahasusu as the winter temperatures fell to 11 degrees below, with winds of force 8. Both sides suffered terribly from the cold although all troops involved were acclimatised. Losses in the battle were reported by the Soviets at 300 Manchurian dead and several thousand wounded. According to the Soviet reports the Russians lost a ridiculously low 3 killed and 11 wounded. More significant for the Manchurians, they had lost the use of the *Kiang Chin* and all the remaining river vessels. Although the land war was not yet over the Manchurians could

A rare photograph of a unit of the Special Far Eastern Army, or ODVA, preparing to go into battle with the North-Eastern Army. The mix of uniforms shows that in 1929 the Soviet Red Army was still trying to standardise weaponry and uniforms. It appears, however, that every man has been issued with a pair of thick winter boots, a godsend in Manchuria.

not stop the Soviet fleet from using the Sungari and Amur Rivers in their army's support. They duly used the Amur River to send reinforcements to the frontline with the *Lenin* and two battleships moving troops in early November. The ships were transporting two infantry divisions, two artillery divisions and four MS-1 light tanks to take part in the coming offensive.


## The Red Army Final Offensive

On the 17th of November ODVA under General Blyuker began their major offensive into Western Manchuria. The main Soviet thrust was undertaken by the Trans-Baikal Group of the ODVA, which comprised 10 divisions. Blyuker's plan was to sweep past Manchouli and head for the fortified region around the city of Chalainor. Once Chalainor was taken the whole force would wheel around and take Manchouli from an easterly direction. The advantage was that all Manchouli's fortifications were west facing. Soviet strategy was to divide the action into two stages with a strong emphasis on secrecy. With this in mind the troops were forbidden to smoke and were told not to use bullets or bayonets. In order not to alert Chinese sentries all the wheels of the Soviet carts, cars and trucks were to be muffled. Their main objective was the destruction of the 40–60,000 Chinese troops stationed along the Chinese Eastern Railway. Fighting began far to the west on the 17th of November as the Soviets attacked Chalainor the railway town 20 miles south-east of Manchouli. The 7,000 Chinese defenders faced three hardened Soviet divisions well equipped with MS-1 tanks, R1 light bombers and plenty of artillery. In one of the fiercest clashes of the war the town was taken and only 1,000 Chinese troops escaped from the battle. The Red Army now surrounded Manchouli on the Manchurian-Soviet border and took the town killing the defenders' commander, General Liang Chung-chia. Eight thousand of Liang's troops were captured during the battle and sent to the growing Soviet prison camps.

With the exception of some heavy resistance by the Chinese at Hailar on the 27th, the plan went according to plan. On the same day the Japanese consul at Manchouli had persuaded the Manchurians there to surrender to avoid more bloodshed. By the 20th of November Soviet troops had surrounded the township around Manchuria Station. The garrison commander of the station was given two hours to consider surrender but before he could respond the Soviet Army attacked. Stepan S Vostretsov, the commander of the Trans Baikal Group, entered the town with some of his staff in two cars. The Chinese defenders were too busy looting the town to react and most had abandoned their rifles in the process. According to some eyewitnesses the soldiers were changing into civilian clothes with a few wearing women's clothes. The town itself was in ruins after Soviet bombing raids and the Chinese garrison soon abandoned it. They fled east in complete disarray towards the city of Tsitsihar, looting as they went. When they reached the bridge over the Nonni River 10 miles from Tsitsihar they were faced by disciplined Chinese soldiers. Under the command of General Wan Fu-lin the troops on the bridge held their ground and prepared to fire. When their comrades who had now turned into a rabble tried to force their way across the bridge, they opened fire on them.

## End of the War

On the 27th of November the OVDA occupied the city of Hailar and within 48 hours of the start of the Red Army Offensive, Chang Hsueh-liang was ready to sue for peace. He had not received any of the expected support from the Nationalist Government and he could not sustain any more losses of men and territory. Chang was aware that the Soviet control of much of his northern border and the increasing threat in the South by the Japanese left him vulnerable. A peace was brokered on the 3rd of December by Britain, France and the USA calling simply for an end to the fighting. The settlement called for the complete restoration of the Soviet Union's position regarding control of the CER. Further more substantive talks were supposed to take place in Moscow but these never materialised. The Red Army had waged its war against the Manchurians on a 200-mile front at each end of the CER. They also bombed and occupied most of the Manchurian towns along the border but did not penetrate beyond the Hinghan Mountains. This was because the Japanese gave them a friendly warning not to cross them into their sphere of influence.

Official Soviet losses during the war were reported to be 143 killed, 665 wounded and 4 missing in action. Manchurian official losses were quoted at 2,000 killed and 1,000 wounded with 8,550 prisoners taken. They lost most of their river fleet along with much of their heavy weaponry, which was difficult to replace in the short term. The casualties quoted by both the Manchurian and the Soviet Army were probably inaccurate. Russian official losses were particularly low in view of the ferocity of the fighting and the conditions the campaign was fought in. They did have the advantage of reasonable medical care for the wounded while the Manchurian wounded were often left to die in the field. Peace was formally agreed on the 22nd of December between Chang's representatives and the Soviet delegates. It eturned the Chinese Eastern Railway to its previous position, although the Russians insisted on selecting a new head.

# 5

# 'SELF DEFENCE': THE MANCHURIAN CAMPAIGN, 1931–32 AND MANCHURIAN RESISTANCE, 1933–37

The three provinces which made up the vast territory of Manchuria had been ruled since 1916 by the Manchurian warlord, Chang Tso-lin. Manchuria had a population of 30 million with territory as large as France and Germany covering 380,000 square miles. Its three provinces, Heilungkiang, Kirin and Liaoning were each the size of a large country. It had been the homeland of the last ruling dynasty of China, the Qing, whose last Emperor, Pu Yi, had abdicated in 1908. The Qing Dynasty had ruled China for 300 years having invaded from Manchuria in the 1600s. During the last years of the 19th and early years of the 20th Century, Manchuria, 'land of the Manchus', had been a theatre of war on several occasions. During the 1894–1895 Sino-Japanese War it was the scene of some of the fighting. Ten years later its territory was used by Japan and Russia as a battleground as they fought for control of the Far East during the war of 1904–05. After the fall of the Qing Dynasty in 1912 Manchuria became the fiefdom of one of the most powerful warlords in China. It was ruled by Chang Tso-lin, the 'Manchurian Tiger', who had begun his career as a bandit and had risen through the ranks to lead one of the largest armies in China. He had become the leader of the Fengtien Warlord clique in 1916 and had led it until his death in 1928. Chang, one of the most powerful militarists during the 1920s, had been supported by the Japanese with arms and money. They wanted to use Chang as a puppet to gain control over the three provinces of Manchuria and large parts of northern China that he controlled. His Army's defeat by the victorious Nationalists in 1928 caused the Japanese some embarrassment. It also made him expendable, especially when he began to withdraw his army back into Manchuria. The Japanese reaction to his defeat was to blow up his train as it entered Mukden station. Chang's Japanese military advisors who were aboard the train had been warned about the bomb and wrapped themselves in carpets and survived. The Japanese expected the Fengtien clique to fall apart on Chang's death and hoped to exploit the power vacuum created to take over Manchuria to 'restore order'. They totally discounted Chang Tso-lin's successor, Chang Hsueh-liang, who was known as a playboy and opium addict. He had spent his youth as a playboy, chasing women, taking drugs and generally being debauched. In the western press he was known among other nicknames as the 'Jazz Dictator'. Although he did hold military command in his father's Fengtien Army and was officially the head of the air force for a while, his mind was usually elsewhere. The death of his father concentrated his mind and saw his rapid metamorphosis from playboy into a military leader. Chang Hsueh-liang, the Japanese surmised, would either run away to a comfortable exile or agree to be the puppet ruler of Manchuria. They were to be disappointed by his reaction; Chang was not going to forgive the Japanese for betraying his father.

Following the assassination of his father in 1928 the 'Young Marshal' had struggled to deal with the power vacuum created by his death. In fact he concealed Chang's death for seven days while he busied himself consolidating his hold on power. Gaining the respect of his father's senior commanders would not be easy for the young upstart. The North-Eastern Army was a large military force with various cliques within its complicated command structure. Some of the commanders of the cliques had ambitions of leading the Army themselves. Chang Hsueh-liang heard these rumours and dealt with this problem in a manner that his late father would no doubt have approved of. He invited two of the suspected generals to a banquet at his headquarters to talk over their disagreements. Before the first course was served he had both of them dragged outside and shot. If any other disloyal commanders had underestimated their new leader before this they soon changed their minds.

One of Chang's first acts as military governor of Manchuria had been to establish friendly relations with Chiang Kai-shek and the Nationalist Government. In July 1928 after long talks between Chang and Nationalist representatives the Manchuria leader formally pledged his loyalty to Chiang. He had been holding secret talks with the Japanese as a counterweight despite his hatred of his father's murderers. Chang was in a powerful position and insisted on a number of conditions which would allow him to rule Manchuria under the umbrella of the Nationalists. His main stipulation was not surprisingly that he should retain command of the former Fengtien Army, now known as the North-Eastern Border Defence Army.

## The North-Eastern Border Defence Army

Chang Hsueh-liang was now in command of one of the most powerful military forces in China. While officially part of the Nationalist military establishment, nobody was under any illusions that Chang was in command. Although it was officially the army of Manchuria, its sphere of operations in 1929 reached as far South as the Peking–Tientsin region. After Chang Hsueh-liang had reorganised, it had been divided into two separate forces, the National Defence Army and the Provincial Army. The National Defence Army had the role of protecting Manchuria's borders while the Provincial Army maintained order in the provinces. In total the National Defence Army had 30 Infantry Brigades, 6 Cavalry Brigades and 10 Artillery Regiments. Provincial Army units were made up of 19 Infantry Brigades and 7 Cavalry Brigades which had less heavy equipment than their NDA comrades and no heavy artillery. Chang had tried to improved the quality of his army with a number of measures including reducing the number of units and dismissing some of the pre-1928 commanders. These were generals who had been loyal to his father Chang Tso-lin but whose

A unit of cavalry under the command of General Chang Hai-peng rides through a town in Manchuria. These troops from the North-Eastern Army were taken into Japanese service by Chang at the start of the invasion of Manchuria. Some of these soldiers went on to form the core of the Manchukoan army once the Japanese had occupied Manchuria. Traitors like General Chang were being pragmatic about the situation they faced in 1931. They saw joining the Japanese as simply changing employer, as they had done throughout the warlord period.

loyalty to him was uncertain. Chang also tried to improve the quality of the lower ranking officers by putting more young officers through the North-East Military Academy at Shengyang. Between late 1928 and September 1930 the academy turned out 4,038 graduates whose loyalty to Chang was less suspect than many of the older officers. Arms for the North-Eastern Army had always been produced at the huge munitions factory at Mukden. In 1931 the factory with 20,000 workers and 1,000 technicians was still turning out sufficient rifles, machine guns, mortars and artillery. The army was particularly well equipped with mortars of every calibre made in the factory set up in Mukden by Chang Tso-lin in the 1920s. These included monster 120mm mortars which made up somewhat for shortages in conventional field guns. The Manchurians also had a number of FT-17 light tanks left over from service with the Fengtien Army. They were slightly modernised in the late 1920s with new 38mm main armaments to replace their machine guns. Apart from the new weaponry the changes were mainly cosmetic, with a coat of paint and new insignia added.

In a further attempt to modernise his army Chang placed large orders with foreign arms companies. In April 1930 he placed one order with French companies for 20 light bombers, 20 field guns and 40 machine guns. He specified 1,700 tons of shells for the field guns and 5,500 tons of small arms ammunition. This particular order did not find its way to the North-Eastern Army however, as Chang had agreed to unite his forces with the Nationalist Army. As part of this agreement between Chang and Chiang Kai-shek, the latter paid the bill for the weaponry, which was added to the Nationalist armoury. The North-Eastern Army's Air Arm had also been thoroughly modernised with 100 modern aircraft and the same number of Manchurian pilots trained to fly them. These new aircraft included 26 DH60 Gypsy Moth trainers, 20–25 Potez 25 light bombers and a single French Breguet 19 light bomber. Over 70 Breguet 19s had been ordered by Chang Tso-lin in the mid 1920s but were never delivered. This one had been sold to the North-Eastern Air Arm when its French crew could not get permission to fly over neighbouring Siberia and ran out of money. They were taking part in one of the numerous long-distance flights that were all the rage in the 1920s and 1930s. Estimates of the strength of the Army in September 1931 vary. The Japanese intelligence agencies claimede there were 250,000 regular and 80,000 irregular troops. They estimated that out of the total of regular troops 110,000 were stationed in North China with the remaining 140,000 in Manchuria.

## The Kwangtung Army and the Mukden Incident

Early in July 1931 the Japanese newspapers carried a lurid story of the murder of a certain Captain Nakamura somewhere in the vast wilderness of Inner Mongolia, China. The Captain was in the company of another Japanese officer, a White Russian and a Mongolian guide and had $50,000 in his pockets. No one knew what the captain or his companions was doing in Inner Mongolia when he was killed but Japan had long coveted the region. It was rich in furs and its grazing land was vital to the food supply in northern China with huge herds of cattle. Nakamura's death

A battery of medium field guns of the Japanese Imperial Army fire across an open plain during their advance through southern Manchuria in early December 1931. The guns are Model 38 75mm field guns, introduced into Imperial Army service in 1905. Most of the Model 38s were sent back to the Osaka Arsenal for extensive modifications during the First World War. Much of the Imperial Army's aging weaponry was in need of replacement when they first went to war against China.

The crew of a Japanese Imperial Army Vickers-Crossley Type 87 armoured car stop outside one the gates in the walls of the city of Mukden in September 1931. These British-built armoured cars were first bought by the Japanese in 1927 and modified slightly. They were widely used by the Japanese during their campaigns in the early 1930s until they could produce their own models in 1932.

was a mystery but the Japanese military and press used it to stir up anti-Chinese feelings. In a typical Sino-Japanese scenario the Chinese had to apologise to the Japanese over the Captain's death. There was no mention of course of what he was really doing in their territory and the story fizzled out. If the publicity surrounding Nakamura's death was intended to give the Japanese a justification for military action it failed. The Japanese military plotters and schemers in northern China and Manchuria were disappointed but they were patient. They would have to wait a few more months for the excuse they needed to 'light the touch paper' in Manchuria.

The Japanese Kwangtung Army had been originally formed in 1906 as the Kwangtung Garrison to defend territory obtained by the Japanese after the conclusion of the Russo-Japanese War in 1904-05. It was named after the leased territory which was adjacent to the South Manchurian Railway. Its 100,000 men were mainly tasked with defending the Japanese-owned railway and was renamed the Kwangtung Army in 1919. Its officers in the 1920s were regarded as being highly nationalistic and independently minded. They paid little regard to their political and military leaders in Tokyo and were determined to expand their control over as much of Manchuria as possible. Their actions in Manchuria in 1931 were against the express wishes of the country's leadership. Once the Kwangtung Army had begun their invasion of Manchuria, the Japanese establishment had little choice but to go along with their actions.

On the night of the 18th of September 1931 an explosion went off close to a line of the South Manchurian Railway in the city of Mukden. The charge which went off was set by a couple of Japanese officers but was so small it did not cause any substantial damage. It was intended however to give the Japanese Kwangtung Army a pretext for beginning hostilities against the North-Eastern Army in Mukden. The explosion was set off near to the Peitaying Barracks where Chang Hsueh-liang's best troops were garrisoned. The Chinese North-Eastern 7th Brigade was stationed in the North Barracks with 10,000 men. On the 6th they had been issued with an order from the commander Chang Hsieh-liang not to provoke the Japanese stationed in Mukden in any way. This non-provocation was taken to extremes with the sentries guarding the walls of the barracks being armed with dummy rifles! Japanese attacks on the Mukden Garrison began the same night with many Chinese sentries being disarmed or killed. Heavy fighting began on the morning of the 19th with Japanese artillery shelling the Chinese barracks. The same day over 100,000 Mukden citizens left the city and moved into the surrounding villages and towns to await developments. Most Manchurian troops gave up to the Japanese without fighting back, on the orders of the officers. The only Chinese unit to offer any real resistance to

An Imperial Army crew of a Type 11 70mm mortar prepare to fire towards Chinese positions in the spring of 1932. This weapon was not in the true sense a mortar as it was really a high angle infantry gun that was a little too heavy to be portable. As the Japanese did not have any modern mortars in 1931–32 this weapon had to be used in the mortar role. When the Japanese occupied Manchuria they captured large numbers of the primitive but useful mortars produced in the Mukden factory.

the Japanese in the first hours of the incident were the 620th Regiment. The policy of non-resistance by the North-Eastern Army came directly from Chiang Kai-shek himself. His rationale was that he wanted the Japanese to be seen as the aggressor to be dealt with by the League of Nations in due course.

The Japanese had been planning for the taking of Manchuria for months with a variety of ruses to hoodwink the Chinese garrison in Mukden. They had infiltrated a large number of Japanese in civilian clothes who, when the incident began, were armed and issued with armbands. Overlooking the Mukden Arsenal was a 'secret battery' of field guns hidden inside a large shed in the centre of the city. The guns had been smuggled into the city in pieces during the previous months under the eyes of the Manchurian troops and police. The field guns were smuggled in crates labelled 'Mining Machinery'. The Japanese Intelligence service in Tokyo were aware that something was about to happen. Just before the Incident the Chief of the Intelligence Section of the General Staff was sent to Mukden for a 'quiet word'. He took a letter to the Kwangtung command saying that they should rein in their plans for Manchuria, but it was politely ignored.

## Manchurian and Japanese Forces in 1931

At the start of the hostilities in Manchuria the Japanese had very few troops available and were heavily outnumbered by the Chinese. In fact, in the whole swathe of territory from Changchun in the North to Port Arthur and along the South Manchuria Railway they only had just over 10,000 men. These were made up of the 2nd Infantry Division with 5,400 men and 16 field guns, the Railway

This crewman of a Manchurian armoured train stands proudly on its armour-plated gun wagon with a machine gun in its turret. The soldier is armed with a C-96 automatic pistol and a fighting sword. His pistol is inside the hollowed-out wooden stock, which doubled as a holster for this popular weapon. Uniforms worn by many of the soldiers in Manchuria were often a mix, as here, of different shades of padded cotton.

Guard with 5,000 men and the Gendarmarie with 500 men. When the fighting began the Railway Guard and Gendarmarie stayed in their positions and the 2nd Division moved into Mukden. The 2nd Division was reinforced by the 16th and 30th Regiments who helped them capture the Chinese Army's East Barracks. On the 21st of September the 39th Mixed Brigade crossed the Yalu River at 10.00 am and was in Mukden by midnight. The Mixed Brigade had been substantially strengthened almost up to divisional size with 4,000 men and an artillery regiment.

When the Japanese invaded Manchuria the main North-Eastern Army formations were made up of the following: Chang Hsueh-liang's personal army, which totalled 50,000 of whom 10,000 were garrisoning Mukden; General Wu Fu-lin's Army in Heilongjiang province of 30,000 men (but when the invasion began he was ill in hospital in Peking); and 80,000 men under the command of General Chang Tso-hsiang in Kirin province. Chang Tso-hsiang was one of the old generation of Manchurian generals and had served Chang Tso-lin and now his son faithfully. He was trusted by the Young Marshal and had since 1928 been vice-commander of the North-East Frontier Defence Forces.

## The Early Japanese Campaign in Manchuria and General Ma Chan-shan

After the Mukden Incident the Kwangtung Army now moved quickly to take the cities of Southern and Central Manchuria. They were to face little or no resistance from the North-Eastern Army. A few Manchurian generals joined the Japanese either by prior arrangement or when their garrisons were threatened by Kwangtung units. These included General Hsi Hsia of Kirin province, General Chang Hai-peng of Taonan and General Chang Ching-hui of Harbin. Chang Hsueh-liang and his army withdrew southwards and westwards ahead of the advancing Japanese. By the end of September the Kwangtung Army had overrun the provinces of Liaoning and Kirin and most of South Manchuria. Other Manchurian commanders and local patriots were not prepared to give up their homeland without a fight and began to gather forces around them. These resistance leaders still held northern cities like Harbin. On the 31st of December Chang Hsueh-liang announced his decision to withdraw inside the Great Wall. He is quoted as saying that he was doing so 'in order to afford Japan no pretext for further aggression in North China'. From now, on any resistance to the Japanese would be in the hands of Manchurian guerrillas who had already begun to fight them.

The main personality to emerge on the Manchurian side during the resistance campaign was Ma Chan-shan. General Ma was a northern Chinese Muslim who had been brought up in extreme poverty as the son of a shepherd. He had joined in his youth one of the many bandit bands which operated in Manchuria. Ma soon had command of the bandit group and like many other leaders of these brigands he took his men into Army service as irregular cavalry. He had been in command of them at Taheiho on the Amur River near to the Soviet border when the Japanese invaded Manchuria. As the Military Governor of Heilungkiang was

An armoured train belonging to the North-Eastern Defence Army sits in a railway station getting up steam in 1931. It formerly belonged to the Fengtien army, which had used a number in their war against the National Revolutionary Army between 1926 and 1928. Although these trains were a potent weapon when used against ground forces, they were susceptible to air attack. Their very size made themt an easy target for Japanese Imperial Army aircraft, especially if they lacked any anti-aircraft weaponry. This train does have several 75mm guns mounted in turrets and machine guns mounted in various firing ports along its superstructure.

ill in hospital in Peking, Ma was hastily given command of all Chinese forces in the province. Unlike most Manchuria military leaders Ma was not at all daunted by the thought of fighting the Japanese. As one writer noted Ma was the 'first Chinese commander since 1895 to have courage enough to fight a pitched battle against the Japanese'. As the Kwangtung Army began to move northwards into North and West Manchuria in, Ma and his men prepared to fight them.

## Nonni Bridge, November 1931

Early in October General Ma Chan-shan in an attempt to defend the city of Tsitisihar blew up the 800ft bridge over the River Nonni. He was trying to stop the advance of the 'turncoat' General Chang Hai-peng and his irregulars. This action turned what had been a dispute between two Manchurian generals into an affair which affected the Japanese. The bridge was of great strategic importance as it was in the vicinity of the junction between the Chinese Eastern Railway and a trunk line which linked it to the South Manchurian Railway. Because of the importance of the railway system to the Japanese control of Manchuria, they immediately sent Ma a demand that he repair the bridge before the 28th of October. The Japanese force of 3,000–5,000 men attacked the defences around the damaged bridge on the 4th of November. They were well supported by artillery and armoured cars and had air support from the Imperial Air Force. Ma had a 25,000-strong but poorly armed cavalry force with little if any heavy weaponry and few machine guns. The Chinese were running low on ammunition from the beginning of the battle but still managed to resist the Japanese for two days. During the fighting the Japanese suffered relatively heavy casualties but the result was never in doubt. By the 19th, Ma's men were completely out of ammunition and had to withdraw from their positions. Ma had sent messages to the Nationalist Government in Nanking asking for assistance but to no avail. Chiang Kai-shek was sticking firmly to his policy of non-resistance and didn't reply to Ma's telegram. The General also sent a rather poignant message to the League of Nations asking them to intervene. He told the League of his plight and ended his message with a final plea for help, as the Japanese 'had such big guns'. Ma now moved back to take part in the defence of Tsitsihar having lost 400 killed and 300 wounded and refused the Japanese demand to surrender the city.

## The Battle of Tsitsihar

As soon as the Japanese crossed the Nonni River they pushed on to take the important city of Tsitsihar. General Ma's troops now joined a numerically strong but disunited defence force of 20,000 men with 24 field guns and 100 machine guns. Other estimates gave the number of defenders at 8,000 but the exact number is lost in the fog of propaganda issued by both sides. The Chinese defenders had prepared a well constructed four-mile-long series of entrenchments which had been finished several weeks before the fighting began. For a change, the units defending the entrenchments had good telephone communications between the battalions, brigades and their headquarters. Gun and machine gun positions were well sited with good fields of fire and there were bomb proof shelters at 80-yard intervals. These shelters had been well built and were said to be impenetrable to anything apart from a direct hit from a heavy artillery shell or the largest bomb carried by the Japanese light bombers. The Japanese assault force was only 4,500 strong with 8 aircraft and 6 light tanks of the FT-17 type in support. They also had a few heavy artillery pieces which were found to be barely adequate for the role they had to play.

The battle began with a two-hour bombardment at dawn on the 17th of November by the Japanese artillery which did little damage to the Chinese defences. At 8.30 the light tanks began their advance but all but one broke down before they reached the Chinese lines. The few Japanese aircraft available were split into two 4-plane units. Four were told to act as observation planes while the other four were to continue to bomb the Chinese entrenchments. Although the bombers targeted the Chinese forward headquarters they were wasting their time. There were no high-ranking officers anywhere near the front, they were safe and sound in the rear area. Planes flying in the reconnaissance role were frustrated by the fact that the Japanese units only had white identification strips to show their positions. These were useless as the battlefield was covered in snow

A trench full of soldiers of the Manchurian North-Eastern Army prepare to defend their position against Japanese attack in 1931. The infantrymen are armed with Chinese rifles but their machine gunner has a Japanese Type 11 light machine gun. This may have been captured from the enemy or may have been supplied to the Fengtien army when its main arms supplier was the Imperial Army. These men are better armed than some of their comrades who defended the main barracks in Mukden, clutching bamboo spears when the Japanese fired on them. Others could not fight back because their rifles had been locked in the guardroom after the evening parade!

and no one had thought to replace the white strips with coloured ones. Bearing in mind that it had been snowing for several days before the battle this was a major oversight by the Japanese command. Included in the Japanese forces were 400 cavalry which in other actions had performed a useful role in scouting and outflanking Chinese positions. In the battle for Tsitsihar the cavalry were given a free role by their commander General Taman. They proceeded to ride around the outskirts of the battlefield and their only positive contribution was to capture a battery of Chinese artillery.

At first General Ma's troops on the right flank held firm and his cavalry tried to outflank the Japanese but were destroyed by artillery fire and air attacks. When the Japanese infantry advanced in force they only got to within 800 yards of the Chinese positions before the defenders turned and ran. After crossing the abandoned Chinese trenches the Japanese continued their advance meeting no resistance until they entered Tsitsihar. Although the Japanese Army did not get to prove their fighting ability in this battle, they did prove their fortitude. From 8.30 they marched 22 miles in atrocious weather to enter the centre of Tsitsihar before midnight. Japanese losses in the battle were 30 killed and 80 wounded with the majority of the casualties a result of the severe weather. Chinese losses were 150 dead and most of these were killed in bombing attacks with only a handful of stragglers slain by the Japanese infantry and cavalry. Ma's remaining troops retreated northwards along the Nonni River valley, fighting a number of rearguard actions. They fought in the defence of two towns further east and suffered heavy losses in both battles. Although his men continued to fight, General Ma decided that at least temporarily he should cross the Soviet-Manchurian border.

## The Beginning of Resistance to the Japanese, 1931–32

When the Japanese invaded Manchuria in late 1931 they were faced by little opposition from the North-Eastern Army. They were soon faced by a different threat in the form of newly raised irregular volunteers. In addition they had to deal with the large number of endemic bandits in Manchuria. The three provinces of Manchuria had always been a hot-bed of bandit activity for centuries and these outlaws were often ex-military. Some had been allowed to join the warlord armies raised by Chang Tso-lin after starting their careers as bandits. Of the 58,000 bandits estimated to have been active in Manchuria in 1929, thousands

Two resolute-looking soldiers of the North-Eastern Defence Army wearing wadded cotton uniforms with winter fur hats steel themselves for a Japanese attack. They are armed with Japanese-made Arisaka rifles supplied to the Manchurians in the 1920s. One man has been fortunate enough to buy a pair of woollen gloves or had them sent in a care package from his family. Many Chinese soldiers lost contact with their families when they enlisted or were conscripted into the army and were considered as already dead by their relatives.

had seen service in the army before 1928. Many of these outlaws now became 'patriotic' bandits, willing to fight the Japanese. Others chose to try and join the newly formed Manchukuoan Army, which in its early days was taking anyone. As time went on the vast majority of these undesirable recruits were weeded out by the Japanese advisors in the Army.

Patriotic Manchurians were soon raising volunteer guerrilla bands throughout the three provinces. Many of these bands were led by army officers and had ex-soldiers in their ranks. Despite the presence of a cadre of military men, the vast majority of the volunteers were civilians. Policemen and other civil officials who did not want to serve the Japanese usually joined the volunteers. This was the only alternative to agreeing to continue in their previous role but under the command of the Japanese and their 'puppet' officials. Almost all of the volunteers were peasants and artisans who did not want to live under Japanese rule. At first there was a rush to join the volunteer armies and by early 1932 they were the only effective armed opposition to the invaders. A large number of the volunteers came from amongst the refugees from the north-east of China who had found their way to Manchuria. These refugees were responsible for forming the North-East National Salvation Society. The Society tried to put pressure on the Nationalist Government to resist the Japanese invasion. Chang Hsueh-liang was a secret supporter of the NENSS who tried to assist its work without letting his

Exhausted Anti-Japanese volunteers take shelter in the house of a friendly peasant family in 1932. Many of these irregulars were former soldiers of the North-Eastern Army and brought their rifles with them. Winter combat in Manchuria was brutal and men like this began to lose their will to fight after a year constantly on the move. As more Japanese and Manchukuoan operations were launched, their lives became even grimmer.

Two members of an Anti-Japanese volunteer army fire from the shelter of a village wall in 1932. At first, volunteers like this would often be able to arm and feed themselves from donations from friendly villagers. As the guerrilla war in Manchuria continued, civilians were severely punished by the Japanese for any support they gave to these men.

superior Chiang Kai-shek know. The Society decided to support the formation of the 'North-East People's Anti-Japanese Volunteer Army'. In command of the Army was General Tang Chu-wu who had previously commanded an infantry regiment in the North-Eastern Army. Tang was helped by the NENSS to make contacts with the commanders of smaller army's and bands. These were usually persuaded to join his larger formation and led to its rapid expansion until it was one of the largest volunteer armies. With this army Tang was able to threaten the Japanese-held territories to the east of the city of Shengyang.

Japanese estimate of the number of resistance fighters in 1931 was 60,000 including 14,000 in Jehol province. In June 1932 it was estimated that there were 122,000 resistance fighters in Liaoning province, 107,000 in Kirin province and 70,000 in Heilingkiang province. Japanese estimates went from a high of 360,000 in 1932 dropping dramatically to 52,000 by 1933. Within a year many fighters had been killed or had deserted the cause having been forced to survive on little food and other supplies. Claiming that their anti-bandit operations were having an effect, the Imperial Army said that the number of resistance fighters fell to 42,000 in 1934 and only 21,000 by 1935. Whatever the truth of these figures, the volunteer armies were taking heavy losses with many resistance leaders having been killed by 1933. Overall losses for the year from 1932 to 1933 were claimed to be 16,000 killed and 7,000 wounded. By 1935, any remaining fighters were surviving on little in the way of ammunition and other supplies and most were operating in small bands.

## The Different Anti-Japanese Volunteer Armies

Led usually by North-Eastern Defence Army officers these large and unwieldy armies fought at first as conventional forces. In most cases these large armies soon had to reduce to a more manageable size so that they could feed their men. The armies included one led by General Sun Ch'ao-yang of several thousand

Spear-wielding Manchurian resistance fighters pose outside the village they are defending in October 1932. They may well be members of the Red Spears, a self-defence group that tried to defend their villages against all armed groups in Manchuria. As with all poorly armed units, these men would be happy to replace their spears with rifles if they could capture them.

fighters but he was killed in action in the autumn of 1933. The 'North-Eastern Volunteer Righteous & Brave Fighters' were organised in March 1932 at Linkiang in Southern Kirin province. It was led by the 37-year-old Wang Feng-ko who managed to expand his army from 1,000 to 5,000 men in a short space of time. Wang wanted his force to have a proper military organisation and formed his men into six brigades. It was one of the longest surviving anti-Japanese armies but was finally destroyed in 1937. Wang was captured by the Japanese and he, his wife and child were executed. Another of the many volunteer armies was the 'Chinese People's National Salvation Army', which began as a small band of 200 men in February 1932. Like many other volunteer armies it was inundated with new recruits and soon reached a strength of 1,000 men and within a month 10,000 men, 30,000 men by July 1932. Its commander was a relatively older Wang Teh-ling, who was 57 when he organised the army, which soon found itself in a dispute with the 'Kirin Self Defence Army'. When the CPNSA came under Japanese pressure Wang decided to cross the border into the Soviet Union in mid-January 1933. The 'Anti-Japanese Army for the Salvation of the Country' had 10,000 men and operated in Southern Kirin province. It was under the command of General Li Hai-ching but was defeated in a major battle in May 1932. The remnants of the army were reformed as a 3,000-strong guerrilla force but soon had to withdraw into Jehol province. Some armies like the 'North-Eastern Loyal & Brave Army' which was 15,000 strong later fought in the Sino-Japanese War.

The 'North-East Anti-Japanese United Army' was organised in North Eastern Manchuria and was organised by the Communist Chinese Party. It was under the command of Chao Shang-chih and included a large number of Korean exiles. This army was to survive the 1930s fighting and form the core of the Communist forces in Manchuria.

During the resistance to the Japanese invasion and occupation a number of existing defence societies fought against them. These groups were generally anti-Japanese rather than pro-Nationalist and fought simply to defend their families from the Imperial Army. The Red Spears operated throughout Manchuria and were raised on a local basis to defend their villages and towns. They tended to be poorly armed and often went into action armed only with spears or swords. During the Manchurian insurgency they had a reputation for suicidal charges, even attacking Japanese armoured cars with hammers and axes. Another popular defence movement in Manchuria was the Big Sword society, which had operated since the 1890s and was revived when the Japanese invaded. Like the Red Spears, they tended to be poorly armed and some relied on charms; some claimed to be immune to bullets. They of course used any rifles that they could get hold of, either by capturing them or buying them from the volunteer armies. By the end of the 1932–33 winter many of the original volunteer army commanders had either retreated into the sanctuary of the Soviet Union or had fallen in battle.

General Ma Chan-shan was a Muslim opium addict who commanded North-Eastern troops in 1931. After fighting the Japanese at the Battle of the Nonnni River, he then spent over a year leading a large irregular army against them. He was courted by the Japanese and double-crossed them, taking large amounts of money from them as a bribe. Eventually he had to admit defeat and withdraw across the Soviet border, leaving his army behind.

General Feng Chan-hai, the commander of a large anti-Japanese volunteer army, with his staff officers. Feng, wearing the fur hat in the centre, led his army in the stubborn defence of the city of Harbin before been forced to withdraw. His officers are a mix of North-Eastern Army regulars and civilian volunteers who have joined him since the Japanese invasion.

## The Taking of Harbin

In late January 1932 the Japanese and their Manchurian allies were advancing on the city of Harbin. Harbin was the vital rail junction in the North of Manchuria in Kirin province and was important to control to quash any further resistance to the Japanese. In an attempt to consolidate the province's general defence a Kirin Provincial Anti-Japanese Government was organised. The garrison of the city was made up mainly of the 'Kirin Self Defence Army' under the command of General Feng Chan-hai and General Ting Chao. In overall command of the city's defences was General Li Tu with a small number of soldiers of the North-Eastern Defence Army. In total the garrison had 30,000 men including the city's police and other officials as well a large number of poorly equipped and untrained civilian volunteers. The garrison had 16 artillery pieces which were dug-in in the centre of the city and a small number of machine guns. The city was under siege from a large Manchukuoan force from the 25th of January before a general assault started on the 3rd of February. General Hsi Ch'ia's Manchukuoans formed the initial assault force but the city's defences held firm. It was reported that the Manchurian defenders believed they were more than a match for the 'puppet' Manchukuoan soldiers. Everything changed when the Japanese joined the battle and their infantry advanced. The defenders were then estimated to number 14,000 men. As with a lot of estimated strengths of troops at this time this may figure may be too low – but they had lost men through desertion. The 2nd Japanese Division moved into the frontline on the 3rd reaching the Nangchengtze River 20 miles north of Shaungcheng by nightfall. Heavy fighting with the Harbin defenders began the next morning and by the evening the Chinese defences had been partly taken. Reports said that in many positions the Chinese fled as soon as they saw the Japanese approach. It still took until noon on the 5th for the Japanese to advance into the outskirts of the city and Harbin was occupied by the afternoon. The city was abandoned by the surviving Chinese defenders who withdrew in the direction of the town of Sanhsing.

On the last day of the battle a newsman and the local British Military Attaché witnessed the final assault on Harbin. They were surprised to see a press report about the fall of the city which proclaimed 'victorious advance of the tanks'. As they noted, only one light tank took part in the attack, which succeeded in killing half a dozen Chinese soldiers. It then drove into a cement-lined ditch which acted as a tank trap. The tank was abandoned by its crew and was out of action for several days before an Imperial Army tractor hauled it out. When summarising the battle the two observers noted that the morale of the Japanese soldiers had remained high throughout. They did say, however, that at no time did the Imperial Army soldiers face heavy fire of any kind. Although impressed by the soldiers'

Japanese troops firing their Type 3 medium machine gun fire from a sandbagged position at a railway station in February 1932. This six-man crew is manning the gun on the loo- out for the Manchurian volunteers who were still active in large numbers in early 1932. All the crewmen are wearing the cherry blossom model steel helmet, which one of several models used in Manchuria. The helmet had a cherry blossom-shaped pommel at the top, hence the name. Their 1930 model winter woollen uniform would be supplemented with fur hats and fur lined jerkins in the worst weather.

A Japanese cavalry officer climbs on the metal framework of a recently captured building in the Manchurian town of Kaopangtze in February 1932. He has taken the Japanese battle flag to a high point so that his comrades attacking the town can see that this position has fallen. The town was a vital railway junction and was taken as part of the Japanese campaign to expand the territory they held in Manchuria.

marching skills they were less impressed by the planning of their attacks. Their criticisms of the Japanese concerned the haphazard way that they organised their offensive. They opined that if the Japanese advanced in that way against a more determined enemy, they would come unstuck. As the city fell the survivors of the 'Kirin Self Defence Army' withdrew into the surrounding countryside. General Ting Chao's troops took up new positions along the Chinese Eastern Railway occupying a number of towns running from Harbin westwards to the Soviet Border. Feng Chan-hai took part of the army into Western Kirin and formed a new force, the 'North-Eastern Loyal and Brave Army', with 15,000 volunteers.

## The Sun Ping-wen Rebellion

Several of the volunteer army commanders flirted with joining the Manchukuoan Army at times during their resistance campaign. General Sun Ping-wen was one of those who decided to throw in his lot with the Japanese and their Manchukuoan puppets. But on the 28th of September 1932 Sun Ping-wen decided to rebel against his new employers. Sun had been put in charge of the troops guarding the Western Section of the Chinese Eastern Railway. When he revolted his army took control of the border town of Manchouli where the junction between the CER and the Trans Siberian Railway was situated. General Sun was soon joined by the forces of General Wan Fu-lin, who had also been flirting with joining the Manchukuoan regime. Sun now renamed his Army the the 'Heilungkiang National Salvation Army' and took his 80,000 men to capture the border city of Manchouli. When they took the city his troops massacred a large number of the hated Koreans who had acted as 'spearheads' for the Japanese in Manchuria.

He also captured a number of Japanese civilians and workers in Manchouli whom he held as hostages. The Japanese Imperial Air Force dropped a number of messages to Sun demanding the safety of their citizens. In addition they made Sun an offer that if he returned to the Manchukuoan fold he would be granted a full pardon. This offer was immediately rejected by Sun but he did release 120 Japanese women and children as a gesture. The hostages were escorted to the Soviet-Manchukoan border where they were handed over to the Soviet authorities. For the next few months Sun was at the zenith of his power as his army moved eastwards along the CER almost to the suburbs of Tsitisihar. Commentators at the time said that General Sun was managing to keep the peace in this newly won territory. The Japanese were never going to countenance the continued defiance of Sun and began preparations to attack him. A new headquarters was established at Tsitsihar and new units were moved up to the frontline. On the 29th of November the Japanese offensive began with a series of bombing raids on the rebel-held cities of Hailar and Chaluntun. In anticipation of the kind of terrain and weather that they would face in the coming campaign the Japanese had gathered together a large number of lorries. Their first ground move was to send this improvised motorised force to the main obstacle in the way of their advance, the Khingan Mountain range. Once they got through the mountain passes they advanced quickly towards Sun's 'capital' at Manchouli. They encountered few of Sun's troops as he had stationed most of his men along the Chinese Eastern Railway. It had seemed obvious to Sun and his staff that the railway was the route that the Japanese would follow. Once Sun had been outmanoeuvred by the Imperial Army it was only a matter of time before he was beaten. After the Japanese captured several of the towns held by Sun's troops the rebel leader pragmatically decided to withdraw. He managed to reach the border with some of his units, where he handed over his hostages and his troops were disarmed and interned. Most of them were taken to the Siberian town of Tomsk.

## The Return of General Ma

Even though his army had been defeated in November 1931 and he had fled across the Soviet border, General Ma's reputation was still intact. The Japanese tried to give some legitimacy to their new state of Manchukuo by buying Ma's services. Ma had become an international celebrity for his resistance to the Japanese and they wanted him to change sides. He was offered the huge sum of $3,000,000 in gold, which he accepted. He brought his troops back over the border to join the Manchukuoan Army. Ma played along for a while and might have stayed loyal to the Japanese if they had given him a legitimate role. He attended the inauguration ceremony of the former Chinese Emperor Pu Yi as Chief Executive of Manchukuo. The Japanese suspected Ma's true intentions and although they made him War Minister of the new state, it was a purely honorary title. Japanese suspicions were proved correct when in early April 1932 he announced his intention to rebel against his new masters. Using the money given to him by the Japanese he raised a new army, having evacuated the wives and children to safety beforehand. In addition, he had moved arms and ammunition out of the arsenals he controlled and had bought other military supplies with his personal fortune. His army was reorganised into nine brigades and thousands of new recruits flocked to his banner. His forces were renamed the 'North-East Anti-Japanese National Salvation Army' with a reported strength of 300,000 men. Not surprisingly, the Japanese Kwangtung Army was out for revenge and launched a series of military campaigns against Ma's Army. Eventually the intense Japanese pressure told, with the initial enthusiasm of Ma's men fading after a number of defeats. Once again, General Ma saw the reality of the situation and in December 1932 he recrossed the border, not returning to China until June 1933.

## Report on the Resistance

In a detailed report of the situation in Manchuria by H.G.W. Woodhead, the pro-Japanese author, breaks down the types of irregulars fighting the Japanese in April 1933. He considered that there were four classes of 'bandit' who were arranged in order from 1 to 4 with the 1st class being the volunteers. He describes this 1st class as being made up of scattered units of the former Manchurian Army, who were organised and numbered 69,000. According to Woodhead the 2nd class of bandit was made up of the 'fanatical organisations' such as the 'Red Spears, Big

During an anti-bandit operation in the newly established state of Manchukuo in the early 1930s a unit of soldiers from the puppet army hold an entrenchment fortified by a stone wall. As the war against the volunteer armies intensified after 1932 more and more of these troops were employed alongside Japanese units. The Manchukuoan Army had a poor reputation in its early days but after reorganisation and retraining, a number of units did perform reasonably during some campaigns.

Swords and Great Souls'. These men were motivated by religious fervour. Most were poorly armed with roughly made spears and swords used alongside any rifles they could capture from the enemy. The author estimated the number of this type of bandit at 16,000 operating mainly in eastern Fengtien province. Third class bandits were the 'Hunghutze' or Red Beards, the traditional bandits of Manchuria who had plagued the three provinces for many years. Numbering according to Woodhead 62,000 they were hardy, used to adversity and often well armed with captured rifles. The final 4th class were 'peasant bandits' who usually fought the Japanese to eat, as they had often been forced from their land by the war. Numbering according to the author 65,000 men, he maintained that they received more sympathy from the Japanese than the other three types of bandit. Woodhead was either deluded or biased if he thought any type of resistance fighter-bandit would have received any mercy from the Imperial Army in Manchuria.

One little known aspect of the volunteer armies was the number of females amongst their ranks. In several newspapers of the time headlines like 'Chinese Amazons who Revel in War's Grim Carnage' are common. In July 1932 it was reported that some of these women were recruited into regiments when their commanders realised that they could 'loot as well as the men'. Some of the stronger women had taken control of volunteer bands when their husbands were killed in action. One woman commander was described by a European hostage taken by her band. She was he said as large as most of her men and her 'snarl' frightened him more than any of her male comrades. What the Japanese thought of wopmen fighting against them can be seen by their treatment. They suffered the same fate as their male comrades and were swiftly executed upon capture.

## Japanese Anti-Bandit Operations 1932–1935 and Weaknesses of the Volunteer Armies

Between March 1932 and November 1933 there were at least 14 large-scale bandit suppression operations aimed at the various volunteer armies. After the defeat of the regular forces of the North-Eastern Army the Japanese were now having to deal with large guerrilla armies. They did this in their usual determined and brutal way, employing thousands of Japanese and Manchukuoan troops. All the instruments of war at their disposal were used including armoured trains, artillery and aircraft. Any civilian who got in the way during these operations could expect little mercy.

The main aim of all these operations was to reduce the size of the volunteer armies into manageable guerrilla bands. These began with the operation to destroy the volunteer armies in Kirin province in March 1932. It involved 7,000 Japanese and Manchukuoan troops who were fighting a force of volunteers estimated at 20,000 fighters. It was supported by the River Defence Fleet and the operation succeeded in pushing the Kirin armies further North and secured control of the Sungari River. Another operation in the late spring and summer of 1932 was aimed at 6,000 of Ma Chan-shan forces and involved mainly Manchukuoan troops totalling 5,000 men. The puppet troops performed terribly and the volunteers had no trouble slipping past them to reform and fight another day. A series of three operations were launched against mutinous Manchukuoan troops under the command of General Tang Chu-wu in the Tungpientao region. The first operation against these rebels took place in May 1932 and the last one ended in early December the same year. Starting with 20,000 men the rebel force was reduced to 1,800 by the end of the third operation. When the operation was completed any rebel officers were beheaded by the Japanese while some of the ordinary soldiers were recruited into the Manchukuoan Army. Two operations were launched against Feng Chang-hai's Army between June and July 1932 with the second one clearing 15,000 volunteers from Kirin province. In May 1932 a 10,000-strong force of volunteers led by Li Hai-ching was cleared from their base in Southern Heilungkiang province. This offensive was launched by 6,000 Manchukuoan troops with a small Japanese force in support. It was successful in clearing the rebels from their area of operations.

The volunteer armies were difficult to command. Many of the men had previously served in small military units or guerrilla bands and still owed loyalty to their old commanders. These old leaders had been given commands in the larger armies but personal loyalty was hard to break in China. Some of the volunteer army commanders had also served in the 1920s in warlord armies in which the only loyalty was to the officer who 'filled their rice bowls'.

As the fighting against the Japanese continued the complete lack of support for the volunteers from the Nationalist Government was telling. The only way for these armies to get arms and ammunition was from the enemy and most of these came from the Manchukuoan Army. In 1932 out of the 150,000 estimated volunteers only 60,000 had any type of rifle and the rest were armed with spears, swords and hunting rifles. Although many Manchukuoan soldiers would have been willing to help the volunteers with munitions they were under the watchful eye of the Japanese. The wide variety of rifles in use with the volunteers also meant a logistics nightmare for the officers. Machine guns were rarely acquired by the volunteers and ammunition for them would have been hard to find. It was hard enough to find the few rounds of ammunition for the volunteers' rifles and pistols.

After their initial shock at facing Chinese resistance the Japanese were by the end of 1932 learning how to counter successfully. The sheer size of the volunteer armies meant there were not the resources to feed, clothe and arm them. Without support from the Chinese government it was always going to be an impossibility to keep the armies in the field long term. Once the Japanese Imperial Army had organised anti-bandit units and begun military operations against them, the fate of the volunteer armies was sealed.

From 1935 onwards the pro-Communist 'North-East Anti-Japanese United Army' absorbed most the surviving volunteers. These men were the core of the Manchurian Communist forces who fought for Mao Tse-tung during the 1946–49 Civil War. How many of the original volunteers went on to join the Communists is unknown but it was said that by 1938 there were a total of 10,000 guerrillas fighting the Japanese in Manchuria.

## The Manchukuoan Army, 1931–1937

On the 18th of February 1932 the independence of Manchukuo was declared and a new pro-Japanese state was created. The last Chinese Emperor, Pu Yi was installed first as Chief Executive and then in 1934 as puppet Emperor of Manchukuo. This made Manchukuo a legal entitys, at least according to the Japanese. In a short space of time Manchukuo had a large army, a navy and even an air force to defend itself with help from its Japanese Imperial Army sponsors. It soon became obvious to the Japanese Imperial Army that keeping order in the vast new Manchukuoan Empire would require substantial military forces. In the early days of their invasion and conquest of Manchuria they employed many irregulars who were mainly recruited from amongst the defeated North-Eastern Armies. Several former Fengtien Army commanders were more than willing to bring their units to serve the Japanese. The substantial financial bribes and promotion on offer to these 'turncoat' generals was usually enough to convince them to betray Chang Hsueh-liang. In any case, many did not feel that they owed loyalty to the 'Young Marshal' but to his deceased father, Chang Tso-lin. Although some may have been angry about the Japanese involvement in Chang Tso-lin's assassination, they were pragmatic.

By 1932 the Japanese were making real efforts to raise a more reliable and better trained Manchukuoan Army. They began the process of getting rid of the more undesirable elements within the army and initially settled on a 110,000-strong force organised into four armies. Manchukuoan troops were still not trusted by the Japanese and there were a series of mutinies and rebellions which were ruthlessly put down by the Imperial Army. Some heavier equipment and weaponry was gradually introduced including small numbers of field guns, improvised armoured cars and a few aircraft. Over the next few years the Manchukuoan Army was employed by the Japanese in a series of anti-guerrilla operations. In nearly all cases the Manchukuoan troops were used in support of Japanese units, which took the lead in all actions. The quality of some of the better units of the Manchukuoan Army did improve and its cavalry raised from amongst the Mongol population was often praised by the Japanese advisors. By 1935 the process of streamlining the regular army was complete and it had been pared down to 80,000 men. As part of the reorganisation the weaponry was updated with Chinese rifles and machine guns replaced with Japanese ones. Officer and NCO training schools were set up by the Japanese and the standard of the army in general improved greatly in the mid-1930s. The troops were issued with smart new uniforms and on the surface the Manchukuoan Army was now a professional, well trained, well armed military force. Under the surface, the lack of trust never changed and constant reports of co-operation with the enemy guerrillas undermined any that did develop. The first thing that a mutinous unit did when taking to the hills was to kill any of their Japanese advisors they could find.

# 6

# 'Outrage': The 28 January Incident
# and the Battle for Shanghai

The worldwide condemnation of the Japanese Kwangtung Army's invasion of Manchuria had taken them and their government by surprise. Their flouting of world opinion was beginning to cause problems for the Japanese government. A planned assault on the Manchurian city of Harbin was expected to evoke more condemnation. In order to take the world's attention away from the final stage of the conquest of Manchuria, a diversion was called for. The plan was to cause an incident somewhere else in China that would portray the Chinese as the aggressors. On the 10th of January 1932 the Japanese master spy Colonel Tanaka Ryukichi was given instructions to provoke just such an incident in the city of Shanghai. He was told 'The Manchurian Incident has developed as expected, but the opposition of the major powers is still giving certain persons at the centre doubts. So please use the current tension between China and Japan to bring off your incident and turn the eyes of the powers towards Shanghai.'

Shanghai, the thriving coastal city on the coast of Chekiang province, was the commercial capital of China. It modern waterfront contained the Asian headquarters of several international banks, shipping and publishing companies. There were significant French, US, British and Japanese interests in the city and all had large communities living there. Shanghai was divided into districts, some of which had been established as foreign settlements in the early 20th Century. It really was a cosmopolis where much of the trading in China was done and goods were imported from the rest of the world. As well as Chinese businesses there were a large number of Japanese firms established there. Shanghai was divided into five parts with several 'native' districts: Chapei, Nantao, Lunghwa and Pootung. There were also two foreign districts or settlements, the French and the International with the latter having separate Japanese and British districts within it. The Chinese population was approximately 3,100,000 while the foreign population was 58,688, many being Japanese citizens.

The Japanese relied heavily on selling goods to the large Chinese population and arrogantly expected them to continuing buying from them regardless. Ordinary Chinese were angry about the Japanese invasion of Manchuria and began to vote with their feet. In protest at the Japanese aggression in Manchuria the Chinese people reacted in a way that their leader was not prepared to do. They boycotted Japanese goods and even resigned from firms with connections to the invaders. Many of the Japanese living in Chinese cities were subject to verbal and physical abuse. The Japanese were left under no illusions as to how the Chinese felt about their behaviour and began to feel the effects of this anger.

The boycott by the Chinese of Japanese goods had been highly effective and had resulted in a drop in sales of nearly 40%. As China was the main market for Japanese goods, any drop in sales had a dramatic effect and in Shanghai it resulted in the closing of 90% of Japanese factories. Over 50,000 Shanghai residents demonstrated against the Japanese and demanded death for anyone who traded with them. Chiang Kai-shek meanwhile continued to put his trust in the League of Nations and hoped that they would pressure the Japanese. He thought that the sympathy building in Great Britain and the USA would prove too strong for the Japanese to resist.

The Japanese populations of some Chinese cities were attacked by rioting protestors and several were murdered by the mob. On the 19th of January five Japanese Buddhists including two priests were badly beaten by a crowd of about 60 in Shanghai. These 'rowdies' as the press described them were probably in the pay of Tanaka and his associates. Three of the Buddhists were badly injured with one of them, a priest, dying in hospital six days later. This 'outrage' sparked a Japanese reaction when 400 of the Japanese Youth League rampaged through the Chinese districts. They targeted the area where the Buddhists had been attacked and in particular the Sanyue Towel Company. According to the mob leaders they suspected that the attackers had come from amongst the workforce at the factory. On their way home from the attack the Japanese were confronted by a few Chinese police and stabbed several of them with one constable dying. The Chinese responded by shooting three of the Youth Leaguers, with one dying of his wounds. Both sides blamed the other and it was obvious that this clash was not going to end peacefully. All this was distracting attention away from events in Manchuria. In the meantime the Japanese Consul General in Shanghai visited the Mayor of Greater Shanghai, Wu Tieh-chen, and issued him with demands: 1 a formal apology; 2 the immediate arrest of the Chinese assailants; 3 payment of any hospital expenses incurred by the Japanese wounded. The Mayor was just about able to meet the first three demands even if they were totally unjust but it was the fourth that was the sticking point. It demanded the suppression of all Anti-Japanese movements and the closing of all pro-boycott associations.

A battery of medium field guns of the Special Naval Landing Forces fire across open ground towards the Chinese positions. The naval troops seconded from the Imperial Fleet to take part in ground operations were not well trained. These marines have obviously been given some artillery training but in the early fighting they had little enemy artillery to deal with.

Wu knew that if he agreed to this last demand he would have to face the full wrath of the people of Shanghai. The Chinese authorities were slow to deal with the 'rowdies' although three were arrested after three days and sent for trial.

(Colonel Tanaka Ryukichi, the Japanese spymaster in China in the early 1930s was responsible for engineering the Shanghai Incident. He also masterminding the Inner Mongolian independence movement in the mid-1930s. After the war Tanaka proudly accepted that he was almost solely responsible for the Shanghai Incident and showed no remorse over the thousands who died during it.)

## The Chinese Army at Shanghai

### The 19th Route Army

The 19th Route Army had begun its life as the 4th Nationalist Regiment formed in 1921 and predated the Whampoa Military Academy. The date of its formation was important as it meant that the 19th had a history that made it politically separate to most Nationalist units. Most Nationalist Armies were full of officers who had been trained at Whampoa and had been indoctrinated by Chiang's political officers. 19th Army officers considered themselves as distinct from, even a cut above their fellow officers in the other Nationalist armies. This distinction made the 19th Army in Chiang Kai-shek's eyes politically suspect. Its leaders were seen as potential rebels and after their success at Shanghai as potential rivals to Chiang. Its officers were also regarded as being left-wing, which in Chiang's eyes was sufficient to make the whole army disloyal.

The accusation that the 19th Route Army's leadership was hungry for public acclaim was made during the fighting. Indeed, the army opened its own publicity department and issued leaflets and other handouts to pressmen alongside the

Japanese Naval Landing Forces man a sandbagged position at the side of the main railway in Shanghai. The sailors are wearing their winter navy blue shirts and trousers with the khaki Navy model steel helmet. At first all the fighting in Shanghai was done by these naval infantry but owing to the heavy resistance of the Chinese defenders, the Imperial Army had to join them.

canapés. Its commanders, especially General Ts'ai T'ing-kai, were far from publicity-shy and posed for 'heroic' pictures at the front line.

The Army was fresh from fighting the Communists in Kiangsi province and its men had learnt some hard lessons during that campaign. Some of these lessons were used to employ tactics in Shanghai which copied some of the ruses used against them in the past. In late January there were in fact plans to remove the 19th Route Army from Shanghai to try and avoid confrontation with the Japanese. Commanders of the 19th had stated their intention to fight the Japanese if necessary, which was seen as a provocation. Soldiers of the army were unhappy with Chiang as they had not been paid for several months when the fighting began. In addition, they were starved of new weaponry and equipment. Although the army had 22,500 men, it had only a handful of light mountain guns to form its artillery element.

During the Shanghai fighting the Chinese artillery was far inferior to their Japanese foe's with only a few light guns. The 19th Route Army had brought their mountain guns that they had been using against the Communists with them to Shanghai. The Chinese did have one larger gun, which was mounted on an armoured train in Shanghai's North Station. This train was confined to the station under the command of an officer from the 19th Route Army, Captain Chang Ch'un-sung. Using what local knowledge he had, the captain had the train's gun firing in support of his comrades from the first day of the fighting. With no reliable air reconnaissance available the train gun was firing with little information and relied on spotters and runners to range it.

A British-made Crossley armoured car of the Special Naval Landing Forces moves at speed through the rubble-strewn streets of Shanghai. The Rising Sun flag with rays emanating from the red disc in the centre signifies that the car belongs to the navy.

## The 5th Army

The 5th Army had only been formed on the 22nd of January, six days before the Battle for Shanghai began. It was put under the command of General Chang Chih-chung a well trusted subordinate of Chiang Kai-shek. This new army was formed from units that were available locally and at first only had the 2nd Division of the National Guard. They had been undergoing specialist training under German instructors at Hangchow in late 1931. All the troops were gathered together from their various sub-units and were then moved up to the Soochow District of Shanghai. Their task was to guard the approaches to Nanking including the canals and railways running from the capital to Shanghai. When Chiang Kai-shek announced the formation of the 5th Army he decided to add two of his best divisions to it. These were the 87th and 88th Infantry Divisions, which were two of the first units to receive German training and new equipment in 1930–31. They had formed the 'Capital Guard' for Nanking and were politically the most trusted Nationalist units. Chiang Kai-shek's distrust of the 19th Route Army was now balanced by the presence of the two divisions in Shanghai. Chinese public opinion was that the 87th and 88th were spoilt by Chiang and were provided with all the best equipment and weaponry. This was proved by the fact that all public donations during the battle were sent to the 19th Route Army, as people felt the 5th Army did not need any help. In reality, the under-strength army of only 13,000 men was not given any particular favouritism at this stage.

Japanese Imperial Army artillerymen fire their light field gun down the road on the outskirts of Shanghai. The five-man crew are fairly exposed to enemy fire, even though they are sheltered behind the gun's armoured shield. When the Imperial Navy had to call for reinforcements the inter-service rivalry meant that they were loath to accept help from the army.

## Irregular Chinese Forces

Shanghai defence forces included many local policemen, customs staff and other uniformed officials included the Military Police. The fighting for Shanghai also served as a unifying force for the various political factions that had formerly clashed in the city. These included the cotton mill workers of Japanese-owned mills who had been laid off when the fighting began. These and other workers formed volunteer units which acted as auxiliaries and support workers for the regular units. There were 60,000 Chinese employed in the mills and out of these a fifth were on strike when the fighting began. The 4,000 volunteers who came from the striking workers dug trenches, brought up supplies and ammunition to the frontline. They basically performed any r task that released the troops for frontline duties. Other volunteers came from amongst the students of Shanghai University and other higher education institutes. Some press reports at the time claimed that the majority of Chinese soldiers were 'mere boys'. The Yi-Yung Chun or Volunteer Corps was a force of 12 armed units given rifles and a few rounds of the ammunition by the Army. The Volunteer Corps of from five to eight hundred was highly motivated. They received training at Shanghai University. The Student Military Training programme gave the students basic instruction on small arms and other weaponry. Japanese pressure was put on the Chinese to disband the Yi-Yung Chun, as they said they were irregulars. On the 14th of February the Mayor of Shanghai bowed to the pressure. The volunteers presumably simply

Three cheerful pilots pose in front of a Japanese fighter during the Shanghai Incident in 1932. Japanese fighters and light bombers had total air superiority over Shanghai and strafed and bombed its built-up areas almost daily. They had little regard for the civilian casualties during these attacks, with military targets being close to built-up areas.

handed in their rifles and continued their previous support role. Other civilian volunteers in Shanghai included a number of 'snipers' from the criminal 'Green Gangs' that dominated the city's underworld. Although not particularly patriotic these criminals certainly did not want the Japanese taking over districts which they controlled. They brought with them both rifles and machine guns they had previously used in their illegal activities. Many of the civilian and student volunteers arrived in Shanghai with no weapons and dressed in light summer uniforms.

## The Japanese in Shanghai

When the battle for Shanghai began in January 1932 the Japanese forces in the city were made up almost entirely of Special Naval Landing Forces landed from the Imperial Fleet off the coast. There were soon 2,000 men in 6 Battalions, the 1st, 5th and the 7th with some field guns, light infantry guns and a few Crossley armoured cars. The total of naval personnel in Shanghai was 5,000, which included all support and non-combatants. They were supported by civilian volunteers or Ronin (see below) who were armed by the local Japanese authorities. When the SNLF proved incapable of dealing with unexpected Chinese resistance, Japanese Army units were landed in and around Shanghai. First was the 24th Mixed Brigade, which was soon joined by the 9th Infantry Division bringing a Mountain Artillery Regiment and six 150mm heavy mortars. Other artillery in Shanghai during the early fighting were twelve 150mm Howitzers and eight 100mm field guns. As the battle progressed the Japanese sent two more divisions to Shanghai, the 11th with a Mountain Artillery Regiment and the 14th Division with a Field Artillery Regiment.

An officer of the 19th Route Army issues orders from the back of his horse exposing himself to enemy fire. His horse may not have been much use against the Reds in the confined streets during one of the Nationalist Army's Encirclement Campaigns.

A Nationalist Chinese machine gun crew fires towards Japanese lines from the natural cover of a hillock. Three officers watch the machine gun fire while one of them observes its target with a pair of binoculars. Men of the 19th Route Army wore a mixture of peaked caps as worn by the gunner and ski type caps worn by the officers; one has a pair of driving goggles.

The Japanese did not have a large armoured force in 1932 but brought in their 2nd Independent Tank Company to Shanghai. With no armour on the Chinese side they hoped that the presence of a few tanks would help them as it had in Manchuria in 1931. Under the command of Captain Shigemi the company had five Type 89 medium tanks and ten Renault NC27 light tanks. Although the Type 89 was a powerful tank in 1932 its use was limited due to the compactness of much of the battlefield. Outside the built-up areas of Shanghai the many creeks and wetlands meant that the Japanese tanks were impractical and stayed parked up for most of the battle. The NC27 was a poor design known in Japan as the 'Otsu B' light tank which stayed in Imperial Army service until 1940. Its over-complicated suspension system meant that it would easily break down in the mud around Shanghai so it also remained unused during the fighting.

### The Ronin
The Japanese use of 3,000 civilian volunteers from their community in their Yangtzepoo Settlement was organised by Major Tanaka Ryukichi. In the initial stages of the Shanghai Incident their role was mainly as agent provocateurs staging local incidents under Tanaka's instructions. There were army reservists who were businessmen in Shanghai and vigilante groups known as Jikeidan and civilian volunteers known by the Chinese as Ronin. They wore civilian clothing but were issued with armbands as identification and were given modern rifles

Reinforcements for the 19th Route Army advance through the suburbs of Shanghai. The tightly packed streets and alleys were the scene of much of the fighting for the city. It is easy to see that any civilians caught up in the fighting would have little protection from artillery fired by both sides or bombs dropped by the Japanese air force.

by the Japanese military. Besides their combat role the Ronin were employed as drivers and performed other support roles during the fighting. One of their roles was to force Chinese labourers into service with the Japanese Navy and Army in Shanghai. The Japanese were short of labour to help in the support of frontline troops and forced labour was organised by the Ronin. They also acted as an unofficial police force, executing suspected Chinese snipers and saboteurs on several occasions. During the Incident the Ronin gained an unsavoury reputation through their treatment of defenceless Chinese civilians.

## 25 January–30 January

On the 25th, units of the 19th Route Army began erecting defences and digging trenches in the Chapei district. The Japanese were aware that the Chinese had been instructed from Nanking to withdraw if they attacked. For this reason the Japanese thought that the 19th Army's preparations were some kind of bluff and that they would obey Chiang. The next day the Shanghai authorities began to comply with some of the Japanese demands in an effort to avoid fighting. These measures included the closing of the anti-Japanese boycott association offices, which were sealed by the Chinese police. Unsatisfied by these token measures, the Japanese consul-general sent the Shanghai Mayor a 22-hour ultimatum. It said if the Chinese did not comply with all the Japanese demands then they would have to take the 'necessary action'. When the ultimatum ran out at 6.00pm on the 28th, hostilities became inevitable.

The official intention of the Japanese Navy was to take control of a defensive sector to protect the Japanese citizens of Chapei. During the night of the

28th–29th, 2,000 Japanese blue jackets formed up in the streets of Shanghai. They were backed by armoured cars, trucks and a number of light artillery pieces and at 11.00 pm the Mayor was informed that this force intended to occupy Chapei. Only 30 minutes after forming up and before the Chinese had time to react to their last message, the Japanese advanced. Knowing that the Chinese units in Chapei had orders to withdraw in face of their advance it was obvious that the Japanese intended to attack them regardless. It was hoped that even a short exchange with the 19th Route Army would give the Japanese Imperial Navy a victory to boast about. Accompanying the Marines were a number of Japanese Ronin or armed civilians sent in to Chapei to cause as much mayhem as possible. These agent provocateurs aimed to provoke the Chinese into fighting and therefore escalate the situation. As the Marines and Ronin moved into Chapei the only opposition they faced was a handful of Chinese police, who were disarmed. A few shots were fired, probably by confused Gendarmes; but this was all the excuse the Japanese needed.

Japanese Naval aircraft appeared overhead and began to drop incendiary bombs onto the Chapei and other Chinese districts causing heavy casualties. This indiscriminate bombing destroyed factories, houses and the large Commercial Press Library with its 600,000 books. Under cover of this bombing the Japanese started to push further into the Chapei District from the Szechwen Road. Heavier fire came from the now fully alert Chinese police as they came into contact with the Nationalist 5th and 6th Regiments of the 78th Division. Fighting now became more serious with attempts by the Japanese to outflank the Chinese regulars thwarted by heavy fire from the defenders. The Chinese armoured train began firing its main gun in the general direction of the Japanese as it moved up and down a branch line of the Woosung Railway. By the 29th the Japanese had managed to secure the defensive sector but this could have been achieved without bloodshed. The Japanese Navy was embarrassed that its superior fire power and air support had failed to intimidate the 19th Route Army in their first encounter. Both sides now rushed reinforcements into Shanghai. The 19th Route Army brought in some of its units that had been stationed outside the city. Its 78th Division was close to Shanghai but the 60th and 61st Divisions were as far away as Nanking. Many of the Chinese troops now moving into the city were reported to be National Guard Militiamen not 19th Army veterans. Attempts at mediation by British and US officials failed. The Japanese offered to cease firing if the Chinese would also stop and they agreed to stay on the east side of the Shanghai-Woosung Railway. Chinese officials responding by saying that the Japanese had no right to be in their territory and that they should withdraw. At the same time the Japanese Commander said that his forces were not at war with China, they were only at war with the 19th Route Army. This was because the Nationalist Government did not want the 19th to fight, so their argument was with this 'rebellious' unit, not the Chinese people. The situation changed on the 30th when Chiang Kai-shek publicly announced his support for the 19th Route Army and his determination to resist Japanese aggression. Any attempt at conciliation with the Japanese was met with more aggressive actions by them. It became apparent that the only policy was to fight. The same day Chiang Kai-shek met with his military advisors in Nanking to discuss the situation in Shanghai. It was decided to move the nation's capital

The Chinese crew of a Swiss- made 20mm Oerlikon anti-aircraft gun prepare their position in the heart of Shanghai. The Japanese had complete air superiority and a few light guns like these were the city's only protection from air raids. Every type of light anti-aircraft gun to be found on the world arms market was used by the Nationalist Army during the 1930s.

to Luoyang temporarily as Nanking was deemed to be too close to Shanghai. The government worried that the Japanese Navy's ships sitting off their coast could bombard the capital if full-scale war broke out. If the Japanese were to break out of Shanghai they were only a short march away from the Nationalist capital. Chiang was adamant that the 19th Route Army should continue to resist the Japanese no matter what the cost. He also ordered that the 61st, 87th and 88th Divisions should prepare to defend Nanking if necessary.

## The Japanese February Offensives

In the first few days of February there was a change in the command of the Shanghai defences. The 19th Route Army's commander, General Chiang Kuang-nai, was promoted to the command of all Chinese forces in Shanghai. He was replaced in his command of the 19th by General Ts'ai T'ing-k'ai, who was to become the 'face' of the Nationalist defence in the press. On the 6th of February the Japanese 24th Mixed Brigade with about 3,000 men landed South of Woosung Creek. They were supported by naval detachments from Shanghai with several armoured cars but were confronted by Chinese forces on the creek's north bank. The Japanese were meeting heavy resistance in the Woosung area of the city in the first week of February and the treacherous mud on the battlefield made movement difficult. The bridges over Woosung Creek had been destroyed and the Chinese had sited machine guns at crossing points. Japanese forces were gathered for a general assault in the sector in an attempt to take Woosung village but again, the Chinese managed to push them back. In the Chapei District in the first days of February the Chinese defenders were well dug-in amongst the ruins. In the Woosung District on the 7th a heavy assault was launched by the Japanese. They laid down heavy fire from artillery, machine guns and rifles before launching an attack. To reinforce this attack the Japanese had landed a mixed brigade at the entrance to the Woosung Creek from small boats. It was estimated that about 5,000 men landed with a force of Marines moving behind the Chinese positions. They blew up bridges at the rear of the Chinese defenders trapping them in a small area that was then bombarded by destroyers from the Japanese Navy.

On the 14th of February in an attempt to counter this build-up of Japanese units the 19th Army command requested similar reinforcements. The newly organised 5th Army made up of the 87th and 88th Divisions along with multiple independent units had been earmarked for Shanghai. Chiang's determination to defend his country's commercial centre was shown by his commitment of two of his 'elite' divisions. They had both been trained by the German Military Mission and he was reluctant to risk them in the battle.

On the same day a company of Japanese Infantry from the 24th Brigade crossed to the north bank of Woosung Creek. They crossed by means of an ingenious floating cork bridge but their commando raid was soon beaten back with heavy losses. The same day the Japanese received vital reinforcements in the form of the Imperial 9th Division with a number of mountain guns, several tanks and support troops. This division of 14,300 men was installed in the Japanese Yangtzepoo Settlement. The division under the command of Lieutenant-General Uyeda had mountain artillery and some tanks. By next day the 9th Division was installed in its billets in the Japanese sector of the International Settlement. Using the International Settlements as military bases contravened the neutrality of these districts of the city. Despite protests by the Chinese Foreign Minister about Japanese use of their Settlement to station troops, nothing was done.

On the 18th of February the Japanese had assembled a 16,000-strong force to launch a major offensive. The Nationalist 5th Army had also arrived in the suburbs of Shanghai and were taking up positions. The bulk of the Japanese were positioned south-east of the Chiangwan Race Course which was half-way between Shanghai city centre and the Woosung Forts. It was planned that the offensive would break through the Chinese defences at Chiangwan. The Japanese would then wheel southwards towards Ch'entsu. On the 20th of February the Japanese 9th Division launched an attack on the village of Chiangwan, which was central to the Chinese defences. The attack began at 07.30 am. The Japanese began a heavy bombardment of the 88th Division's trenches.

At the same time aircraft from the Imperial Navy's carriers off the coast began bombing their positions. The bombardment was followed by an attack by the Japanese 24th Mixed Brigade which was countered by the well trained Chinese troops. The Japanese advanced behind a screen of light tanks but these could not break through the well prepared entrenchments. Eventually, the Japanese did gain a foothold in the eastern part of Chiangwan and for the next seven days tried to extend the territory they controlled. The Japanese ground attacks supported by air and artillery bombardments began to wear down the defenders. Soldiers of the 60th Nationalist Division defending Chiangwan stood firm and stopped the Japanese getting their tanks into the village. They were helped by the anti-tank defences they had prepared and by the fact that the area was crisscrossed by creeks and ditches that tanks could not cross. Progress by the Japanese on their right wing was easier until they came up against the trenches filled with 60th Division troops. By the 22nd the Japanese had committed all the troops they were willing to and their lines were now thinly stretched through Chiangwan. The Chinese then began a counter-attack which was intended to roll back the 24th Mixed Brigade and the 9th Division but this soon broke down. A feature of this offensive was the resistance put up by Chinese troops defending the Fuhtan University campus. In the grounds of buildings of the university a resolute group of Chinese troops held out. Press reports said that the Japanese were unwilling at first to bomb a 'cultural institution' but they soon dropped their scruples and the facilities were attacked. After giving the Japanese a good fight, the defenders of the university withdrew. The assault on the University saw effective co-operation between the Japanese air and ground forces. Planes flew low above the battlefield giving instructions to their navy and artillery about exact Chinese positions. When the Japanese bombardment was over, a huge area of the city had been reduced to ruins 'from the mouth of the Whangpoo River to the Woosung Creek'. In the ruins the 19th Route Army had built a well designed and built system of entrenchments and a network of tunnels. The Chinese artillery shelled Japanese positions in the stronghold they had established in the Changwahpang Railway Station. This bombardment was answered in kind by heavy shelling from the Japanese fleet, which caused further damage and started numerous fires in the Chinese-held suburbs. A fierce battle developed with Japanese planes flying overhead and shells coming in from their ships off the coast. The only Chinese response was to fire their machine guns from their coastal positions towards the Japanese ships, which were out of range. Casualties from this heavy fighting soon piled up at the hospitals with wounded lying in the corridors. Japanese estimates of the Chinese dead from five days of fighting were 500, with 400 of these killed in one day. Witnesses told of the Japanese killing any civilians who they came across during the fighting, often with bayonets. This did not deter the Chinese from wanting to join the army. A thousand men trying to get into the war zone through the French Settlement. Women volunteers also came forward to join the Red Cross with several who had lost their families saying they wanted to die for China.

From the 25th of February the Japanese shifted tactics, with the units fighting in the city centre holding their positions. They began their attack on the Nationalist

87th Division at 06.30 am with an hour and a half artillery bombardment. The assault then began and the Japanese soon reached the largely destroyed Chinese trenches. Their assault had caught the shell-shocked Chinese unprepared but it took until 11.00 to force the 87th to begin to fall back. Chinese reinforcements were rushed up by the 19th Army from the city centre including units from the 78th and 61st Divisions. These reinforcements arrived just in time and the Japanese were forced back to their starting point.

The fighting for Chiangwan continued but it became apparent that the Japanese were going to win. Some reinforcements which had been destined for Chiangwan were sent instead to Chapei. It was thought that the position in Chiangwan was lost and that they would be wasted in a futile gesture. This heavy fighting continued into the last days of February with some cut-off Chinese units in Chiangwan fighting to the last man. Three companies of hand-picked Japanese troops had been chosen to mop up the last of these Chinese fighters. With no food or water supplies left, the Chinese expected little mercy from the Japanese, so carried on fighting. The Japanese under the command of Colonel Hayashi launched a bayonet charge with their commander at the front. According to an eyewitness the defenders 'fought with extreme courage and ferocity during the bayonet charges, using machine guns and hand grenades, realising that all retreat was severed, and their lives were forfeit'. Japanese attacks were launched on three sides with desperate hand-to-hand fighting as the Imperial troops 'leaped on each other's backs and scaling the ruined fortifications'. Tanks led the attack firing their guns into the houses which had been turned into strongholds. Within the ruined fortifications the Chinese held out with ammunition running low and many on the verge of starvation. When the fighting was finished the defenders were paid a rare compliment by the Japanese commander, General Uyeda: 'They were equal to anything but our artillery, which was superior and eventually told.'

## March Fighting

On the 1st of March the Japanese launched a major offensive along the northern flank of Chapei district. As usual, the attack was supported by the superior Japanese artillery and there was plenty of air support. During the bombardment the Chinese defenders had to remain in their bunkers as they had no guns to fire back. The Japanese stopped any Chinese reinforcements getting to the frontline by shelling the railways in the rear. The 8,000-strong Japanese force had Marines from the SNLF in the forefront who wanted to show their fighting abilities after failing in the early actions. Marines operating in small assault groups did make some progress in the ruined streets of Chapei. They managed to infiltrate Chinese positions where they found that the heavy shelling had affected the fighting spirit of some of the Nationalist troops. Casualties suffered by the Chinese meant that some positions were poorly manned as some troops withdrew. In the middle of the fighting for Chapei the North Railway Station fell to a Japanese assault. The station had been a symbol of the Chinese resistance but it had been bombed throughout. It is difficult for any soldier to suffer continuous bombing, especially when there is no way to reply. Although the Chinese did have some light anti-aircraft guns these were too few in number to trouble the Japanese air force.

The Chinese had tried to launch a counter-attack in the Chapei fighting but this failed to break the Japanese lines. By the 2nd the 19th Route Army told the press that they were running out of ammunition and they began to prepare to leave their defences. On the 3rd some units of the 19th and 5th Armies began gradually to withdraw from the city. Chinese forces had been making a slow and well organised withdrawal in the last 10 days of February. The Chinese commanders and General Tsai in particular were disillusioned by the lack of support from Chiang Kai-shek. The promised reinforcements did not arrive and air support which was supposed to have been sent from Canton never materialised. The 5th Army now began withdrawing from their frontline positions to the west of Chiangwan as well. Japanese forces moved up behind them but do not appear to have pressed them too hard. After their performance during the battle, the Japanese were quite happy to let the Chinese withdraw.

As the Chinese were retiring from their positions the Japanese launched an amphibious operation behind the Nationalist lines. An 8,000–10,000-strong force from the 11th Division was transported by eight ships upstream from Shanghai and landed on the shores of the Yangtze River. They were opposed by a skeleton force of Chinese cadets who were soon brushed aside and they then began to advance southwards behind the Nationalists.

## The Woosung Forts

The three Woosung Forts to the north of Shanghai were positioned on the Yangtze River. There was one either side of the junction with the Wangpoo River that ran past the city. The third and most important fort was on the headland at the point where the two rivers met. The forts were garrisoned by 2,000 Nationalist troops, most of whom were from the 19th Route Army, as well as some local National Guards. The forts were armed with a number of large 8-inch coastal guns but some of these appear to have been out of action in 1932. A strong naval landing force was gathered and was landed on the banks of the Yangtze and Wangpoo Rivers ready to begin an assault. For five days from the 2nd to the 7th of February the 10,000 strong force tried to capture the forts. Their attacks were beaten back on several occasions. Then the Japanese Imperial Navy's destroyers bombarded the forts from point blank range. Protected by concrete emplacements and bunkers the garrisons held out despite heavy casualties. The Japanese fleet bombarding the fort was made up of 2 destroyers, 2 cruisers and 12 aircraft. By the 10th of February it appeared that the forts were about to fall but the stubborn resistance of the garrisons continued. Even after weeks of air bombing and bombardments from the Japanese fleet, the forts still held out. The troops holding on in the ruins of the fort were cut off from Shanghai from early February but resisted a number of frontal assaults. In fact it was not until 8.00 am on the 3rd of March that the fort closest to Shanghai fell, after the landing of a new assault force including a regiment from the 11th Division. The remaining Chinese troops withdrew under fire from the fort and tried to make their way back to their lines at Shanghai. The Japanese blew up the main guns on the forts on the 5th of March and shipped the lighter ones back to Japan as war trophies.

## The End of the Fighting

In the middle of this fighting the League of Nations demanded that both sides should observe a ceasefire but clashes continued into the first week in March. On the 6th of March the Chinese agreed to the League demands but the Japanese ignored them and continued their attack. A few days later a one-sided ceasefire agreement was reached, which called for Shanghai to be off-limits for Chinese troops while the Japanese were allowed to keep some units there. They would be stationed in the designated Neutral Zone, which rather undermines the concept of nueutrality. The peace was nearly disrupted on the 10th of March when the Japanese heard false rumours of an attack by 30,000 Chinese troops who had arrived in the region. The Japanese threatened to renew the fighting until it was shown that the rumour was untrue and things calmed down again. In the ever changing situation the Japanese were prepared to retire from Shanghai by mid-March. This change of attitude was prompted by the increasing cost of the campaign. On the 14th, League of Nations representatives arrived in Shanghai to

A Nationalist heavy mortar crew are about to fire towards Japanese positions from their fire base in a railway goods yard. Weapons like this were often fired during the battle for Shanghai without sufficient intelligence as to where the Japanese were. Large calibre mortars were mass-produced in Chinese arsenals in the 1920s.

try and make the Japanese negotiate. On the 18th the Japanese began withdrawing their forces from the city and once this was completed hostilities formally ended.

The peace treaty called for the demilitarisation of the Settlement Zone and the end of the Anti-Japanese boycott. It caused anger amongst the vast majority of the Chinese and the official who signed it on behalf of the Government was badly beaten up by outraged students.

## The Air War over Shanghai

The Chinese had a single Boeing 218 fighter, 8 Junkers K47 heavy fighters and pair of Blackburn Lincock fighters. They also had 20 two-seater light bombers including Corsairs, Douglas O-2MCs and Wacos. Facing them over the city were 40 Japanese fighters, 25 reconnaissance planes, 40 light bombers and 10 seaplanes. Types used by the Japanese included the Nakajima N1A1 fighter and several models of light bomber including the Type 88. Throughout the incident Japanese air raids caused large numbers of civilian casualties. On the 29th of January an air raid on the crowded Chapei district caused 1,000 civilian deaths. On the 31st of January the Japanese sent a 'show of force' flight of 30 aircraft over Shanghai

On the outskirts of Shanghai Chinese troops of the 5th Army prepare to defend their entrenchments from a Japanese assault. Apart from the Maxim M1908 machine gun in the foreground, all the men are armed only with rifles and stick grenades. Their officer crouched at the back of the trench looks for any movement in the distance, armed with a C-96 semi-automatic pistol.

Although the defenders of Shanghai had few artillery pieces, they did have a handful of German-made mountain guns like this Rheinmetall 75mm M14. They also had a few more modern L/13 infantry guns, which, being lightweight, were ideal for an army with few vehicles. The 10-man crew seen here would have to manhandle their gun from one firing position to another during the battle.

to cow the population. The Japanese launched a number of raids throughout February. On the 5th two Japanese bombers and three carrier-borne fighters from the 'Hosho' engaged in dogfights with Chinese fighters over Shanghai. Two days later aircraft from the Japanese carriers *Hosho* and *Kaga* flew over the city supporting their ground forces. On the 22nd of February three Mitsubishi B1M3 light bombers from the *Kaga* escorted by B1M2 fighters was attacked by Chinese fighters over Shanghai. Although the Nationalists did receive some help from the 2nd Squadron based at nearby Nanking they were always outnumbered and out-gunned in the air by the Japanese. In early February the Chinese received a strong reinforcement of 26 fighters along with a group of pilots trained in the USA, Britain, France and Germany. The pilots made their wills and said that they would fight to the death to defend the skies above Shanghai. Japanese bombing of the crowded districts of Shanghai was roundly condemned by the press. When Admiral Shiozawa was questioned about the indiscriminate bombing of the crowded districts of Shanghai by a western journalist he was relaxed in his reply: 'You know your papers call me the baby killer? But after all they should give some credit. I used the 30 pound bombs, and if I had chosen to do so I could have use the 500 pound variety.' During the battle the Japanese did not restrict their air attacks just to the centre of Shanghai, bombing several towns near to the city. On one occasion their bombers strafed a refugee camp set up by the League of Nations but this was described by the Japanese as a 'mistake'. They then repeated their mistake every day for four days killing a total of 50 civilians.

A young grenadier of the Nationalist Army in Shanghai prepares to throw his stick grenade for the camera. The boy who is probably not even in his teens has no weapon other than the two grenades he holds. Several eyewitnesses commented on the youth of some soldiers of the 19th Route Army. Most of these were probably volunteers who had joined during the battle.

## The All-American Hero

Although neutral in the war in China, in 1932 the US Government quietly 'encouraged' certain military aircraft companies to supply the Chinese with planes. Boeing agreed to supply aircraft to the Nationalists and sent one of their latest products to China. So in mid February that year a Boeing 218 P-12 fighter arrived in Nanking flown by an American Army Reservist, Robert Short. He was in China to demonstrate the P-12 to the Nationalist Air Force but was soon made aware of what was going on 60 miles away in Shanghai. Short decided that a good way to help the Chinese and demonstrate his fighter's prowess was to take it into battle. He had already endured one Japanese air raid on the airfield he was flying from and when three fighters came back he took off in his P-12. In no time he had shot down one of the Japanese planes killing its pilot, Lieutenant Kidokoro, and chased the other two fighters away. The shocked but grateful Chinese feted him as a hero. For two days no more attacks came but on the 22nd a Japanese force returned to attack Suzhou Train Station with a force of three bombers and three fighters. Despite the odds Short took off to face them alone again and flew straight into the middle of the three Nakajima A1N1 fighters. His target was the bombers they were escorting and he did manage to kill the pilot of one of them without downing the plane. Led by the co-pilot of the damaged bomber, the bombers flew off leaving Short outnumbered three to one by the fighters. In an intense two-minute dog fight Short put up a good fight but his plane was hit and set on fire. It crashed into the city centre killing Short, whose brave fight had been witnessed by thousands watching from below. Robert Short became a national hero in China and his sacrifice was featured in the world and especially the US press. This one courageous act changed the attitude of many Americans about what was going on in China. From now on millions more Americans took more notice when they read about China's fight with Japan.

## The Cost and the Aftermath

During the battle the Chinese lost 2,449 dead amongst whom were 117 officers, and 6,343 injured, 401 officers. Other estimates give the total casualties at 24,000 but this includes the civilian losses. The western press and Japanese official sources claimed that Chinese casualties were 11,427 dead and wounded out of the total engaged of 63,000. This is a high casualty rate of 18%. If you calculate the total number of troops involved using the smaller divisional organisation this figure gets worse. This would give a figure of 40,000 troops making the casualty rate as high as 30%. During the battle about 320,000 Chinese civilians fled Shanghai with casualties estimated by the League of Nations at 13,000. Other reports put the figure of civilian deaths at much lower but with air bombardment, artillery shelling and summary executions, a large number of people were killed or wounded. Women captured by the Japanese military and especially their Ronin auxiliaries were ill treated and often killed.

The Japanese committed several outrages during the fighting in Shanghai which went largely unreported. One western eyewitness saw at firsthand how the Japanese treated civilians who 'got in the way' during the battle around the city's racecourse.

An armed policeman stands in the ruins of the Woosung District in Shanghai having fought as part of the defence force. The Shanghai garrison included civilian volunteers as well as uniformed forces like custom guards and police. This constable is armed with an older type of rifle and has spare clips for it in his leather bandolier. He also has a bayonet or dagger stuck into his belt and looks proud to have fought against the Japanese invaders.

The entrance to my favourite stand at the racecourse is littered with corpses, fresh corpses newly made before my eyes ... There are women and children among them; women shot through the back, their padded coats run through with military sabres, children whose bodies are riddled with bullets; men garbed as peasant farmers heaped grotesquely about, their wounds soaking the ground ... The houses are burned, with neat precision – not a wasted match. (T.O.Thackery, editor, *Shanghai Evening Post & Mercury*)

Although the Japanese eventually won a victory in Shanghai it was an unmitigated propaganda disaster. For the first time their behaviour was not only in full view of a large number of western eyewitnesses but also of the whole world. Their earlier outrages had been conducted in remote and far-off places like Korea and Manchuria, which created little interest outside the region. Many westerners who had sympathised with Japan's previous actions in Manchuria as a legitimate protection of their rights were shocked. The big publicity winner of the fighting in Shanghai was General Tsai Ting-kai who was featured in magazines as a popular hero. On the 26th of March he made a speech to a parade of 89,000 Nationalist troops during which he issued a rallying cry. He told the assembled troops that thousands of farmers were digging trenches in preparation for more fighting at Shanghai. Although he received a rousing reception no one expected the fighting to resume as Chiang Kai-shek would not support it. Chiang meanwhile had noted the popularity of Tsai with the Chinese people and began to plan how to remove him from the limelight. It was not long before Tsai and the survivors of his 19th Route Army were on their way to Fukien province to fight the Communists. He was to get back into the press in 1933 at the head of an anti-Chiang rebellion in the eastern province where he had been sent (see chapter 10).

The European and US press were full of reports of the bravery of the Chinese 19th Route Army as well as the indiscriminate bombing of civilian areas by Japanese aircraft. While previous massacres in China beginning in 1894 had been largely ignored by the west, by 1932 attitudes had changed. Although both sides in Shanghai had fought their battle in areas crowded with Chinese civilians, the Japanese were now seen as the aggressors. This played into Chiang Kai-shek's hands as he finally evinced the sympathy he had expected when the Japanese invaded Manchuria. For the rest of the 1930s Japan was seen, especially in the US, as a vicious nation trying to dominate fellow Asians. The sympathy created in Shanghai was to turn into a longstanding bias against the Japanese Empire in the west. This antipathy towards Japan was to lead directly to the outbreak of the Pacific War in December 1941.

# 7

# 'THE FORBIDDEN PROVINCE':

# JEHOL, 1933

When the Japanese Kwangtung Army invaded Manchuria in September 1931 it effectively sealed the fate of the neighbouring province of Jehol. Jehol was situated to the north-west of Manchuria and had long been acknowledged as its effective fourth province. The establishment of the new state of Manchukuo by the Japanese in 1932 gave them the opportunity they were looking for to acquire this vast province. Claiming that Jehol was part of Manchukuo the Japanese lobbied for its peaceful transfer to the new state. Jehol was known as the 'Forbidden Province' and had largely been ignored by the Nationalist Government. It had been left by Chiang Kai-shek under the rule of one of the most corrupt military governors, General Tang Yu-lin. As far as the Japanese were concerned, no one would really care if Jehol was taken over by Manchukuo. They argued that all they would be doing if they incorporated it into Manchukuo was returning it to the fold. The Japanese proffered a justification that they were to give many times over the next few years. They said that the Manchukuoan Government had asked for military assistance to aid them in their legitimate claim on territory that was historically theirs. In typical Japanese diplomatic language, their officials said 'The affairs of Jehol province are unquestionably an internal problem of Manchukuo.'

Jehol was a huge province of 65,000 square miles covered with mountains and deserts with stifling hot summers and freezing winters. It was one of the most isolated and underdeveloped provinces in China with no paved highways. Its only roads were the old caravan routes. Some 200 miles of these tracks had been slightly improved but were barely suitable for motor transport. Even though northern China generally was well connected by railways there were none in Jehol, the mountainous terrain making it difficult to build any. Most of the routes into Jehol were easily defensible as they ran through numerous passes ideal for ambush. The province had little in the way of industry and the only crop of note grown there was the opium poppy, the cultivation of which basically provided all the finance of Jehol. As one press report put it 'Opium is its main export; opium keeps up its army, its aeroplanes, its ammunition, motor trucks and locomotive factories. Its special opium train runs or did run every week under military escort to Tientsin and the Foreign Concessions. Opium maintains the province which is China's Northern Defence.'

A Japanese FT-17 light tank in the town of Shanhaikwan after its occupation by the Kwangtung Army in January 1933. The coastal town was taken by the Japanese as a precursor to their attack on Jehol a few weeks later. It had to be secured to stop any Chinese reinforcements moving northwards through its pass into Jehol. The tank has a single machine gun in its turret.

## The Kwangtung Army, 1933

In preparation for the invasion the Japanese Kwangtung Army had distributed their forces all along the Manchukuo-Jehol border. They were stationed as far north as Kailu in the north-east to the far south at Shanhaikwan on the Great Wall. These forces included the 8th Division under Lieutenant-General Nishi with the 4th Brigade 'Suzuki' and the 16th Brigade 'Kawahara' totalling 12,000 men. The 9,000 men of 6th Division were under the command of Lieutenant-General Sakamoto, with the 11th Brigade 'Matsuda' and the 4th Cavalry Brigade 'Mogi'. In addition there was the 14th Infantry Brigade under Major-General Hattori with 4,000 men giving an overall total of 25,000. To defend the strategic coastal town of Shanhaikwan the 33rd Infantry Brigade under Major-General Nakamura was sent from the 10th Division stationed in Harbin in Manchukuo. During the campaign the Japanese were to be reinforced by the 28th Brigade of the 14th Division under Lieutenant-General Gamaboku in March. This gave the Japanese a grand total of just under 40,000 troops who were to be involved directly in the campaign. The morale and performance of the Japanese Imperial Army and its soldiers in 1933 was at an all-time high. They were supremely confident in their abilities and had no doubts about the outcome of the coming campaign.

In support of the Japanese Imperial Army were the rather dubious allied troops of the newly recruited Manchukuoan Army. Various figures have been given for the number of these 'puppet' troops available for the invasion, with between 25,000 and 43,000 involved. The number of Manchukuoan troops was almost immaterial as they were to prove of little real use to the Japanese. The Japanese simply did not trust or respect their allies, most of whom had been in the service with the enemy until very recently. The Manchukuoan contingent of the invasion force was made up of seven Detachments of the Taoliao Army, three Detachments of the National Foundation Army, the National Salvation Army and the National Protection Army. Its best formation was the 1st Brigade of the Guard Corps, which had been given training and better equipment and weaponry by the Japanese.

Manchukuoan cavalry were better regarded by the Japanese than the infantry and these did see some action during the campaign. Officially, the Manchukuoan Army was under the command of General Chang Hai-ping, one of the chief 'turncoats' in 1931. When the fighting began he was given a limited command role in charge of a force of 4,000 cavalry. The Japanese attitude to the Chinese defenders in Jehol was that they were bandits, not regular soldiers. Some Kwangtung Army officers regarded the coming campaign as simply a masive anti-bandit operation. Presumably, any captured Chinese troops would receive the same treatment as their Manchurian comrades had from 1931 to 1933.

Japanese armoured vehicles used in Jehol were limited to the 11 Type 89 medium tanks and two Type 92 combat cars. The type 92 was despite its name a light tank which had only been brought into Japanese service in 1932. These fought in a single 1st Special Tank Company under the command of Captain Hyakutatake. Records say that this unit advanced a remarkable 320km in three days but by the end of this advance none of these tanks was serviceable. It was reported that all of the Japanese tanks broke down in the first 36 hours of their being operated. The reason given for these breakdowns was not the terrible weather but was blamed on the 'lack of sympathy on the part of the ordinary soldier with machinery'. It appears that none of the 500 armoured crewmen and mechanics of the 1st Special Tank Company had been adequately trained to deal with adverse weather conditions.

## The Taking of Shanhaikwan, January 1933

The preparations for the invasion of Jehol began in January 1933 with a Japanese attack on the fortified Chinese garrison at Shanhaikwan. Situated at the eastern-most end of the main section of the Great Wall, the town of Shanhaikwan guarded the main route from northern China to Manchuria. The Japanese had been given the right to have a small garrison in the town under the terms of the Boxer Treaty of 1900. Japan had taken advantage of the Boxer Rebellion, like many European nations, to impose conditions on the defeated Chinese. In a typical Japanese ruse, soldiers of the Japanese garrison staged an incident on the 1st of January involving a grenade attack. According to reports a provocative night manoeuvre by the Japanese was followed by an accusation of 'misbehaviour' by Chinese troops. They claimed the Chinese had planted two bombs in their barracks and that 'someone hurled two bombs and fired two rifle rounds' from Chinese positions. In reality, the Japanese had ordered one of their troops to go out and fire a few rounds off towards his garrison. This 'attack' on the Japanese garrison was blamed by their commander on Chinese 'terrorists'. The Japanese commander was suitably indignant and ordered all Chinese troops to be withdrawn from Shanhaikwan Pass. When the Chinese commanders in the town issued their expected refusal to withdraw, units of the Japanese 8th Division began their attack at dawn. In three days of hard fighting the Japanese were able to push the defenders out of town using their overwhelming firepower from tanks, armoured trains and artillery. The poorly armed Chinese garrison only had a few heavy machine guns and mortars. Why such a strategic position should be so poorly protected is probably down to political issues between Chiang Kai-shek and his northern generals. Even though the Chinese had fortified some of the Great Wall's towers and forts, they were blasted out of them by Japanese artillery. When Japanese aircraft bombed the defences and the Imperial Navy's 2nd Fleet joined in by shelling them from the nearby coast, the defenders surrendered. They had put up a good fight but with no support coming from other Nationalist units in the region the outcome was inevitable. Losses on both sides in the battle were heavy with a reported 600 Chinese killed or wounded and 300 Japanese also casualties.

It was expected that the Japanese would now advance on Peking along the southern side of the Great Wall. To everyone's surprise, apart from the Japanese themselves, this new offensive did not materialise and the 8th Division was prepared instead for another operation. This new conquest would be Jehol. Chiang Kai-shek was aware that the Japanese had taken Shanhaikwan for good strategic reasons and tried to react. He sent five troop trains of 8,000 reinforcements to bolster his armies in the region of the Great Wall. Everything that Chiang did was measured by his fear of provoking more aggression by the Japanese if the sent too many reinforcements to the region.

## The Japanese Air Force in Jehol

The air element on the Kwangtung Army in Jehol was made up of two Air Regiments of Kawasaki Type 88 light bombers and one Air Regiment of Nakajima Type 91 fighters. Without any air opposition on the Chinese side the Type 88s had a free hand in the campaign, bombing concentrations of enemy troops whenever they spotted them. One of their tactics was to frighten Chinese troops into taking shelter in the forests and gorges. They would then drop incendiary bombs into the middle of them spreading more panic amongst

General Tang Yu-lin in typically sinister pose outside his headquarters in his provincial capital, Chengteh. Tang was certainly not camera-shy and there are numerous photographs of him on horseback. In the few short years that he was military governor of Jehol he managed to acquire a huge personal fortune. Unfortunately for the people of Jehol, he was largely left to his own devices by his immediate superior, Chang Hsueh-liang.

the already demoralised soldiers. Although the ground campaign did not begin until February, the Japanese Air Force had been bombing a number of towns in Jehol for a few weeks previouly. They used their airbases at Chinchow and Tungliao to launch their attacks, which included the dropping of incendiaries on towns. In a typical propaganda spat the Chinese press reported that a large number of civilians had been killed in these raids. Japanese press releases said in contrast that the raids had been welcomed by the people of Jehol as the first step towards their liberation from the Chinese 'yoke'. Even when the Chinese did fire at Japanese bombers, it was often a half hearted effort as they did not want to provoke another attack.

The Kwangtung Army had enough fighters and light bombers to support their troops in Jehol but was short of transport aircraft. They looked to the newly formed 'Manshu Koku Kabushiki Kaisha' or Manchurian Aviation Company Ltd for assistance. Known by its initials MKKK, this company was formed in September 1932 to provide transport throughout the new state of Manchukuo. It started with 145 employees and four Fokker Super Universal single engine transport planes which was soon expanded to eight. By the time of the Jehol campaign it had a total of 18 planes including six De Havilland DH80 Puss Moth light transports. When the Jehol Campaign began the Kwangtung Army asked the MKKK to form a transport squadron to support their troops. It consisted of six Fokker Super Universals and a single Fokker VIIb-3m trimotor transport. This main unit was supplemented by a smaller unit that had three DH80s used to transport Japanese officers to and from the frontline. During the campaign the bigger transports were used to drop food supplies to forward units and to fly in supplies when air strips were available. They also took wounded back to military hospitals and sometimes moved troops from one unit to another. One of the MKKK's main jobs during the winter fighting was supplying warm shoes and winter clothing to units. Some units had gone into the field without the full winter kit and frostbite was a major problem for the army.

## General Tang Yu-lin

The defence of Jehol was in the hands of one of the most unscrupulous generals in the whole of the Nationalist Army. General Tang Yu-lin, the 'Opium King' who was in his sixties was the epitome of the worst kind of Chinese general. Born in 1871 in Jehol, Tang had risen through the ranks of the Fengtien Army of Chang Tso-lin, the effective ruler of Manchuria. During his military career he had spent some time on active service with Chang's Army but also spent a lot of time in charge of his own province. In the mid-1920s Tang and his 40,000 'braves', his personal cavalry force, had been sent to Jehol to deal with a rebellious bandit leader. This bandit had reneged on a deal with Chang Tso-lin and Tang soon dealt with this in the customary way. Tang had then been allowed to stay on in Jehol and become its military governor with the blessing of Chang. After his employer's death he had been appointed military governor by Chiang Kai-shek in 1928 and given free rein to rule his fiefdom.

Elite Chinese cavalry prepare to move out in the early stages of the Japanese invasion of Jehol. They are well uniformed with padded cotton jackets and hat, l armed with modern rifles and mounted on hardy ponies. Some Chinese cavalry fought effectively when well led but their officers were often not worthy of the rank they bore.

Tang had a rather inflated view of his military ability and was happier to publicise his nom-de-guerre of the 'Chinese Napoleon'. He had taxed the poor population of Jehol during his governorship to death, putting taxes on frying pans and water buckets. Tang had looked for any product or activity that he could tax, including new-born babies. Taxes, as in other badly run Chinese provinces, were collected years in advance, the 'Crop Anticipation Tax'. He also forced the people to change their standard currency for his provincial notes, which were worth 5% of their face value. Any Manchu treasures that fell into his hands were immediately sold at auctions in the various treaty ports of China. He hunted and ate the last of the Qing Emperor's famous deer and reestocked their pastures with horses and Guernsey cows. Opium was Tang's personal vice and was also his main source of income. One of his first acts when taking power was to dig up the region's famous lotus gardens. The soil in these ancient gardens was ideal for the growing of poppies and soon he had a bumper crop to sell. He also introduced a 'Poppy Anticipation Tax' – £6 per acre for anything grown on fertile oasis land. The only way to pay such a high tax was to plant the land with poppies, which added to his quota to export. As he had decided that only he could export opium from Jehol, he was able to take a cut from its growers when they sold it. He took money from the opium crop at every turn, with taxes and duties on every ounce leaving the province. The crop was so important to his control of Jehol that his army's main role was its protection. The best units in Tang's Army were permanently stationed outside of the government-owned opium factories. General Tang even had his own personal opium and cocaine factory in the grounds of his provincial palace. Tang's ill-gotten gains were to used to host regular banquets for his officers and their concubines. Regularly on the menu were swallow nest soup, lotus buds, pork with crisp crackling, shark's fin and other delicacies. Drink served at the banquets included French champagne and cognac from General Tang's cellar. Entertainment was provided by his hungry military band, which played outside while the guests feasted. It was reported that Tang forced his concubines to practise horse riding every morning. He was a good horseman and liked to entertain visiting pressmen by performing a Wild West rodeo act, in which he shot from the saddle with great accuracy.

After the takeover of Manchuria Tang had been approached by Japanese officials who tried to persuade him to unite his province with Manchukuo peacefully. Thinking always of his opium empire Tang did sign under Japanese pressure the Manchukuo Declaration of Independence on the 16th of February 1932. In typical Chinese fashion he was then persuaded by Chang Hsueh-liang to repudiate this support for Manchukuo and re-join the Nationalist fold. Tang's reversal of his position was by no means unusual. Chang Hsueh-liang was not happy about having to rely on this tyrant and his army to defend Jehol but had little choice.


## Tang Yu-lin's Army, 1933

The 68,000-strong Army of Tang Yu-lin was a chaotic mixture of poorly armed and trained irregulars and well drilled Manchurian regulars. Between 15,000 and 20,000 of his troops were Manchurians who had served in Chang Tso-lin's Fengtien Army before 1928. About 38,000 of them were local volunteers who could just about fire their rifles but had been given no real training. Most of these irregulars were cavalry whose main role was keeping the population of Jehol under control. Another 15,000 of his men were described as being reinforcements from Peking and these may have been former North-Eastern Army soldiers. Tang did have a core of good troops and his well disciplined and immaculately uniformed bodyguard were armed with the latest Czechoslovakian ZH-29 semi-automatic rifles. Most of his army had the modern Mauser rifles and a large number of Czech ZB-30 light machine guns. It appears that Tang had little conventional artillery apart from a few old mountain guns but did have large calibre mortars. In some ways Tang was prepared for the Japanese invasion, having stored munitions in secret dumps throughout the province. He had also bought a fleet of new US trucks but these were probably intended for opium transport rather than for military duties. Without motor transport the Chinese Army relied completely on bullock carts and baggage camels to move supplies. Without a proper central command large camel trains carrying precious boxes of ammunition were moving across the province without proper instructions. Often when they arrived at their destination no one was earmarked to unload their cargo and it was just dumped on the ground. Soldiers refused to unload the cargo and there was usually no logistics officer to deal with the ammunition or arms anyway.

Irregular Manchukuoan cavalry of General Chang Hai-peng ride through a town in Jehol during their participation in the province's conquest. They were regarded by the Japanese as auxiliaries who were not expected to take much of a combat role against the Chinese. Mounted on Mongolian ponies the Manchukuoans did serve as useful scouting troops under the command of Japanese officers.

Tang had one main advantage over many of his fellow Chinese military commanders: he paid his men! He may have been a rather odious and totally corrupt man but he knew that a sensible general, especially in China, pays his men on time. The lack of command and organisation in the Chinese Army in Jehol led to some surprises. When the Japanese captured the provincial palace at Chengte it contained according to their reports $10 million worth of opium and other 'treasure' belonging to Tang. He had earlier sent eightr trucks full of his booty for safe keeping in the city of Tientsin in northern China. Tientsin was renowned as a 'bolt hole' for defeated warlords who retired there with the loot they had managed to salt away during their career. He was using the few trucks available to the Chinese defenders during the fighting. His hard-pressed troops were desperately short of ammunition, which could have been delivered by the trucks. A Reuters despatch described the chaotic situation in General Tang's palace just before it fell to the advancing Japanese: 'Concubines passed in and out of the palaces and an occasional telephone call disturbed the sleepy orderly. General Tang looked 'all in'. He was still talking about fighting to the last man but … asked about his army, he said he did not know where it was.'

## The Campaign Begins

The Japanese issued a 24-hour ultimatum to Chang Hsueh-liang in Peking and to the central Government in Nanking on the 23rd of February. This called for the withdrawal of all Chinese troops from Jehol and was issued with a 'reasoned'

Poorly uniformed Manchukuoan troops in Jehol wait in the dark to go into action in Jehol. They are led by the officer on the left and have a flag based on those used by the pre-1928 Fengtien army. Most early Manchukuoan troops had formerly seen service in the Army of Chang Tso-lin. They have carried this style of banner from their previous service into use with the Manchukuoan army.

explanation of their claim to the province on behalf of Manchukuo. Twenty four hours later having received a Chinese refusal the Imperial Army launched its offensive across the Manchukuo-Jehol border. Fighting had already been taking place at various points along the border for a few days with clashes occurring on the 21st and 22nd. Japanese units had been moving into position and obviously had no respect for the border, crossing it to establish forward positions. On the eve of the fighting the Japanese formations and their objectives were:

1 The 33rd Brigade with 4,000 Japanese infantry and 1,000 Manchukuoans were to contain the Chinese Army of General Ho Chu-kuo south of the Great Wall.
2 The 14th Brigade with 4,000 infantry and 1,000 cavalry along with 500 artillerymen and 500 armoured troops with 13 tanks. The Japanese had considered bringing some armoured cars with them but the roads were considered too poor. Their objective was to cross the border in the south-east of the province and advance along the Suichung-Lingnan-Lingyuan road to captured Lingyuan.
3 The 8th Division with 12,000 men including a small armoured unit, artillery and cavalry was to advance towards Lingyuan from Nanyang in

Imperial Army Field-Marshal Muto stands and watches his troops march across the hills of Jehol during their advance into the province. The Field-Marshal does not appear to be receiving any special privileges regarding clothing and wears the same balaclava as his men. Japanese troops had to deal with freezing weather, icy roads and high winds during the campaign.

    the east of Jehol. Once Lingyuan was taken they would then advance on the Jehol provincial capital Chengteh.

4 The 6th Division was to enter Jehol in the north-east and then advance south-westwards along the Kailu-Hsiawa-Chihfeng road towards Chengteh. This force had 10,000 Japanese troops with 2 infantry and 1 cavalry brigade along with some Manchukuoan light artillery and 4,000 puppet cavalry.

The Japanese-Manchukuoan Army included an exotic unit of irregular cavalry commanded by a Manchurian Princess. This larger than life character known as the 'Manchurian Joan of Arc' was Kawashima Yoshiko. Although Manchurian by birth she had been adopted in 1912 by a Japanese family in her youth at the request of her father Prince Su. She grew up proud of her royal Manchu blood but loyal first and foremost to her adopted homeland and willing to act as a spy for the Imperial secret service. In 1933, at the age of 26, after already having undertaken missions for the Japanese she raised a cavalry unit to take part in the Jehol Campaign. Although pictured with her unit in military uniforms it was never established how men were under her command. It appears that Kawashima struggled to raise her unit and had to resort to bandits who were willing to fight for plunder. She was probably advised by several of the Japanese adventurers who had been involved with bandit groups in Manchuria for years. Japanese looking for adventure and riches had joined bandit groups in Manchuria since the Russo-Japanese War of 1904–05. They often formed their own bands and plied their trade in the vastnesses of Manchuria sometimes with, sometimes without official Japanese support. One famous example of these desperadoes was Date Junnosuke often known by his Chinese name, Chang Tsung-huang. Born in 1892 Date was known to have advised bandit forces taking part in the Jehol campaign probably including Kawashima's unit. What Kawashima and her unit did in the fighting is a mystery but they seem to have disbanded and reformed at will. They were certainly disdained by the Imperial Army who regarded them as nothing more than a publicity stunt by their fame-hungry commander.

Chinese defence plans for Jehol did not exist as such, with General Tang neither knowing nor really caring where his forces were positioned. Most of his troops were scattered in groups along the frontier with each commander defending however much territory he wanted to. Some commanders simply kept their units gathered around their headquarters probably hoping the Japanese would not advance in their direction! Chang Hsueh-liang's grand defence plan appeared to have entailed Tang holding out long enough for him to bring in reinforcements from south of the Great Wall. As far as Chang and Tang were concerned the only strategic place that needed defending was the provincial capital at Chengteh. Over the 12 days that the campaign lasted Chang was able to send a few thousand troops to the aid of Tang. These were wasted amongst the thousands of demoralised soldiers they were asked to fight alongside.

Two heavy 120mm mortars of the Chinese Nationalist Army fire from an exposed position towards advancing Japanese troops. These weapons had been made in large numbers in a factory which had been set up by Chang Tso-lin during his control of Manchuria. This type of artillery had to make up for the lack of field guns in most Chinese armies in the early 1930s.

Chiang Kai-shek was never under any illusions about his governor's ability to hold Jehol as things stood. In the paranoid situation that existed in Nanking in 1933 it would probably quite suit the Nationalist leadership if the province fell to the Japanese. As Chang Hsueh-liang had overall command of the situation of north-east China his prestige would be affected by its loss. The loss of face that Chang and his supporters would suffer would effectively end any threat they could offer to Chiang Kai-shek and his clique. Chiang's plan was to march to rescue the situation by consolidating the hold on China to the south of the Great Wall. He had also calculated that even if the Japanese moved south and took the old capital at Peking, his sphere of influence did not extend to Hopei province. This was all part of Chang's long-term policy of keeping the Japanese in the role of aggressor in China. His hopes that the League of Nations would eventually deal with Japan were however crushed when, on the 20th of February, a speech was given in Geneva. The Japanese foreign Minister announced to the gathered representatives that his country was withdrawing from the League forthwith. This shock move by the Japanese now signalled that the 'gloves were off' and from now on there was little that could halt their aggression in China. On the same day that Japan was leaving the League of Nations, Chang Hsueh-liang was in Chengteh making a defiant speech. Chang repeated his determination that he and his army would defend Jehol 'to the bitter end'. As if to answer Chang, Japanese aircraft were at the same moment bombing the city of Chaoyang to soften it up for the advance of their 4th Brigade.

In the early morning of the 21st General Nishi ordered his 16th Brigade to begin an attack on Nanling supported by 4 light tanks and 10 armoured cars. This advance was also supported by a few light bombers that dropped their bombs over Chinese defence positions. Waiting for them were the heavily reinforced Chinese 38th Brigade of General Tung Tu-t'ing's Army. Fortunately for the Chinese the terrain they were defending was difficult for the Japanese to cross and at the end of the day's fighting their advance had been stalled. Another attack was launched by the Japanese 4th Brigade supported by two armoured cars and six aircraft. Their target was the Chinese defences at Kowpangtse, which were also manned by General Tung's troops. This offensive was more successful with the Chinese having to withdraw to Chaoyang which they in turn had to evacuate on the 25th of February. General Tung tried to halt the Japanese advances by setting up a strong defence position at Tamiao 10 miles west of Chaoyang. He tried to keep contact through his outposts with the nearest fellow commander, General Liu Hsiang-chin. General Nishi was bringing his 16th Brigade up the main road to attack Tung's positions after its reverse at Nanling. On the 26th the Japanese gathered their forces at Chaoyang in preparation for the next day's attack on Tamiao. When the assault on Tamiao began at dawn on the 27th the Chinese fought bravely even though the Japanese were advancing under the cover of a heavy artillery bombardment. This shelling was kept up for the full 48 hours of the battle and surprisingly the Chinese held firm. Chinese troops could often be stubborn in defence but the Japanese were shocked that their foes did not turn tail and run this time. Their resistance was however broken by a renewed Japanese frontal attack on the 28th starting at dawn.

This attack was combined with an outflanking movement to the North, which panicked Tung's troops into retreating. Japanese rapid advances now chased the now demoralised Chinsesw, who had performed so well in the first engagements. General Nishi's 8th Division now had an open road to Chengteh with only poorly armed irregulars to fight them. The only problems they would face would be the rugged terrain and the terrible weather, which would slow their advance.

Meanwhile to the south on the 21st of February 1,000 Japanese cavalry of General Hattori were moving along the Suichung-Lingyuan road in a north-western direction. This formation had been given the role of probing the rumoured defences set up by the irregular Generals, Peng Chen-kuo and Cheng Kwei-lin. Japanese scouts clashed with irregular cavalry just to the north of the road but otherwise their advance was unmolested. On the 26th of February the 14th Brigade attacked entrenchments defended by the Chinese 51st Brigade of General Liu Hsiang-chin. The Japanese were reinforced by the dubious presence of a few detachments of Manchukuoan cavalry. This joint attack on Wutzushan was thrown back by the defenders who again put up a strong showing on the first day of the battle. As in the clash with Tung's troops, the Japanese simply outflanked the defences and Liu's men retreated in panic. A pattern was developing where the Chinese could stand a frontal attack when their line of retreat was open. Once they were in danger of being cut off it was every man for himself.

The retreat of Liu's force was followed by an aerial bombardment of Yehchikou, which fell to the Japanese. A further advance by the 14th Brigade took them to Lignan on the 1st of March which was halfway to their target, the

An Italian news magazine of 1933 provides a romantic image of the Manchurian princess Kawashima Yoshiko. She is shown leading the cavalry she raised for Japanese service in the Jehol. Although she did command an 'exotic' irregular cavalry unit, it is not known whether they ever went into battle. The whole unit may have been a propaganda exercise by the Japanese, in which the princess was happy to participate.

city of Lingyuan. Retreating in front of them were Liu Hsiang-chin's troops who were bombed at intervals by any available Japanese planes. By now any viable defence in the South of Jehol was over and Chinese formations either retreated in some kind of order or simply disappeared into the countryside.

In the north-east of Jehol Major-General Mogi's 4th Cavalry Brigade was joined by 'turncoat' General Chang Hai-peng's Manchukuoan cavalry. They crossed the border and began to advance south-westwards along the Kailu-Hsiawa- Chihfeng road towards Chengteh. This large cavalry formation was first sent to deal with General Tsui Hsin-wu's 9th Cavalry Brigade who were defending the border town of Kailu. The Japanese-Manchukuoan force drove the 9th Brigade out of Kailu on the 24th of February, which was left in the hands of a small garrison. Over the next two days Mogi's cavalry continued their advance while the Japanese 11th Infantry Brigade moved south from Kailu. They were supported by Chang Hai-peng's Manchukuoans who had been seconded from the joint cavalry formation for the purpose. The 4th Cavalry Brigade was in the process on the 27th of a difficult march in terrible conditions through the gruesome and unusual interchange of snow and sand storms. Their destination was the city of Chihfeng, which they occupied with little resistance on the 2nd of March. They were now poised to begin the final advance on Chengteh as the best placed Japanese formation. The plan was for the Cavalry to move at a steady pace down the Chihfeng-Chengteh road. No real opposition was expected as the main Chinese units had already been beaten in the border regions.

There were still many thousands of armed Chinese troops roaming around the Jehol countryside. However there were no competent Nationalist officers who were resolute enough to lead them against the Japanese. A contrary Chinese report did claim at the time that a large body of their cavalry managed to defeat a Japanese cavalry force at a place called Black Mountain Pass. The Japanese were surprised and routed by the Chinese cavalry after a Japanese reconnaissance plane had failed to spot them. Whatever the truth about this rare victory for the Chinese, it did not alter the situation and the Japanese continued their steady advance.

The last fighting in the conquest of Jehol continued with the 8th Division led by the 4th Brigade advancing through Lingyuan to Pingchuan. Japanese aircraft bombed the road between Lingyuan and Pingchuan on the 2nd of March, which was crammed with Chinese reinforcements moving towards the frontline. The following day they startled the population of the provincial capital Chengte when a squadron of fighter bombers flew over the city without dropping any bombs. What meagre anti-aircraft guns the capital had were not fired at the circling planes as they did not want to provoke the Japanese air crews. Instead their crewmen waited until the planes were just about out of sight before firing off a few desultory shells. General Sun Tien-ying and his 30,000 men who were defending Lingyuan laid down their arms. This allowed the Japanese to enter the city without only isolated resistance from a few die-hard units. Accusations of the payment of 'Silver Bullets' to Sun and his command were at first denied by the Chinese high command. This denial had to be retracted when it became obvious that General Sun had taken a bribe to hand over the city to the Japanese. Lingyuan was just to the east of Chengteh, which was almost totally undefended by the now totally demoralised Chinese. In the capital Tang was finally organising something – but this was only his escape from the city. On the 3rd of March Tang had ordered every available truck in Chengteh to take his loot out of Jehol. He had requisitioned 160 trucks, which were supposed to have been moving ammunition to the soldiers at the frontline. As he fled to the south to the Great Wall he was still issuing optimistic statements to the western press. These were full of boasting about his men 'fighting to the death' while he deserted them to their fate. He did make an offer of a formal surrender to the Japanese but they refused largely because of his double dealing with them before the war began. Meanwhile, the countryside was now full of newly unemployed soldiers who would be dealt with later by the victorious Japanese. There were still a few Chinese units in the field but these were being bypassed by the rapidly advancing Japanese. One regiment from General Sun Tien-yang's Army was encountered by a US journalist marching northwards. They told him they were marching to defend the city of Chihfeng but the city had fallen many days before, nobody had bothered to tell them. Many soldiers turned, as Chinese troops often did in these circumstances, to banditry, with the local population suffering as usual. Some of these were local irregular cavalry who by signing up to defend Jehol had gained rifles. They now used these to ply their new trade having never fired a shot in the defence of their province.

The crew of a Japanese Kawasaki Type 88 light bomber prepare to go on another raid over Chinese positions during the 1933 fighting. Its maximum speed of 138 miles per hour would have been a problem if faced by modern fighters but it had a good payload of up to 550lbs of bombs. This type of aircraft flew numerous sorties over Jehol in 1933 and had total air superiority. One of the crewmen has borrowed an Imperial Army winter hat to protect him from the cold.

## The Fall of Chengteh

On the morning of the 4th of March the Japanese 4th Brigade entered Chengteh having defeated a rearguard action by 3,000 diehard Chinese. These troops were dug-in at Tienchaoshan just outside the city and at least gave a token defence of their capital. According to Japanese reports, their troops were met by enthusiastic crowds as they marched to the city centre. The people were said to be relieved to be liberated from the corrupt rule of General Tang. For many the despotic rule of Tang was simply being replaced by a better organised Imperial tyranny. Other press reports said that lorries full of Japanese troops drove into the city spraying the streets with machine gun fire. This according to an eyewitness effectively disposed of any 'possible resistance by stragglers and compelled civilians to remain indoors'. In one of the trucks the troops brought a precious commodity, a lorry full of Korean prostitutes. The campaign was over and there was little mopping up to do as a resistance movement in Jehol did not materialise. If the Kwangtung Army had in fact encountered more resistance there were plenty of reinforcements on hand to finish the job. The Imperial Army had a total of 45,000 more men available if needed including the 10th Division, the 14th Division and the 1st Cavalry Brigade all stationed in various parts of Manchukuo. Another two divisions, the 19th and 20th, were ready if needed over the border in Japanese-ruled Korea. The conquest of Jehol was completed on the 4th of March 1933 with the Japanese now in control of 250 miles of the Great Wall. The Kwangtung Army now had the whole of northern China at its mercy and the next step was to cross the Great Wall and move into the lands on the southern side of it.

The Kwangtung Army had conquered Jehol and added it to the territory of their growing empire on the Asian mainland. It had been a relatively easy campaign and their main foe had been the weather and its effect on their troops and machinery. As in previous wars the Japanese had employed a series of tricks during the fighting in Jehol. These included psychological warfare. They encouraged local secret societies to resist the Chinese defenders and to try and perform sabotage acts behind Nationalist lines. Japanese agents also set up a radio station which broadcast on Chinese frequencies sending fake orders to already demoralised and confused Nationalist commanders.

Their press emphasised the joy with which the population of Jehol greeted them as they advanced through the province. According to the Japanese propaganda both their troops and those of the Manchukuoan Army were met with 'joyous demonstrations'. The people were so happy that they had been freed by the Kwangtung Army and they 'blessed them for delivery from the tyranny and exactions of native rule'.

On the Chinese side the fall of Jehol was another blow to the prestige of Chiang Kai-shek and his Government. The Nationalist Army was not well represented in Jehol and the poorly trained troops that defended the province were a sorry bunch. Some did fight but with poor leadership, lack of heavy weaponry and general low morale the result was inevitable. Most soldiers tried desperately to get away from the advancing Kwangtung Army and those near the Great Wall headed for safety to the south.

Thousands and thousands of defeated Chinese troops fearing slaughter at Japanese hands and abandoning everything in their wake are now frantically scrambling for safety inside the Great Wall. Every pass from Jehol into North China is choked with uniformed humanity and transports composed of camels, oxen and horses and every description of vehicles … All routes from Peking North are blocked by the fleeing troops which are in an indescribable state of panic. (*Western Mail*, 9th March 1933)

Casualty figures for the Jehol Campaign are difficult to find although *Time* magazine in 1933 listed the Japanese losses at 1,479 dead and 3,468 wounded. Tthe *China Weekly Review* only listed the Japanese dead which it estimated at 1,000. It can only be assumed that most of the casualties were from non-combat causes with frostbite being given as a reason for many. On the Chinese side the official Japanese figures ran into tens of thousands. There simply wasn't enough serious fighting to warrant these numbers of dead and wounded.

## The Aftermath

In the aftermath of the fall of Jehol there was a certain amount of soul searching by the Chinese military and political establishment. Even though the province had from the beginning been given up as a bad cause its easy conquest was a stain on the Chinese military. The poor performance of the Jehol defenders was particularly stinging a year after their comrades had fought so well at Shanghai. One commentator, Rodney Gilbert in *Asia* magazine a few months after the end of the fighting summed it up: 'If Tang Yu-lin, Chang Hseh-liang or any other Chinese commander had had the slightest thought of putting up an effective resistance at Jehol, the Japanese campaign against it would have been not a motor truck jaunt but a hard fight through road-less passes, in which mechanised equipment would have been of little avail.' T.V. Soong, the Nationalist Finance Minister:

Steeped in the traditions of old fashioned warfare where vast armies marched and counter-marched with little bloodshed, doing their fighting by telegrams and proclamations, our military minds could not imagine a modern battle with its weeks and months of ceaseless preparation behind the lines, enabling the deciding of the issue to develop to a crescendo in the space of a few days. Our generals who strut in field-grey uniforms and Sam Brown belts neglect the universal principles of warfare, enunciated by our greatest strategist that soldiers are trained for a thousand days to be employed for a single day. The highly mechanised Japanese forces supported by every possible killing device on the land and in the air won a hollow victory. Now that the debacle has come, the public demands scapegoats, which will be provided but the blame lies not with individuals, but with the system which permits the existence of vast armies of ill-fed, ill-armed and ill-trained soldiery. Which in a time of crisis degenerate into helpless mobs.

Nevertheless, I maintain that we did right in fighting. If only to prove that Jehol is part of Chinese territory, and did not let it go by default. But we need not despair. There will arise from the anvil of Japanese aggression something great and pure, fashioned from blood and tears of the nation writhing under the heel of aggression. This time last year the world was hailing as an epic the heroism of the Chinese soldier at Shanghai. Today it looks with wondering eyes on the rabble fleeing to Peking. The two came from the same stock, but one was quickened with the spirit of nationalism and the other was corrupted and paralysed by the taint of archaic and incompetent military professionalism. Until our military leaders discard their eighteenth century conceptions of warfare, we will continue to be the prey of any nation that desires to impose its wishes upon China.

The political fall out from the Jehol debacle were far reaching with both Chang Hsueh-ling and Tang Yu-lin taking the blame from the Chinese people. Mass demonstrations were held in various Chinese cities where the crowds chanted 'Death to Chang and Tang!' Tang was variously reported to have been assassinated, shot by Chiang Kai-shek or to have simply fled. On the diplomatic front the Japanese as mentioned chose the height of the Jehol Campaign to announce their withdrawal from the League of Nations. The Lytton Report written about their invasion and occupation of Manchuria was too critical for their liking so they left the league in protest. The head of the Japanese delegation said the League must understand their 'desire to help China as far as is within our power. This is the duty we must assume.'

# 8

# 'To the Last Bullet!':
# The Great Wall, 1933

On the 6th of March 1933 Chiang Kai-shek took a plane to Peking to try and assess what had happened during the Jehol campaign. He had now to try and formulate a plan to stop the Japanese from advancing across the Jehol border into northern China. Chiang met Chang Hsueh-liang who apologised for his failure in defending Jehol and resigned his offices. He said he would like to travel abroad in the time-honoured warlord way of saving face, 'completing his education'. His subordinate Tang Yu-lin had fled to Shanghai despite rumours that he had been shot by Chiang Kai-shek. He was to turn up later in Chahar province where he got involved with the 'Christian warlord' Feng Yu-hsiang. The Japanese now that they were in control of the northern side of the Great Wall looked to consolidate. They very quickly came to the conclusion that the only way to safeguard the wall was to control its southern side as well.

Chiang was now determined to protect northern China from the Japanese and tried to re-organise forces there to defend the region. For hundreds of years the Great Wall had protected northern China from invasion from Manchuria. Now it was to form the defence line which the Nationalists had to hold of they were to stop the Japanese Imperial Army. After three centuries of neglect the Great Wall was in a sorry state in 1933. The vast stretches standing still formed a serious obstacle to anyone attacking it. Built to follow the natural contours of the mountains it effectively blocked most of the passes that ran through them. Any passes that were still open were heavily fortified and in the past would have been protected by large garrisons. Armies which broke through the passes in the past had the plains of northern China laid out in front of them. The main passes in the wall from east to west were Hsinfengkow, Lowenyu and Kupeikow. Other passes that needed defending were Lengkow and Chiumenkow and all would have to have large garrisons. An abortive plan to move northwards into Jehol was seriously considered but instead the Nationalists started to prepare their defences. The organisation and co-ordination it would take to plan an offensive were simply lacking. Chiang knew that his troops were better in defence and hopefully the Japanese would be worn out after their exertions in Jehol.

The Nationalists only had a few days to prepare their defences on the wall and in the passes before the Japanese attacked. China's foreign minister in March was confident of the Nationalist army's ability to defend northern China. His confidence it seems was based on the ability of the Chinese soldier to take a bullet – and the fecundity of China's mothers: 'China may not have shot and shells, but each Chinese can stop one! Our soldiers are unarmed, unclothed, but we have our lives

Relaxing 'Big Sword' soldiers of the 29th Army look down on Hsifengkow Pass waiting for the Japanese to attack in March 1933. When ordered to attack Japanese positions with their swords which they carry on their backs, they would move forward without rifles. Well-disciplined troops like these would be sacrificed in pointless charges against dug-in Japanese trenches.

to give. Let the enemy come, even throughout China, and kill a hundred million! We are very productive and will send more. Lives are China's ammunition!' Nationalist Government agencies tried to stir the population into a new patriotism with posters and leaflets saying 'To The Last Man and the Last Bullet!'

## The First Battles

The Japanese had already begun to move up to the Wall to secure the passes which would allow them to advance into North China when they wanted. There was no plan for a general offensive into China, only for the seizing of the passes. Once the passes fell each would be a sword of Damocles threatening northern China. The Japanese manoeuvred their forces into position between the 4th and 10th of March. At the same time more and more Chinese units were also moving into position, most of whom were made up of regular troops. Japanese preparations were under the command of General Nishi whose 8th Division's headquarters was established at Chengteh. He sent his 16th Brigade to the Kupeikow which was situated on the main road into Peking. They arrived on the 7th of March and immediately went into action against the Chinese defending the town and its pass. The Nationalists under the command of General Wang I-che were pushed out of the outskirts of the town after what was described as a 'sharp engagement'. Japanese troops then began to prepare for a siege of the town while skirmishes continued. On the 14th Japanese engineers blew up the North Gate of the town and after some street fighting the Chinese had to leave Kupeikow. According to press reports they suffered a staggering 4,000–5,000 casualties during this fighting. They did not, however, flee and dug in further along the pass, which they held until the 12th of April. During the month they held these positions Wang's troops launched several suicidal attacks by his 'Dare-to-Die' Corps on the now Japanese-held town. These commando units were made up of volunteers who attacked the Japanese usually with large fighting broadsword in one hand and a C-96 automatic pistol in the other. These units had been a major feature of many of the warlord armies of the 1920s but the outcome of their headlong charges against dug-in machine guns can be imagined.

On the 10th of April a major offensive was launched all along the length of the Great Wall bordering Jehol. At Kupeikow General Wang's dug in forces were attacked by the Japanese under General Kawahara. Over two days a series of ferocious hand to hand fights continued around Wang's positions with the Japanese launching bayonet charges. Wang's troops were finally driven back towards the town of Shih-hsia to the south-west while the Japanese consolidated their hold on Kupeikow, moving reinforcements into the town. As the Chinese withdrew towards the town, Shih-hsia was hit on the 17th and 18th by Japanese bombers which dropped 60 bombs. The intention was to demoralise the population before their soldiers arrived. The Japanese Air Force was busy over

Chinese officers pore over plans in their forward trench during the fighting along the Great Wall. As the Japanese moved further south beyond the wall they encountered more resistance from those who were now defending their own territory. These smartly turned out officers belong to the staff of General Sung Che-yuan's 29th Army. The 29th Army was made up mainly of ex-Kuominchun troops and their loyalty was primarily to China, not to Chiang Kai-shek.

the next few days softening up the Chinese in other parts of northern China. They bombed the town of Tungchow on the 18th of April, which at 12 miles away was close enough to Peking to terrify the city's population. Propaganda leaflets were also dropped in the vicinity of Peking, which appealed to the people of northern China to support the Japanese. These emphasised that Japan had no problem with the Chinese people and they should throw off the 'yoke of their oppressor', Chiang Kai-shek. On the 20th of April the Japanese took stock and decided that no further advances into North China should be launched. The Imperial Army commander Field Marshal Muto was satisfied with his offensive and now sought to turn back and take all the other passes on the Great Wall. Field Marshal Muto (1868–1933) was the Commander-in-Chief of the Kwangtung Army and was in direct command of the Jehol Operation. During the Jehol Campaign Muto was said to be ill with jaundice and he officially died of the illness in July 1933. (It later came to light that the Field-Marshal had committed ritual suicide. He had held command in Manchukuo and his death was a courageous if futile protest about the treatment meted out to its people by the Kwangtung Army.)

The 16th Brigade of General Kawahara now made a strategic withdrawal back to Kupeikow, which was reached on the 22nd. A Chinese counter-offensive was launched by General Wang I-te's forces totalling five divisions. It was aimed at units of the 16th Brigade dug in at Nantienmen at the southern point of the Kupeikow Pass. Nationalist General Hsu Ting-yao's division attempted to outflank the Japanese at Nantienmen and the town fell to the Chinese. The Japanese were furious with this unexpected setback and began a heavy artillery bombardment of the Chinese positions. Fighting around Nantienmen was particularly ferocious with the heights above the pass changing hands several

A Chinese soldier stands guard outside his sangbagged position in one of the towns fought over during the Great Wall actions. He is wearing a rather rough-looking uniform, made from padded cotton and his hat has a fur lining. His rifle looks like one of the older types in service with the Nationalist Army and he carries spare five-round clips for it in his ammunition bandolier.

times. On April 25th another attack was launched by the Japanese to re-take the town, again preceded by a heavy artillery bombardment. Again the Chinese held out, even after several heavy attacks. Unable, because of the terrain, to influence the battle for Nantienmen, the Japanese Air Force took it out on Shih-hsia. The stricken town was subjected to a bombing raid in which 40 bombs were dropped. Finally on the 29th Wang's troops had to withdraw from their positions at Nantienmen after being softened up by four days of continuous artillery attacks. The Chinese withdrew south-westwards to prepared defences at Hsinkailing. The Japanese did not follow as the 16th Brigade was ordered to hold its positions to defend the southern end of Kupeikow Pass, which it did until May.

On the 9th of March Chiang Kai-shek had emergency discussions with Chang Hsueh-liang about the situation on the Great Wall. During this meeting Chiang agreed to strip some units away from the attacks on the Kiangsi Soviet to reinforce Chang's troops. The forces of Generals Huang Chieh, Hsu T'ing-yao and Kuan Liz-heng and the Suiyuan 7th Corps of General Fu Tso-yi were ordered to move to the battle zone. These reinforcements were not large enough to change the situation at the Great Wall and by the 11th the Japanese had pushed up to it. On the 12th, Chang Hsueh-liang under pressure from Chiang resigned his post and was replaced by General Ho Ying-ch'in as commander of the North-Eastern Army. General Ho was now given the responsibility of defending the passes of the Great Wall against the Japanese.

Nationalist soldiers of the 88th Division march towards the fighting in northern China in the spring of 1933. This Division was one of Chiang Kai-shek's best units, which had already seen action as part of the 5th Army at Shanghai in 1932. The troops are marching uphill along the verges as the deep mud on the road makes it more or less impassable. The cyclist coming into the picture on the left wasn't going to find the going any easier.

The Japanese took the pass at Lowenyu, which was occupied by the 4th 'Suzuki' Brigade on the 12th of March. General Nishi, the 8th Division's commander, was ordered to hold the pass against any attacks by General Liu Ju-min's Nationalist forces. On the 19th the Chinese launched an attack on the Japanese positions which was thrown back and followed up by a Japanese counter-attack next day. The situation at Lowenyu stabilised and there was no major attack by either side. The Japanese had to send elements of the 4th 'Suzuki' Brigade to reinforce the 16th 'Kawahara' Brigade at Kupeikow. The Japanese 14th Brigade had taken the town of Lingnan on the 1st of March before turning south to occupy Lengkow Pass. The occupation of Lengkow was immediately followed up by an attack by the Japanese on Hsifengkow Pass. It was here that the Japanese came across the Nationalist 29th Army under the command of General Sung Che-yuan. This well disciplined army was made up mainly of former units of the pre-1929 Kuominchun Army of Feng Yu-hsiang. Sung and his troops were firmly dug in at Hsifengkow Pass and were being strengthened all the time by reinforcements that drifted into the sector. On the 9th of March the 14th Japanese Brigade began an all-out attack on the Chinese defences. The men of the 29th Army stood firm and repulsed not only this attack but fought the Japanese to a standstill in skirmishes on the 11th and 12th. General Hattori tried to tip the balance by bringing fresh troops to Hsifengkow from those he had left at Lengkow. These

Chinese soldiers stage a fight for the press from their positions on the Great Wall in early 1933. Although strong points and sandbagged positions were built on top of the wall, they were vulnerable to enemy fire. The firing points used historically for shooting arrows from were now being used to fire rifles and machine guns. These troops have their rifles, fighting swords in their scabbards on their backs and several have German style stick grenades, 'potato mashers'.

were used to launch another major attack on the 13th, which again was repulsed by the Chinese who were gaining in confidence. The Chinese now gathered their forces together for a counter-attack the same day. This attack by soldiers of the 29th was dominated by the charge of 1,300 men of the 'Dare-to-Die' Corps. Stripped to the waist the volunteers armed only with long swords made a desperate but futile attack on the Japanese who mowed them down. The sight of so many 'crazy' swordsmen charging towards them may have startled the Japanese defenders but they soon recovered. There was never much chance that this suicidal attack would succeed and these brave Chinese were sacrificed with only 30 returning to their lines. When the Japanese had recovered from this attack they again moved forward on the 15th. Once again their attack failed and over the next few days the two combatants battled for control of the heights over the pass. Japanese losses began to mount and even the presence overhead of 30 Imperial Air Force planes did not subdue the Chinese. Nationalist troops under Sung Che-yuan now turned the flank of the Japanese and occupied the heights in front of Hsifengkow. Three days later the Japanese sent a detachment from the 14th Brigade which crossed the Great Wall south-east of Hsifengkow. They occupied the town of Sahochiao until their commander General Hattori had taken the pass. Having achieved their objective the Japanese withdrew from Sahochiao, which was 'liberated' by Sung Che-yuan's troops in return. After the fighting on the 18th the Hsifengkow sector remained quiet for almost a month until the 10th of April. On that day General Hattori began an offensive which was to coincide with other attacks at Lengkow, Chielingkow and other places along the Great Wall. The 14th Brigade's objective was again the town they had recently occupied, Sahochiao, and neighbouring Panchiakow. Sahochiao was

A Nationalist soldier leans against the rough stonework of the Great Wall during the March-May fighting. He is armed as far as we can see with just his brutal looking 'da-dao' fighting sword gripped tightly in his hand. Neither the sword nor the steely glare would save him in the futile charges along the passes and heights south of the wall.

taken by the Japanese but changed hands several times before the Imperial Army finally chased the Chinese out of the town. This time the Japanese air support was vital with several squadrons combining to create a powerful bombing force. Having gained their objectives the 14th Brigade dug in along the wall, which it held for a month.

In the middle of March two brigades of the Japanese 16th Division had arrived at the coastal town of Shanhaikwan. This allowed the 33rd Brigade under General Nakumura to be transferred to the Cheihlingkow and Lengkow Passes. On the 21st of March the Japanese launched an attack on the Nationalist 32nd Army under General Shan Shen holding the Cheihlingkow Pass. This attack against a determined Chinese defence was repulsed with the Japanese having to return to their starting point. Toward the beginning of April the 11th 'Matsuoda' Brigade of the Imperial 6th Division was moved to Shanhaikwan from Jehol. This allowed the 27th 'Takata' Brigade to reinforce the 33rd Brigade, which thus strengthened was able to overcome the Nationalist forces of General Shan at Chihlingkow on the 4th of April. This was followed up by an advance by the 27th Brigade and part of the 14th Brigade on the 10th towards Lengkow, which fell at 7.00 am next morning. Other advances took place on the 11th with Kienchening to the south-west of Lengkow falling later in the day. In

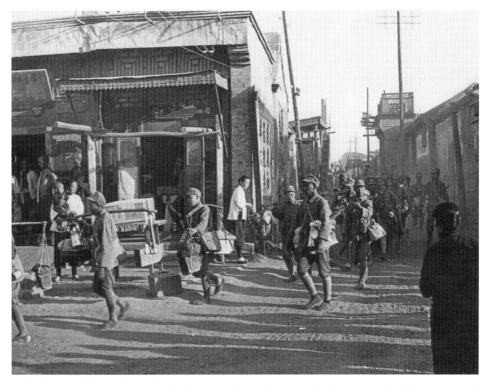

Nationalist troops move through the town of Tungchow at the northern end of the Great Wall near to Peking in May 1933. Once the Japanese had captured the passes along the Great Wall, their forces moved towards the old capital. Japanese aircraft flying overhead and artillery firing in the distance convinced the Nationalist Army to withdraw from the area.

a day of successes for the Japanese, the 33rd Brigade moved southwards from the recently captured Chihlingkow to Taitouying. This town fell after some heavy fighting on the 12th with the assistance of some Manchukuoan troops. During the fighting along the eastern section of the Great Wall the Japanese had been supported by over 7,000 Manchukuoan soldiers. Japanese success in the Lengkow-Chihlingkow sector meant that units could now be sent to Shanhaikwan further east.

In the Shanhaikwan sector the Chinese forces there had been steadily reinforced between the 1st and 24th of March. Under the command of General Ho Chu-kuo the Chinese had prepared positions along both the Tashih Ho River and the Shih Ho River. The rivers ran parallel to each other with the Tashih Ho River a little further to the north. The frontline of the Chinese defences was at the town of Shihmenchai on the main road from the region to Peking. On the 24th of March a large Manchukuoan cavalry force swept in to take Shihmenchai but were soon pushed out by the Chinese. A Japanese force along with Manchukuoan support advanced from Chumenkow along the Tashih Ho River and took the town of Shahochai. On the 1st of April an 18-strong force of Japanese bombers attacked the town of Shihmenchai. The town was also subjected to a heavy bombardment from Japanese artillery, which was followed by a determined attack. Chinese troops finally broke and retreated leaving the Tang Ho Valley open to any further advance by the Japanese.

A Japanese Imperial Navy aircraft carrier had arrived off the port of Chinwangtao on the afternoon of the 1st of April. Its planes, along with those of the Imperial Air Force already in theatre, began a heavy bombardment of Haiyang and Hsiaopulao in the Tang Ho Valley. This bombardment was followed in the early hours of the 2nd by the renewal of the Tang Ho Valley offensive. Supported by a squadron of armoured cars the advance cleared the area between the Tang Ho and Shih Ho Rivers of Chinese troops. Any troops that got away withdrew to the town of Haiyang, with those dug in along the Shih Ho forced to leave their trenches. With all Chinese troops now withdrawn from the Chinwangtao region the Japanese were satisfied that Shanhaikwan was safe from any attacks. The Japanese did not move to occupy Chinwangtao even though the city was undefended, as they saw no tactical or strategic advantage. A Manchukuoan cavalry force did come to take charge in the city on the 7th of April but this was without Japanese approval.

On the 9th a major Chinese counteroffensive was launched all along the Shanhaikwan Front under the command of General Ho Chu-kou. It liberated Shihmenchai and Chinwangtao and Ho's troops were also able to take up their old positions along the Shih Ho River. On the 13th of April the pendulum swung again in favour of the Japanese with yet another counter-attack taking Shihmenchai, Haiyang and another town, Peitaho. This offensive under the command of General Gamaboku was possible because of the release of Japanese forces from the Lengkow-Chihlingkow sector. In the early morning of the 15th a strong Manchukuoan force supported by a small number of Japanese troops but with heavy artillery and air support attacked the Chinese on the Shih Ho front. By the afternoon of the same day Chinwangtao was again occupied by the

Japanese and the front was finally stabilised. Another Manchukuoan force moved southwards from Taitouying to threaten the demoralised Chinese Army's rear. The town of Changli was captured on the 17th while the Japanese Army's advance southwards took Haiyang. By the 19th, General Ho Chu-kuo and the remnants of his army were on the right bank of the Luan River licking their wounds.

The end of fighting along the Great Wall saw Chiang Kai-shek leave North China to resume his anti-Communist campaigns in Kiangsi at the end of March. Before he left he appointed the reliable General Ho Ying-ch'in with his 50,000 men to take charge in northern China. Ho's main role was to try and stabilise the situation in North China in light of the Japanese domination over the region. General Ho Ying-ch'in's troops withdrewl to the line of the Pai Ho, or White River, close to Peking and waited for the next offensive by the Kwangtung Army. Although the Nationalist Army had been finally defeated, many of its units had put up a surprisingly good fight against the Japanese. During the initial fighting along the wall itself they had according to eyewitnesses used its ramparts and forts to good effect in hand- to-hand combat. One platoon under the command of an NCO, Ho Chu-kuo, even earned the grudging admiration of the Japanese. Ho and his men managed to hold off a superior and better equipped Japanese force for three long days armed only with rifles and fighting swords.

During the fighting along the Great Wall many units of the Nationalist Army were to prove their tenacity and bravery. In late March one Chinese unit repelled 20 Japanese with their defence being led by a 'dare to die' unit of sword-wielding troops. There can be no doubting the courage of the Nationalist troops during the fighting and their ability to hold firm even when taking heavy casualties. In mid-May in a three-day period of fighting at Nantienmen, 3,000 Chinese troops were killed. This did not affect the resolution of the defenders who continued to resist.

## Japanese Ruses de Guerre

In May the rather underhand tactics used by the Japanese in and around the Great Wall came to light. These included the use of a 300-strong force of Chinese in plain clothes who were reported to be under the command of the maverick General Shih Yu-shan. This undercover force attacked Chinese garrisons and planted bombs and booby traps to cause confusion and chaos. They had been sent out of the Japanese concession in the city of Tientsin and returned there after their mission was over. Twenty of them had been captured by the Chinese in the confusion caused by the turning off of all lights by the Japanese in the concession. Other tactics included the attempted killing of high ranking Nationalist officers by assassination squads. Several teams of Koreans were involved in these missions including one four-man team who tried to assassinatc General Ho Chu-kuo.

The Japanese had a Special Agency in Tientsin set up to try and bribe the Nationalist generals or high ranking officers in northern China. At the same time they tried to encourage local secret societies and associations to resist the

Chinese. They also set up a radio station on Chinese military frequencies which they used to confuse the Nationalist commanders. Their Chinese speaking agents gave fake orders to Chinese field commanders.

## The End of the Fighting and the Tangku Truce

Once the Japanese had reached all their objectives the question for the Kwangtung Army was whether or not to capture Peking. The fall of the old Chinese capital was fully expected and government officials packed their bags and tried to leave the city. Japanese aircraft flew over Peking on a daily basis flying low over the streets to frighten the population. It seemed obvious that the next step for the Japanese was to occupy Peking and a large swathe of northern China. One saving grace for the Chinese was the performance of their troops at the Great Wall. It must have been apparent even to the arrogant Japanese that

Soldiers of the Peace Preservation Corps line up for inspection in the aftermath of the signing of the Tangku Treaty in May 1933. These officially neutral Chinese troops were supposed to keep the peace throughout the entire period to the outbreak of the Sino-Japanese War in July 1937. In reality, these men found themselves being exploited by the Japanese, who persuaded some to act as the military force of several puppet regimes in Northern China.

Chinese resistance grew the more they advanced into the heart of the country. Kwangtung Army strategists did not really want to fight another urban battle after the difficulty they had faced in Shanghai in 1932. The Japanese knew that they were best when using their superiority in mechanised warfare with their tanks and air support. Chinese troops had proven their expertise at street fighting and an assault on Peking could be very costly. On the 25th of May the Nationalist Government finally sued for peace to stop any threat against Peking and Tientsin.

Lists of casualties suffered by both sides in the fighting along the Great Wall are either non-existent or ridiculously inaccurate. The official Tokyo War Office figures do not distinguish between the Jehol Campaign and the fighting along the Great Wall. They say that the Kwangtung Army lost 467 dead and 2,005 wounded while they report Chinese losses in both campaigns to be 120,000! We don't have any other figures on the Japanese casualties. We do have a realistic figure of 20,000 casualties suffered by the Chinese Army in the Great Wall fighting.

Despite having often put up a good fight against the Japanese along the Great Wall the Chinese were ready to sue for peace at the end of May 1933. The Kwangtung Army had begun to advance threateningly across the Great Wall towards Peking. If the Chinese were in any doubt about the Imperial Army's intentions this march indicated that they needed to make peace quickly. Japanese demands were outrageous; they wanted the demilitarisation of an area of 115,800 square miles. This would leave them with a Chinese population of 6 million under their occupation and a strong foothold in North China. Japanese 'negotiators' held the possibility of their occupation of Peking over the heads of the Chinese. With little choice and without support from Chiang and his government the result of the talks on the 30th of May was a foregone conclusion. The talks lasted a whole hour Having caved in to Japanese demands, a date was chosen for the official signing of the truce, May 31st.

A group of 24 Chinese delegates duly turned up at the signing meeting arriving by train and then having to walk through the streets of Tangku to the meeting hall. To compound their humiliation they were met at the gates of the Japanese Consulate, which had been chosen as the venue. After being searched they were led into a hall where one further humiliation awaited them. Japanese negotiators had been carefully selected all to be one rank below that of their opposite number in the Chinese delegation. This classic Oriental insult was to make their already nervous counterparts feel inferior. To put on a little more pressure the Chinese were under constant watch by the Consulate Guard and the Imperial Navy. As the delegates talked several Imperial Navy ships sat menacingly at anchor a mile off the coast.

The rough terms of the truce were summarised in press reports which said that the Nationalist Army was t; 'withdraw behind a line 130 miles long which runs parallel to and from 25 to 35 miles east of the Tientsin-Peking Railway'. Japanese observers were to ensure that the withdrawal had been carried out by 'airplane, reconnaissance or other means'. The Chinese were guaratee the protection of the Japanese observers. When the observers were happy that the

Nationalist troops had completed their withdrawal they would make their move. Their forces would retire from their positions in North China south of the Great Wall, which would then became the boundary between China and Manchukuo. In the absence of either Chinese Nationalist or Japanese Imperial troops to keep the peace in this demilitarised zone a new neutral force was to be created.

## The Demilitarised Zone Peace Preservation Corps

To police the newly established demilitarised zone in the north-eastern corner of Hopei province the Japanese demanded the raising of a 'neutral' armed force. This force was to be recruited from former Chinese soldiers with the 'correct attitude' to the Japanese. As they put it, the Chinese Peace Preservation Corps could not be 'constituted of armed units hostile to Japanese feelings'. They were armed only with rifles, pistols and bayonets with no machine guns or heavier weaponry allowed. Peace Preservation Corps troops were in an invidious position. Their commanders were often men of dubious backgrounds with several having taken part in earlier Japanese intrigues in northern China. Its recruits could effectively be vetted by the Japanese and would include troops from the several collaborationist forces demobilised from the Jehol garrisons. The political affiliations of anyone wishing to serve in the PPC would be carefully scrutinised. No Manchurians were allowed to join the PPC in case they were found to be ex-anti-Japanese volunteers. A thousand of the PPC came from the ranks of the rebel General Shih Yu-san's army and another 2,000 came from the army of General Li Chi-chun (see chapter 11). The PPC served in their role from May 1933 until the formation of the puppet East Hopei Autonomous Government in the demilitarised zone in 1935. Most of its troops then became the army of this early puppet regime overnight.

# 9

# 'IT'S ALWAYS DARKEST BEFORE IT BECOMES TOTALLY BLACK': THE NATIONALIST EXTERMINATION CAMPAIGNS, 1930–34

After the Communist-Kuomintang break in 1927 the young Marxist revolutionary Mao Tse-tung gained prominence in the Chinese Communist Party (CCP). Born in 1893 to a lower middle class family Mao had received a good education in his native Hunan province. He came under the influence of a veteran Marxist while working at University and joined the CCP. When the CCP formed an alliance with the Kuomintang in 1921 he was the representative for Hunan province. Unlike most Chinese Communists Mao favoured a peasant revolution in China breaking with the usual international Marxist strategy of urban revolution. When Chiang Kai-shek turned against his Communist allies in April 1927 Mao, like other surviving revolutionaries, went into hiding. In the autumn of 1927 Mao and his followers in Hunan launched a poorly organised 'Harvest Uprising', which was swiftly crushed. This rural rebellion was a test for Mao's policy of peasant-led revolution but along with other simultaneous revolts in several cities it failed. Thousands of the rebels were tortured and executed by the Nationalists and local warlord troops and Mao was criticised by his opponents within the CCP. Undeterred, Mao and a few hundred followers de-camped and set up a base in the remote Chingkangshan Mountains. His ramshackle guerrilla band was given the rather grand title of Red Army and Mao began planning for his next move. He began to develop his own version of Chinese Communism, which was suited to the particular conditions of the undeveloped country.

Until late 1930 Chiang Kai-shek was preoccupied with dealing with his rebellious former allies in the North of China. He saw powerful warlords like Feng Yu-hsiang and Yen Hsi-shan as the main threat to his control of China. The Communists he regarded as 'bandits' who could be dealt with by local military commanders. This is not to say that he did not realise that they could eventually become a threat to the Nationalist Government if they were allowed to expand their activities.

In the late 1920s and up until 1930 one of his preferred tactics against the Communists was to send his agents into territory controlled by them to foment unrest. These agent provocateurs did have some success but they were usually disncovered by the Communists and executed. In 1931 over 1,000 of these agents were unmasked by Communist intelligence and were either turned or executed. One major success that the agents did have was in helping to stir up problems within the 20th Red Army, which led to a mutiny in 1930.

Military action was of course also undertaken against the Communists and this had been ongoing since the crushing of their presence in the National Revolutionary Army in 1927. In 1928 Chiang Kai-shek ordered an 18-regiment-strong offensive to wipe out the 'troublesome' Communist base in the Chiangkangshan Mountains. This base had been established in 1927 by the young revolutionary Mao Tse-tung who had been joined by an ex-Nationalist officer Chu Teh and his guerrilla band. Their ragged Red Army had only a few hundred rifles and had no chance of resisting the Nationalist offensive. Fortunately for the Communists, the troops taking part in this operation were poorly disciplined ex-warlord troops. They were led by commanders who had only recently been defeated by the Northern Expedition and had no stomach for the fight. None of the various commanders was willing to co-operate with another because of old rivalries from their recent warlord army service. This meant that they were even willing to see the Communists escape rather than see a rival general gain a victory. The sheer scale of the Nationalist offensive did mean that the Communists were forced to leave their base area. The Nationalist commanders' ineptitude in pursuing the defeated Communists meant that they would soon regroup and establish safer bases. The Communist leadership during this period was far from united and power struggles leading to purges of leaders and ordinary soldiers were a regular occurrence.

The Communists were able to establish a new mountain base in the Tapiehshan Mountains in the Oyuwan region and in South Kiangsi province. These new bases were well organised and Chiang Kai-shek's intelligence soon informed him that these, if unchecked, could develop into a real threat to the Nationalists. Chiang may have seen the new bases as a danger but was not willing to involve himself

Nationalist troops man trenches which are part of the blockade around the Kiangsi Soviet during one of the Extermination Campaigns. The number of troops used in the five campaigns grew from 40,000 in the first to over 500,000 by the fifth. These soldiers are from one of the regular Nationalist Divisions used, rather than from the provincial or militia units.

or his best troops in destroying them. Instead, his policy was to launch old fashioned anti-bandit sweeps against them using soldiers who were unreliable and had little loyalty to him. These ex-warlord troops were in Chiang's mind expendable and the more of them that died fighting the Communists the better. His loyal 'elite' divisions meanwhile would be kept in reserve. There was only one problem with this strategy; the ex-warlord troops he employed against the Communists were not up to the job.

## The Li Li-san Offensive, 1930

The leader of the Chinese Communist Party in 1930, Li Li-san was one of the old school of Chinese revolutionaries. Unlike Mao and his followers, Li still advocated the Bolshevik form of revolution that depended on urban rebellion. Mao recognised the different demographics of China and believed that rural revolution was the answer. In an effort to prove the superiority of his theory Li Li-san demanded the launching of a series of urban rebellions in the summer of 1930. Li and his followers surmised that the internal problems that the Kuomintang was undergoing in 1930 gave the Communists an opportunity to strike. He ordered a large percentage of the Communists 65,000 armed men to foment rebellion in the three main cities of Central China. These three cities, Nanchang, Changsha and the tri-city region of Wuhan were to be attacked by three armies. P'eng The-huai and his 3rd Group of armies were to attack Changsha while Mao Tse-tung and Chu Teh were to move against Nanchang. A third army based in Western Hupei province under Ho Lung was to attack the three city complex of Wuhan. All three offensives were to be launched simultaneously on the 28th of June but the only success came for P'eng's troops who captured Changsha. The city fell on the 27th of July and P'eng set up his headquarters in the American Bible Institute. Disappointingly the population of Changsha did not support the revolution and a victory meeting attracted a paltry 3,000 workers. This was in a city that was regarded as 'sovietised' and should have provided a large number of volunteers for the rebels. On the 29th of July P'eng announced the formation of a Chinese Communist Republic but there was little popular acclamation. In fact the citizens were, if anything, hostile to these self-proclaimed revolutionaries who had invaded their city. With Nationalist forces approaching P'eng and his army evacuated the city on the 5th of August. The Nationalists were led by General Ho Chien whose artillery shelled the rebels as they left. When the Nationalist Army entered Changsha they took their revenge on genuine or suspected Communists, killing 5,000.

   The other two revolutionary armies had both been repulsed in their attacks on Wuhan and Nanchang. Reports at the time said that these offensives were half hearted and led by men who did not believe in their orders. Li was furious about the failure of his three attacks and ordered Mao, P'eng and Ho to combine to launch a second attack against Changsha. With 20,000 poorly armed men the Communists were now faced by large Nationalist forces who had been moved into the region. All Communist assaults were thrown back and the remnants of

A uniformed village guard during the Anti-Red Extermination Campaigns armed only with a spear. In most cases the Nationalists were able to arm all their men with rifles, whether regular or irregular. The Communists captured a lot of their weapons from local troops like this man, although they could make their own spears.

the combined force withdrew into the mountains. In the cities they left behind, a major purge took place of all organisations associated with the Communists. Thousands died – including Mao Tse-tung's second wife who had been captured during the fighting and was shot outside the walls of Changsha.

The total failure of the offensives spelt the end of Li Li-san and his leadership of the Communist Party. At the Third Plenary Meeting of the Sixth Central Committee in September 1930 he was removed from office. With the fall of Li, the urban policy he has espoused was dead and the rural revolution policy promoted by Mao was now to come to the fore.

## The Nationalist Army, 1930–1935

The huge number of Nationalist troops that fought during the five Encirclement Campaigns from 1930 until 1934 came from a wide variety of sources. Some were 'elite' units which had proved themselves during the Northern Expedition and the Central Plains War. Others were poorly trained and armed local provincial troops who had served until recently in the ranks of the warlord armies. In the early campaigns Chiang Kai-shek thought that he could defeat the Communists using the poorer quality ex-warlord troops. This would have the added advantage of depriving some of his rivals of their troops while leaving Chiang's loyal divisions untouched. Other Nationalist troops were drawn from the militia system that had been introduced in July 1929. Many used were from the various para-military formations formed in the early 1930s. They were basically uniformed militia who were recruited on a local basis and were poorly organised, trained and armed. During the Encirclement Campaigns all local government organisations from the village to the city had to organise defence forces or 'Pao-Wei'. Beginning in 1932 all males between the ages of 20 to 40, if not in the regular army, were liable for service in this organisation. This age range was widened in 1933 so that any male between the age of 18 and 45 would serve. There was little chance of getting out of this part-time military service and by 1935 there were 2,000,000 serving. A better trained and armed formation, the Peace Preservation Division or 'Pao-an T'uan' was formed in 1932 with a strength of 14,000 men. Recruits to the Pa-an T'uan received six months training which included political indoctrination before being sent into action beside regular troops. These para-militaries and militia were not always reliable and often ended up more of a liability than an asset. Although the Peace Preservation Units were usually armed with rifles their militia counterparts often had to make do with a spear.

## The First Extermination Campaign, December 1930–January 1931

The 1st Encirclement Campaign involved the Nationalist 9th Route Army led by the Kiangsi Governor, General Lu Ti-p'ing whose headquarters was in the city of Nanchang. General Lu Ti-p'ing was a Chiang loyalist and his 100,000-strong

Nationalist troops pile their personal equipment on the back of an already overloaded mule as they prepare to go out on an anti-red operation in the early 1930s. Units like this would often march aimlessly across the Chinese countryside in a fruitless attempt to locate and destroy the Red Army. Even when they did find Communist units these were usually able to slip past them and then out-march the encumbered Nationalist formations.

12-division army was deployed around the Soviet. This regular force was supplemented by second-line troops formed into special forces known as the 'Anti-Bolshevik Group'. This force was joined by the 6th Route Army from Hunan province and commanded by Chu Shao-ling and the 19th Route Army under Chiang Kuang-nai. In total the Nationalists were to employ 44,000 men in 5 divisions during the operation which crucially were supported by 3 light bomber groups. The vast majority of the Nationalist troops involved in the 1st Campaign were described as 'rag-bag' ex-warlord troops, which did not bode well. The Nationalist plan was a simple one: to encircle the Kiangsi Soviet forcing the Red Army into the Tapiehshan mountains and stopping them from outflanking the Nationalist armies. As soon as the Soviet was surrounded the Nationalists would attack the towns of Tungku, Tungshao and Lungkang.

The operation, launched in December 1930, was doomed from the start. The higher ranking officers were still basically warlords who were steeped in the bad habits of their previous service. They were unwilling to sacrifice their troops in battle as any losses would deplete their personal power base. Although attempts had been made to re-educate these former warlords the effect was negligible. The intelligence for the campaign was almost non-existent. Little or no information was available on the number or quality of Communist troops. Maps of the country they were operating over were basic if available and locally gathered intelligence was unreliable. Any information that the Nationalist troops got about the Communists was usually beaten out of the local peasants. The heavy-handed treatment by the soldiers of the population only served as a recruiting sergeant for the Communists. Peasants who may have worked as porters for the Nationalists now avoided doing so and if press-ganged escaped at the first opportunity to join the Reds. Lack of transport and other support services like medical care in the Nationalist Army lowered morale further. Supplies were erratic and soldiers did not trust their officers to feed them. The lack of even basic medical care meant that if a soldier was wounded he could expect to be left behind by his comrades to the tender mercies of the Communists or angry local peasants. Nationalist deserters were given good treatment by the Communists in a well calculated policy to encourage them to turn.

At the start of the campaign the Communists controlled Chian, a town on the Kan River in Central Kiangsi. This strategic town sat astride the main line of communication for the province and was an obvious target for the Nationalist offensive. Mao and his advisors insisted that the town be abandoned and that the main body of the Red Army move into in the remote and hilly territory in the south-east of the province. Three Divisions, the 18th, 24th and 50th, were ordered to advance southwards from the starting point to the region north of Ningtu on the Mei River. These better quality divisions were veterans of recent fighting against the Kuominchun in the Central Plains War. The rest of the 12 divisions were made up largely of Kiangsi and Hunan provincial troops of poor quality. The field commander of the campaign, General Chang Hui-tsan, moved his 18th Division from their positions in the north-west of the Soviet in a south-eastern direction towards Ningtu. In support of the 18th he also had the 5th and 77th Divisions and these three divisions were intended to perform a pincer movement with General Lu's force. The Nationalists followed the Red Army across the Kan River on the 18th of November and advanced in three columns. The 1st Column soon occupied the towns of Yungfeng and Chishui, while the 2nd Column occupied Lean and I'huang and the 3rd occupied Chian. Red Army units withdrew in front of the Nationalist columns making hit and run raids on their strung-out units. By the 26th of November the Red Army had withdrawn successfully to new positions but were then hit by a mutiny within their ranks. This large-scale mutiny at Futien completely disrupted their efforts and gave the Nationalists an opportunity to attack. Nationalist intelligence had found out about the mutiny so General Lu Ti-p'ing ordered the 50th and 18th Divisions to attack the Communists at Tungku. The 50th Division took the town and the Red Army withdrew into the surrounding hills. Now a costly confusion took place. During their advance the two divisions had become separated either side of a high ridge and neither side radioed to give the other their location. When the 18th Division reached Tungku they attacked it killing many of their comrades who had arrived earlier before they realised they were Nationalists.

After this catastrophe the 18th Division stayed in Tungku while the recently arrived 28th Division occupied Futien. By the end of December the Nationalists were now in possession of most of the Kiangsi Soviet with the 50th Division advancing towards the town of Yuantou. Nationalist units were strung out

In a scene typical of the various anti-Communist campaigns of the early 1930s a winding column of Nationalist troops goes out in pursuit of the Reds. Long, trundling columns like this were easily followed by the more mobile Communists. When units were isolated during their march the Red Army would make hit and run raids on them causing confusion and damaging the whole army's morale.

over a vast area amongst a population that was generally hostile. 65% of the Nationalist troops were being employed in occupation duties and receiving no co-operation from the people. Their harsh treatment of the locals now meant that they became even more sympathetic to the Communists.

In late December two Brigades of the 18th Nationalist Division planned an attack against the city of Langfang for the 30th. Unfortunately for the Nationalists, Communist intelligence discovered the plans for the offensive and moved forces to surround the 18th. On the 30th as the 18th Division moved into Langfang the 1st Red Army Corps moved its troops in an encircling movement around the city. At the same time the Red Army's 4th Army Corps and elements of the 3rd Corps positioned themselves to block any retreat by the 18th Division. By the end of the day the Nationalists trapped in the city were in total disarray and 9,000 of them capitulated. Their commander, General Chang Hui-tsan, was to feel the full wrath of the Communists, who put him on trial. To serve as an example to the rest of the Nationalist Army General Chang was publicly beheadedHis head was put in a bag and was floated down the Kan River towards the Nationalist lines.

A few days later the Nationalists' 50th Division commanded by General T'an Tao-yuan began a southern advance in reaction to the defeat of the 18th. As they advanced towards the town of Yuantao on the 2nd of January their deployment was again discovered by the Communist spy network. As soon as they received the news the Communists sent a force to intercept the 50th in an attempt to repeat their success of few days before. Next day they launched a fierce attack on the Nationalists at Tungshao from three different directions. Many Nationalist troops abandoned their heavy weapons and even threw their rifles down as they tried desperately to escape the closing Communist net. The Nationalists were fortunate that the 3rd Red Army Corps was late arriving at its blocking position, which allowed many to get out of the trap. Nevertheless the Red Army was able to capture 3,000 prisoners and more importantly 4,000 precious rifles, 40 machine guns and a large cache of small arms ammunition.

The destruction of the two Nationalist divisions at Langfang and Tungshao virtually ended the 1st Campaign with Chiang's troops receiving a bloody nose. His army lost 15,000 made prisoner and an estimated 12,000 rifles, along with some machine guns.

In the four-month interval between the end of the 1st Campaign and the launch of the 2nd both sides tried to strengthen their forces. The Red Army had a large amount of captured weaponry to distribute. Of course the large number of Nationalist prisoners of war were one source of possible new recruits but the Communists were wary. Any prisoners who said they were willing to join the Red Army were vetted by the Communist political officers. Political officers were also responsible for trying to improve the discipline of the Red Army soldiers. Generally speaking, the Communist troops were superior to the Nationalists they had fought in 1930 but some did not fight well. The Red Army commander Chu Teh took the opportunity to try and reorganise his disparate forces into divisions. Although the divisions were of different strengths they were all organised on the Soviet 3-regiment system. Chu also organised one of the first specialist units when he recruited former coal miners into an engineer unit.

## The 2nd Extermination Campaign, 1 April–1 May 1931

For the Second Encirclement Campaign the Nationalist Army employed four Route Armies to surround the Kiangsi Soviet. The armies were deployed at four points around the Soviet with the 5th Nationalist Route Army's HQ near Chian to the west of the Red base. To the east of the Soviet at Nanfeng was the 6th Route Army and to the North was the 26th Route Army with its headquarters at Le'an. Finally the 19th Route Army was stationed to the south with its HQ at the town of Hsingkuo. In total 200,000 Nationalist troops had been committed to this second attempt to destroy the Communist base. The plan for the campaign was to make a slow and steady advance into the Soviet without reacting to Communist guerrilla attacks. Some lessons had been learned by the Nationalists from the recent fighting but most troops now involved in the 2nd campaign were of the same low standard.

The Communists were happy with their defeat of the 1st Campaign but they were under no illusions about Chiang Kai-shek's determination to crush them. Because of the overwhelming odds against them the Communists knew that the survival of their Kiangsi stronghold was in the balance. In an attempt to formulate an agreed plan a series of four 'crisis' meetings was held in March and April 1931. They had to decide whether to stay at Kiangsi and fight or to withdraw and set up a new base. Various options were discussed but the majority agreed that if they did evacuate the Soviet, then Szechwan province was best option to establish a new base. At the third meeting military commanders were invited and the decision was made to divide the Red Army into small units to fight the Nationalists with guerrilla warfare. It was also decided to make a strong attack against the Nationalist 19th Route Army to the south of the Soviet. The attack was intended to weaken the 19th enough to create an escape corridor for the Communists to evacuate the Soviet if necessary. Mao argued that the better option would be to attack the 5th Route Army in the west instead. His reasoning was twofold: first, the 5th Route Army was made up of Northern troops who were unfamiliar with the country they were stationed in. He believed the troops of the 5th were homesick and that their morale had suffered because of this. Second, regarding the 19th, Mao commented that they had been garrisoning Hsingkao for a while and had built good fortifications in and around the city. In the end it was decided to attack either the 5th or 19th with the final choice being made once the military situation became clearer. At the fourth and final meeting Mao outlined his defence plan for the Soviet, which involved the reduction of its perimeter. The Red Army was to withdraw from some of its outlying posts and to re-deploy to three main bases. By the 23rd of April the army had finished its relocation with the 3rd Red Army Corps at Lungkang. The rest of the 1st Front Red Army was stationed at Ningtu and the 3rd and 4th Armies were entrenched in the mountains.

In early May the Nationalist Army went on the offensive and occupied the town of Futien to the west of the Soviet and then advanced south-eastwards towards Tungku. As the Nationalists advanced along the main road towards Tungku they were unaware that Mao and Chu's forces were in the Juichin

A flight of Nationalist Douglas O2MC light bombers fly over the Kiangsi Soviet during one of the regular air raids on the Communist base. These planes are part of a 20-aircraft group that arrived in China in 1931 and provided an important element in the Nationalist air effort. With no air opposition and little anti-aircraft fire to deal with, they could concentrate on identifying and bombing targets.

Mountains above them. By the 11th of May the 28th and 47th Divisions were in the jaws of the well laid Communist trap. It was five days before the Communists attacked the lumbering Nationalist column. The Red Army units chose the town of Chungtung for their attack and began by rolling boulders down the mountains onto the exposed Nationalists. This primitive tactic worked well with many troops being killed and many more panicking and fleeing. Nationalist officers tried desperately to wire for help but the Communists succeeded in blocking their communications. Even though no ground support was forthcoming the Nationalists still had total air superiority with their light bombers. In a cruel blow for the desperate Nationalist divisions poor weather conditions throughout the fighting meant that no air support was available. By the 17th of May the two divisions were beyond help and both capitulated and handed over large amounts of arms – 5,000 rifles, 50 machine guns and 30 artillery pieces and mortars.

Two days after this defeat another battle took place at Baisha to the north of Tungku where the Nationalist 43rd Division was the target. The Division had been had been heading towards the town of T'an-tao when its commander heard about the defeat at Chungtung. He decided to withdraw northwards towards the town of Shuinan with the intention of crossing the Hsiaolung River. On the north bank of the river he planned to establish a defensive position and wait for a Communist attack. As the Nationalists approached the only bridge over the river they found that it had been occupied by irregular Communist forces. With no heart for the fight to take the bridge the 43rd had to continue their march to Baisha; but they were ambushed before they reached the town. As with the previous defeat the large amounts of armaments lost to the Communists was a significant blow to the Nationalist war effort. This time the Red Army gained an impressive 4,000 rifles, 30 machine guns and 2 mountain guns. In a worrying development for the Nationalists the 19th Route Army which was supposed to go to the 43rd Division's aid, chose not to. They stayed out of the fighting and then withdrew back to their base at the city of Hsingkao. With the loss of its three divisions over a few days the mighty 5th Nationalist Route Army had effectively been wiped off the map. When the fighting ended on the 31st of May the Red Army had in captured 30,000 prisoners as well as 20,000 small arms. The weapons and other supplies were enough to equip the entire 1st Front Red Army with up-to-date Mausers or Gew-88s. Older weapons were handed over to militia and guerrillas who had formerly been armed with spears and swords.

## The 3rd Extermination Campaign and the Ningtu Uprising

The heavy defeat of the Nationalists in the 2nd Campaign infuriated Chiang, who now realised that his powerful army was being repeatedly humiliated. In the first two campaigns the Nationalists had been out-fought and out-thought by the Red Army. He decided to take over command of the upcoming 3rd Campaign and made preparations to fly to the Kiangsi region. Within a few days of the end of the fighting he flew along with his military advisors to Nanchang arriving on the 21st of June. In a summit meeting it was decided to launch another large offensive as soon as possible so that the Communists did not have time to regroup. The remaining large armies which had taken part in the previous campaign were reinforced to 300,000 men in 24 divisions. This figure is disputed with some sources saying that there were only 130,000 troops involved. It may well be that there was the larger number of troops in the war theatre but only the lower figure of troops were actually involved. Two Army Groups were formed to lead the offensive while other formations were to be positioned to stop any Communist breakouts from the Soviet. Both Army Groups were 7 divisions strong with the Left Flank Army Group under the command of General Ho Ying-ch'ing. The Left Flank Army Group was made up of the 5th, 6th, 8th, 9th, 11th, 14th and 24th Divisions and its headquarters was at Nanchang. It was to attack south-westwards along the line of the Ju River outflanking the Soviet then meeting up with the other Nationalist formations.

The Right Flank Army Group was made up of the 25th, 27th, 47th, 52nd, 54th, 60th and the 61st Divisions. This force was under the command of Ts'ai T'ing-k'ai and was to attack northwards from its base into the heart of the Soviet.

To the west of the Soviet holding the line of the Kan River were two divisions, the 28th and 77th along with the 34th Brigade of the 12th Division. On the right of the Soviet was another holding force made up of the 49th and 56th Divisions with the 14th Brigade. This Brigade was made up of newly recruited troops who, like many of the Nationalist soldiers, could not be relied on in battle.

Large numbers of Nationalist troops were to be held in reserve to the west of the Soviet. Nationalist formations began moving into the Kiangsi Soviet in late June and the operation officially began on the 1st of July. During this month of manoeuvring the Nationalists took control of five towns on the outskirts of the Soviet. When the Nationalist offensive began the Communist leadership was still undecided about how to try and counter it. In the end, Mao's already proven strategy of withdrawal in front of the advancing enemy was accepted. Communist units would again retreat as the Nationalists advanced until there was an opportunity to attack isolated and strung-out units. Long Nationalist columns weighed down with all the paraphernalia of war would be picked off one by one in hit and run attacks. When Nationalist units then came to the aid of their comrades, well laid Communist ambushes would cause further confusion amongst their usually demoralised foes.

At the start of the Campaign Red Army units went on the offensive and made several large-scale raids into Nationalist-controlled areas. These were meant to confuse the Nationalist commanders and to gather recruits and supplies for the coming fighting. On the 6th of August the Nationalist 47th Division moved into Lient'ang and the 54th Division took Huangpi. The Communist command saw an opportunity to strike and attacked the Nationalist division garrisoning the town of Lungkang. They struck with overwhelming force employing the 3rd, 4th and 12th Armies against the single division. After destroying the troops in Lungkang the Red Army moved on to attack the 54th Division at Huangpi. This second division was devastated with its Headquarters staff walking into an ambush and by the 7th of August the Nationalists had lost 2 Brigades, 1,000 dead and 3,500 prisoners. Red Army booty included 3,000 precious rifles and pistols and 14 field and mountain guns. The Red Army then continued its attacks on Huangpi having decided not to move against Lungkang, which was too well defended. Huangpi was now defended by the 8th Nationalist Division and the 4th and 12th Red Armies attacked this unit. At the same time the 3rd Red Army and 7th Communist Division cut of the 8th's escape route. The fighting took place in filthy weather with rain and thick fog. The Nationalists suffered over 1,000 dead and 4,000 of them were taken prisoner with war material captured including 3,000 small arms and 11 field guns. Even more importantly, the Communists captured wireless sets and a large cache of ammunition.

Chiang was now desperate to try and reverse the series of defeats his troops had faced and decided to attack the Red Army concentration at Huangpi. His troops quickly moved around the Communists and completely encircled the town with its defenders soon facing starvation. The siege of Huangpi lasted a month before the Red Army decided to break out and during the night of the 16th of August most of them slipped past the blockade. Communist troops from the 12th Red Army now played cat and mouse with the Nationalists, just managing to keep ahead of their pursuers. The Nationalists were totally exhausted having chased the more mobile Red Army over mountains and through ravines. All along the route Communist guerrilla units had been attacking them and they had taken heavy casualties. While the Nationalists had been otherwise engaged the 1st and 3rd Red Army Corps had moved to the town of Hsingkuo where they prepared

The crew of a Junkers K-47 fighter prepare their German-supplied plane during the early 1930s. Planes like this were used in air attacks against the Red Army in the early 1930s with only ground fire to worry about. Unfortunately for the Nationalist Air Force, the K-47 was unreliable and had to be withdrawn after a series of crashes.

for the next round. When Chiang realised that the main Communist force was in Hsingkuo he turned his army around and headed west to attack it. Just as he was approaching the town Chiang heard about a rebellion in Kwangtung province and called a premature end to the 3rd Campaign. The Red Army was not finished yet and in early September made a series of attacks on the withdrawing Nationalist Armies. In a series of victories the Communists destroyed the 52nd Division and took a total of 7,000 prisoners, 6,500 rifles, 10 artillery pieces and 200 horses. In one final encounter on the 7th of September the 4th Red Army and the 3rd Red Army Corps suffered heavy losses when they took on three Nationalist divisions at Kaohsinghsu. Although the Red Army's success looks impressive on paper, with 17 Nationalist Brigades destroyed and 30,000 soldiers killed, they had also suffered. Their losses at the battle of Kaohsinghsu were harder for them to replace and for a while they not in a fit state to resist any more Nationalist attacks.

The Communist war effort was given a significant boost in December 1931 when the 26th Nationalist Route Army revolted. Of the 20,000 men of the 25th and 27th Divisions who made up the 26th, most were ex-soldiers of Feng Yu-hisang's Kuominchun. Many came from Feng's elite 'Big Sword' units which had formed the assault force of the Kuominchun Army. The leaders of the uprising were General Tung Chen-t'ang and General Chao Po-sheng, who had been loyal subordinates of Feng. A bonus for the Red Army was the presence in the 26th Army of five doctors including Doctor Chi P'eng-fei, who went on to form the Red Army's Medical Corps.

## Improvements to the Nationalist Army, 1932–34

Chiang Kai-shek was painfully aware of the weaknesses of his Nationalist Army during the early Extermination Campaigns. The use of poorly motivated, trained and armed ex-warlord troops had proved to be a disaster. All of the Nationalist command badly underestimated the Red Army during the 1st and 2nd Campaigns. They thought that the warlord troops alone could defeat the Red Army in a kind of police action. His policy of padding out his forces with inferior troops may have looked good on paper but it was ill conceived. This did not mean that Chiang was not going to try and use his overwhelming superiority in numbers to defeat the Communists, but the men must in future be better prepared. With his military advisors Chiang had studied in detail the first three campaigns and had identified where changes needed to be made. His new policy was supposed to be 70% political and 30% military, with an emphasis on winning the 'hearts and minds' of the population. The new policy al;so called for 'Total War' against the Red Army with any resistance broken by overwhelming numbers of better trained troops. Chiang still heavily relied on the surviving officers of the former National Revolutionary Army. These had been mainly trained at Whampoa Military Academy and their numbers had been badly depleted over the years. Veterans of Whampoa had received a good basic training in the 1920s and early 1930s but none of them had received any instruction in anti-insurgency tactics. (To take a wider view, you would be hard-pressed at the time to find many militarists who were, in any army in the world.) Chiang set up a new academy at Lushan, which quickly retrained 5,400 Nationalist officers in the tactics it was thought they would need to defeat the Communists.

He not only tried to improve the training of his troops but also wanted to make sure that they were better armed than their opponents. This was of course a double-edged sword, as so much Nationalist weaponry had fallen into the hands of the Red Army during the disastrous early campaigns. Throughout the early 1930s Chiang placed orders with any arms manufacturer who was willing to sell. Most of the time, priority for new armaments was given to the loyal divisions fighting in the Anti-Communist campaigns. In January 1934 a large shipment of arms was unloaded in Canton including 70 machine guns. The machine guns were sent straight to the Nationalist forces encircling the Kiangsi Soviet.

## The 4th Extermination Campaign, January–March 1933

After a break of a few months during which Chiang was distracted (a little) by the Japanese invasion of Manchuria in September 1931 and its aftermath, the 4th Campaign began. Of course the Nationalist Army had maintained pressure on the Kiangsi Soviet and other Communist bases in the interim. In fact it could be more accurate to say that the five extermination campaigns were one long campaign with five large-scale operations punctuating the almost four years of fighting. For the 4th Campaign Chiang used tactics which were a mixture of hearts and minds and slow strangulation of the

Communist base. He consciously adopted the same tactics used 70 years before by the Qing Commander, Tseng Kuo-fan. Tseng had finally surrounded the 19th-century Nien rebels who, like the Communists, had raided from their bases. The Nationalist hearts and minds policy included attempts to make the local officials, magistrates and landlords more honest and generally kinder to the population. Rents were to be fairer and local committees were to share goods and tools and were to loan money to peasants at fair interest rates. Any progress that was made with hearts and minds was immediately ruined by the forced conscription of people to labour for the army. They were made to build the roads, air fields and blockhouses which were part of the next encirclement campaign. New taxes were also imposed to pay for all the building work being done around the Kiangsi Soviet. In total 1,500 miles of road and 14,000 block houses were being built around the Kiangsi Soviet. Blockhouses were built from stone or brick and all were manned by regular troops and peace preservation corpsmen.

In December 1932 Chiang had committed over 400,000 troops in 30 divisions to the crushing of the Soviet. This time he did not trust the operation to his subordinates and moved down to the city of Nanchung to supervise it himself. He established his forward headquarters at the town of Fuzhou and began the final planning for this mammoth operation. The main Central Nationalist force was made up of three huge columns, 150,000 men in 12 divisions under the command of General Chen Cheng. The 1st Column had 3 divisions, the 11th, 52nd and 59th while the 2nd Column had the 10th, 14th, 27th and 90th Divisions. Its 3rd Column had the 5th, 6th, 9th and 79th Divisions while the 43rd Division was in reserve. Another 240,000 troops were allocated to manning the blockhouses and barricades built to enclose the Red Army. Each flank was assigned approximately 70,000 men in 6 divisions to block any Communist retreat. These forces were concentrated in the Kwangtung-Kiangsi and the Fukien-Kiangsi border regions. Another 100,000 troops were given the task of conducting anti-bandit operations in outlying regions of the theatre of operations. These were in north-east and north-west Kiangsi as well as the south-east Hunan–south-west Kiangsi border areas. As soon as the various blockades were in place the 12-division, 3-column Nationalist force would advance southwards along separate routes. They would then concentrate for a massive attack on the Red Army's rear crushing them between their formations and the blockading formations.

The Red Army on the eve of the 4th Extermination Campaign had expanded to 70,000 men with its main base at Lichuan. It was organised into the 1st, 3rd and 5th Red Army Corps as well as the 11th, 12th, 21st and 22nd Armies. In the period leading up to the 4th Campaign the Red Army had been undertaking a series of attacks on Nationalist-held cities in the region. In December 1932 the next designated target for these attacks was Nancheng but Nationalist reinforcements were rushed to the city and pushed the Red Army out of the outskirts. Nanfeng was then chosen for a Red Army offensive and this was attacked on the 1st of February 1933. The Red Army began encircling the city and besieged it for about a week but it was held by a determined Nationalist garrison. A large part of the

Central Nationalist Force under Chen Cheng was sent to relieve the city and the Red Army was forced to withdraw by mid-February.

In order to allow the main body of the Red Army to withdraw from the city the Communists used an old tactic of fooling the Nationalists into thinking they were still active in the area. The 11th Red Army attacked the city of Lichuan while the rest of the army marched away. The main Nationalist force reacted as expected by moving its three columns against the city. Its 1st Column including the 52nd and 59th Divisions became isolated from the other two and fell into a trap. On the 25th of February the 52nd and 59th Divisions advanced towards the city of Huangpi but their march took each either side of a mountain. Two days later the Red Army caught the 52nd Division on the march in torrential rain and devastated it. At the same time the 59th Division had reached Huangpi where it was attacked by a large Communist force. The Nationalists were completely routed and their commander, General Chen Shih-chu, was taken prisoner. After this victory the Red Army moved back to its base at Lokou to reorganise and prepare for the next operation.

The defeated Nationalists now changed their plans and brought together the remaining two columns into one large force. They were to remain in their original columns but advance one behind the other towards their objective. On the 16th of March the Nationalists began to advance towards the centre of the Soviet. The 11th Red Army performed the same type of feint as had previously fooled the Nationalists. This feint was towards the city of Kuangchang; but this time the Red Army turned and attacked the advance units of the pursuing Nationalist column. Because of the effective Communist attack the two Nationalist columns became separated by a 31-mile gap. Now the rear column was isolated. The Nationalist 11th Division, part of the rear column, was attacked and decimated. Fighting alongside it was part of the 9th Division, which was similarly destroyed in a running battle.

The battle of Tsaotaikang as it became known was the last major encounter of the Fourth Encirclement Campaign. For the remainder of March 1933 the Communists concentrated on political work in the Soviet. Nationalist resolve had been been affected by their reverses and by April they were slowly withdrawing. This time, however, their spirit was not completely broken and there was now a resolve on the Nationalist side to get revenge. Instead of marching right back to their starting points many Nationalist troops were ordered to begin preparations for yet another campaign. These preparations involved the building of more blockades around the Soviet and the reinforcement of existing fortifications, fences and palisades to 'fence' the Communists in.

The Nationalists had of course suffered damaging losses during the fighting with three divisions effectively put out of action. The Red Army took 10,000 Nationalist prisoners, the rank and file being offered the chance to change sides. Nationalist officers were usually either executed or sent for re-education, which often ended in their deaths. War booty taken by the Red Army included 10,000 rifles, 300 'new' German machine guns and 40 artillery pieces of various types. Nationalist losses during the 4th Campaign were quoted as 30,000 killed, missing and taken prisoner.

In a rare frontline photograph, the Nationalist Army defend a position near the city of Nanchang in 1933. The ZB-26 light machine gun was imported from Czechoslovakia in the early 1930s. Chiang Kai-shek armed his troops as well as possible and imported modern weapons like this mainly from Belgium, Czechoslovakia and Germany.

## The 5th Extermination Campaign, September 1933–June 1934

Even though the crushing of the Communists was Chiang Kai-shek's main priority in the 1930s, he could not ignore the Japanese completely. The advances of the Imperial Army in Jehol and in Northern China in early to mid-1933 had taken his attention away for a short while from the Red Menace. Chiang's policy of destroying the Communists first and dealing with the Japanese later soon brought him back to the planning of a Fifth and hopefully final Extermination Campaign. Although the four previous anti-Communist campaigns had failed to some degree, the Red Army had been worn down by the almost constant fighting. Unlike the Nationalists who could keep renewing their armies the Red Army had a finite number of men. Chiang had been listening to the advice of his German advisors this time; both Hans von Seeckt and Alexander von Falkenhausen suggested the same tactics. Their strategy involved a total blockade of the Soviet with a series of hundreds of fortified concrete blockhouses. As well as the garrisons of the blockhouses there were thousands of troops held in reserve to counter any Communist attacks on them. Ever since the end of the Fourth Campaign large numbers of troops and pressed civilians had been working on the construction of the blockade. When one line was built, any advance by the Nationalists would see another line constructed, which meant double or even triple lines of blockhouses, barbed wire and wooden fencing. New roads were also constructed so that motorised Nationalist units could be moved to a section of the blockade if attacked. Some armoured cars were sent to Kiangsi and these would be sent on patrols to stop any infiltration through Nationalist lines.

In an attempt to break the Nationalist blockade a number of costly attacks were made on some of the larger fortified blockhouses. The Communists lost some of their best troops during these futile assaults and gained little. As soon as gaps in the blockade were made, they were plugged by Nationalist reinforcements. At the same time the economic blockade that went hand in hand with the physical one was taking its effect on the surrounded Red Army. Rice and salt were specifically banned from being transported into the Kiangsi Soviet zone. All goods were effectively stopped from entering the blockaded area and in many areas the Red Army and their families began to starve. While the Communists began to feel these severe effects of the blockade the Nationalists began to gather their forces to deliver the coup de grâce.

The Nationalist Armies now concentrated around the Soviet were vast, in excess of 700,000 men. Some estimates said that 1 million men in regular and irregular units were preparing to attack the Soviet. These were supported by five Air Corps equipped with large numbers of light bombers imported mainly from the USA and Germany. Douglas O2MC light bombers were most numerous and were to become the scourge of the Red Army during the coming campaign.

The Nationalist Army had deployed their largest formation, the Northern Route Army of 33 divisions and roughly 500,000 men, to block the north. It was deployed on a rough line from the city of Yungfeng in the west to Nancheng in the east. The 11-division and 150,000-strong South Route Army as its name suggests blocked any possible Red Army escape in that direction. This army was made up largely of troops of the Kwangtung warlord General Chen Ji-t'ang, who was not 100% committed to the coming operation. Like several former warlords he valued his army too much to risk it fighting for the Nationalist Government. The Western Route Army, again of 150,000 men, mainly from Hunan province, controlled the region to the north-west of the Soviet. Its units were stationed mainly along the Kan River to stop any Red Army withdrawal that way. Finally the North-East escape route was blocked by the Army of the Fukien-Chekiang-Kiangsi Region with about 50,000 men.

The Red Army waiting to face this huge force had expanded despite its precarious situation to 100,000 men using weapons captured in recent campaigns. Many of its new recruits would have previously fought for the Nationalists and would be regarded as untrustworthy. This enlarged force needed more food and military supplies and its command had little time to prepare for the coming campaign.

On the 25th of September 1933 the Nationalists began the campaign by sending three of the Northern Route Army's divisions south from their base at Nanchang. Their objective was the town of Lichuan which quickly fell and the Red Army's

Central Front Army withdrew in shock. They waited for reinforcements from their Eastern Front Army before beginning a counter-offensive on the 6th of October. This attack near Hsunkou was a success with the destruction of three Nationalist Brigades during the battle. Further advances, however, now came up against the fortifications of the blockade with desperate assaults against dug-in Nationalist troops failing. For two months the Red Army tried to break through the blockading Nationalists in various sectors but without success. From their well prepared entrenchments and blockhouses the Nationalists bombarded the Communists with artillery and mortar fire. Their machine guns had been well sited on the advice of the German military advisors and thousands died trying the breach their defences. At the same time well co-ordinated air strikes by the Douglas O2MCs, Junkers K47s and other light bombers taunted them from above.

It was much to the Red Army's relief when the outbreak of the Fukien Rebellion in the neighbouring province broke out in late November 1933, temporarily diverted the Nationalists. During this lull the Communists met to discuss their options; the normal 'lure the enemy in deep' tactic would not work now. Instead, they decided on commando-type assaults on the blockade. The Communists' German advisor Otto Braun suggested the conscription of every able-bodied man and youth in the Soviet. With this 'million strong army' he said they could overwhelm the Nationalists even if they had to arm themselves with spears.

With the defeat of the Fukien Rebellion in January 1934 the full-scale campaign resumed with fresh attacks on the Northern Front. The line of blockhouses was strengthened and the Nationalist Army using 35 divisions began to advance southwards. As they advanced they undertook a methodical clearing sweep pushing any Red Army units in front of them. The first objective of this offensive was the city of Kuangchang, which was heavily defended by the Red Army. They tried to build their own lines of fortifications but with no concrete and few other materials it was difficult. Usually the only materials to hand were wood and mud and they tried to build blockhouses out of these. When the Nationalists attacked the sub-standard fortifications were easily destroyed by artillery. Some were simply washed away in the rain.

While the Nationalist southward offensive continued a new threat came from their eastern front forces. These had been reinforced both by troops returning from defeating the Fukien Rebellion and by some units formed from former 19th Route Army troops. The westward offensive of the eastern front armies involved 14 Nationalist divisions, which soon joined up with their northern front comrades. When the two forces joined up at Tengkuang in March 1934 they began a co-ordinated advance on Kuangchang. This united Nationalist army regrouped before beginning the offensive on the 9th of April led by 10 divisions from the 3rd Route Army. They started from Nanfeng and were well equipped with artillery and had plenty of air support. The route of their advance was along both banks of the Ju River and took two weeks to achieve. Communist defences were easily pushed aside with many defenders dying in their poorly constructed bunkers as the sheer weight of numbers told. By the 23rd of April the Nationalists were in control of the high ground around Kuangchang.

A Nationalist sentry guards his
unit's headquarters during one of the
Encirclement Campaigns. His smartness
and his modern Gew-88 rifle suggests
that this man is from one of the
better Nationalist formations used in
the 1930–34 campaigns. During the
Anti-Communist campaigns the quality
of Nationalist troops varied greatly from
unit to unit.

Inside the perimeter, the Red Army desperately tried to construct new defences but these again were poorly constructed owing to the lack of materials. On the 27th the Nationalists began to bombard the Communist defences with artillery and several air attacks finished the job. Many were killed manning those poor defences when they would have been better employed fighting guerrilla warfare. The next day, the city fell. The Red Army had suffered 5,093 casualties, 20% of their strength. In a rare victory the Nationalists had taken the city having only lost 2,000 or so troops.

The victory at Kwangchang was now followed by a general offensive from all directions by the Nationalists. Within a few days they had taken all their initial objectives and the Red Army was in retreat. On the 16th of May the Nationalists took the city of Chienning on the eastern side of the Soviet sealing off that route of withdrawal for the Reds.

The Nationalists now had sufficient troops of a reasonable quality to occupy territory it took from the Communists. In previous campaigns any gains taken by the Nationalist Army were often lost when units moved forward because they did not have enough troops to properly garrison the areas vacated by the retreating Red Army. Fighting continued throughout May and June with the Red Army now in a desperate situation. Several months of fighting had begun to tell on the Communists and on the local population, whose support for the Red Army was waning. Losses meant that new recruits had to be found to fill the Red Army ranks and these often had to be pressed into joining. Obviously the desertion rate went up accordingly and the size of the army did not really increase despite their best efforts. Many officers had been killed and their replacements did not have the experience of their predecessors. Food was desperately short and requisitioning from the peasants only made the Red Army more unpopular. The territory controlled by the Red Army contracted as the Nationalists began sweeps to clear the Communists out of their strongholds.

## The Plight of the Communists in 1934

The almost 'watertight' blockade of the Kiangsi Soviet was taking a heavy toll on the Communists by the summer of 1934. Within the beleaguered Communist base there was a shortage of everything including food and medicines. Although the Communists had won victory after victory they had also suffered heavy casualties. Even when new recruits were found there were few weapons to arm them with and there were fewer captured Nationalist ones available. Within the Soviet and in the countryside outside it, the peasants were suffering from Nationalist requisitions of crops and other goods. There was less food to bring into the Soviet even when the smugglers could get it past the Nationalist blockade. For the ordinary people of Kiangsi province, whether they supported the Communists or not, it was a miserable existence. As with any other civil conflicts in China during the late 1920s and early 1930s, the years of fighting had caused devastation. It was estimated that the death toll of civilians through fighting or by disease and starvation was in excess of 1 million people. The Communists as well as the Nationalists were ruthless when it came to the effect of their struggle on the civilian population. Once the Red Army moved out of the Soviet, the lot of the peasants would not improve as the Nationalist Army chased them across the country.

# 10

# 'In Waking a Tiger, Use a Long Stick': The Fukien Revolt and the Long March, 1933–35

The Nationalist campaigns to defeat the Communists obsessed Chiang Kai-shek and his leadership in the early 1930s. In 1933 however, the Nationalists were faced by a new and dangerous challenge to their authority in eastern China. This threat did not come from the Communists and their Red Army but from a disgruntled and rebellious Nationalist Army. In 1933 the famous 19th Route Army and its commanders, General Tsai Ting-kai, General Chen Ming-shu, General Chang Kwang-nai and General Li Chei-sen went to war with Chiang.

## The Fukien Revolt, 1933–1934

The survivors of the 19th Route Army had quite rightly in most people's opinions been feted by the Chinese and world press. They had stood up to the hated Japanese during the Battle for Shanghai in 1932. Some observers at the time did (quietly) point out that the 19th Army had been given too much credit for its part in the battle for the city. Other commentators noted that as a Cantonese unit the 19th Army received little support from other Nationalist units at Shanghai. For this reason some people say the 19th had little choice but to fight well, when they could not depend on their comrades. Even some of Shanghai's population was not particularly fond of the 19th in the time-honoured Chinese way of being wary of people, especially soldiers, not from the same province. They regarded the 19th as an alien army regardless of its performance against the Japanese. Whatever its motives, the 19th did show what determined defence against the Japanese Imperial Army could achieve.

Chiang Kai-shek now saw the popular leadership of the 19th as a political threat and in particular its commander General Tsai Ting-kai. General Tsai was a popular hero throughout China and Chiang decided to remove him and his army from the scene. Against the army's wishes the 19th was sent to the eastern coastal province of Fukien, where it was to prepare for operations against the Communist Kiangsi Soviet.

Fukien was a poor coastal province and it was to prove difficult for the 19th Route Army to raise the money to pay the troop and feed them. The disgruntled Route Army leadership already had left-wing political sympathies and their treatment by Chiang Kai-shek simply pushed them further towards outright rebellion. Once

General Tsai Ting-kai during his command of the 19th Route Army at the Battle of Shanghai in 1932. In late 1933 he was one of the military leaders of the Fukien Rebellion in opposition to his former leader, Chiang Kai-shek. During the revolt, troops and their officers would have replaced their Nationalist insignia with new badges. These would have featured the red, blue and gold colours that were on the flag of the rebel People's Republic.

established in its garrisons in Fukien the Army's leadership began to establish contacts with the local Communists. The army's leadership never intended that the 19th would join the Red Army but it was hoped that the two anti-Chiang forces could at least co-operate against the Nationalist Government. Any co-operation between the Kiang Soviet and the 19th Route Army was, however, frowned upon by the Communist leadership.

The leader of the commanding triumvirate of the 19th Route Army, General C'hen Ming-shu, went on a visit to Europe in the summer of 1933. When he returned he had decided to take military action against the Nationalist Government. He instructed his two subordinates, Generals Chiang Kuang-nai and Tsai Ting-kai, to start making preparations for a rebellion. Unsuccessful attempts were then made to make an anti-Chiang alliance with the leaders of the Kwangsi clique. They had revolted against Chiang in 1929 and were not willing to risk his wrath so soon after their defeat by him. The Route Army leadership did manage to agree a non-aggression agreement with the leaders of the Kiangi Soviet. Some meetings took place between the two parties and an agreement was reached to barter goods between the two rebel forces. Communist negotiators even asked if they could buy some of the aircraft in Fukien with gold to form a Red Air Force in the Soviet. Any co-operation between the two anti-Chiang forces was stopped at the insistence of both the Chinese and Russian Communist leaderships. They did not trust the three generals who were in command of the 19th Route Army and ordered that no assistance should be given to them. Even without any substantial aid coming from the rest of China and with a semi-hostile Communist force to the north, the rebels were still determined to form a left-wing government in Fukien. The Social-Democratic 'Peoples Revolutionary Republic' was formally declared on the 20th of November 1933. Its government included a group of prominent left-wing politicians as well as the three military leaders Tsai, Ch'en and Chiang. Politicians who backed the new republic included Eugene Chen, the former Nationalist Foreign Minister and Hu Hammin, who gave it his backing from his exile in Canton. The leadership of the Republic called fort for the overthrow of the Nationalist Government. They also asked formally for an alliance with the Chinese Communist Party and friendly relations with the Soviet Union. Apart from their dislike of Chiang Kai-shek himself, the People's Republic abhorred the Nationalist' policy of appeasement of the Japanese. Looking around for possible allies in their fight with the Nationalists, they were fast running out of options. Having failed to get support from Kwangsi, the rebels now approached the powerful Kwangtung General Chen Chi-t'ang for support but he was not willing to help. They now knew that they would have to rely on their home-grown military to defend their newly formed republic. The republic was also under pressure from foreign interests including the British and US, who did not want the Fukien ports of Amoy and Foochow closed to their shipping companies. Britain threatened to send her China Naval Squadron into the area if Foochow was bombarded by the Nationalist Navy.

## The People's Revolutionary Army, 1933–1934

The only substantial military force available to the Fukien rebels was the 19th Route Army itself estimated at the start of the revolt at between 22,000 and 30,000 men. It is a misconception that the 19th in 1933 was made up of battle-hardened veterans of the 1932 fighting in Shanghai. Many of its troops had been recruited after the battle for Shanghai and most of these would see their first action in 1933. The Army was made up of the 60th Division under the command of General Shen Han-kwang, the 61st under General Mo Wei-shou and the 78th Division under General Ou Shou-nien. Just before the fighting began, the 19th was reorganised into six divisions, the other three divisions under the commands of Generals Chang Yen, Tan Chi-shui and Oong Chao-huan. These three new commanders were capable officers who had seen service during the Shanghai Incident. Their men, however, were mostly raw recruits who had arrived from Canton to join the revolt or were locally raised volunteers from Fukien. The Army was well equipped according to eyewitnesses with trench mortars, light artillery and machine guns. These arms were under the control of separate egiments within each of the six divisions. But the People's Army could not match the Nationalists in heavier weaponry. There were some reports of armoured cars in use with the People's Army with some being captured at the end of the war (see below). If this is true they can only have been the improvised type used by several Chinese warlords – basically trucks with armour plating added.

It was obvious to the rebels that the full might of the Nationalist air force would be used against the People's Republic so attempts were made to raise its own air arm. The People's Army did have its own air element made up in late 1933 of 12 assorted training aircraft. They had three Avro 637 trainers and one Armstrong Whitworth Atlas light bomber, as well as a donated Farman 291 transport. This

Soldiers of the 19th Route Army march through a town in Fukien province shortly after their arrival there in 1933. The troops, who were mainly from Canton, were always going to be regarded by the population of Fukien as an 'alien' army. It was always the case that the population of a province would never accept its occupation by soldiers who were not native to it. Despite efforts by the 19th Army to establish friendly relations with the Fukienese, they were never accepted by the vast majority. Few civilians of Fukien joined the People's Army voluntarily during the rebellion and conscription would have been a waste of time.

improvised rebel air arm was going to be of little use against the Nationalists' modern fighter bombers. The rebels placed orders in Japan, France and Britain for aircraft to bolster their air arm; some of the orders predated the declaration of the People's Republic. In anticipation of the large Nationalist air force gathering around their borders the PRA tried to purchase some anti-aircraft guns. This proved impossible and the only defences they had against air attack were a few heavy machine guns fitted with anti-aircraft sights. Sympathetic overseas Chinese did donate money to purchase a few modern aircraft but none of these would arrive before the end of the fighting. Some pilots and flying officers also found their way to Fukien including Colonel Chang Hui-chang, the former director of the Nationalist Air Department. Colonel Chang was immediately named as the commander of the People's Army's Air Arm. Attempts were made to buy other war materials abroad and to finance these purchases a 10% increase in taxes was introduced. At the same time they optimistically placed an order for a large shipment of ammunition from an arms company in Shanghai.

## The Nationalist Expeditionary Army in Fukien

Opposing the rebellion was a 100,000-man, 11-division Nationalist Army which had the massive advantage of 60 aircraft. The Nationalist force was made up of a mixture of regular and irregular provincial troops and elite units sent from

Nanking. These elite units included the German-trained 87th and 88th Divisions, who had a number of light tanks. In 1933–34 these were ex-French FT-17s and a handful of Carden-Loyd MkVI tankettes. The Nationalist air arm sent to Fukien was made up of the 3rd, 4th and 5th Squadrons later joined by the 1st. In preparation to crush the rebellion the Nationalists had built a few new air strips in Southern Chekiang province. The Nationalist Navy was also important in the war as Fukien was a coastal province with several large ports in rebel hands. The People's Republic had no naval units and the Nationalist Navy was able to operate virtually without hindrance. The Nationalist Army was made aware from agents within the People's Republic that the rebels intended to launch offensives against it. Military preparations in the neighbouring provinces of Chekiang to the North and Kiangsi to the west were made. In Kiangsi the local forces at Nanchang were reinforced by 10,000 crack troops along with 20 anti-aircraft guns and 19 anti-aircraft machine guns. A leaflet was delivered to the rebellious troops which was straight to the point: 'To the 19th Route Army – Comrades! Either clean up the bogus Fukien Government or the Nanking Government promises you utter annihilation. Chiang, Commander-in-Chief.' The leaflets were dropped by the thousand over the People's Revolutionary Army lines. Chiang also threatened to bomb the rebel capital at Foochow and in response the government of the People's Republic was moved inland to Changchow. This was as a precaution not only against air attack but also naval bombardment. To counter Chiang Kai-shek's propaganda the People's Republic sent radio messages to all parts of Fukien and southern China. These asked for assistance for the people's struggle against the Nationalist Government, which was preparing 'to bomb its own people'.

## Fighting Begins

At first the hostilities between the Peoples Army and the Nationalists were confined to the bombing of several towns in Fukien, beginning in the first days of December. Planes based in South Chekiang province bombed these undefended towns while avoiding the well defended provincial capital at Foochow. These attacks included the bombing by three government planes of the town of Chuanchiu killing 20 people and injuring about 100. The townsfolk were in the middle of a ceremony to celebrate the formation of the People's Revolutionary Republic. Nationalist Armies moving up to the Fukien-Chekiang border now halted their advance for a few weeks on Chiang Kai-shek's orders. This was so that his officials could speak to the Cantonese leadership and gauge whether they would support the 19th's rebellion. When they were more certain that the Cantonese would stay out of the war, the army was told to renew its offensive.

The real fighting began on the 21st of December. Large numbers of Nationalist troops began to advance into Fukien from neighbouring Chekiang and Kiangsi provinces. Nationalist losses during these early clashes were high, with the hospitals at Kuichow and Pucheng full of wounded. The shock of the People's Army resistance caused the initial Nationalist advances into Fukien to be halted.

The Nationalist Air Force was heavily involved in subduing the rebels by late December. Eleven aircraft attacked the town of Yengping on the 27th. Air raids continued during the last days of 1933 as support for the rebels waned even amongst the population who supported them. All the political and military leaders of the People's Republic were aware that support for their cause was failing and they looked for a way to rejuvenate their cause. In an effort to change their fortunes they launched their own large offensive. The offensive was led by a 10-regiment force called the 'Right Flank' Army under the command of General Chin Shao-shen.

Three People's Army regiments already stationed on the Fukien-Chekiang border crossed into Nationalist territory on the 28th of December. With few Nationalist troops in the immediate vicinity, the People's Army's offensive made some early progress capturing the town of Kingyuan.

The PRA sent plain clothes agents in front of their Army to try and drum up support from the Chekiang population, this failed dismally. Some Nationalist deserters did join the PRA but to balance this out a similar number of rebels also joined the Government forces. In fact, a whole Brigade of the PRA under the command of General Chung Shao-kwei defected to the Nationalists. These troops had not been paid for six months. All soldiers of the PRA had received a single dollar to help them celebrate the formation of the new republic but that was all they had been paid.

Regardless of the morale of its troops the PRA's offensive was soon running out of steam anyway. As soon as the Nationalist command in Chekiang were able to react to this incursion they had moved troops against the invading force and its advance was halted. After the failure of the offensive the PRA was now on the defensive and tried to prepare for the inevitable Nationalist push. The whole of the Nationalist Army in the region was ready to launch a major offensive by New Year's Eve. Most of the Navy was in a position to support the

Rebel soldiers of the People's Republican Army are brought into Nationalist Army lines as prisoners. During the 1933–34 fighting soldiers from both armies deserted; the PRA's troops changed sides when it was obvious the war was lost. Few of the PRA rank and file were imbued with the revolutionary fervour of their leaders and were happy to surrender when possible. It's surely a trick of the camera – but this POW seems to be smiling.

Army when necessary. Over the next few days the Nationalists steadily advanced into Fukien meeting resistance but not enough to stop their advance. There were local successes for the PRA which was after all made up partly of veterans of the Anti-Communist campaigns and the Battle of Shanghai. Several of these victories were however against provincial troops, who were not of the same calibre as the regular Nationalist formations. Preparations were made to defend Foochow with a system of sandbagged emplacements and trenches built on the heights above the city. These fortifications were straw houses because of the lack of machine guns and artillery with which to defend them.

By early January 1934 the People's Revolutionary Republic was looking doomed with town after town falling to the advancing Nationalist Army. On the 6th of January a Nationalist force took the town of Chuchow after its defences had been largely destroyed by a series of air raids. Most of the remaining People's Army forces were now concentrated at the city of Yengpu. Yengpu was a port on the Min River, 85 miles north-west of the capital Foochow. Soldiers in the Yengpu garrison were now losing their will to fight as reports reached them of other defeats. The troops' morale was further affected by the constant bombing of their positions by a 10-strong bomber force. Over a few days these bombers dropped hundreds of bombs on the town causing heavy military and civilian casualties. Any town or village in the war zone was levelled. The Nationalist Army also shelled the town from distance with their heavier field guns; the rebels only had lighter mountain guns. At the same time a large Nationalist Army was massing to storm Yengpu and another force was outflanking the city's defences.

## Defections, False Promises and the End

The Nationalists received further reinforcements made up of 'loyal' Fukien troops under the command of General Liu Hing-pang. These joined the troops who had advanced eastwards through northern Fukien to block any retreat by the PRA at Kingyuen on the Chekiang-Fukien border. Yengpu fell on the 7th of January after a fierce 30-hour battle with many of the garrison fighting to the last. Newspaper reports said that the garrison commander, a General Tang, defected to the Nationalists just before the city fell. Another rebel formation was isolated and destroyed at Shuikow, 40 miles from Foochow. In yet another reverse three regiments of the PRA under the command of Chen Chei-shan went over en masse to the Nationalist side on the 10th. Other more determined PRA formations did not give up without a fight and hostilities continued for another week. General Tsai said he was determined to defend the besieged Foochow with its hospitals full of wounded. Field hospitals were being improvised in preparation for the expected heavy fighting for the city. The civic leaders of Foochow had begged General Tsai Ting-kai and his troops to evacuate the port before the Nationalist Navy bombarded it. To hammer home the futility of further resistance one of the largest air raids of the war was launched against Foochow involving 20 Nationalist planes. Panic amongst the civilian population now reached its height with all shops and other businesses closing down. Anyone with the means fled the city but many did not have the transport and had to stay. By the 9th of January the Nationalist Army was only 25 miles from Foochow and was advancing down the Min River. During the course of their advance they had isolated two large columns of PRA troops who were cut off from their supply lines.

On the 13th of January a significant battle took place between their forces and a 3,000-strong Nationalist force at Kutien. The PRA had launched an offensive towards the town but had been repulsed by the superior Nationalist force. For the first time during the fighting Nationalist FT-17 tanks were employed alongside a Marine force. The hero of the battle of Shanghai, General Tsai Ting-kai, was reported to be in the frontline during these decisive engagements but in reality he was fleeing with other commanders out of the province. After this last gasp of resistance the People's Revolutionary Army began to withdraw. On the same day large numbers of rebel troops were evacuated from Foochow by sea with other troops heading towards Amoy. Amoy was defended by one of the few remaining PRA formations that still kept its discipline while their comrades crowded any available ships or junks. During the retreat of the PRA the Nationalists captured several large caches of arms, the largest including 5,000 rifles, 100 machine guns and intriguingly, 20 armoured cars.

Proclamations of support for the dying rebel state from various Chinese regions were still coming in to their headquarters. These promises of support did not turn into actual military or other aid and the Communists stood back while their fellow left-wingers struggled. One or two rebellious Nationalist commanders sent empty promises of support including the Ninghsia General Ma Hung-kuei. General Tam Kai-shau had been given command of the 19th Route Army by Chiang Kai-shek once it had returned to the Nationalist fold. He issued an appeal to Tsai Ting-kai by telegram asking him to repent his 'mistake' and bring his troops back to the government side.

On the 15th of January Foochow finally fell as the People's Republic leadership fled by various means. The city was taken during the night by a landing party from the ships of the Nationalist navy anchored off the coast. General Tsai was reported to have fled on horseback with a small retinue while Eugene Chen the politician embarked on a steamer in disguise. Other leaders of the revolt escaped in the Republic's only transport plane while others gave themselves up to the Nationalists. One 2,000-strong PRA force did hold out briefly on Nantai Island, a short distance from the port. These soon gave up when they found out that they had been abandoned by their leaders. Another force of the PRA fled towards the Kwangtung border but General Chen Chi-t'ang was waiting with a substantial army and they turned back into Fukien.

After its defeat the remnants of the People's Revolutionary Army were reported to be wandering aimlessly around the province. Some of the veterans of the 19th Route Army were reported to have found their way to the nearby Kiangsi Soviet. When they reached the sanctuary of the Soviet they were allowed after screening to join the hard-pressed Red Army. The four main military commanders of the rebel army now asked for terms from the Nationalist command. In typical Chinese fashion the rebel leadership went unpunished having sought immunity

The handwritten caption on the back of this photograph reads: 'Retreating rebel troops with all their belongings & probably some loot, Foochow China January 1934'. This was written by the photographer, one of the few European witnesses to the fall of Foochow and the retreat of the People's Republic Army.

from prosecution from their hiding places. Although they had been in rebellion against the government of Chiang Kai-shek they were allowed to go into exile. The civilian leaders of the now defunct People's Revolutionary Republic had meanwhile taken shelter in Hong Kong. Chiang Kai-shek was particularly keen to retain at least the name of the 19th Route Army even if many of its troops were dead or on the run. Divisional commanders of the PRA also asked for immunity from persecution if they brought their remaining troops back into Nationalist service and this was accepted. A reported 10,000 of the defeated soldiers were moved by the Nationalist command to Honan province while others joined the Kwangtung Army.

The Communists' lack of support for the Fukien Rebellion was to prove one of their worst strategic decisions ever. Just as the rebellion was defeated the gap left in the encirclement of the Kiangi Soviet by the 19th Route Army was snapped shut. Chiang Kai-shek had sent his elite 88th Nationalist Division to the Chekiang-Fukien border. With the encirclement of the Soviet now again in place it was time for the Communist leadership to consider the future of their Kiangsi stronghold.

## The Long March

Of all the events in modern Chinese history the Long March is one of the most discussed and argued over. Some claim that the story as told by the Communist propaganda machinery since the 1930s is true and historically accurate. Others say that events during the March were invented to boost Mao Tse-tung's image. The truth is probably somewhere in between. As the whole of Mao's early career rested on his part in the Long March we can assume that much licence has been taken.

After the conclusion of the 5th Extermination Campaign in the summer of 1934 the Communist leadership knew that sooner rather than later they had to leave the Kiangsi Soviet. Mao Tse-tung advocated breaking out of the Soviet and the break-up of the Red Army into small guerrilla armies. These would work around the Nationalist forces on the northern and eastern fronts of the encirclement where there were fewer blockades in place. Mao was supported by Chu Teh in this mobile policy but the dominant '28 Bolsheviks' group rejected this plan. They insisted on holding what positions they had in the Soviet and digging in for a long siege. In April 1934 the Red Army suffered a disastrous defeat on the Fukien-Kiangsi border at the Battle of Kuangchuang where they lost 4,000 dead. They also suffered 20,000 wounded and the Red Army was now on the brink of total destruction. The Communist capital at Juichin was now open to any Nationalist attack and the morale of the soldiers reached an all-time low. Red Army troops were deserting in large numbers, some were shooting themselves in the throat by pulling the trigger of their rifles with their toes. Small armed groups began breaking out of the Soviet without orders but the vast majority waited for their leadership to make the hard decisions.

These Nationalist soldiers are marching through a Fukien town taken from the defeated People's Republic Army in January 1934. They belong to an elite division of the Nationalist Army, as is evidenced by the wearing of the British or US steel helmet. Chiang Kai-shek was determined to crush the Fukien People's Republic before its left-wing message could spread throughout eastern and southern China.

It has been debated how much planning went into the Long March but there is no doubt that preparations were made. In fact, some preparations had been started as early as six months before the start of the march. Within the limitations of their situation the Red Army had been trying to bring in new recruits for the coming campaign. The civilians in the Soviet were expected to marshal all the resources available. Harrison Salisbury in his book *The Long March* describes these preparations:

> A parallel campaign was launched to collect foodstuffs: heavier requisitions were ordered; the peasants were appealed to for contributions. There was a drive for loans. More silver dollars were struck. Winter clothing was made. Workshops began repairing guns and weapons. Old battlefields were scoured for spent cartridges. The brass cases were refilled with powder and lead. When lead ran out, wooden heads were whittled. A propaganda drive was launched to get peasant women to make straw sandals for the soldiers. Sandals wore out rapidly. Soldiers tried to start a march with a couple of pairs in their knapsacks. The women were told to make the new sandals of extra thickness, a certain hint of a long march.

In the summer of 1934 other Communist forces in Central China were trying to break out of smaller scale blockades imposed by the Nationalists on these regional Soviets. The 7th and 10th Red Armies totalling 10,000 men tried to move out of their base in Fukien province. The plan was that they would move into neighbouring Kiangsi and unite with the larger Red Army forces there. This movement was a complete disaster as the two armies were surrounded and in the words of one commentator were 'torn to pieces'. A few survivors escaped and fled into the countryside to form smaller guerrilla bands. Another Communist force, the 6th Red Army, had a base on the Kwangtung-Hunan border and was under the command of Hsiao K'o. It was decided in August to try and unite the 9,000 men of the 6th with the 2nd Red Army under Ho Lung, which was based in Northern Hunan. Again, the 6th Army was caught on the move by the Nationalists. Its 4,000 survivors met up with the 2nd Army. Their combined force was renamed the 2nd Front Army and began to move southwards into Kweichow and Yunnan provinces. They were then to turn northwards avoiding the dangerous Tibetan borderlands crossing the Yangtze River. After crossing the Great Snowy Mountain Range they were to join with Chang Kuo-t'ao's 4th Front Army in north-western Szechwan province.

As the Red Army marched along they knew that they would have to raise money and feed themselves in any way they could. This would include asking for ransoms for two captured wives of European missionaries who were released for $10,000 in silver. These eyewitnesses said the Communists stole 'everything they could lay their hands on'. This included the crops and livestock of the Lolo, or Yi, and other indigenous tribesmen whose lands they marched through. They also traded opium for food and other goods. At times they were marching through areas where *any* Chinese were unwelcome, never mind an army of tens of thousands.

## Leaving the Kiangsi Soviet

The break-out from the Soviet was led by the 1st and 3rd Red Army Corps which were regarded as two of the best formations in the Red forces in Kiangsi. For their mission to break out of the Soviet the two Corps were given priority in arms and equipment by the leadership. In command of the 1st Corps was Lin Piao with about 15,000 troops and the 3rd Corps was led by P'eng Te-huai with 13,000 men. Each Corps had only about 9,000 rifles, many of which were of questionable quality and each soldier only had 100 bullets each. Total ammunition stocks were reported to be a meticulously enumerated 1,800,640 bullets, 2,523 mortar shells and over 76,000 grenades. Two field guns captured earlier from the Nationalists were taken out of the Soviet. This meant that the 60 or so field and mountain guns captured in the early 1930s were abandoned. They also had 300 machine guns with only 500–600 rounds per gun and 30 mortars with little ammunition. Two aircraft, a single Vought V-65 Corsair known as Lenin and a Douglas O-2MC captured from the Nationalist Air Force would also be left behind. The Red Army's only pilot, a Nationalist deserter, would presumably be on the March. Much of this weaponry would be abandoned in the early stages of the March despite the best endeavours of their crews. Following the two Corps was the administrative 'Command Column' in which travelled the Kiangsi Soviet's Central Committee. In addition this column included a small anti-aircraft unit with a handful of heavy machine guns fitted with anti-aircraft

The Red Army sets out on its Long March on the 15th of October 1934 in a column that stretched for several miles. These marchers are probably from one of the rear columns as they are not wearing any kind of uniform. When the march began any type of firearm at hand was taken along and there were too few to go around. Later they captured rifles from the Nationalists. There are so many myths surrounding the march; but this photograph reflects the reality of the Red Army in 1934.

sights. Behind this column marched the Red Army's field hospital and its Medical Corps and lower ranking government officials in the 'Support Column'. In total the Command and Support Columns had 14,000 personnel which included only 35 women. In addition there were smaller columns which carried everything portable that a 'mobile' government could carry. These included printing presses to produce newspapers and propaganda leaflets and machinery for repairing small arms and producing primitive bullets. Out of these support columns at least 4,000 men were expected to take their place in the frontline when required. The females in the columns were the wives of the leadership including Mao's third wife, Ho Tzu-chen. Ho was an experienced guerrilla fighter known as the 'two gunned general' presumably because of pistols she carried. Every long marcher was issued with a new uniform before setting off on the journey made up of one or two pair of strong shoes, a blanket or quilt and a quilted winter uniform. End each man had a drinking cup. Each had 'a pair of chopsticks stuck into their puttees and a needle and thread fastened under the peak of their caps. All wore big sun hats with two thin layers of bamboo with oiled paper between them, and many had paper umbrellas stuck in their packs.' According to reports of the time everyone going on the Long March was to be dressed and equipped the same. Photographic evidence rather than propaganda paintings does show that this level of uniformity was not achieved by everyone.

More importantly though, each man carried a rifle of some kind although some were older ones, including flintlocks. These would hopefully be replaced with newer ones as they travelled through China over the next year.

It was decided to leave most of the women and the children in the Soviet. They were under the protection of the 28,000-strong rearguard, of which 20,000 were wounded and deemed unfit to travel. The 6,000 or so fit rearguard were ordered to try and continue the guerrilla war against the Nationalists. Out of the men left behind only a third were armed and that tended to be with damaged or older rifles. It was hoped that the survivors of the rearguard would keep some kind of base operational in case the Red Army were forced to return. Only the youngest and fittest of the Communists were considered by the leadership to be fit enough to survive the ordeal of the March. Many of the troops were barely teenagers, the youngest soldier recorded as being 11 years old. Just over half the marchers were between 16 and 23 while 44% were between 24 and 40 with only 4% over the age of 40. Strict discipline was officially to be imposed during the March including death sentences for looting the local population. In the dire situation, it is doubtful if this rule was often applied.

At about 5 pm on the 16th of October 1934 Mao Tse-tung and his entourage walked out of the Soviet. They marched westwards towards the part of the blockade held by the Kwangtung provincial troops who they hoped would turn a blind eye. The Kwangtung troops who had no love for Chiang Kai-shek didn't offer any resistance and moved away from the advancing column. Travelling only at night at first, the marchers divided into two columns that crossed the first blockade line at Hsingfeng. They then had to cross the Hsingfeng River by boat and ferry before dividing again, arriving at the second blockade line on the 5th of November. This line was on the Hunan-Kiangsi border, also guarded by troops who had no real argument with the Communists. The different groups took slightly different routes but crossed the third blockade line on the Canton-Wuhan Railway guarded by Kwangsi troops. They were now being pursued by Nationalist divisions that would not be so friendly, under the command of Generals Chou Hun-yuan and Li Yun-chieh. This meant that the marchers had to increase their pace and abandon some of their heavier equipment. In front of them now was the first of their many challenges, They approached a waiting Nationalist Army at the Hsiang River in late November.

## The Battle of Hsiang River

Just a few weeks after the breakout from the Soviet the Red Army was nearly destroyed at the Battle of Hsiang River in a trap arranged by Chiang Kai-shek and his staff. The Red Army's unwieldy column stretched for 50–60 miles as it moved towards the waiting Nationalist Army at Guilin in Southern Hunan province on the 25th of November. Strung out along the banks of the Hsiang River were a total of 15 Nationalist divisions, 150,000 troops. Although many of the Nationalist troops were unreliable ex-warlord soldiers they still made up an overwhelming force. The Nationalists were over-confident about the outcome of the coming battle. They even used their aircraft to drop propaganda leaflets instead of bombs on the Red Army as it drew near to the Hsiang River. These told the Communist soldiers that they were doomed and that the Nationalists were waiting for them with eager anticipation. Chiang had reinforced his army with soldiers of the Kwangsi and Kwangtung generals who were not considered loyal to his cause. He had ordered the southern generals to move their divisions from their provincial bases in the South.

There followed a week-long running battle which almost saw the end of the Red Army as it suffered disastrous losses of up to 30,000 men. The Communist leaders fell out amongst themselves during the bloodletting. Many Red soldiers either tried to desert to the Nationalists or simply melted away when the opportunity arose. It was estimated that out of the 30,000 lost to the Red Army about 15,000 took the opportunity of the confused fighting to desert. Despite these severe setbacks the surviving Red Army managed to break through the Nationalist blockade and marched through southern Hunan and northern Kwangsi provinces. The next port of call for the army was the impoverished d Kweichow province.

Here they were faced by a large number of poorly led, trained and armed Kweichow troops under weak Nationalist control. The Red Army spent several weeks marching north-westwards towards their next objective, the town of Tsunyi. Just over the Kweichow-Hunan border at Liping the marchers divided again into two columns. They had to cross a number of rivers and mountains, often under pressure from local troops. It was reported that the Kweichow and Szechwan troops they encountered were not pro-Chiang. They were, like many provincial Chinese anti anyone who was not from their province. The marchers continued towards the town of Tsunyi, garrisoned by 3,000 Kweichow troops.

Having interrogated captured soldiers, the 1,000 men of the Red Army's 4th Regiment entered the town disguised as the enemy. Most of the garrison fled and the rest of the Red Army marched in behind them for a few days well earned rest. While the rank and file slept and ate, their leadership discussed the progress of the march.

## The Tsunyi Conference

After breaking through the Nationalist blockade it took a month's march for the Red Army to reach a safe area to rest. When the exhausted Red Army reached the town of Tsunyi in Northern Kweichow province they had managed to shake off the pursuing Nationalist Army for a while and the local provincial forces were some of the weakest in China. The Marchers were at a low ebb so a crisis conference was held in the comfort of the residence of a local warlord. Heated discussions took place over a number of weeks with Mao criticising command decisions made up to that point. He and his supporters criticised the command of the Moscow-dominated '28 Bolsheviks' group and their German advisor Otto Braun, both while at Kiangsi and on the march. At first influential commanders like Chou En-lai were in support of the 28 Bolsheviks group and Mao and

Mao Tse-tung makes a speech in the mid-1930s after the end of the Long March. Mao was only one of the leaders of the Communists in the early 1930s and he often found himself outnumbered in policy debates. It was his winning of the arguments over vital policy decisions that saved the Red Army from destruction in 1934 and brought him to prominence. After his leadership of the march he was never again challenged for control of the party, although he was not officially Party Chairman until 1942.

his small coterie were isolated. Mao however managed to change many of the Politburo's minds somehow and by the end of the conference he had persuaded the people who counted. Chou En-lai even took a demotion, sharing military command with Chu Teh while Mao was given overall command on the 6th of January 1935. This appointment of Mao was not only a personal victory for him but was a de facto acceptance of the guerrilla tactics he had espoused for many years. It also meant that from now on the Moscow-dominated groups within the Communist Party and Red Army were to lose most of their influence.

While in Tsunyi the Red Army was to take the opportunity to expand their depleted forces. They launched a recruiting drive amongst the populations of Kweichow, Szechwan and Yunnan provinces. Amazingly, they did manage to recruit about 20,000 young men; what their motivations for joining the struggling Communists were is not known. The opportunity was also taken for the ordinary soldier to to re-supply. Each soldier was issued with a little money to buy new shoes, some medical supplies and other personal gear they would need in the coming campaign. The new plan for the Red Army was to leave Tsunyi and march north and cross the Yangtze River to meet up with Chang Kuo-t'ao's 4th Red Army. Ma intended top wrest the command of the 4th Army from his long-term political rival Chang. The 4th Army was known to be a larger and better armed force the control of whom Mao believed could be the key to leadership of the Communists. The Communists managed to outwit the Nationalist Army and crossed the Golden Sands River, as the Yangtze was known in the region.

## Crossing the Tatu River

The crossing of the Tatu River in the remote province of Sikang was probably the biggest single challenge faced by the Red Army. When they arrived at the fast flowing mountain river in May 1935 there were three possible crossing points. The extremely fast and powerful current made it almost impassable by boats and the only way to get large numbers of troops and civilians across was over the bridges. All three crossings were guarded by Nationalist troops with six regiments positioned at various points. Three of the Nationalist regiments were described as 'backbone regiments' who could be relied on to stand firm. At the small town of Anshunchang the crossing point was too well guarded by Nationalist troops, as was the crossing point at Fulin, guarded by the Szechwanese troops of the local warlord General Liu Wen-hui. The only remaining crossing point was at Luting where the river was crossed by a chain bridge. The 120ft long chain and planking bridge strung across the river was of a type built across high gorges as the only means of connecting mountain communities. They swayed terribly when light traffic was crossing. For once as they approached the bridge the marchers had a stroke of good fortune, as it had not been blown up as expected. The locals, who were not sympathetic to the Red Army, or the warlord troops guarding it, could easily have destroyed the bridge. But its destruction would have been little short of a disaster for the local population and it would not have been replaced

Soldiers of the 25th, 26th and 27th Red Armies assemble at Yung P'ing-chun in northern Shensi province on the fourth anniversary of the Japanese invasion of Manchuria. The men are part of the elite of the Red Army and they have been given the pick of weaponry. In the foreground are two ZB-26 light machine guns captured from the Nationalist Army during a battle.

for months. Instead of destroying the bridge the defenders had tried to make it impassable by removing a number of planks from its floor.

A hand picked squad was given the task of crossing the bridge under fire; they had to crawl across the chains hand over hand. All the time the Nationalist troops on the other bank were firing on them and several either fell or were shot off the bridge. When the survivors reached the planking that was still in position the Nationalist troops began pouring kerosene on the boards and setting fire to them. According to first-hand accounts the surviving squad leader drew his sword and his C-96 automatic and charged into the flames. His comrades followed and in minutes the bridge was taken and the defenders had fled. The boards were replaced and the army shuffled across the bridge to continue their journey. What a spectaclular sight that must have been.

The Red Army often took routes during the Long March which involved crossing mountainous terrain and wide rivers. Some have argued that at times it was unnecessary to cross some of this terrain with all the attendant suffering. Mao would of course argue that it was unlikely that the Nationalists would be willing to follow the Red Army over such terrain. On many occasions there was in fact only one route and that was over the mountains or across the river. Rivers could sometimes be crossed by ferry but getting thousands of men across on a single or a handful of boats was tortuous. There were 24 to cross during the march. Amongst the mountains crossed was the Old Mountain in Kweichow province and the Snow Mountains in Szechwan province, which rise to 18,000 feet. The Red Army crossed in June 1935 with many marchers poorly dressed for the journey. As Dick Wilson pointed out in *The Long March*, these were not mountain people: 'Many of the poorly-clad, thin-blooded Southerners in the ranks, unused to high altitude, died of hypothermia and exposure.' Wearing flimsy straw sandals or cloth shoes, others simply slipped and fell to their death.

## The Meeting of the Red Armies

When the Red Army had crossed the Great Snow Mountains they rendezvoused with the Communist 4th Front Army under Chang Kuo-tao. This army was between 40,000 and 45,000 strong and had been pushed out of its Oyuwan Soviet in Northern Szechwan province.

They had been ejected by large Szechwan provincial armies who acted independently of the Nationalist Government. Although they had left their base they had not suffered the same deprivations as their Long March comrades. Although strong on paper, only 50% of Chang's troops were armed with rifles. Chang expected to absorb the Red Army into his 4th Front Army but Mao and the other leaders would not allow this to happen. In a series of meetings between the two men their animosity towards each other soon became obvious. It also became apparent that they had many political and military differences, which made a unification of their armies impossible. Chang insulted Mao by pointing out the better condition of his men compared to Mao's and implied that this proved he was the better commander. Mao's riposte was predictable and reasonable: his men had fought every step of their march and it was amazing that they had survived their ordeal. Chang and Mao were as arrogant as each other and there was no way that either man would back down and accept the other as his superior. They disagreed on the first decision – where to establish a base. Mao wanted to continue north to the existing base in Shensi province, which he thought would be just remote enough to guarantee safety. Chang thought that a base in the Sinkiang-Szechwan border region would be better. He was influenced by the fact that Sinkiang was a province dominated by the Soviet Union on its borders. When it became obvious that no settlement would be reached Chu Teh

A Red Army machine gun crew in the period after the end of the Long March with a Browning M1917 heavy machine gun. This weapon was produced in a number of Chinese arsenals and was used in large numbers by the Nationalist Army. With the Government Army serving often as an unwilling quartermaster for the Red Army, they also used them whenever they could capture them.

the military leader imposed an agreement on both men. Mao was to keep his 1st and 3rd Corps and take 2 Corps from Chang's Army to to create an 'Eastern Column'. Chang took the remainder of his 4th Front Army, renamed the 'Western Column', and was joined by Chu. The Western Column soon departed after a public but insincere reconciliation between Mao and Chang. They marched westwards to find somewhere they could establish a new base to rest up for the winter. Mao and his Eastern Column followed shortly afterwards and continued their march northward to the wild lands of Chinghai province.

## The Chinghai Grasslands, the Latzukou Pass, Shensi at Last

The crossing of the apparently benign grasslands of the remote Chinghai province was surprisingly difficult for the Red Army, which they acheived in August and September 1935. It was described by Mao himself as the most difficult episode of the Long March. The high grasses grew in several feet of black water and swampy black soil. Some weakened soldiers who lost their footing drowned in the brackish water unless a comrade had the strength to pull them out. With no fresh water to drink and little food to eat, the freezing and snowy cold nights were spent in the open sleeping on any patch of hard ground they could find. Dry patches of ground were at a premium and there was no firewood. The soldiers suffered for weeks from these conditions. Having faced more obviously challenging high mountains and raging rivers, the grasslands nearly ended the Red Army with thousands of soldiers dying from hunger and hypothermia.

The last major hurdle for the Red Army before it entered Shensi was the Latzukou Pass on the White Dragon River. A mile and a half wide defile between cliffs barred access to the North-East and was heavily guarded by well trained Nationalist troops. The Nationalists had a division dug in with trenches and field guns and any frontal attack along the pass would have been fatal for the Red Army. The defenders had also constructed lookout towers to stop any chance of a surprise attack. To make matters worse the only route through the defile was a single-file wooden bridge which would become a death trap if used by the Red Army. The only answer was to outflank the Nationalist defences. This was done by a picked unit of climbers who scaled the cliffs on the right side of the bridge. On the 18th of September, with grappling hooks and ropes the Red Army assault team managed to scale the heights and attacked the Nationalists from behind. Although the Nationalists were surprised it still took a large-scale and costly assault to take the bridge and expel the defenders.

After moving the troops through this pass the Red Army still had several other bridges and other obstacles to cross before they reached their base. At the Pailung River their engineers had to build a new bridge after the original one had been destroyed by the Nationalists. A final natural obstacle were the Liupun Mountains, which, although not on the scale of the Snowy Mountains were still a daunting challenge. Many were now ill with malaria and other conditions. Once they had crossed the mountains over winding paths they were soon faced by more Nationalist troops.

The Nationalists were a mix of first line units and local militiamen and many of them were Muslim cavalry. These mobile troops now harried the Red Army with hit and run attacks in the same way they had previously done to the Nationalists. Although these attacks caused casualties the Red Army's advance could not now be stopped. At the end of October the vanguard of the Red Army column began to come across Communists venturing out from the existing Shensi Soviet. As the column began to limp into the relative safety of the Shensi Soviet it must have presented a tablesu of human suffering and endurance. The highest estimate of the number of Long Marchers who reached their destination was 20,000. This estimate is thought however to include the 10,000 or so Communists who were already in the Soviet. Some say the total that entered the Soviet was 8,000 but this includes about 2,750 who had joined the march along its route. This would mean that out of the 100,000 who set off in October 1934 only 5,000 original marchers reached Shensi. Many of these would of course be higher ranking officers and political leaders who had been kept away from the worst of the fighting. Out of the original 100,000 a large number had been left behind to begin guerrilla warfare in the provinces they passed through. Some wounded had been left in the hands of friendly peasants and a few of these would eventually reach Shensi. Others were with Chang Kuo-t'ao and some of these would also eventually reach the relatively safety of Shensi. Whatever the figures one thing is certain: the Red Army had survived as an idea but many of its soldiers and supporters had died in the process.

Chou En-lai seen here at the end of the Long March was a long-standing revolutionary with wide military experience. He was the main organiser of the Communist withdrawal from the Kiangsi Soviet and his intelligence network was invaluable during the march. In the early 1930s he was recognised as one of the leaders of the Chinese Communist Party as being senior to Mao. When Mao rose to the leadership of the Party, Chou was happy to serve as his vice chairman until both their deaths in 1976.

## The Straggling Red Armies, 1935–1936

The arrival of Mao and his men in Shensi was not the end of the Communists' efforts to find safe havens for their army. Chang Kuo-t'ao and his army was still looking for somewhere to establish a new base. Mao Tse-tung radioed all the other Red Army units telling them to enter Kansu province and follow his army to Shensi. But the passes that the Red Army had used to get to Shensi had now been blocked by large formations of the Nationalist Army. The pursuing Nationalists were now under the command of much better officers including the wily Cantonese General Hsueh Yueh. Other commanders of these more efficient Nationalist divisions included General Hu Tsung-nan. Chang Kuo-t'ao's forces tried in vain to break through the well established fortified lines of Hsueh Yueh in September 1935. After marching to the west they spent the winter in the remote region of Sikang on the border with Tibet. This region was so remote that Chang's Red Army was able to rest there from November 1935 to June 1936. It was a lawless country and the only threat was from poorly armed government militias and Tibetan tribesmen. Chang now had a plan to take his army to distant Sinkiang, a province of China under the strong influence of the Soviets. If Chang could get his forces there they were personally promised military and other assistance by Joseph Stalin himself. In June 1936 Chang was joined by the 5,000-strong force of another Red Army commander, Ho Lung. Ho and his men now joined a summer march towards Sinkiang that faced little opposition from the poor local government forces. They entered Kansu province, finally reaching the Yellow River at a town called Chingyuan. There Chang started to ferry his army across the river to the west bank in small boats, a thousand per night. He had managed to get 22,000 soldiers across when the Nationalist Army caught up with them in September. When the superior Nationalist forces closed off this crossing there were still 35,000 men on the east bank. With the stranded Communists were Chu Teh and other Red Army leaders. The trapped Red Army now turned around and began the long journey to Yenan, where most eventually arrived. Meanwhile, Chang and his men continued their exodus and as they travelled westwards through Kansu they came under continous attack from the province's famous cavalry. These were under the command of the provincial military governor, General Ma Pu-fang, a Muslim who hated the Communists. Ma's Muslim horsemen harried Chang and his fast depleting force for months and finally wiped most of them out in a vicious battle at Chiuchuan in January.

## 11

# 'LITTLE LOCAL DIFFICULTIES': GENERALS AT WAR, 1929–1935

Besides the larger scale wars and revolts that plagued China between 1928 and 1937 there were numerous minor conflicts. Chiang Kai-shek's newly installed government was supposed to have imposed strong rule from the centre on all of China. In reality, the country was still fractured with only a few provinces truly under Chiang's control. Other provinces were ruled by un-reformed warlords who flew the Nationalist flag over their palaces. Many Nationalist military governors had no real loyalty to Chiang and were willing to challenge his rule militarily when the opportunity arose. The main opponents of Chiang were defeated during the Central Plains Wars of 1929–1930. There were, however, still troublemakers throughout China who chanced their luck in a series of rebellions. In addition provincial military governors fought their own local conflicts over territory, as they had throughout the 1910s and 1920s. Some of these wars were fought in outlying provinces and hardly troubled Chiang and his rule at all. They threatened Nationalist control regionally but few were a direct threat to his political base at Nanking. Chiang rarely interfered in regional conflicts as these often weakened his rivals. The Nationalist leader's 'divide and rule' policy was helped by the constant falling out of the more powerful of the provincial leaders. No matter what the magnitude of, or reason for, the various wars fought over nine years, the effect on the population of China was often devastating. The ordinary Chinese were pawns in the power games of the ruthless generals.

## Warlord Rebellion in North-eastern Shantung, 1929

In the spring of 1929 there returned to Shantung province one of the most reviled of all the warlords who had dominated China since 1916. General Chang Tsung-ch'ang who had controlled the rich province for several years had gone into exile in Japan when defeated by the National Revolutionary Army in 1928. While some warlords accepted their enforced retirement after their defeat by the Nationalists, others still dreamed of returning to power. General Chang Tsung-ch'ang, the notorious 'Dog Meat General', had held sway over Shantung province for most of the 1920s. He was given a variety of non-complimentary nicknames, including the 'Monster'. Of all the vicious warlords of China in the 1920s and 30s Chang was the basest who held Shantung through sheer fear. His reputation for once was not exaggerated and he was infamous for lopping off the head of anyone who opposed him. Besides his cruelty he was known for for his love of money and women and had several dozen concubines of every nationality. In a strange touch, each of his women had the flag of their home country painted on their wash bowls. There were a reported 26 different nationalities featured on the bowls with several 'spares' from the same country. After Chang went into exile in 1928 he was said that have murdered a diplomat in Japan whose wife he coveted. The still ambitious 'Dog Meat General' saw his defeat as temporary and gathered a group of his former allies and subordinates around him in an attempt to regain power. His allies included General Chu Yu-pu who had been the military governor of Hopei province with its 30 million people. Another was General Huang Feng-chi who had managed to raise a force of 26,000 ex-soldiers. Former warlord generals like Chang, Chu and Huang would not accept their new reduced circumstances and were willing to risk everything to regain power. There was also unsubstantiated reports that Chang had contacted two White Russian commanders to help him. These were Ataman Semonov who had fought his own campaigns against the Bolsheviks in Siberia until 1922, and Colonel Netchaieff. Netchaieff had commanded a division of White Russians for Chang Tsung-ch'ang in the mid-1920s and may well have joined his venture. When the rebel generals landed in eastern Shantung province they brought with them only a small retinue but soon gathered their loyal soldiers together. Although some of their defeated soldiers had been recruited into the Nationalist Army, most were now unemployed and more than willing to fight. The outlook for an ex-warlord soldier or officer in 1929 was bleak, especially when the Nationalist Army was being reduced. Soldiering was usually out of the question for Chang's former troops and it was hardly surprising that so many of his former fighters flocked to his banner. The rebellion frightened the foreign residents of Chefoo, the major city in north-eastern Shantung province. Plans were made by the foreign community to evacuate their families from the city if the rebel army threatened to take it. There was panic in Chefoo when the distant sound of artillery reached the outskirts of the city. The bombardment turned out to be coming from the town of Kusien 25 miles to the west. Clashes there had begun on the 22nd of February as both armies moved their troops towards the frontline. After several days of skirmishes a large-scale battle took place on the 24th of February between General Huang's 26,000 men and a much smaller Nationalist force of 7,000 under General Liu Chen-nien. General Liu had history with Chang, having served in his personal bodyguard in the mid-1920s. Although the rebel army was ostensibly much larger, its troops were poorly armed and trained. General Liu was to receive only half-hearted support from Chiang Kai-shek during his struggle with Chang. He was given a war chest of 50,000 Yuans and 200,000 rounds of ammunition in February. The rebels were not at this time under the command of their former commander, whose whereabouts were unknown. The presence of the 'monster' Chang Tsung-ch'ang in the field might have made a difference to his troops' performance. The Shantung rebels lost 200 killed during the brief battle and 300 of them were taken prisoner. More importantly for the poorly armed rebels they also lost 2,000–3,000 rifles and 15 precious machine guns.

This first defeat for the rebels did not deter Chang and his fellow warlords, who moved to support Huang's still large army. The defeated rebels marched

General Chang Ts'ung-chang, the 'Dogmeat General', disappeared from the Chinese military scene for a short period in 1928 before trying to make his comeback in early 1929. He is pictured here at the height of his power in the 1924–28 period wearing his light blue dress uniform. Chang was unwilling to settle for a comfortable exile in some foreign concession in China. Although reviled by the ordinary population, he did have the loyalty of most of his soldiers, who respected and feared him.

north-westwards towards the city of Tengchow to try and establish a new base. General Liu after his victory began to move more men and supplies up to front to make a fresh attack. Although he was under orders from Nanking he continued to run his own war and ignored several messages from Chiang Kai-shek. Little support came from the central government anyway, apart from the appearance of a gunboat sent from Manchuria.

Over the next few weeks the rebels took out their frustrations, as was usual, on the local population. Half a dozen towns and 50 villages were razed to the ground by the rebels, mostly in revenge for the killing of a popular lieutenant in Chang's army by a villager. The troops of the Nationalist General Liu did not behave much better and the poor peasants were also robbed by their 'protectors'. Citizens of the Chefoo had no confidence in Liu's ability to stop Chang despite his seemingly impressive victory and many fled to the city of Dairen. General Liu, although officially an adherent of the Nationalists, had been ruling the people of Chefoo and the surrounding areas like an unreformed warlord since 1928. Chiang Kai-shek and his government were perplexed by the motives behind Chang's invasion of eastern Shantung. They could not see how Chang Tsung-ch'ang's revolt fitted in to the civil war going on all over China at the time. In reality, Chang simply wanted to get back his former power base in Shantung and was willing to achieve this with our without Chiang's approval. Chiang's main worry was that the fighting in north-east Shantung would persuade the Japan to go back on their promise to withdraw their troops from the province. Since May 1928 the Japanese Imperial Army had controlled the main railways in Shantung and negotiations were taking place for them to leave the area. There were suspicions that Chang Tsung-ch'ang had been given covert support from the Japanese to make trouble in Shantung. At the very least the Chinese accused the Japanese of helping Chang leave Dairen and get to Shantung.

After a few weeks of desultory fighting a five-day truce was arranged between Liu and the rebel generals in early March. The rebels tried to win Liu over to their cause with the tried and trusted 'silver bullets' – a $100,000 bribe. General Liu thought his loyalty was worth at least $500,000 and held out for that amount but the rebels could not or would not meet his price. There was a plan for a typical 'sham fight' outside the city between the two armies to save Liu's face. This non-battle would allow General Liu to claim to have fought hard before surrendering. Sham battles were one of the peculiarities of Chinese warfare during the civil wars of the 1920s. The bribe was not paid and the sham battle did not take place; the truce came to an end without a settlement. When the truce ended the tables were turned as a strengthened rebel army moved in three columns towards Chefoo. Chang Tsung-ch'ang had astutely used the truce with Liu to gather more of his loyal troops from around Shantung. In the meantime General Liu had asked Chiang Kai-shek for reinforcements but he was more concerned with what he regarded as a more tangible threat from Wuhan rebels. It seems that the battle for the city was swung by the defection of one of General Liu's regiments led by a Colonel Liang. The exact strength of Chang's army is not known but it soon overwhelmed Liu's forces defending Chefoo. Chang had been reinforced on the eve of his capture of Chefoo by the arrival of 7,000 troops under the command of General Sun Tien-ying. When the city fell on the 1st of April, Chang's troops immediately hoisted the five-barred flag of the Chinese Republic. This flag was used repeatedly during the various rebellions of the 1930s as a symbol of the good old days of warlord China.

It appears that the victorious rebels were fairly disciplined at first but from the 6th to the 13th of April they ran amok. Their officers tried to control their unruly troops but the worst elements amongst Chang's army could not be controlled and began to loot the city. Western eyewitness told of a period of mass killings, rapes and looting led by bandits who had joined Chang's Army just before the city fell. Even if Chang had really wanted to control his men he probably couldn't as he had used the promise of booty to recruit new soldiers. The looters were eventually dissuaded from continuing their worst outrages and some kind of calm descended on the devastated city. Chang Tsung-ch'ang took full advantage of his temporary ascendancy by trying to fill his war chest through heavy taxes on the already suffering people of north-east Shantung.

General Liu meanwhile had withdrawn with some of his men to the city of Muping, which had a population of 100,000. The city was surrounded by large numbers of Chang's troops who half-heartedly laid siege to the garrison. They soon lost interest and began to drift off to seek easier plunder elsewhere. Chang's cause had begun to flounder anyway, as many of his troops began to lose interest in the fighting. Chang still had a loyal following but he did not have the numbers he would need to defeat Liu. When the siege was lifted General Liu and his army marched to Chefoo and relieved the city. They chased the remnants of Chang's army out into the countryside, who broke up into a series of disorganised rabbles.

As the rebellion collapsed in early April its various commanders scrambled around with their own armies looking for shelter from the vengeful Nationalists and civilians. General Chu Yu-pu found a bolthole in the small walled city of Fushun with the remaining 4,500 of his army. They locked the gates of the city and imprisoned the terrified 20,000 citizens while Nationalist forces laid siege to it. During the 13-day siege the rebels raped and robbed the people. Chu's troops used women and children as human shields. They tied the poor wretches to posts on the walls of the city and fired from behind them at the besieging Nationalists. It was not recorded if the Nationalists refused to fire on the defenders because of their living shields but it is doubtful. Missionaries approached General Liu who was now in command of the siege to allow women and children to leave the city. There was also the problem of the 300 wounded soldiers inside the city walls and the 400 or so lying exposed outside. Neither side recognised the Red Cross workers as non-combatants, so most of the wounded were left to die. It was reported that Liu and Chu did agree to let women and children leave the besieged city but this is doubtful. Such compassion would be out of character.

More horrors were to follow when the city fell; the women and girls of the city committed mass suicide. They could not face the 'shame' (a terrible and tragic misnomer) of their rape and prepared to end their torment in the only way they knew. At a prearranged signal they began to jump down the wells of Fushun until they were filled. When the Nationalists entered the city they took revenge on Chu's troops but not, amazingly, on the General himself. He was allowed free passage to the coast where he boarded a ship to Korea taking $400,000 in silver bars with him. It can be assumed that he left a large amount of his loot in the hands of the Nationalist officers who let him leave Fushun unharmed. The battle for the city had cost the Nationalists 1,500 and the rebels 2,000 casualties. Any of Chu's troops found in the hospital would have certainly have been thrown out

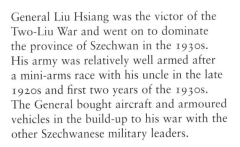

General Liu Hsiang was the victor of the Two-Liu War and went on to dominate the province of Szechwan in the 1930s. His army was relatively well armed after a mini-arms race with his uncle in the late 1920s and first two years of the 1930s. The General bought aircraft and armoured vehicles in the build-up to his war with the other Szechwanese military leaders.

in the street to die. After peace returned temporarily to Shantung, General Liu and another Nationalist loyalist, General Jen Ying-chi, fought a two-day war. In typical warlord fashion this short but still brutal conflict was fought over which general had more authority in Shantung, Liu won.

Chu's arrogance was to be his undoing when a short time later he left his comfortable exile to return to the scene of his crimes. He was soon hunted down by the peasants who had suffered at his hands, dragged off and was buried alive. Another version says he was buried up to his chin and black ants and the searing sun gave him the slow death he deserved. All the time silent peasants formed a circle around him to watch his suffering. His commander Chang Tsung-ch'ang had to wait a little longer to receive his just deserts as he left a train on the 3rd of September 1932 at Tsinan Railway Station. He was shot at point blank range by the relative of one of his subordinate officers from the 1920s. This officer, long forgotten by Chang, had had been executed for some transgression.

## Shih Yu-san, the 'Grey General', 1929–31

General Shih Yu-san, known to history as the 'Grey General', was the archetypal rebellious military leader who plagued China in this period. In 1929, when the general was 38, he began a series of revolts. General Shih was a subordinate of Chang Hsueh-liang and had 40,000 men under his command. He controlled Northern Honan and on Monday the 2nd of December in that year Shih led two divisions of his army in a revolt at Pukow and seized the railway from there to Tientsin. From his headquarters at Pengpu Shih he entered into talks with the Government at Nanking about his peacefully evacuating the railway zone. The Government quickly agreed to his demands to rid themselves of this troublesome general. Instead of accepting the terms, Shih made even more demands and the Nationalist Government lost patience. Nationalist units moved towards Shih's positions on the railway and fighting began with heavy casualties on both sides. The press gauged the level of the fighting, as was often the case, by the number of wounded in the hospitals. Shih had to wind down his campaign as he realised that his army could not win in the end. After the 1929 campaign wound down Shih was still in the field with a substantial army under his command. As newspaper reports of late March 1930 said, 'Rebelling was becoming a habit for General Shih.' Shih had in February opened hostilities against the Nationalists on the Lunghai Railway. This so-called 'Spring War' was of little importance in the great scheme of things at the time. It was just another challenge to Chiang Kai-shek's authority in a time of crisis. Shih's army had occupied the city of Tsaohsien before being chased out by the Nationalist loyalist General Chiang Ting-wen. The Nationalist Government tried the usual tactic of bribing Shih with an offer of $200,000, which was the going rate for stopping rebellions in 1930. Officially the money was to be used by General Shih to pay the arrears owed to his soldiers but at least some of it would have ended up in his bank account. He was also offered without a trace of irony the job of 'Commissioner for the Suppression of Bandits'. Shih agreed to the conditions of the settlement and was said by a government communiqué to have shown signs of contrition. He now found himself in September 1930 fighting alongside his superior, General Chang Hsueh-liang. Chang had finally pledged his North-Eastern Army to Chiang Kai-shek and Shih's army joined the Nationalist war effort as well. Shih was only interested in fighting when it suited him and his army to do so and decided in early December to strike out on his own again. On the 2nd of December he led his two divisions in another revolt, taking the city of Pukow. He seized the railway from Pukow to Tientsin and settled down to await developments.

By early March 1931, in an attempt to make peace with the Government, General Shih had returned all the rolling stock that he had commandeered from the railways of northern China. He had held the rolling stock as collateral for what he regarded as underpayment of funds by his superior, General Chang Hsueh-liang. The $600,000 per month that Shih claimed he needed to maintain his Shantung Army was never going to be paid. He had received $200,000 in total for the three-month period from November 1930 to January 1931. As part of the peace deal brokered between Shih and the Central Government the General was to retain command of only one of his divisions. Chiang Kai-shek insisted that General Shih's other loyal division should be sent to garrison the city of Shenyang. General Shih was never going to accept these conditions but he pretended to agree to them while stalling for time. Throughout March and April Shih issued a number of protestations of loyalty while trying to build up his army's strength for a renewed campaign against the Nationalists. Just before he left service with Chang Hsueh-liang, Shih was in command of the North-Eastern 13th Route Army. This was made up of two so-called 1st Class Infantry Divisions and four 2nd Class Infantry Divisions, he also had a cavalry brigade, an engineer regiment and a 'Special Operations' Regiment which served as a support unit and also had MP duties. He also had an armoured train under the command of Colonel Tuan Chun-tse which had been formerly been in service with the Kuominchun. In total this was an army of 64,000 men; the vast majority were prepared to follow the General into rebellion.

By July 1931 the Government had given up any pretence of a peaceful settlement with General Shih and began preparations for an offensive against him. In mid-July Shih ordered a period of so-called 'intensive training' for his army and a 'practice manoeuvre' along the Peking–Hankow Railway. He established his headquarters at the town of Shihchiachuang and began issuing orders for the confiscation of all the rolling stock he could find. Shihchiachuang was strategically placed as it was where the railway from Taiyuan, the capital of Shansi province, met the main Peking–Hankow Railway. It was 160 miles south of Peking and 125 miles to the east of Taiyuan and was a vital crossroads of the northern Chinese railway network. With nearly all the trains and wagons on the railway in his hands, all traffic had to be suspended. Shih used his newly acquired rolling stock to move his army to the north and on the 13th of July the first clashes occurred with Chang Hsueh-liang's North-Eastern troops at Shunteh, 60 miles to the south of Shihchiachuang. Nationalist forces were now despatched in large numbers to the Shih-controlled zone. These included three infantry divisions, several squadrons of light bombers and several armoured trains to confront Shih's train. Chiang Kai-shek and Chang Hsueh-liang were now determined to deal once and for all with the troublesome Shih. The Nationalist Government issued a 'dead or alive' reward for Shih of $2,000. In the last few days of July Manchurian troops began advancing along the Peking–Hankow Railway towards General Shih Yu-shan's army. The fighting took place along the railways with the armies trying to out-manoeuvre each other. Heavy fighting in the region between the cities of Paotingfu and Chengtingu ended in a stalemate. In order to prevent any threat to Peking, a large Manchurian formation dug in at Changsingtien, close to the former Chinese capital. In an attempt to break the stalemate General Shih sent his 'elite' 'Big Sword' Division eastwards along the Peking–Tientsin Railway. His aim was to try and threaten the rear of the main Manchurian Army but this advance was soon countered. The bulk of the Manchurian forces under the command of General Han Fu-chu had in turn advanced to threaten the rear of the 'Big Sword' Division. Han was the military governor of Shantung province and a former ally of General Shih. There was a remote threat that General Shih would be joined in his revolt by units of General Feng Yu-hsiangs Kuominchun. The defeated troops of Feng were said by the press to be 'skulking' in southern Shansi province and could have joined Shih's latest rebellion. Shih was planning several offensives with his main objective being the capture of the city of Tientsin. This would involve an advance across Hopei province and North-Eastern troops were employed digging entrenchments outside the city. They also built defences on the Tientsin–Pukow Railway to stop Shih advancing from that direction. The Nationalist Air Force tried to take the war to Shih in his Shihchiachuang headquarters with their bombers killing 100 civilians in a raid. The war against Shih was now left mainly to the North-Eastern Army; its propaganda department said it was 'quite capable of crushing General Shih Yu-sa'.

In late July General Chang Hsueh-liang's North-Eastern Army suffered heavy losses in fighting with Shih's forces at Wangtu, 110 miles south of Peking. The Manchurians suffered several thousand casualties and a thousand were taken prisoner by Shih's army. A major bonus for Shih was the capture of large numbers of rifles and a dozen field guns. Shih was also reported to have received $1 million dollars from the southern province of Kwangtung, which was also in revolt against Chiang Kai-shek. General Shih's Army now moved 20 miles northwards to the town of Paotingfu, where they waited for the advancing Shansi army sent to attack them.

## The Paotingfu Campaign

After their victory against the North-Eastern Army Shih's 40,000 to 60,000 troops were now confident and they thought they could defeat all comers. Reinforced by a number of former North-Eastern soldiers and with the captured field guns they waited for the attack to begin. Against them were three strong divisions of Shansi troops under the excellent General Fu Tso-yi, who had travelled 300 miles southwards along the Suiyuan–Peking Railway. An

A column of Liu Wen-hui's army march through a mountain pass during their war with the army of Liu Hsiang. All of the men have locally made cotton jackets and trousers, which most wear with traditional Szechwanese turbans. On closer examination several of the men wear peaked caps and a few have wrapped their turbans around them. Although most men have rifles there was a shortage of machine guns and heavier weaponry in their army.

additional four Shansi divisions were concentrating at Nientsekwan ready to attack Shih's army in the rear. Shih's army won an outstanding victory against the North-Eastern Army on the 29th of July; but this was to be his swan song. Over 50,000 of Chang Hsueh-liang's troops retreated in disorder on the 30th and Chang sent 15 troop trains to transport them out of the area. These arrived too late the men continued their retreat on foot as far away from the fighting as they could get. Shih's army prepared to advance in the direction of Tientsin but then things dramatically changed.

On the 31st Chiang Kai-shek told Chang he was determined to crush this latest rebellion and pledged to send 200,000 troops and 50 planes if necessary. This news was passed down the line and the uplift in morale it engendered led to many of Chang's troops rejoining the lines ready to retake Paotingfu. Overwhelming North-Eastern forces retook the city after several hours fighting and Shih withdrew his headquarters to the town of Wangtu 30 miles to the south. Large numbers of North-Eastern troops were pouring into the area to finish off Shih's 70,000-strong army.

The North-Eastern Army was to be reinforced by up to 300,000 Shansi troops who, although a multitude, were poorly armed, equipped and trained. They were still suffering the effects of their defeats in late 1930 when part of the anti-Chiang alliance. On the 1st of August Shih's troops were attacked in the rear by General Liu-Chih's Honanese Army who had advanced 300 miles from the north. With three armies attacking him simultaneously, even Shih could not hope to survive for long. Chang's North-Eastern Army moved in from the north; Liu-Chih's Honanese forces had outflanked him to attack from the south-east; and an army of Shansi troops attacked from the south-west. After several days fighting, mainly on the Peking–Hankow Railway, Shih's outgunned and outnumbered army finally broke on the 3rd of August. Most of his defeated troops began to head towards Shantung province in a disorganised mob, with every man for himself.

Shih's outnumbered army was totally defeated by the end of the first week of August and most of his troops surrendered on the 6th. The greater of the surrendering rank and file troops were absorbed into the Nationalist Army but their officers were vetted for their loyalty to Shih. The defeated General had fled from the battlefield with a small retinue and took ship to a remote part of northern Shantung. From his hiding place he issued a rather pointless official resignation from all his military posts on the 10th of August. Unfortunately the defeat of Shih did not bring peace to large areas of Shantung province; 5,000 of his soldiers turned to banditry. For over a year these renegades terrorised the population of western Shantung before they were defeated in a series of actions with Nationalist troops. Even at this late stage some surviving rebels, in the age-old Chinese tradition, were accepted into service with the Nationalist Army!

## The Canton Rebellion, 1931

The troublesome southern militarists were once again in rebellion when Dr Sun Yat-sen's old comrade Hu Han-min was put under house arrest in early 1931. This arrest of one of the founding politicians of the Kuomintang was seen as an outrage by the left-leaning southerners. Generals in Kwangtung and Kwangsi provinces joined forces in opposing Chiang Kai-shek and his un-revolutionary politics. They realised that Chiang was no revolutionary and in their opinion the arrest of the revered Hu finally proved it. Their first act was to declare yet another 'National Government' in Canton in May 1931 in opposition to the Nanking Government. Preparations were soon made by Nanking to send an expeditionary army to crush the rebellion. This Army was to be sent to northern Kwangtung province to confront the forces of rebel leader General Chen Chi-tang. As was usual in these kinds of Chinese rebellion, a series of threats alternating with offers of peace were wired back and forth. Kwangtung troops did cross the border into Hunan province in August but there were few clashes between the two armies. By mid-September the Kwangtung Army had reached Hengchow 200 miles inside Hunan but still no major clashes occurred. Up to that point the Hunanese troops had simply withdrawn in front of the advancing Kwangtung troops. It was as if neither side would back down but they did not want to be the one who started a full-scale war.

The Government of Chiang Kai-shek was keen to come to some compromise as their army was busy fighting the Red Army at Kiangsi. Chiang now released

Hu Han-min from house arrest and called a 'reunification congress' to try and settle any disputes. This was an abject failure and convinced Chiang to pursue a military solution to the Kwangtung problem. In September the Nationalist army had released enough troops to launch an attack against Kwangtung but then the Japanese struck. The Japanese invasion of Manchuria delayed any fighting and talks were arranged. These took place in October with a peace deal struck on the 7th of November. The Kwangtung warlord General Ch'en Chi-t'ang refused to comply with the agreement because of Chiang's policy of appeasement and non-resistance to the Japanese. He did, however, withdraw most of his troops back into Kwangtung province by mid November. On the 15th of December Chiang made one of his strategic resignations from all his offices to take the pressure off his beleaguered Nationalist Government. He was to take a short holiday and a month later had returned to the government as its military leader.

## The 'One Eyed General', Yunnan 1931

Since 1929 the western province of Yunnan had been under the control of General Lung Yun 'the One Eyed General'. He earned his nickname having had one of his eyes kicked out by the jackboot of a superior warlord he had rebelled against. The warlord then had Lung put in a wicker cage and hung outside the Temple of the Western Clouds in the Yunnan capital, Yunning. As he sat starving in the cage the people of the city were encouraged to file past and spit on him and throw excrement at him. After 30 days he somehow managed to escape from his torment and began planning another revolt against his captor. This time he made sure that his planning was better and his second revolt was successful. He had the defeated warlord hung in the same cage for exactly the same amount of time that he had been. Lung added a final touch by releasing the warlord after 30 days in the cage but had him publicly beheaded outside the temple.

Lung's rule was always under threat, even with a 40,000-strong army behind him and in 1931 he was briefly deposed. On the 11th of March four of Lung's trusted generals marched their troops into the capital to arrest him but he had gone into hiding. His troops were unhappy with Lung because he had disbanded some units as a cost-cutting exercise. Lung contacted Chiang Kai-shek and asked for help to get back into power; but it was public opinion that helped him in the end. The rebel generals tried to get prominent Yunnan politicians to declare for their side in the attempted coup. General Lung decided to leave the capital Kunming on the 12th of March to let the rebels fall out among themselves while he visited his family's graves. With Lung out of the capital, the men of influence there suddenly realised how much they relied on him and called for his return. When he finally arrived back at Kunming he dealt with the four generals, who were allowed to keep their heads but little else. They were replaced by younger officers who accepted the disbandment of some of their units and the fact they had no say in the province's government. Lung had managed to regain control of his province for another 14 years with little bloodshed simply by going on holiday.

## The 'Han-Liu War' in Shantung

The strategically important central Chinese province of Shantung was the scene in 1932 of another of the incessant local military squabbles. Two equally ambitious Shantung generals, Han Fu-chu and Liu Chen-nien, fought for several months over the province. The war was fought between the incumbent military governor of the province Han and his bitter rival, Liu. Both generals had previously been powerful in the province but Han had stolen a march on Liu to gain Shantung's coveted governorship. Han had previously served in the Kuominchun and had been a protégé of Feng Yu-hsiang before joining the Nationalists. Although officially General Han was in charge of the whole of the province, in reality General Liu held sway over most of eastern Shantung. This was a situation found in many of China's provinces in the 1920s and 1930s as one general was often not capable of controlling a whole province by himself. General Liu had managed to create a comfortable existence in his eastern stronghold with his headquarters in the port of Chefoo. He had co-existed peacefully with the more powerful General Han Fu-chu since 1928 but this was about to come to an end. The situation in Shantung was complicated by the threat of Japanese military intervention to protect their extensive commercial interests in eastern Shantung. For this reason any conflict that took place in the province would have to be fought within certain limits.

The main dispute between the two generals was over the allocation of the monthly allowance they received from Nanking. This allowance was given by the Government to each military governor for the maintenance of their armies. In the regional power struggles that were taking place throughout the 1930s this allowance was vital. General Liu had by far the weaker army of the two with only 20,000–30,000 men against General Han's 80,000 men. Both armies had a

General Liu Wen-hui outside his headquarters during the Two-Liu War in his dress uniform, which was peculiar to his army. His uniform points up the isolation of Szechwan militarily from the rest of China as it did not follow Nationalist dress regulations. Liu's collar ranks are also a leftover from the pre-1928 Republican Army and his sword is from the 1920s. The General fully expected to win his war with General Liu Hsiang but had not prepared for it as his opponent had.

reasonable amount of light artillery and machine guns but Han held the advantage. As the official governor of the province Han had access to more medium and heavy artillery than Liu. It was the Chinese practice for most of the province's artillery to be held centrally near to the military governor's headquarters.

The air arm of Shantung province had not been well developed during the 1920s although there had been four Breguet 14 light bombers in service in 1926–27. It is not known how many were still serviceable in 1932, although they may have been used alongside other planes bought in the 1920s. There were six fairly modern trainers of various makes in service with the Shantung air force in the late 1920s. Some of these probably were used during the Han-Liu War as improvised light bombers.

Han was by far the most aggressive of the two men while Liu would probably have preferred to kept the status quo in Shantung. Liu had managed to instil a certain steel into his troops however with many buying coffins before the war began in preparation for their 'fight to the death'. The main fighting of the short but nasty war took place in mid-September with the first clashes starting on the 17th. A series of small actions took place along the Tisinanfu-Tsingtao Railway, which turned into a bloody stalemate. General Han was trying to move thousands of his troops along the railway while Liu's troops tried to block their progress. General Han in preparation for his advance had sent a number of small forces from his garrisons in the west to reinforce his garrisons on the roads leading to Chefoo. Han now mobilised all his available forces to begin an advance against his rival's 'capital' at Chefoo. Because of the problems with the main railways, any available transport was confiscated to move Han's army along the main roads. Without much motor transport Han's troops had to rely on carts to move their equipment along the poor roads. In an attempt to slow this advance Liu's engineers blew up a bridge on the main road into the Chefoo region. The war turned into a grand advance by Han's army with little to encourage Liu's men that the war was winnable. On the 24th of September a Brigade of Liu's troops voted with their feet and crossed the line to join the enemy. As Han's army advanced they shelled any of Liu's troops who stood and fought with their superior artillery. The Shantung air force also came into play with several small-scale air raids. One raid involving most of the province's available light bombers and with trainers acting as improvised bombers was made on the town of Yikhsien.

The Central Government tried to keep out of the dispute, which Chiang Kai-shek regarded as a local matter. They did however send strong requests to both generals that any dispute between them should be settled at a peace conference at Nanking. Neither general was in the mood to make peace and the fighting continued. Officially the Central Government appeared to be keeping out of the conflict while unofficially favouring the incumbent governor, General Han. The strategic importance of the province and the danger of Japanese involvement led Chiang Kai-shek to make a move. On the 24th a Chinese Naval force landed at Chefoo to take the port for the Nationalist Government. The boats were from Chang Hsueh-liang's Manchurian navy and had been sent to capture the port at Chiang Kai-shek's request. Chefoo's importance as the only port that remained usable during the winter months meant it could not be allowed to remain in the hands of a rebel general. General Liu's troops had made a strategic withdrawal from Chefoo on the night before the landing, probably on the advice of the Nationalist commander. This takeover of Liu's headquarters did not immediately stop the fighting but General Han did offer to suspend hostilities on the 26th. In his view the intervention of the Central Government in the fighting had given his control of the province unarguable legitimacy. Chefoo's fall did not however end Liu's campaign and he simply moved his forces into the hinterland of Shantung province. Throughout October Liu's army created havoc in the countryside taking out their frustrations on the local population. Thousands of terrified civilians flocked to Chefoo where the government had set up refugee camps for them until the fighting ended. General Han's troops were far from innocent and they in turn attacked villages and towns thought to be loyal to General Liu. Although the two armies seem to have rarely clashed on the battlefield a war of words took place between the two bitter rivals. Han claimed in his speeches that Liu was a Communist sympathiser who was in contact with the Red guerrillas. At the time there was no greater insult for a Chinese officer than to be called a Red and Liu replied with equal vitriol. General Han appealed to the elders of the province saying he regretted the privations caused by his campaign against Liu. He however proclaimed that 'My conscience will not feel at ease as long as General Liu Chen-nien remains in Shantung for a single day. I am determined to subjugate him and will not stop half way.'

For such a bitter conflict, the end of the fighting in early November saw a relatively bloodless outcome. Under the terms of the peace treaty General Liu's defeated troops were put on a small fleet of ships and sent to the south of the country. They were forbidden from returning to the province. Han Fu-chu went on to be a popular military governor of Shantung, who became known as the 'Benevolent Despot' in the western press. This was because of the way he ran his province with a strange mix of humane and cruel policies. He was an educated and well read man who had studied Fascism, Communism and Roosevelt's 'New Deal'. Adopting facets from all types of political philosophies he mixed them all up to produce rules for the people of Shantung. These rules could be rather eccentric and included, for example, the prohibition of hair curling by women. Other rules met the approval of the people – like a tax system that did not bleed them dry! Another popular policy was the immediate execution of any captured bandits, which resulted in a substantial drop in the practice. He personally organised the execution of all 60 of a bandit gang outside the wall of the provincial capital, Tsinanfu. Han Fu-chu's demise came in 1938 when he was accused by Chiang Kai-shek of giving up Shantung too easily to the Japanese. As an example to other Nationalist officers who were unwilling to fight to the death, he was taken out on the 24th of January and shot.

## The Two Liu's War, Szechwan 1932–1933

The large, remote and mountainous south-western province of Szechwan had seen many small-scale conflicts in the early 20th Century. Since the 1911

Revolution there had been hundreds of conflicts fought there, even if most were small-scale affairs. With little outside influence the belligerents of Szechwan had been settling their own scores for decades and constantly vied with each other for territory. Szechwan had been roughly divided over time into six distinct territories like the slices of a huge pie, each controlled by one or more warlord. These generals had hardly acknowledged the victory of Chiang Kai-shek in 1928 and did not see why it should affect affairs in Szechwan. These military commanders were of course officially under the control of the Nanking Government. In reality they were all only interested in controlling as much territory as possible and in building up their own military strengths. There were almost constant conflicts between the various Szechwan generals throughout the 1920s. In 1929 Yang Sen, the dominant warlord, had been defeated by General Liu Hsiang, who was now the most ambitious of the Szechwan generals. When all military commanders under Nationalist control were ordered to make reductions in their troop numbers in 1929, the Szechwan commanders ignored the command. Instead, some began actively to increase the size of their armies and to buy weaponry to make them more potent. On the eve of the main conflict in Szechwan there were six main combatants in the province. In the north-west was General Teng Hsi-hou who controlled the city of Chengte, and in the north T'ien Sung-yao. Controlling a small territory in the north-east was General Liu Ts'un-hou. In the centre of the province controlling a relatively small territory was General Yang Sen, whose former prominence in the 1920s had now faded.

The main rivalry in 1932 in Szechwan was between General Liu Hsiang and his uncle General Liu Wen-hui. Liu Wen-hui controlled most of western Szechwan while his nephew Liu Hsiang controlled the east of the province and importantly, the provincial capital Chungking. The two relatives had co-operated over the years and had built up a small joint air force with a handful of transport planes. They also had at great expense purchased a fleet of armoured cars built in Shanghai on truck chassis. Although the armoured cars were not the greatest, they faced little opposition from other four generals who had little heavy weaponry. Most of the Szechwan armies had a handful of aged mountain guns in their armouries along with a few machine guns. For this reason the purchase of any modern weaponry by any of the Szechwan generals was bound to start a mini-arms race. Liu Hsiang's ambitions took no account of family loyalties and by 1932 he was heading for all-out war with his uncle. Liu Wen-hui had been annoying his nephew for a while by luring away army officers from his army with higher wages to serve in his army. Liu Wen-hui had done the same to the other warlords in the province, so Liu Hsiang assumed he could call on their support if it came to a war. Liu Hsiang's control of the major city Chungking gave him a financial advantage, as some taxes had to be paid through there. With the extra funds he gained he began to buy French military aircraft from 1930 onwards and by 1932 he had five Potez-25 and six Breguet 14A2 light bombers. At the same time Liu Hsiang made sure that none of the other Szechwan warlords was able to purchase large arms shipments and certainly not aircraft. With his aircraft and with small arms he had purchased from unscrupulous arms dealers, in October 1932 Liu Hsiang launched a war against his uncle. Liu Hsiang called it the 'war

Officers of Liu Wen-hui's Army take shelter behind a hillock during fighting in the Two-Liu War of 1932–33. The officers wear the field caps characteristic of the Szechwan armies of the early 1930s. Weaponry used in this remote conflict was mainly purchased by the two warring generals themselves. The junior officer on the left is armed with the C-96 semi-automatic, imported into China in vast numbers in the 1920s.

to Stablise Szechwan' although in the press it was commonly known for obvious reasons as 'The Two-Liu War'. Involving over 300,000 men, the war may have been restricted to one province but it was a large-scale conflict.

Besides his aircraft, Liu Hsiang also had the advantage of a small fleet with two warships to support his campaign. Fighting began in October 1932 with Liu Wen-hui's 24th army having a strength 200,000 men while Liu Hsiang's 21st Army had about 100,000 men. Liu Hsiang was supported by Generals Li Chih-Hsing & Lo Tse-chou with their 18,000 men while Tien Sung-wao and his 24,000 supported Liu Wen-hui. Liu Hsiang was reinforced in late October by the 30,000-strong 20th Army of General Yang Sen.

The fighting began in early October with local skirmishes in the Tungnan area in which both sides suffered heavy casualties. General Liu Wen-hui won the first major action of the war on the 8th of October at Chengte, the provincial capital. Undeterred Liu Hsiang's forces began to gain ground over the next week and on the 10th won a battle at Yungchen. This battle was a particular blow to Liu Wen-hui; 7,000 of his troops first retreated and then decided to join the enemy. These men belonged to the 2nd Division of the 28th Army and the 36th Division of the 24th Army. While this battle was going on, a further clash took place 120 miles east of the capital, Chengte. This battle at Shunking was one of the many local engagements which took place during the war that were more or less unrecorded. All that was reported was that both sides had suffered heavy casualties and that the wounded had nowhere to receive treatment. These vicious early battles and the heavy casualties suffered led General Liu Wen-hui to claim that he was doing all in his power to avoid further conflict. Tibetan tribesmen had taken advantage of his predicament. They had been renewing their large-scale raids on his territory in the neighbouring province of Sikang. Liu Hsiang noting his opponent's difficulties and called for him to stop the fighting and concentrate on his Tibetan raider problems. Before any constructive peace moves could be made by either side, a brigade of Liu Hsiang's Army had moved to outflank Liu Wen's Army. This movement by General Fang Shao-tseng and his Border Defence Division restarted the fighting. On the 21st of October another battle took place at the town of Chailingkiang, with the usual mutual commitment resulting in at least 1,000 deaths on either side. While the battle was underway Liu Wen ordered his forces to evacuate Shunking, the principal city of eastern Szechwan. The war so far had displaced thousands of civilians who had no real stake in the war and didn't really care which particular despotic warlord ruled over them. Many of these refugees found themselves in Chungking, where they waited for the fighting to cease.

It was far from over, with the majority of Liu Wen's army now entrenched at Tungnan, Tachu, Kiangchun and Yungchan. Liu Hsiang's army and those of his allies were advancing towards these strongholds gathering more troops as they went. As always, civilians were press ganged into either serving as soldiers or acting as unpaid porters for the armies. The war in Szechwan was a low tech affair with most armies having rifles and little else. Machine guns were few and usually older models with little ammunition. Artillery used by all Szechwan armies was confined to a few modern mountain guns and older 'museum piece' field guns. A few raids were undertaken during the war by Liu Hsiang's Potez 25 light bombers on the towns of Yungchan and Kiangchung. Liu Hsiang also had the only naval vessels of any size during the war, a handful of gunboats. The only opposition they would have faced would have been from any armed junks that Liu Wen-hui had. Liu Wen's artillery did manage to sink one of Liu Hsiang's gunboats in a battle at Kiangtsin.

By the last few weeks of October the war was coming to an end. On the 28th, the 29th Army of General Tien Sung-yao had taken the western gates of Chengte. Several times the attackers were thrown back and heavy fighting took place in the suburbs of the city. The defenders had some successes: in one skirmish hundreds of Tien's troops were captured and their rifles issued to Liu Wen's troops. Several bombing raids were launched by Liu Hsiang's small air force but these did not cause significant casualties. Superior numbers and firepower did eventually tell against the defenders and Liu Wen-hui's troops began to evacuate the city and move to their outlying strongholds. Street fighting continued for a few days with the last of Liu Wen's army heading for the town of Yungchan. The combined forces of Liu Hsiang and General Tien Chung-yau had penetrated Yungchan's defences and Liu Wen's defeated troops were in retreat there as well. The 21st Army of Liu Hsiang took the towns of Kiangtsin and Tungnan in the Yangtze Valley near Chungking. Liu Wen-hui tried desperately to get new weaponry to continue the war but the Central Government had prohibited arms sales to Szechwan. Although he could have probably bought arms from abroad he did not have time to do so before he was defeated. Fighting was to continue into November with a battle at Luchow on the 9th which ended in a bloody stalemate. Liu Wen-hui now gathered his 90,000-strong army on the west bank of the Tokiang River and waited for Liu Hsiang to attack. In the meantime he appealed for peace and in this even received the support of two war-weary rival generals. Both General Tien Chug-yau of the 29th Army and General Teng Shih-hou of the 28th Army called for peace talks.

Their appeals did not sway Liu Hsiang, who now dealt the death blow to his enemy at the Battle of the Tokiang River. During the battle Liu Hsiang's army suffered a loss when one of the troop ships was ambushed by Liu Wen's men as it approached Chungking. Liu Wen's men opened fire with machine guns, sweeping the crowded decks, cutting down more then 200 men. When the ship pulled into its berth in Chungking the decks were 'choked with dead bodies and the scuppers running with blood'. Despite setbacks like this for Liu Hsiang, the fortunes of war were definitely running in his direction and Liu Wen was on the verge of defeat. The defeat at Tokiang was too much for Liu Wen to bear and he took a phial of poison. His life was saved against his will by the speedy actions of a local doctor and miraculously he made a full recovery. This near-death experience seems to have clarified his mind as to the real situation. By mid December Liu Wen had accepted defeat. On the 29th of December he cabled his decision to resign his post as Szechwan governor to his enemies and the government in Nanking. He promised to give up any territorial claims in Szechwan and to move the remains of his army into neighbouring Sikang province. There he hoped with the support of his still powerful army to establish his own fiefdom. As he evacuated his thousands of troops and their dependents into Sikang, a few more clashes with his rival armies did occur. Reports of sporadic fighting continued

Yunnanese soldiers of General Lung Yun's army parade on the border with Kwangtung in the mid-1930s. Troops like these were loyal first and foremost to their general and then to some degree or other to Chiang Kai-shek. Lung Yun armed and equipped his army from money largely raised from his illicit trade in opium. During the Second World War he did get some military aid from the USA, as his province was one of the few not occupied by the Japanese.

until July 1933 when his army had safely migrated iton Sikang and he had set up his new regime there. Liu Wen and his army were to face more struggles in their new home in the wilds of Sikang. The fighting had been extremely costly with a reported 10,000 dead by the end of December. The cost to the civilian population, of course, was never estimated.


## 'Spear Soldiers': Kweichow 1932–1934

Kweichow in south-west China was one of the smallest and least developed provinces in the country. Its remoteness and poverty had kept out of many conflicts in the 1910s and 1920s.

By the 1930s its electric supply was only switched on for five hours a day. Its corrupt civil servants turned up at their offices for an hour or two in the afternoon. In 1928 the then governor, General Chou Hsi-ch'eng, decided to build the first paved road in the province at great expense. He then purchased a limousine from Shanghai and had it brought to his capital Kweiyang. It had to be transported across mountains by several hundred porters, having been broken down into pieces. When it arrived with its precious supply of petrol he could then drive up and down his newly built road to nowhere. The people of Kweichow were always on the verge of starvation and the provincial or any army was often the only source of employment. When the Red Army advanced through Kweichow during their Long March in 1934–35 thousands of men from the province joined them. This was not because they had any revolutionary sympathies but simply because they wanted to 'fill their rice bowls'.

Kweichow armies had a terrible reputation with most of the troops hopelessly addicted to opium. Soldiers in Kweichow were known as 'Two-Gun Men', one a rifle, the other an opium pipe. They were also known as 'Spear Soldiers', which indicates the shortage of rifles. It was difficult to enough to provide the province's soldiers with rifles, so heavier weaponry was a rare feature of Kweichow armies. In the mid-1920s the various Kweichow armies had a total of 24 artillery pieces. These would have been exclusively mountain guns of various types and ages with some being antiques. The possession of one or two artillery pieces in the wars of south-western China could keep a general in power. Machine guns were also in short supply, with the figure of 24 again recorded. These would be leftovers from the 19th century alongside a few modern Maxims, Hotchkisses or Brownings.

As with many of the remoter Chinese provinces, Kweichow was largely left to its own devices by the Nationalist Government. In 1932 General Wang Chieh-lieh was the incumbent military governor surrounded on all sides by rebellious subordinates and devious politicians. By October that year Wang was under threat from the previous governor of the province, General Mao Kuang-hsiang, who had the backing of several units still loyal to him. Mao had been governor of Kweichow from October 1929 until March 1932 when Wang took over control. Wang mobilised a strong force to counter this rebellion with eight battalions of reasonably well trained troops. He told his neighbours in Szechwan province not to interfere in any conflict as they had done in the past. At the same time Wang received a message from Chiang Kai-shek telling him not to fight yet another civil war. When it came the civil war was short but brutal, with heavy fighting between rebel irregulars and Wang's army outside the capital Kweiyang. The rebels were led by General Mao personally but it was his subordinate, General Yu Kuo-tsai, who took the city in late November 1932. Wang decided to live to fight another day and withdrew into the countryside with one division of his loyal army with him.

By mid-May 1933, after spending the winter preparing for a comeback, General Wang had returned in triumph to his capital. His political rival General Mao and his irregulars had disappeared from the scene with their commander going into exile. Wang was now under attack from another quarter: two Generals, Chiang Chai-chin and Chia Ming-yi, were in revolt against him. In this month Wang tried to up the ante by forming his own air force – with the acquisition of one plane. At the end of May this Canadian-built light bomber was in Kweichow flown by a pilot of unknown nationality. Whether this secret weapon tipped the balance or not the two rebel generals had been defeated by August. By the end of the month however, Wang was made aware of the formation of another rebel army under the command of one of his 1932 rivals, General Yu Kuo-tsai.

Yu was on the Kweichow-Hunan border with his army preparing for an invasion of Kweichow. Wang did not wait for Yu to attack him and sent a strong Expeditionary Corps up to the western border to fight him. The rebel was defeated at a battle at the town of Tungen and was pushed back. Wang now had a little breathing space in his constant struggle with one rebellion after another. Early October saw a major boost to his war effort with the arrival of 1,000 modern rifles and 300,000 rounds of ammunition. This arms shipment arrived just in time to help Wang in his fight with a large army of five regiments of infantry led by one of the defeated generals of the May war, General Chia Ming-yi. Chia's army may well have contained a number of mercenaries from neighbouring provinces, as the press described them as coming from 'certain quarters'. The rebel general Chia was now joined by the recently defeated General Yu, whose army had been armed and equipped by his Szechwan allies. This unified army now attacked the province from two directions with a battle taking place at the town of Changyuen. General Yu Kuo-tsai's army and Wang's army fought a fierce battle which ended with a stalemate and 1,000 dead. Wang returned to Kweiyang and Yu returned to the border area to lick his wounds ready for the next round. This was a disappointment for Chiang Kai-shek, who had decided covertly to back anyone who attacked Wang. The fighting ended for the winter with Wang's loyal troops exhausted by the years of fighting.

In February 1934 three Generals, Chia Min-yi, Lei Min-chu and Yang Chi-chang, attacked the capital. Wang must have been a determined character. He continued to resist all the challenges against him regardless of the odds. In late February the rebels were joined by a strong army from Hunan province under the command of General Chen Chu-chen. Details are sketchy on how Wang did it but what we do know is that he managed somehow to heavily defeat this rebel Hunan army. Wang's victorious army then pushed the demoralised Kweichow rebels and their Hunan allies back to the border. On the way they liberated all the towns which had been in rebel hands and punished anyone who had aided the rebellion. Under agreements between Wang and the Hunanese provincial government the rebel troops were disarmed in mid-April. General Wang was always looking for ways to strengthen his position and wanted to add to his single plane. He ordered three Stinson O type trainers from the USA with the intention of turning them into improvised light bombers. The planes did arrive at Canton during 1934 but Wang did not receive them and they were eventually requisitioned by the Nationalist Government.

A new threat now appeared to Wang and Kweichow in August 1934 when a large force of troops from Yunnan province crossed the border. They established a base at the town of Panhsien in June and ignored Wang's protests but did not move against him. Wang soon had his hands full anyway with yet another rebellion, this time under General Chiang Tsai-chen. A battle took place in mid-August at Sungtao in eastern Kweichow. Wang survived this rebellion but Chiang Kai-shek's patience was running out with this troublesome province and its constantly warring generals. Chiang was prepared to do whatever it took to impose some kind of discipline on the various Kweichow armies. In May 1935 he imposed a new training programme on them in an attempt to form one unified force. This course trained 400 junior and other officers up to the rank of brigadier at a training camp at Keiyang.

## Bunraku: Li Chi-chin, the Unknown General

General Li Chi-chin was one of those mysterious figures who found themselves involved in various intrigues in northern China in the early 1930s. In 1933 Li was in his late 50s, a native of Hopei province and had had a long but unremarkable military career. Li was described in intelligence reports of the 1930s as being a 'well educated man of pleasing personality'. During the late-Imperial and Revolutionary period he had served in various military roles and had risen through the ranks. By 1913 he was reported to have reached the rank of general although it is not known which Republican army he was serving in at the time. After 1913 he disappears from the records, although he must have continued his army service, probably in an administrative role. Then in early 1933 he emerges in command of a cavalry force of 'several thousand men' under the pay of the Japanese. The only available information is that his troops had been raised in the border region between Manchukuo and northern China. General Li and his men were sent into the Luantung area to the south-west of the border town of Shanhaikwan on the Great Wall. They were under orders from their Japanese paymasters to make mischief in the disputed region south of the Great Wall. Li's force's main period of activity was during the interim between the end of fighting on the Great Wall and the signing of the Sino-Japanese Tangku pact in May 1933. His army was given the purious legitimacy of the title 'National Salvation Army' and his men fought under the five-barred flag of the 1912–28 Republic. Li claimed rather ridiculously to be fighting the Japanese and that his ambition was to set up an independent state in northern China.

As was often the case with these irregular armies, desperate men did join Li and his was reported to have grown to a strength of 10,000. During Li's short career as army commander his troops laid siege to several small towns and briefly occupied them. Li occupied the towns of Tongshan and Chinwangtao and set up what were called 'Administrative Organisations'. It was said that the General had ambitions to set up a permanent state in the coastal triangle he was allowed by the Japanese briefly to occupy. As was common, his men were allowed to loot the towns unless the population paid General Li a bribe to leave them in peace. All Li's various activities were shadow boxing to confuse the issues being discussed by the Chinese and Japanese. He had managed to create the type of turmoil that the Japanese were hoping for – but with the signing of the Tangku Treaty his usefulness to them was over. Under the terms of the treaty the Japanese were supposed to withdraw their troops to the Great Wall by mid-June. Even the Japanese could not get away with leaving behind a large body of troops led by the 'unreliable' General Li. So Li was requested/commanded to attend a Japanese conference in the city of Dairen where the situation in North China was discussed. The maverick General's force was now an embarrassment to Japan and a deal between Li and the Imperial Army was done at the conference. This involved the recruitment of 2,000 of Li's 10,000-strong army into the Peace Preservation Corps.

The Peace Preservation Corps was the armed police force recruited from the demobilised Chinese armies (see Chapter 8). Armed only with rifles, the PPC was to keep the peace in the de-militarised zone created by the Tangku Treaty. Although the PPC was officially neutral, it was largely controlled by the Japanese and was often commanded by Chinese with pro-Japanese sympathies. Whatever Li's involvement in the formation of the Peace Preservation Corps, he does not appear to have been given a command in it. He simply disappeared from the scene in the summer of 1933 as quickly as he had emerged on it in the spring. He was suspected of having gone into a comfortable retirement in the Japanese concession of Tientsin with his pockets full following his dubious military career.


## General Sun Tien-Ying, Ninghsia 1934

Ninghsia, the westernmost of the three provinces that made up Inner Mongolia, was the scene of a military campaign beginning in January 1934. It was a young province formed in 1929 with a territory covering 100,000 square miles and with a population of less than a million. The war in Ninghsia began when General Sun Tien-ying, who had commanded his 41st Army against the Japanese in Jehol in 1933, invaded the province with his 60,000-strong army. General Sun had supported Feng Yu-hsiang's 'Chahar People's Anti-Japanese Army' after withdrawing from Jehol. This role of the 41st Army, performed against Chiang Kai-shek's wishes, had led to the military formation being effectively outlawed by the Nationalist Government. Sun advanced his army through Suiyuan province with the hope of gaining some territory that he could control in the western provinces of China. In June 1933 Chiang offered Sun and his men the opportunity to move to remote Chinghai and help develop the underpopulated province. With little option, Sun and his officers agreed to the deal and as they marched westwards loyal Nationalist troops were moved in behind them. This effectively cut the 41st Army off and removed any perceived threat that they posed to the government. As far as Chiang was concerned, the local military commanders would deal with Sun and his men in due course. Sun's army made slow progress through the deserts of Suiyuan province taking food and other supplies from the population. These privations caused a tirade of complaints from local officials to the Nationalist Government. Local people and of course the military did not want the presence of an 'alien' army in their province. In November 1933 the 41st Army was ordered by Chiang to stop its advance and settle where they were for the time being. Sun had no choice but to move on as his troops were starving with no supplies coming from the government, and were on the verge of mutiny. In early January 1934 the 41st Army crossed the border between Suiyuan and the province of Ninghsia. General Sun Tien-ying immediately set up a rival regime at the town of Shihtsuishan and stated that his ambition was to conquer the whole province. This was a direct challenge to the Muslim General Ma Hung-pin, the resident governor. Ma was supported in his rule in Ninghsia by his three brothers, Generals Ma Hung-k'uei in Kansu province and Ma Pu-fang and Ma Pu-ch'ing in Chinghai province. Together they formed the Ma clique which had ruled the north-west of China since the 1910s. In addition the forces of the provinces of Shansi and Suiyuan were instructed by Chiang Kai-shek to mobilise. Although Chiang was hoping that the Ma

Nationalist soldiers on parade in Ninghsia province during the 1934 war. The primitive nature of the fighting in this 'backwater' of China is summed up by the arms carried. As far as can be seen all the regular Ninghsian soldiers are armed only with these roughly made spears. The further that he was from the centre of China, the worse the soldier was trained, equipped and armed.

clique would soon defeat Sun, he wanted one of his own men in the region. He sent General Chu Shao-liang to the north-west to take up the role of Kansu Pacification Director. Chiang's intention with this appointment was that Chu would check on the Ma Generals' resolution in dealing with Sun's Army.

The 41st Army soon moved on from its base at Shihtsuishan and began an advance on the provincial capital, Ninghsia. By the 24th of January they were only 13 miles from the capital at Likangpu as Ma Hung-pin's troops struggled to deal with the battle-hardened opposition. Another battle between the two armies took place at Pinglo near the capital, where again the local troops were close to defeat by the 41st Army troops. General Sun was nevertheless frustrated at his army's failure to capture Ninghsia, as he knew that time was running out. Without any hope of replacing losses his army would only get weaker while the Ma army would only get stronger. Reinforcements were on their way from the other Ma armies with additional troops being available from Shansi, if necessary. In addition,n the arrival of a few light bombers from Nanking tipped the balance in favour of the defending forces. Eventually General Ma Hung-pin's army moved to attack the 41st Army and by the end of January the invaders began a long retreat. In March, Yen Hsi-shan, the Shansi General, sent troops to cut off any line of retreat for Sun's 41st troops. By April General Sun was staring defeat in the face and accepted Yen's offer of sanctuary in his capital, Taiyuan. Sun's surviving troops were offered service in the Shansi Army and most happily accepted while their commander lived quietly in a modest house given to him by Yen.

## General Liu Kue-itang, January 1934

China in the early 1930s was full of military commanders who were really still no better than bandit leaders. One such character was the notorious General Liu Kue-itang, who began a rebellion against the Nanking Government in the Peking region at Christmas 1933. Liu was a former goat herder who had become a full-time bandit in 1915 at the age of 23 in the mountains of southern Shantung. After joining the Republican Army with his men, he gathered arms, ammunition and other supplies and then took to the hills. This trick was repeated several times by Liu, who used the regular army when he needed them to arm and feed his bandit army. In 1931 he and his men were incorporated once again into the army, this time in northern Shantung province. He revolted again and went on the rampage in Hopei province before agreeing to take his troops into Jehol to fight the Japanese. Next, he joined the Manchukuoan Army and was responsible for taking the city of Dolonor in Chahar province in May 1933 (see Chapter 13). In yet another switch of 'allegiance', if the word is applicable at all, Liu and his ever-loyal troops now joined the Army of the Nationalist Governor of Chahar, General Sung Che-yuan. Sung gave him the rather ridiculous title of 'Bandit Suppression Commander of Eastern Chahar'. Bandit suppressor Liu and his men set up their own protection racket demanding money from towns and villages in the territory they controlled. Having asked Sung for a better posting for his army, Liu decided that he had had enough of the quiet life and revolted again. Liu's rebellion broke out on Christmas Day 1933 at Chihcheng in eastern Chahar province, with the insurgents sacking the city. Having caused devastation in the city they advanced southwards into the Japanese-Chinese demilitarised zone. Liu's 5,000-strong army clashed with Government troops at the town of Kaoliying, 15 miles north of Peking. Liu and his men had travelled 120 miles from Chahar and fought at least a dozen skirmishes with Nationalist troops along the way. Both sides suffered casualties during the fighting around Peking and withdrew to regroup. General Liu Kue-itang's troops withdrew into the de-militarised zone south of the Great Wall where the Government troops were unable to follow. Under the terms of the Tangku Truce no Chinese troops were allowed to enter this zone and their commanders were frightened to antagonise the Japanese. Some of Liu's troops had reached as far as a few miles from the gates of Peking before being turned back. The gates of the city were closed and the soldiers moved into the villages around Peking to loot them instead. They captured a British engineer who was driving through the suburbs of Peking and took his watch and wedding ring. By early January, Liu's forces, having pillaged every area behind them, crossed the Peking–Tientsin Railway before heading southwards. They were moving in the direction of Shantung province where they hoped to take refuge in the mountains. Their straggling column included hundreds of camels and pack animals piled high with loot from plundered villages. It was expected that Liu and his men would revert to type and form a large bandit group in their mountain fastness.

Liu, like so many troublesome generals before him, went into retirement in the Japanese concession in Tientsin. He was to make a nuisance of himself two years later when he led a bandit force in armed clashes with Government troops. This armed clash took place in the vicinity of the Imperial Ming tombs, close to Liu's old stomping grounds in Peking. The clashes with General Sung Che-yuan's 29th Army were a result of Liu's move through western Hopei province into northern Honan province. His next move was expected to be into Shantung province. Governor General Han Fu-chu offered a reward for ex-General Liu of $50,000, dead or alive.

Liu Kwei-tang survived this campaign and was still active in January 1936 leading a 2,000-strong bandit force. This 'rag-tag' army made a nuisance of itself in northern Hopei taking the town of Laiyuan, just outside the Great Wall. When a strong force of the 29th Army turned up at Laiyuan to chase him away, Liu split his army into two and retreated with 1,000 men to the Hopei-Shansi border region. Here Liu's army was surrounded by two regiments of the 29th Army and three regiments of the 53rd Army and was annihilated. Liu the survivor was able to escape, whether by luck or by bribing the victorious Chinese commanders to let him flee. Seven years later in 1943 he was at last killed while in the service of the Japanese-controlled puppet government of Wang Ching-wei. This 'turncoat' General had changed sides so many times it was surprising he had any coat left – and that he managed to reach the age of 51.

# 12

# WAR IN THE WESTERN PROVINCES, 1928–37

The territory covered by the Chinese north-western provinces of Kansu, Chinghai, Ninghsia and Sinkiang was a vast and barren land of mountain and desert. These remote provinces, some of which had only recently come under the official authority of Nationalist China, were largely lawless. Here the military governor had full power over the people he ruled with little or no interference from Nanking.

Ninghsia was the most westerly province of Inner Mongolia and was controlled in the 1930s by one of the infamous Ma warlord clique, General Ma Hung-kuei. The Ma clique were an extended family of Muslim warlords who were sometimes allied and at other times at war with each other. Another of the Mas, General Ma Pu-fang, ruled the vast region which had recently been given the provincial title of Chinghai. Ma Pu-fang's brother General Ma Pu-ch'ing ruled parts of Kansu and assisted his brother, when necessary taking his troops into Chinghai.

Separated from the other north-western provinces by Tibet, Sinkiang was controlled by a series of military governors who had little recourse to Peking or later Nanking. For 17 years until 1928 Sinkiang was reasonably well ruled by Marshal Yang Tseng-hsin but he was assassinated. For the next five years his usurper General Chin Shu-jen faced some of the most bloody rebellions seen in China in the entire century. General Sheng, who overthrew Chin in 1933, brought peace of a kind to Sinkiang but at the cost of 100,000 political killings.

## War in Kansu, 1926–1936

Kansu province was one of the most remote but troubled in China with 125,000 square miles populated with approximately 6,500,000 people. During the 1920s and 1930s the province was hit by three major earthquakes, in 1920, 1930 and 1936. A famine which began in the late 1920s lasted into the early 1930s with millions dying. A second famine in 1936 – less severe – meant three million, or almost half of the population, being dependent on what little relief reached them. During the 1928–30 famine it was reported that people ate their children, as well as the dead. Kansu province had come under the control of Feng Yu-hsiang and his Kuominchun in 1925 on the death of the previous military governor, General Lu Hung-tao. Feng tried to rule the province with a lighter hand at first but the people of Kansu were never going to let themselves be ruled by a non-believer.

The population was against any alien army being in their province, never mind a non-Muslim one. A low level rebellion began in 1926 under the command of a rival of the last governor, Li Chang-ch'ing. This revolt was soon dealt with by the Kuominchun leadership in Kansu, who arranged for Li and his closest followers to be murdered. Kuominchun control over Kansu continued for the next two years with Feng trying to introduce the same reforms he had in the other provinces he controlled.

During the 1926–28 period the Muslim resentment against Kuominchun rule built and erupted into one of the most savage rebellions. An earthquake in 1927 caused much suffering and the continuing demands of Feng Yu-hsiang's tax collectors were the final straw. When Feng tried to raise the level of taxes in the spring of 1928 the traditional hatred between the Muslims and Han Chinese meant war. Muslim armies now rose up all over the province under the leadership of Ma Ting-hsiang. The famed horsemen of Kansu flocked to join the rebellion and Ma's armies laid siege to the city of Hochow. Hochow was under siege on three separate occasions, Kuominchun forces coming to its relief each time. Every time the Kuominchun subdued the rebellion in one part of the vast province it broke out somewhere else. The main centre of the rebellion was in the south-west of the province where thousands died in the brutal fighting. Cruelties committed by both armies were described at the time as medieval. Men, women and children were killed without mercy and often after torture. When the main rebellion apparently ended in September 1928, it was estimated that at least 100,000 were dead.

The rebellion itself was, however, far from dead; it started again in January 1929 but this time the fighting was even more intense. In February a 20,000-strong Muslim army took the city of Tangar. Five thousand Han Chinese families living there. In a two-hour occupation the Muslim troops killed 2,000 people, mostly putting them to the sword. The frenzy of the swordsmen often left the victims still alive with terrible wounds, which meant a slow death as there were not even any bandages, let alone surgeons. Their killers were too busy looting to give them the coup de grâce. When they left the city it was totally destroyed and hundreds lay dying. Wars in Kansu had always been brutal with no tradition of taking prisoners and civilians treated abominably.

In May 1930 a particularly savage Muslim group the Salari took the town of Tsinchow. The Salari took the town so easily that it was reported that they suffered no casualties. This did not save the population; 4,000 of the townspeople were killed and another 2,000 were wounded. All possessions and food was stolen. According to a correspondent in Kansu at the time, the Salari were capable of raising an army 50,000-strong when necessary. They simply ordered every non-soldiering male to fight regardless of age or infirmity, and then gave them a sword or lance.

In October 1930 in a typical action a large bandit army besieged the town of Lihsien in Southern Kansu. The townspeople put up a stiff resistance as they knew that if their town fell they would be shown no mercy. When the army finally took the town they killed 8,000 of the inhabitants and dragged off most of the women. With this fate in mind some cities and towns put up a fanatical resistance with women fighting alongside men. In March 1929 the people of one town decided to take revenge on their tormentors, ambushing a 2,000-strong army. The Muslims were slaughtered to a man. Women fighters amongst the avenging townspeople were said to have taken particular pleasure in despatching the prisoners. As with most rebellions, the one in Kansu gradually lost steam but not before the death of a reported 2,000,000 people. Many of these deaths were from starvation as the agonies of a horrific famine were added to the people killed. Every time the rebellion was supposed to be under control it broke out again in another part of the province.

After the defeat of the Kuominchun in the war with the Nationalist Government, in August 1931 General Ma Hung-ping was appointed governor of Kansu. His rule was going to be short as on the 31st of the same month he was overthrown by a coup in the provincial capital, Lancchowfu. The coup was organised by General Ma Wen-chu, whose troops took the capital and imprisoned Ma Hung-ping. There was some fighting in the capital but the transfer of power was relatively peaceful compared to the usual Kansu bloodbath. Another Ma, General Ma Hung-kuei, marched his 15th Army into Kansu to sort out this local feud before Chiang Kai-shek could get involved. The arrival of that Ma's troops from neighbouring Ninghsia province settled the affair peacefully. In January 1932, Ma Wen-chu was himself overthrown by General Kao Chen-pang in 1936. General Yu Hsieh-chung was installed as governor. Between 1931 and 1936 there were at least four different civil governors but this was par for the course in China at the time.

## Ninghsia and Chinghai Armies

Ninghsia and Chinghai provinces were remote from Nanking and the Nationalist Government. The advantage for the military governors of these provinces was that they faced little interference from the government; the disadvantage was that they could expect little help with internal or external threats. Ninghsia was threatened by maverick General Sun Tien-yang's army in 1934 (see chapter 11) and Chinghai was under attack by the Tibetans in the early 1930s. Because both provinces were under threat during the 1930s they had to maintain reasonably strong armies. Ma Hung-kuei's Ninghsia army in the mid-1930s was about 40,000 strong and was largely made up of poorly armed cavalry. The General paid little attention to his superiors in Nanking and ran his province and his army how he saw fit. When the Red Army moved across his territory in 1934 he proudly boasted that he would annihilate them. His long-suffering soldiers had other ideas and most refused to fight or simply melted away back to their villages. This was hardly surprising when most of them had not received any pay during their service and had even to buy their own uniform! If the average soldier could have afforded his own rifle then it is pretty certain that Ma would have insisted on it. As it was, they often had to borrow money to pay for their uniforms and any equipment they had. On paper Ma Hung-kuei had a sizeable army but because of its unreliability he had forcibly to recruit a large number of irregular 'gate guards'. These men were responsible for guarding towns and forts that Ma controlled and were able to exploit the local population to pay for them.

A soldier of the Kansu army in the middle of a market crowd in the early 1930s. Soldiers in the remote north-western provinces of China were not renowned for their spit and polish. This soldier is wearing a padded cotton jacket and trousers with a yak fur hat and he has a canvas bandolier and blanket roll. His rifle is an older model which could be any type used by the pre-1908 Imperial Army or the post-1911 Republican Army.

Ma Pu-fang's Chinghai army fluctuated in size in the 1930s but was about 30,000–40,000 strong. Recruitment was a constant problem so his army was much smaller than he would have liked. Conditions in his army were terrible. Even when Ma reduced taxes on the families of all his soldiers the number of recruits coming forward did not increase. He had to resort to recruiting or press-ganging tribesmen from Tibet and the border region, where the people were more desperate for employment.

## War in Sinkiang and Chin Shu-jen's Army, 1928–1933

Sinkiang, also known as Chinese Turkestan, was a vast province to the north of Tibet and covering 550,500 square miles with a population of 2,500,000 in 1931. Its population was nearly all Muslims but was divided between the ethnically Chinese Tungans and the Turkic Uyghurs. Although the Uyghurs and Tungans were co-religionists, they differed in every other way and often fought each other. As Sinkiang was close to the Russian border its governors had often come under the sway of first, the Imperial Russian, and then Soviet, governments. On the 7th of July 1928 the Governor of the province of Sinkiang, Marshal Yang Tseng-hsin, whose seat of government was in the city of Urumchi, was assassinated. Yang Tseng-hsin had started his career in Sinkiang in the late 19th century serving in various Qing Imperial positions. At the time of the Revolution in 1911 Yang was in command of 2,000 Tungan troops, the strongest military force in Sinkiang. In 1912 Yang swore his loyalty to the new Republic and was rewarded with the military governorship of the province. Over the next few years Yang was able to bring a sort of peace to the restless province using his military strength to crush any rebellions that surfaced. These rebellions were usually motivated by a mixture of religious and ethnic disputes between the Chinese and Turkic peoples. Over the next 16 years Yang earned a reputation as an able but harsh administrator who tried to improve conditions in Sinkiang. His autocratic rule in Sinkiang obviously made him enemies and Yang himself realised that his power was waning as he aged. The victory of Chiang Kai-shek's Northern Expedition in far-off northern China in 1928 was greeted by the raising of the Nationalist flag in Sinkiang. The province's allegiance to Chiang did not go down well with many of Yang's officials and his days appeared to be numbered. Yang was well aware of the rising opposition to his rule but before the 61-year-old could leave the province he was gunned down at a banquet. He was quickly replaced by a non-Muslim Han Chinese from Kansu province, Chin Shu-jen. Chin immediately asked for recognition from Chiang Kai-shek as he purged his government of both pro-Yang (and even anti) officials. These were replaced by a number of fellow Kansu officials, which did not endear him to the people of Sinkiang.

Chin knew that he needed to build up his military strength if he was to survive as military governor. The appointment of his two sons as the highest ranking military officers in his expanded army was a poor decision. He also promoted his body servant to command a regiment and other loyal members of his entourage to other military commands. These appointments may have guaranteed his commanders' loyalty but most of his army officers were complete novices. Recruits to his army were also of poor quality and were described as a pack of 'undisciplined rowdies'. This ramshackle army was supplemented by the arrival of several thousand Manchurian troops from across the Soviet border. In Manchuria in 1931 as units of the North-Eastern Army pushed towards the Siberian border, a number crossed it and were interned by the Russians. They were well treated as they were seen as a useful military force which could be used to the Soviet Union's advantage. The Manchurian troops were led by General Sheng Shi-tsai, who was more than willing to co-operate with the Soviets. In March 1933 the Manchurians under the title of the 'North-Eastern National Salvation Army' were taken by Russian trains to the Sinkiang border. These 2,000 troops were described by eyewitnesses as 'regular soldiers, well disciplined, well trained and full of fighting spirit'. They were to make a huge difference to Chin's military strength. In 1931 Chin Shu-jen decided to form an air arm to help him hold on to power and in September he purchased two Soviet R-1 light bombers. These planes, copies of the British DH-9A, were ideal in the anti-insurgent role and were flown by two Russian pilots. In May 1932 Chin bought another eight aircraft, two more R-1s, 3 Polikarpov U-2 trainers and 2 Kalinin K-5 passenger planes. Chin Shu-jen also tried to improve the weaponry of his army and imported weapons mainly from British India. These arms shipments included in 1932 the receipt of 4,000 Lee Enfield .303 rifles along with 4 million rounds of ammunition. He also received some weaponry from the Soviet Union under secret agreements he kept even from his closest advisors. Chin's army included a number of White Russian refugees who had escaped to the province after the Russian Civil War in 1922. These desperate men formed a 250-strong foreign legion, which on several occasions saved Chin from defeat. Under the command of a Colonel Pappengut, a former Tsarist and White Russian officer, this mainly cavalry force was eventually expanded to 1,500 men. All the White Russians were eventually formed into three regiments which were mainly cavalry but there were some infantry units as well. Most of the White Russians were not willing volunteers but had little choice when faced with Chin's conscription policy. The only alternative was forced repatriation together with their families to Stalin's Russia and a gruesome fate. Chin had also tried to supplement his forces with the elite Buddhist cavalry of the Torgut leader Sengtsen Gegen. Sengtsen, who was the spiritual leader or 'Living Buddha' of the Torgut Buddhists, refused to put his men at Chin's disposal when asked to send them against the rebels at Hami. The Sinkiang Governor later got his revenge when he had Sengtsen and his entourage shot at his headquarters in 1932.

## The Kumul Rebellion, 1931–1934

The city of Hami became a hotbed of anti-Chin feeling, resulting in rebellions that devastated Sinkiang in the early 1930s. For centuries the city had been ruled by a Turkic vassal king with little interference from the provincial capital at Urumchi. When the last of these kings, Shah Maqsud, died in 1930, Chin took the opportunity to abolish this archaic institution. About the same time a small number of refugees from fighting in Kansu province asked for sanctuary in the Hami region. Chin not only gave the 100 refugees from his own province shelter, he also handed them land that belonged to the local Turkic citizens. They were compensated with desert land that needed to be worked before it was suitable for crops. Turkic resentment was finally pushed to the limit by a marriage which took place between a Han Chinese tax collector and a local Turkic girl. In March 1931 the locals killed the tax collector, his innocent bride and every Kansu refugee they could get their hands on. Chin despatched a military force to the region, which put down the rebellion with the same kind of barbaric brutality. They killed every Uyghur they could get their hands on and burned down villages and destroyed crops and livestock. The survivors of Chin's revenge attacks withdrew to the mountains and prepared to get their own revenge in due course. The last King of Hami's advisors, Khoja Niaz and Yolbars Khan, now became the leaders of the rebellion. These men were desperate for assistance in what they knew would be a long and bitter struggle with Chin. They sent messengers to neighbouring Kansu province, where a local young warlord had been making a name for himself over the past few years. The young warlord was a 25-year-old Kansu native by the name of Ma Chung-yin, who had been fighting since his early teens. Ma was a distant relative of the members of the Ma clique who dominated north-western China in the 1920s and 1930s. He was a ferocious fighter who, according to one western eyewitness, was 'child-like, naïve, helpful and sympathetic, but he could also display barbarous cruelty and kill the whole population of places he captured … If he was annoyed, he could shoot down with his own pistol an officer or soldier who had committed an error. He was said to have shot down his own cook in this way when dinner was not ready at the appointed time.' He was pleased to receive this invitation from

This Chinghai provincial soldier poses proudly outside his barracks during the war against the Tibetans in 1932. He is wearing a typical winter uniform worn by most Chinese troops with his yak fur hat and wadded cotton jacket and trousers. His footwear and puttees were designed to keep his feet warm in the severe conditions faced by both armies in the 1930–32 war. He has a spare pair of cloth shoes tied to his back pack and has a German-made MP-28 sub-machine gun slung over his shoulder.

Sinkiang as his campaigns in Kansu were failing and he wanted a new challenge. Preparations were made by Ma and he managed to gather a small army of 500 cavalry but could only arm about half of them with rifles. The rest had their traditional sabres with the intention that they would soon capture brand-new rifles from the enemy. It was 350 kilometres from his base at Anhsi to Hami and it was the middle of the summer when he set off. With insufficient provisions his hardy horsemen suffered terribly in crossing the waterless desert. When they arrived in the Hami region they did not take time to rest and recuperate but went straight into action. His army took the town of Barkul, the population welcoming him as a liberator and giving him the 2,000 rifles from the local arsenal. Gathering volunteers he could now arm, he advanced towards the city of Hami and prepared to lay siege to it.

When Ma arrived with his 2,000 or so Tungan troops in front of the walls of Hami the Chinese garrison did not, as he might have expected, open the city's gates for him. Instead they put up a desperate resistance expecting little mercy at the hands of the besiegers if they were defeated. In command of the defenders were two officers, General Chu in charge of the new parts of the city of Hami and General Hsiung the old quarter. The siege of Hami was to last for six months before Ma realised that he did not have the men or the weaponry to capture the city. Both armies had rifles and a few machine guns but there was no mention in any of the reports of artillery in either army. Two English lady explorers, Mildred Cable and Francesca French, were trapped in the city. According to the explorers the defenders, when running low on ammunition, checked the city's ancient armoury. In there they found old fire arrows, which the defenders used to good effect against the Tungan positions. Other primitive weaponry employed by the defenders included boiling oil, which was poured over the attackers and until it ran out. The attackers dug trenches close to the wall and began to dig tunnels under the walls to undermine them in the sapper method used for centuries. Scaling ladders were used but in a reported 48 assaults Ma's men were unable to breach the walls. Any small breach that was made in the walls were soon filled with bales of wool by the defenders. After six months the defenders were running out of food and all cattle had been slaughtered long ago. Both armies were out of ammunition and swords were the main weapons used in the skirmishes. Ma had grown tired of the siege and held a meeting with his officers about what to do next. They realised that with the resources they had the city would never fall and the morale of their unruly army was at breaking point. Ma decided to take what remained of his army back to Kansu in order to equip and re-arm them ready for the next campaign.

### The 36th Division and Tungan Weaponry

In a twist Ma Chung-yin now sought employment with the Chinese Government and was surprisingly given command of the Nationalist 36th Division. Nationalist thinking was that it was better to have Ma in their pay and to use him against the too-independent Chin in Sinkiang. Chiang Kai-shek had long been unhappy with Sinkiang's burgeoning relationship with the Russians. He was worried that the province was fast becoming a satellite of the Soviet Union, dealing directly with Moscow without reference to Nanking. Ma established his Divisional HQ in the city of Soochow in February 1932 and began to recruit soldiers for his unit with the aid of Nationalist gold. Although an able and courageous soldier, Ma began to show the instability which was a feature of his command. He could be incredibly cruel when campaigning and had no pity for the plight of the civilians his army came across. Any soldiers of his army who transgressed could also expect no mercy and desertion was dealt with the beheading sword. On at least one occasion Ma delivered the punishment personally, beheading five soldiers who had tried to run away. Training for his 36th Division usually included dodging live bullets and even on occasion home-made grenades. As a young man Ma pushed himself hard in training and expected his men to match him in horsemanship, running and shooting.

Ma's division was split into several Regiments of cavalry with his elite unit called the 'White' Regiment armed with both carbines and large fighting swords. The other two units which made up his cavalry element were the 'Black' and 'Brown' Regiments, each about 2,000 strong. They were armed with a wide variety of carbines of all types and ages with some described as antique pieces. In addition Ma had a large infantry force armed with Gew-88 rifles; their officers all had C-96 semi-automatic pistols.

Some weaponry used by the Tungan Army would make a fine museum exhibition of small arms: US-made Winchester repeaters and Snyders, Victorian era Lee Metfords, Japanese Murati rifles, German Gew-88s and Remington M1917 rifles stamped with Imperial Russian eagles. His troops also captured at Urumchi a large number of Moisin-Nagant M1930 rifles fresh from the factory. Most artillery was mountain guns dating from the 19th century. Ma's troops captured an armoured car from the Sinkiang Army but this was abandoned in early 1934 having not seen action. Ahmad Kamal, who spent several months with the Tungan Army, was taken by General Ma Chung-yin to inspect his primitive armoury. All of Ma's munitions were stored in an ancient warehouse with separate rooms for each type of weaponry. Ma had a large number of Mauser semi-automatics, a popular side-arm with all Chinese armies. His modern rifles were a mixture of British, German and Russian types with the Lee Enfield .303 one of the most numerous. Other rifles included Savage sports rifles probably left behind by an expedition in the 1920s. Rifles were in a dozen different calibres from .22 to .440 and were in various conditions from brand new to rusted away. The thousands of grenades in his armoury were all live and were described by Kamal. There were 'Russian bombs that looked much like wine bottles, and others like baby rattles. Most were of local manufacture and round as the proverbial cartoon bomb, with small shielded shank and dynamite fuse.' Machine guns seen by Kamal included crates full of Lewis light machine guns which he saw being unwrapped by the armoury workers. Artillery used by Ma's Tungan Army included a number of ex-Russian mountain guns and one Krupp light gun. One impressive looking gun was mounted on the back of a modern truck but on closer inspection it turned out to be a Russian muzzle loader from the early 19th century.

### Urumchi under Siege, 1933

While Ma Chung-yin was away from the campaign in Sinkiang his second in command Ma Shih-ming continued the fight against Chin. In January 1933 Ma Shih-ming and his army advanced on the provincial capital Urumchi, laying waste the countryside. They were reported to have slaughtered any Han Chinese that they came across. As the murderous forces of Ma got closer to Urumchi the local Chinese were told to take shelter inside the city's walls. The siege began in February with the city defended by a mere 700 men until the arrival of a 300-strong reinforcement of White Russians. Panic ran around the neighbouring villages and all White Russian émigrés fled to the relative safety of the city. Local militias were raised to defend the city with the White Russian men, many of whom were ex-soldiers, taking the lead. An ad hoc force was organised and went out from Urumchi to attack the Tungan forces, whom they managed to push back temporarily. On the night of the 21st of February a surprise night attack by the Tungans penetrated the city's defences and they rampaged through its western suburbs. There followed a massacre in which civilians were tortured to death in 'indescribable ways'. Just when all seemed lost a relief force of Tungpei troops under General Sheng Shih-ts'ai arrived. The arrival of the disciplined troops of Sheng made the Tungans lose heart and they prepared to lift the siege. After a few days more fighting the Tungans had to withdraw and rode off into the mountains carrying loot and captured women with them. During the siege both sides had committed atrocities as age-old enmities rose to the surface. People were summarily shot along ethnic lines. Carts spent days clearing the 6,000 people who were killed in this short but brutal battle for the city.

A second assault on Urumchi began in the spring with the city completely cut off from outside help. Chin now made the fatal mistake of mistreating the

A Tungan irregular Muslim soldier poses in the courtyard of his barracks in 1934 with his Lee Enfield .303 rifle. The rifle is held steady by a stand and also with the stick he holds in his left hand to allow him in theory to fire accurately from a long distance. Behind his comrade is armed with a Moisin-Nagant M1891 rifle.

White Russians who had proved crucial in repelling the first siege. The Russians had previously been given the worst of the weapons available and the worst horses, and were not issued with saddles. When there was a shortage of horses he insisted that they fight as infantry, even though most were superb horsemen. At the same time the White Russians were always given the most dangerous assignments. On the 11th of April the White Russians took matters into their own hands and went to Chin's headquarters to protest. When he refused to see them they returned next day and a fire fight between Chin's guard and 70 White Russians took place. When a few Russians were killed, the main 500-strong cavalry unit of White Russians stormed Chin's palace, which was defended by 250 bodyguards. Chin disguised himself as an ordinary soldier, climbed the palace walls and disappeared into the night. He was accompanied by a handful of followers as he rode off into the desert leaving his brother and others from his entourage behind. The victorious Russians took revenge on a few of Chin's high ranking officers, who were shot, along with the defeated leader's luckless brother.

### Sheng Shih-ts'ai's Rise to Power

Sheng Shih-ts'ai was an unusual character whose muddled politics pushed him into the Soviet camp in the 1930s. Born in Manchuria much of his military education took place in Japan alongside Chiang Kai-shek. He fought against Chiang's National Revolutionary Army during the Northern Expedition and for the Nationalists during the Japanese invasion of Manchuria. When he seized power in Sinkiang he espoused left wing politics and issued Marxist sounding manifestoes. In reality though, he was an unreformed warlord who ruled Sinkiang through fear, killing many thousands of his political opponents. (During the 1940s he would be welcomed back into the Nationalist fold by the ever pragmatic Chiang Kai-shek.)

At a meeting of the civic leaders in Urumchi on the 14th of April it was decided to make the Minister of Education, Liu Wen-lung, the new civil governor of Sinkiang. More importantly in this time of crisis, the Manchurian General Sheng

Shih-ts'ai was promoted to military governor of the province. Former Governor Chin meanwhile had fled to the town of Chuguchaq, where he tried to organise a counter-coup. When only a handful of supporters joined him he realised his political career was over and he crossed the border into the Soviet Union. Sheng soon emerged as the undisputed ruler of Sinkiang and began to kill any political opponents he felt threatened him. In 1934 he instituted a wide-scale purge in which the majority of his political opponents were eliminated. His fanatical hatred of the Japanese after his experiences in Manchuria pushed him further into the arms of the neighbouring Soviet Union. He established trade links with them and gradually, as their influence grew, Sinkiang became a satellite state.

Sheng Shih-ts'ai's army was built not surprisingly around the survivors of the 2,000 Manchurian troops he had brought to Sinkiang. Locally these troops were known as Tungpei, or north-eastern troops, and were probably reinforced during Sheng's control of Sinkiang by other refugee Manchurians. He also had a large number of White Russians who were inherited from Chin's Army, as they were willing to fight for whoever controlled Sinkiang. The White Russian force expanded to nearly 3,000 during 1933. They were under the overall command of a White General Bektieieff who was described as the field commander of the provincial army. He had his own White Russian staff and his troops often operated as a separate 'elite' force within the Sinkiang army. The rest of his army was made up of Mongols and Turkics, who were often press-ganged into service. Sheng would recruit or conscript anyone willing to fight for him from the sparse and diverse population of Sinkiang.

By 1934 it was claimed that the Sinkiang army had expanded to at least 20,000 men with some reports saying 30,000. Unfortunately for Sheng, the only dependable troops were said to be the White Russians who were constantly under the threat of deportation to the Soviet Union. In July 1933 his army was joined by the troops of a defecting rebel leader, Khoja Niyas Haiji. He was one of the two leaders of the 1931 Kumul Rebellion; but Sheng offered him the command of all provincial forces in the southern regions of Sinkiang. When Khoja Niyas Haiji agreed to defect and marched his army southwards from Urumchi he was attacked by a larger Tungan Army. The survivors set up a new headquarters in the Kashgaria Region to act as an auxiliary force for the Sinkiang army. Sheng gave them the task of trying to counter the movement of Tungan forces through their territory.

Sheng knew that it would be a good idea to enlarge the air arm he had inherited from Governor Chin in 1933. He also tried set up a flying school in the capital Urumchi but this was disrupted by the Ma Chung-yin rebellion. When Ma Chung-yin's army took Urumchi they captured two of the Russian aircraft at the airport but with no pilots to fly them they probably destroyed them. During the rebellion Sheng received air support from the Soviet Union who used R-5 light bombers and U-2 trainers against the rebels. The flying school was set up with Soviet personnel and the R-5s and U-2s were sold to Sheng at a knock down price. In 1934 all 18 of Sheng's Russian aircraft were destroyed in a hurricane but these were replaced by the Soviet Union. It is known that 12 of the R-5s were supplied to Sheng as a gift 'from the people of the USSR'.

## Ma Chung-yin's Second Campaign, 1933

With the failure of his army to capture Urumchi, General Ma Chung-yin decided to return to the fray. He had spent 18 months recuperating in Kansu province and felt ready to resume his campaign to conquer Sinkiang. His army had been expanded and his armourers had been working overtime to arm his mainly cavalry force. The size of his army was unknown but it was estimated that it was up to ten times the strength of his 1931 force, or about 20,000. It was also described as being better trained, better armed and better paid and had been joined by many Uyghur recruits. Other troops had been conscripted and had received little training and were to be treated as cannon fodder during the coming fighting. In May 1933 Ma sent his brother Ma Chung-chieh with 2,500 cavalry to capture the town of Kumul, which was done with little fighting. Sheng Shih-ts'ai had positioned 5,000 of his best troops along the line of the Tungan army advance. As the main Tungan Army moved towards their first objective at Kitai, on the 23rd of May Sheng left Urumchi at the head of a 5,000-strong army including 1,000 White Russians. The two armies clashed outside Kitai and the Tungans were victorious, although Ma Chung-chieh was killed. As things went from bad to worse for Sheng, his defeated army limped back to Urumchi and began to prepare for a second siege. He also received reports that several of his commanders in outlying regions were offering to bring their troops over to Ma. The Tungan army began to advance towards the capital with the white banner of their leader carried in front of them with the black character for 'Ma' in the centre. Sheng led his army out again to try and stop Ma's advance and met him in battle at the village of Tzu-ni-chuan in mid-June. This time Sheng's army were victorious and the Tungan army withdrew to prepare for the next battle. Just then the weather suddenly became much colder and the warmlyl dressed Manchurians and White Russians were at an advantage. Ma's Tungan troops were wearing summer uniforms and as they began to suffer in the cold, morale dropped. They withdrew from the frontline to rearm and re-equip and were soon ready to begin their campaign again. The summer and autumn of 1933 saw Sheng back in Urumchi and Ma's Army reorganising for a final battle. After an abortive peace negotiation initiated by Nationalist officials that broke down because of mutual distrust between Sheng and Ma, the war resumed. In December 1933 General Ma made a dash to try and capture Urumchi before Sheng could react. The Tungan army marched 1,500 miles across the desert and Sheng's army prepared its defences in Urumchi. In desperation, Sheng sent appeals to his Soviet friends to come to his aid and fortunately for him, they responded.

## The East Turkestan Republic, 1932–33

The ongoing war between General Ma's Army and the provincial forces of General Sheng was now complicated by another rebellion, this time by the Turkic-speaking Uyghur population of Sinkiang. A declaration of independence was proclaimed on the 13th of February 1933 and its new flag of a white field with a blue crescent and star was unveiled. It was based in the city of Kashgar and a cabinet was organised and it appeared to have all the appearance of a legitimate government. The government called for support from Afghanistan and Turkey and all Muslims around the world. Knowing that the government of Sinkiang was not going to tolerate a breakaway state, the East Turkestan Republic, or ETR, began to raise an army. Within a short time they had two divisions, named the 'Qeshqer' and 'Khotan', with a total strength of 22,000 men. Further formations were added to the ETR army, which may have reached a strength of 60,000 men. Negotiators were sent to Afghanistan to buy arms and ammunition and extra taxes were levied to pay for them. The ETR also asked for any Turkish soldiers or civilians who had lost favour with Kemal Ataturk's government to join them. The emergence of this Muslim state on their southern borders alarmed the Soviet Union, still fighting the last vestiges of their own Islamic insurgency. They worried that if the ETR was to survive it could be used as a base by the Basmachi guerrillas from Soviet Central Asia. As Sheng was struggling to deal with the Tungan rebellion and this new threat from the East Turkestan Army, they decided the help him.

### Soviet Intervention in Sinkiang, 1934–42

As the fighting was going against General Sheng and his army he approached Soviet diplomats in late 1933 about getting some military assistance. Sheng had established close ties with the Soviet Union and it was in their interests to keep him in power.

In January 1934 General Sheng Sheh-t'sai received his hoped-for reinforcement when two Soviet brigades marched south-eastwards across the Sinkiang-Soviet border. These two brigades were the 'Altayiiski', recruited in the Altay region, and the 'Tarbakhataiskii', recruited from the ranks of the GPU. The GPU were the internal security force of the Soviet Union. They were about to take part in a secret mission in Sinkiang. All the men were either wearing civilian dress or in

Ma Chung-ying 'Big Horse' was the cruel and enigmatic Muslim warlord whose wild soldiers devastated large parts of Sinkiang province in the early 1930s. Ma began his military career in his teens and soon won a reputation for cavalry raids against local Nationalist Chinese armies. Although he was seen as a champion of the Chinese Muslim population, anyone who resisted him, no matter what their religion, was slain. He is wearing the uniform of an officer of the Nationalist 36th Division during his command of the unit. Nationalist politicians offered him the command in a classic attempt to employ a 'thief to catch a thief'.

some cases Chinese uniforms, while the cavalry wore Cossack dress. They were, however, all armed with brand new Moisin-Nagant rifles and this secret Soviet army included some armoured cars and artillery as well as a few light tanks. About 7,000 men took part in the Soviet intervention, which was deemed by their command to be sufficient to crush the Muslim rebellion. Air support was offered by some R5 light bombers without markings, which during the fighting were reported to have dropped gas on the Tungan army.

According to the *Times* correspondent Peter Fleming who was in Sinkiang at the time, this Soviet Expeditionary force fought the Tungan army at the Tutun River. In several days of running battles the fanatical Muslim cavalry came close to defeating the Soviet troops. In one engagement a 500-strong Tungan cavalry force ambushed some Soviet armoured cars and pushed some of them off a mountain road. The Soviet force was on the verge of defeat when in a strange twist of fate a White Russian force saved them. Finally the tanks and armoured cars of the GPU troops prevailed and General Ma Ching-ying retreated. They were chased by a mixed force of Manchurian, Chinese, White Russian and Soviet troops. By this time the White Russians were under the command of Soviet officers, who purged any officers who were anti-Soviet. Once they had defeated the Tungans the Soviet expeditionary force was used to defeat the already demoralised ETR Army. It was in fact the 'puppet' troops of the turncoat Khoja Niyas Hajji who finally cornered and defeated the last remnants of the ETR Army and arrested its leaders. Apart from a skeleton force, the Soviet troops were then withdrawn from Sinkiang; but the threat of further intervention kept Sheng in power. He was now advised by a five-strong Soviet team which included two military advisors who had a small GPU force in Urumchi. This situation prevailed for almost 10 years until in 1942 in a complete 'about face' Sheng threw out the Soviets. He demanded the withdrawal of all Soviet military and civilian personnel from Sinkiang. Although he regretted this decision and tried to invite the Russians back in, he had miscalculated badly. Somehow he managed to hold on to power in Sinkiang until 1944 when he was ordered to go to Chungking, the Nationalist wartime capital. Chiang Kai-shek did not shoot him as he might have done – instead gave him the post, bizarrely enough, as forestry minister.

## Ma's 1934 Campaign and Survival of the Tungan Army

Despite several reverses at the hands of the Soviet expeditionary force, Ma Chung-yin's Tungan army was still in the field in January 1934. Besides the Soviet troops Ma also had to contend with Uyghur forces under the turncoat Khoja Niyas Hajji who were now fighting for Sheng. They had been armed by the Soviets with new Moisin-Nagant rifles but their morale was low. Ma captured their Headquarters at Aksu, which was defended by 800 Uyghur troops who were slaughtered by the Tungans. Khoja Niyas Hajji's army now withdrew to Kashgar with 1,500 men on the 13th of January. With his position in Kashgar untenable, Khoja Niyas gathered all his forces together to move to the Oasis town of Yangi Hissar. Yangi Hissar was already under siege by the Tungans and after two weeks the town fell with the whole of the 500-strong garrison killed by Ma's men.

The garrison were only armed with old rifles but managed to kill several hundred of Ma's men. Ma's troops were relatively well armed with modern rifles, machine guns and several mountain guns. It did not take long for the garrison to run out of ammunition and they had to turn to more primitive weaponry: bows and arrows, spears, broadswords and bombs filled with oil as localised Molotov cocktails. The defenders somehow managed to hold off the besiegers with these medieval armaments from their last defences in the town's citadel. On the 26th of March the siege was broken by subterfuge when the defenders stopped fighting to observe a Muslim holy day. Ma's men, although Muslims, decided to take advantage of this one-sided truce to complete the mine they had dug under the walls of the citadel. When the mine was exploded Ma's troops armed with swords rushed through the breach created by the explosion and killed without mercy. The commander of the garrison was captured and beheaded, his head being put to immediate use. As was often the tradition in Central Asia, it was taken to the parade ground and used as a football by the victorious soldiers.

No matter how many towns fell and how many victories it achieved, the Tungan army was now war-weary. Several cities were looted by Ma's troops during the spring including Kashgar Old City, where 2,000 civilians were massacred. By April Ma still had 10,000 men under this command but even he had begun to realise that eventually he would be defeated. His forces took Kashgar and Ma established the city as his new headquarters but he was not sure how long he could hold it. Sheng Shih-ts'ai had the support of the Soviet force for as long as he needed it and Ma would struggle to hold his army together. Suddenly in early July Ma left Kashgar with a handful of his most trusted men and arrived at the Soviet border on the 7th. His 50-strong bodyguard disappeared into the desert and Ma and four of his officers crossed the border into the Soviet Union. Whatever deal Ma had done with the Russians, he appeared to have settled quietly in his exile – but his legend did not end there. According to the most romantic report he went on to fight for the Republicans in the Spanish Civil War. Others believe that like many foreign exiles, he ended up as one of the thousands of victims in Stalin's purges of the late 1930s.

Ma's abandonment of his Tungan troops did not end their war against Sheng and a large force continued to fight for several years. In 1935 the Tungan army was under the control of Ma Ho-san, a 22-year-old in the mould of Ma Chung-yin. He had established bases in a number of oases in the South of Sinkiang and had at least 15,000 men under his command. These were all armed with rifles but there was also a large number of auxiliaries attached to the army armed only with swords. Most of the armed troops were made up of well mounted cavalry giving the army a great deal of mobility. The army's heavier equipment included a handful of machine guns and several light cannon and mountain guns. All the officers were Tungans but the vast majority of the rank and file were Turkic. Tungan soldiers were described as born fighters but the Turkic element had to be constantly trained to keep up to standard. According to Peter Fleming this army still constituted the most 'formidable fighting force in the province' in the mid 1930s.

## War on the Tibetan-Chinese Border, 1930–1937

Tibet, the 'hermit kingdom', had officially been part of China for centuries but it was ruled with a very light hand from Peking in the early 20th Century. Since the late 1700s the Qing Imperial control of Tibet had waned as the Chinese had enough problems without interfering too much in the remote kingdom. The defeat of the Chinese in the Sino-Japanese War of 1894–95 and the British invasion of Tibet in 1904 further reduced Qing influence. Britain's short-term occupation of Lhasa, the Tibetan capital, strengthened their contacts with the Tibetans and their leader, the 13th Dalai Lama. During the Chinese Republic from 1912 to 1928 China did try and re-establish some control over Tibet. The Republican Army invaded and fought a border war in 1917 with the Tibetans but there was no serious attempt to occupy Tibet.

In 1914 a British diplomat had recommended the expansion and modernisation of the Tibetan Army. It was suggested that it should have a strength of 15,000 men and would be supplied with modern armaments by the British. The British government supplied the Tibetans with 5,000 rifles and 5,000,000 rounds of ammunition in 1917 just in time for its army's border war with the Chinese. After the war was over the Dalai Lama resolved to expand his army to 20,000 men but decided to increase it at a realistic rate of 500 troops per year. It was suggested in 1921 that the British should send instructors from their Indian

Tungan soldiers of General Ma Chung-ying on campaign in 1933. All the men wear typical winter clothing, yak fur hats worn with wadded cotton uniforms. The men are armed with a mixture of old Mauser rifles and C-96 semi-automatic pistols, a weapon in widespread use in China.

Army to train Tibetans especially in the use of heavier weaponry. In 1930 the British had supplied the Dalai Lama with 3,000 rifles and pistols to arm his newly raised 1,000 strong bodyguard, whho were trained by British instructors.

As the spiritual leader of Tibet's Buddhists the Dalai Lama was supreme ruler of the Lamaist State in both religious and secular terms. After being acknowledged as the 13th Dalai Lama at three years old he took over his office at the age of 19 in 1895. He ruled Tibet in a difficult time for his country. Unlike the present-day image of a peace-loving cleric, this Llama had territorial ambitions to extend his rule over all territories where ethnic Tibetans lived and sent his army to war in 1917 and in the early 1930s. During his reign, which ended with his death in December 1933, he constantly tried to build up the strength of the Tibetan Army.

The fighting in the early 20th Century between the Muslims of western China and the regular and irregular armies of Tibet took brutality to a new level. General Ma Pu-fang and his 'Divine Army' went to war with the Nogolok Tibetan tribesmen in the late 1920s. This conflict turned into a war of extermination with Tibetan men, women and children slaughtered in huge numbers. One eyewitness to fighting in 1929 described how the heads of 'young girls and children' were staked around the Muslim troops' camps. Every Muslim cavalryman was said to have 10 to 15 heads hanging from his saddle. Heads were also said to be 'strung about the walls of Muslim garrisons like a garland of flowers'. As they advanced, General Ma's troops left a trail of decapitated bodies along the way. Any man of Ma's Army who was unfortunate enough to fall into Tibetan hands was tortured to death in revenge. The favourite way of dealing with Muslim captives was to skin them alive, or to cut open their stomachs and put a large stone in the still living victim. Buddhist temples were not surprisingly a favourite target of the Muslim troops, who always killed all the monks they found. They were also a good source of loot with gold ornaments and other religious items being sold to pay for Ma's campaigns.

## The Sino-Tibetan War in Kham, 1930–1932

The war between the Tibetan Army and the army of the Szechwan warlord General Liu Wen-hui (see chapter 11) was about the control of several monasteries in the border region. General Liu, who at this time was the dominant warlord in Szechwan province, was also in control of the remote Sikang province. He began interfering in Tibetan affairs, which was not a good idea, especially with the 13th Dalai Lama in a militant mood in 1930. Tibetan society was dominated by its large Buddhist monasteries, which besides their religious role also had a major political role. The monks of the large monasteries were often in competition which each other and protected their territory and wealth from each other. In 1930 a dispute broke out over lands belonging to the Nyarong and Targye Monasteries with monks from the latter taking control of the former. The local leader who supported the Nyarong Monastery asked for advice and military assistance from General Liu. In response, the monks from the Targye Monastery asked for help from the Tibetan authorities and in

Five White Russian soldiers pose while fighting for the Sinkiang governor General Sheng Shi-t'sai. These refugees from the Russian Civil War were a useful shock force for the pro-Soviet ruler of Sinkiang. All the cavalrymen in this group are armed with ex-British Lee Enfield rifles, which found their way to western China during the fighting in the early 1930s.

particular the commander of the border troops in Kham. The Tibetans sent a number of troops from the town of Derge which fought Chinese troops in the town of Beri, throwing them out. In October 1930 the furious Dalai Lama sent a telegram to Chiang Kai-shek blaming the fighting on General Liu. General Liu then also sent a telegram to Chiang giving his version of the events saying that the Tibetans were sending more troops in support of the Targye Monastery. Two Chinese negotiators were sent to Tibet to begin peace discussions at the request of the Dalai Lama. But before they could arrive the border war erupted again, with the Tibetans winning a significant victory over the Chinese in March 1931. This victory resulted in the retreat of the Chinese army towards the Nyarong region, with the Tibetans in pursuit. The Chinese officials demanded to know why fighting was still taking place while peace overtures were being made. On the 24th of March the Dalai Lama replied saying that ceasefire orders were still on the way to the frontline when the fighting took place. This excuse about the delayed orders now allowed the Tibetans to move further east while they waited for the arrival of the official order. They defeated the poor Chinese provincial forces in several skirmishes and captured a large tract of land to the east of the Upper Yangtze River. The Tibetan Army took the towns of Kanze and Nyarong and it looked as if all lands which had been traditionally part of Tibet would soon be taken. Liu Wen-hui, however, was not someone who gave in easily and he began to move large numbers of troops into the war zone. By the end of 1931 things were going against the Tibetans, who were gradually pushed back westwards. They lost the two towns they had recently taken and by May 1932 they were losing territory which they had controlled since 1919. A beaten and demoralised Tibetan army now retreated back across the Yangtze River and waited for the Chinese. The situation for the Tibetans had also changed with the outbreak of another conflict, this time with the Chinghai warlord, General Ma Pu-fang, in the Chamdo border region. It now became apparent to the Dalai Lama that the Chinese could advance as far as his capital at Lhasa, so in August he contacted the British asking for them to intercede to end the fighting. British diplomacy brought an end to the fighting in Kham. They told the Chinese that they would take a dim view if their armies crossed the Yangtze. On the 10th of October a truce was signed between the Tibetan leaders in Kham and their Nationalist counterparts. The peace treaty said that the Tibetans would stay west of the Yangtze, meaning they lost the town of Derge and the important Khamba region. From Liu Wen-hui's point of view, he was now facing challenges from rival generals in his home province, Szechwan. The last thing he needed was a war in his most remote domain, so a peaceful solution to the war also suited him.

## The Campaign in Kokonor, 1932

Even as the Tibetans were fighting for Kham province a new front was opened by a dispute in the north-east of Tibet. Heavy fighting took place in the Tibetan province of Kokonor between March 23rd and late September 1932 between Tibetan and local forces. Kokonor was a huge territory and had been held by the Chinese since the early 20th Century. The disputed territory was in the Yushu district of Kokonor, a plateau more than 15,000 feet high on the Chinese-Tibetan border. During the dispute Tibetan troops had occupied an area of Chinese territory equal to the size of 50% of Kiangsu province. Beginning in the spring the 13th Dalai Lama had ordered his troops to move into the region of Sikang to the west of Szechwan province. To counter this General Ma Pu-fang, who was chairman of the Kokonor Government, ordered local troops to prepare defences. The Dalai Lama misinterpreted the Kokonor troops' movements and saw them as offensive rather than defensive. He claimed they were intended to threaten the left flank of his army and decided to up the ante by ordering 7,000 of his men to invade Kokonor on the 23rd of March. Tibetan troops moved into the Yushu District, the mountains of which were the location of the sources of the Yellow and Yangtze Rivers. Only 400 poorly armed and trained Kokonor troops were available to defend the district and they had to pull back. In the small scale but bitter mountain warfare that took place, 300 of the defenders were killed and no quarter was given by either side.

The local Chinese officials sent officials to Sining, the capital of Kokonor province, pleading urgently for reinforcements. There were plenty of troops in Kokonor, 25,000 men split almost evenly between infantry and cavalry; 5,000 of the cavalry had recently been sent to Kansu province to help to keep order there, but this left substantial available forces. It was not the number of troops available that was the problem for the Chinese but getting them to the frontline. Kokonor was huge and getting troops across the mountainous terrain could take months. Any reinforcements that were sent had no support network and had to carry all their needs with them. Any weaponry and ammunition a soldier needed during the campaign would have to be carried on his back The distances involved in the Kokonor campaign were astonishing and the actual fighting was almost secondary to the logistics involved. It was said that it would take a good rider 20 days to get from the capital Sining to the Yushu front on horseback. This was if he had a change of horse at every messenger station and if he managed to get past the local bandits on the way.

The leader of the Kumul Rebellion in Sinkiang in the early 1930s, Khoja Niyas Hajji in traditional clothing. As a Uyghur, or Turkic-speaking Sinkiang leader, he managed to get the Chinese-speaking Tungan people to join his revolt. He was later to join the regime of his enemy General Sheng and was declared a traitor by his fellow Muslims still fighting.

When the soldiers finally reached the frontline they could expect little re-supply of ammunition and they were very careful with how much they used. They would under strict orders to fire their rifles as little as possible and to use their fighting swords instead. Many soldiers also carried spears, which again would be used before they fired their precious rifles. During the fighting the Nationalist Government did manage to get 100,000 rounds of ammunition to Lanchow in Kansu province. From Lanchow it would take six days to get this ammunition delivered in the seven trucks that the Kokonor Government had. The price of petrol in the region was extortionate at $60 per can, making this a very expensive supply run. When the ammunition finally arrived at Sining it was transferred to horses and mules for the long trek to Yushu. Officially, the 2,500-strong Kokonor army there was waiting for this ammunition to launch its counter offensive. The reality was that they simply could not wait and had to manage with the few rounds each they had left.

## Continued Tibetan Fighting, 1933–1935

The Tibetan border with its neighbouring provinces of Sikang, Szechwan and Yunnan saw a series of border conflicts in the early 1930s. Irregular and regular Tibetan forces continued to raid into these provinces, often killing any Chinese they captured. The death of the 13th Dalai Lama in December 1933 did not stop the fighting between the Tibetans and Chinese. In August 1933 General Lung Yun, the Military Governor of Yunnan, reported what were at first thought to be

Tibetan irregulars invading his province. They had taken a large part of territory in the northe, terrorising the Han Chinese population. Lung's outnumbered troops had been forced to evacuate the region near to the Chinsha River and the Tibetans had taken the town of Chungtien. Chungtien was an important town because properly fortified it stopped any Tibetan invasion of China's western provinces. Situated in the north-west of Yunnan, it was 20 miles from the Sikang border and controlled the main road from Tibet. The town had been held by a strong Yunnanese force until early 1933 but most of them had been sent to the Szechwan border. Rumours of an invasion from the neighbouring province gave the Tibetans the opportunity to overcome the company force defending Chungtien. The total number of Tibetans involved in the invasion was between 3,000 and 5,000, all armed with modern rifles. Most of the rifles carried by the Tibetans were Lee Enfield .303s supplied by the British in the 1920s. Because of the modern weaponry carried by the Tibetans it became clear that these were regular troops, not irregulars or bandits. After taking Chungtien the Tibetans then moved towards the town of Likang, while Lung Yun contacted Chiang Kai-shek asking for help. In reply Chiang ordered Lung to throw the Tibetans out of Chinese territory but he did not offer any assistance. Lung replied that he had defeated the Tibetans, hoping that he could accomplish this before Chiang found out he was lying. It emerged that the Dalai Lama was behind the invasion, as he tried to establish his 'Great Tibetan Empire'. Lung Yun's Yunnanese forces were well trained and armed and proved too much for the poorly armed irregular Tibetans.

The Military Governor of Sinkiang, General Sheng Shih-t'sai, in a formal portrait wearing his Nationalist Army uniform. He spent most of his governorship disobeying Chiang Kai-shek's instructions to cut his province's connections with the Soviet Union. Sheng brought much hardship to the people of Sinkiang, sometimes with the secret support of Soviet troops.

General Sheng Shih-t'sai with a visiting journalist standing in front of the crossed Nationalist Army and Kuomintang flags. Sheng was always officially an official of the Nationalist Government in Nanking but in reality he ruled Sinkiang as a personal fiefdom. The source of much of Sheng's support is shown by the Soviet Moisin-Nagant M1891 rifles.

The war between the Sikang governor General Liu Wen-hui's army and the regular Tibetan army continued into 1934. Tibetan demands that Liu Wen's forces should move out of the town of Khanchingchuo in February were ignored. A 40,000-strong Tibetan army of regular and irregular troops was massing on the Sikang-Tibet border. The Tibetan regulars were armed with brand new rifles and light machine guns and their artillery had a number of mountain and screw guns. Their irregulars were armed with primitive flintlocks, shields and broad swords and their main tactic was a suicidal charge. Liu appealed to Nanking for support. No help was forthcoming as Chiang Kai-shek had little interest in this remote part of China. Tibetan forces crossed the frontier in the first few days of March and a battle between Liu's troops and the invaders took place at Tungkew. After pushing aside the Szechwanese army the Tibetans continued their advance through the Tehkah region and were moving towards the major town of Kangtze. Chinese reinforcements were rushed to the frontline and by the 12th of March the Tibetans were in retreat. Brutal fighting continued back and forth through the rest of March and into early April 1934 and both armies fought to a standstill. After a lull in the fighting in the first days of April the Tibetans renewed their advance and another battle took place at a place called Bahon, where they gained the upper hand. The fighting now was concentrated around a crossing on the Kinha River where the Chinese held strong positions. Several desperate attempts to cross the river were repulsed but the defenders were soon running out of ammunition. Liu wired the Government for more arms and ammunition but even they were sent they would take weeks or months to arrive. He knew that unless they received supplies his men would not stand up to the fanatical Tibetans. The Tibetans were deeply religious and were more than

These tough looking Uyghur fighters of the Army of the East Turkestan Republic gather around their commander. Although they may have been good individual fighters, their army was not well organised and on one occasion a 10,000 strong force was defeated by a 2,000-strong Tungan army. Weaponry carried by this unit varies with a Winchester repeater alongside several types of Mauser and Lee Enfield .303s.

willing to sacrifice their lives for the Dalai Lama. They also listened to their local Buddhist leaders. One, Nionar Hutukutu, the 'Living Buddha of Sikang' gave the soldiers some dubious combat advice. According to Hutukutu, if they were gassed by or shot at by their enemies in battle they should recite the 21 charms of the Goddess of Mercy, Kwan Yin. Reciting these prayers would make them immune to the gas and bullet-proof.

## General Liu Wen-hui in Sikang, 1932–1937

In 1931 the new Chinese province of Sikang was nominally controlled by the Szechwan warlord General Liu Wen-lui. Beginning in April 1931 Tibetan raiders were making regular attacks on Liu's poorly armed militia. The General appealed to Chiang Kai-shek for assistance in defending his province but he was not interested. Soon Liu had other problems when his leadership in Szechwan was challenged by his nephew General Liu Hsiang (see chapter 11). In late October the Tibetans were again threatening to invade Sikang with or without the support of their government. Tibetan politicians were deeply split between belligerent and non-belligerent camps, with many elder statesmen in favour of negotiations with the Chinese. The Dalai Lama and his inner circle were however in favour of

Tibetan militiamen during fighting with Liu Wen-hui's Szechwanese Army in 1930–32. These were the kind of troops who managed to defeat the Chinese army in the early stages of the war. Often the troops they were facing were of a similar standard to these men. The Chinese also using local auxiliaries in their campaign.

continuing conflict and they were the dominant group. By May 1932 the defeated Szechwanese army of General Liu Wen-hui had moved into Sikang and had taken over several cities. Tibetan forces were driven out of the towns of Kanze and Nyarong and other areas that they had been in control of since 1919. Before long, having suffered more defeats, they had been pushed further westwards, as far as the Upper Yangtze River. The Tibetans had massed 50,000 largely irregular troops with the object of launching a counterattack. They soon changed their mind after meeting Liu's battle-hardened troops in a number of engagements. Liu now felt secure enough to bring his family and the dependents of his troops and various other hangers-on into Sikang, away from the advancing Liu Hsiang. Although Sikang was only a fiftieth of the size of Szechwan, Liu decided that he could safely control the province and turn it into his personal fiefdom. Liu still wanted to maintain a relationship with the Nationalist Government and hoped to get support, but without any interference from Chiang Kai-shek. His army, known before 1932 as the 24th Army, was renamed the 24th Division of the Nationalist Army. It still had its official headquarters in Chengte in Szechwan and Liu still maintained a palatial house in the city. Officially the 24th Division was now part of the Nationalist Army although its troops only obeyed Liu's orders. Liu was now given a string of titles including Governor of Sikang, Pacification Commander of Sikang and Commander of the 24th Division. He was only made governor in 1935 after Sikang officially became a province of China under the

Tibetan tribesmen guarding a fortress during the fighting against various Chinese armies in the early 1930s. They are wearing their traditional dress and have bandoliers over their shoulders carrying ammunition for their rifles. In front of the men are a couple of light guns with which they are preparing to defend their stronghold. Much of the fighting in the 1930–32 war was done by irregular troops like this rather than by the regular Tibetan army.

influence of Liu and his officials. When the 24th Division was integrated into the Nationalist Army it was supposed to have been reduced in size but Liu would not allow that to happen. The division was organised into two brigades each with three Regiments, plus one independent regiment. Its 137th Brigade was commanded by General Liu Yuan-tsung, a nephew of Liu Wen, while the 136th Brigade was commanded by his son-in-law. Officially there were a total of 10,000 men in the 24th Division but it was assumed that it was much higher. Liu would have as many men under arms as he could afford, as his army was his only guarantee of power. He also had various para-military forces under this command, made up of the Pacification Corps, 'Security' troops and provincial police totalling about 10,000 men. Most of the officers in the 24th Division were blood relatives of Liu Wen or were relatives through marriage. This gave him in the old warlord tradition the loyalty of his officer corps, who depended on him for their livelihood: a different meaning to the phrase blood and treasure. An eyewitness of the situation in Sikang in 1935 noted that 'The 24th Division's soldiers all are armed at least with modern bolt-action rifles, and they all carry belts full of ammunition. They are relatively well disciplined and wear clean, neat uniforms.' It was also reported that military supplies were plentiful because Liu has had his own financial resources. Every squad of 16 men had 14 rifles and 1 automatic weapon and every company had 2 mortars. Both brigades had a special artillery unit with both mortars and mountain guns but these were stationed across the border in Szechwan. This was the Nationalist Government's not so subtle way of keeping a check on Liu and his army. If his heavy weaponry was under the overall control of Nanking, then Liu's military capacity to make war was strictly limited. Liu's ambitions were also kept in check by the presence in the southern part of Sikang of another 10,000-strong army under the command of General Ho Kuo-kwang. He was a Nanking appointee whose troops were loyal to Chiang Kai-shek. Although on paper Liu was governor of the whole of the province, this force made sure that his ambitions did not get out of control. This was especially the case if he decided to try and regain his former territory in Szechwan, upsetting the delicate situation there.

## The Cadre that Remained a Cadre

In 1932 in the remote Sikang region on the Tibetan-western Szechwan province border, a brutal but small 'war' took place. Local tribal leader Kiseng Tsering organised a separatist militia of 150 men and called for independence for Sikang. His tiny army was recruited from amongst the local bandits and other lawless elements in the region with a small cadre of patriots. Arms were bought or stolen from General Liu Wen-hui's defeated troops who had crossed the border from Szechwan. Kiseng established his headquarters at Pa'an and proclaimed 'Let the people of Sikang rule Sikang!' Kiseng recruited some Tibetan irregulars to bolster his numbers and with the approval of the authorities in far-off Nanking went to war. The Chinese Government's motive for supporting this separatist movement

Soldiers of the regular Tibetan Army in the mid to late 1930s parade wearing their new uniforms. The NCO and his two men wear the fur hat which was worn by the majority of Tibetan troops. Both privates are armed with Lee Enfield .303 rifles which were supplied to the Tibetans in batches from 1917 onwards. Although they were fearless and tough fighters, the men of the Tibetan Army was nearly always outgunned when at war with China.

was simply to cause problems for the neighbouring Tibetan authorities. His main opponent in Sikang was the recently defeated General Liu Wen-hui, who had decided to create a refuge for his army and its dependents there. The war was small-scale with armies involved on each side never reaching more than a few hundred but no less bitter for that. Beginning in April the four-month war was made up of ambushes, skirmishes and sieges. The main action involved a siege of a fort held by 400 of Liu Wen-hui's troops, which was finally taken by the Sikang rebels through trickery. In the armoury of the captured fort was a cache of 700 rifles, which allowed Tseng to expand his forces. Even with the expansion of the Sikang Army it was heavily outnumbered by the experienced troops of Liu Wen-hui. By July 1932 the fighting had petered out and General Liu had established a firm base in the region. Liu's ambition was to use this fastness to plan his eventual re-conquest of Szechwan controlled by Liu Hsiang's Army.

## The Tibetan Army, 1936

In 1936 the Tibetan Army had over 10,000 troops still stationed along its eastern border. These were divided into nine regiments of regulars totalling 5,000 men and 11 regiments of poorly armed militia with each unit having about 500 men. Of the four mountain guns, three had been lost in local fighting in 1934. Modern weaponry used by the regulars were .303 Lee Enfield rifles and they also had six Lewis light machine guns. The militia were armed with older but still serviceable Lee Metford rifles and a few older types. In the capital Lhasa there were 600 troops of the Bodyguard Regiment, 400 Gendarmarie and 600 regulars from Kham province. The Kham troops were stationed in Lhasa while they underwent training on the six mountain guns kept in the capital. Apparently four of the six guns were described as being 'too dangerous to fire'. A total of 5,000 Lee Enfields were kept in the Bodyguard Regiment barracks along with two Lewis light machine guns. In the Lhasa armoury were stored another 4,000 Lee Enfields as well four unidentified machine guns. There was a primitive arsenal in Lhasa which only repaired broken rifles and manufactured .303 bullets that were notoriously unreliable. Throughout Tibet there were a large number of local village militia who, if lucky, were armed with matchlock muskets.

# 13

# 'Defend the City at all Costs':
# The Secret War – Chahar, 1933–36

In the 1930s Inner Mongolia was sandwiched between the People's Republic of Mongolia, the newly installed puppet government of Manchukuo, and northern China. It was a vast territory sparsely populated by descendants of Ghenghis Khan, the great Mongolian conqueror of the 13th Century. The vast majority of the population were herdsmen who lived a migratory life on the plains in their traditional yurts. Like their fellow Mongolians in the MPR, they had spent the early part of the century ruled loosely by the Qing Dynasty from the then Chinese capital, Peking. When the northern Mongolians won their independence in 1912, the Inner Mongolians were left under the rule of the Han Chinese. The Inner Mongolians were divided into tribes or 'Meng', which were further divided into Banners. Each Banner was headed by an hereditary ruler who represented his people at councils where decisions affecting all the tribes were made.

After the Japanese invasion of Jehol and its incorporation into the Manchukuoan Empire in 1933, the situation in the region remained tense. Jehol was the easternmost of the four provinces that made up the region of Inner Mongolia. The region ran roughly across the southern border of the Communist People's Republic of Mongolia. The other three provinces which made up the region were, from east to west, Chahar, Suiyuan and Ninghsia. Even as Japan's Kwangtung Army was ending its conquest of Jehol its strategists had begun planning for a more stealthy takeover of Chahar. This province was now isolated from the rest of China and was ripe for picking by the ambitious Kwangtung Army. The province was garrisoned by the troops of General Sung Che-yuan a former subordinate of Feng Yu-hsiang. Sung was seen by the Japanese and in particular their spymaster Colonel Dohihara as a potential leader of a puppet Chahar regime. The situation in Chahar was now complicated by the presence of an anti-Japanese army independent of the Nationalist Government.

## The People's Anti-Japanese Allied Army, 1933

Feng Yu-hsiang, the leader of the Kuominchun, had returned from temporary retirement and was looking for a new role in northern China. He had only a 3,000-strong bodyguard under this command with the remains of his former Kuominchun spread throughout northern China. Most of his former divisions and their commanders had now been incorporated into other Nationalist armies. Even as the war was ongoing in Jehol Feng decided to establish at his Kalgan base a new army to challenge Japanese aggression. The fact that the other northern strongman Chang Hsueh-liang had lost favour since the defeat in Jehol gave Feng an opportunity. He saw that he could, if he was careful and patient enough, regain his former prominence in the region. In the first weeks and months of 1933 Feng received constant entreaties from the public to lead a fight against the Japanese. In February he formed the core of a new army in collaboration with some of his former generals and some anti-Japanese organisations throughout China.

Many Chinese high ranking officers were infuriated by Chiang Kai-shek's appeasement of the Japanese in the early 1930s. Feng, with the vocal support of other Chinese patriots, began to make constant entreaties to Chiang to go to war with Japan. By April 1933 Feng was receiving many messages of support at his headquarters at Kalgan in Chahar province pleading for him to lead a military force against Japan. The Japanese encroachments into Chahar province and the taking of a number of towns there in early May exacerbated the situation. On the 28th of May Feng finally gave in to this pressure to do something by announcing the formation of a new anti-Japanese army. This Army titled the 'People's Anti-Japanese Allied Army' was never going to be endorsed by the Government, who were trying hard not to antagonise the Japanese. Feng accepted the position of Commander-in-Chief of this new army and began to recruit as many men as possible into it. The army's main core was made up of veterans of Feng's North-Western Army who had usually seen service in the Kuominchun. It also included deserters from the Manchukuoan Army and Mongol volunteers and soldiers who had originally been part of the North-Eastern Army in Manchuria. Over 100,000 volunteers flocked to Feng's army within the first month but he was disappointed by the types of volunteers. He had hoped that students and other patriotic groups would volunteer giving his army a truly revolutionary zeal. In reality, it was made up of units and individual soldiers who had suffered defeats over the previous few years. There was an inevitable lack of armaments with even small arms in short supply. It was estimated that only three-quarters or fewer of his troops had rifles, and machine guns and artillery were even scarcer. Even at the height of his power in the mid to late 1920s Feng's Kuominchun had been short of artillery anyway. Regardless of the condition of his army Feng was now determined to take on the Japanese in Chahar with or without Government support. The presence of Feng's Army in Chahar in 1933 raised a major problem for Chiang and the Nationalist Government. He was in open revolt against Chiang but he was under threat by the Japanese, who were moving into Chahar. This meant that although the Government could not support him, if they did not, they faced losing Chahar to the Japanese.

## General Fang Chen-wu's March, 1933

General Fang was another of those mavericks who troubled the Nationalist government throughout the period under disussion. Fang was a former Kuominchun officer who in 1929 refused to attack his former commander Feng Yu-hsiang, despite Chiang Kai-shek's direct order. Fang suffered for his

Soldiers of Feng Yu-hsiang's People's Anti-Japanese Army go through their sword exercises on the barracks parade ground. Feng's Kuominchun was always well known for its 'Big Sword' soldiers and these men may well be veterans of one of these units. During the fighting in Chahar in the early 1930s some of these men would be called upon again to go into action armed only with these swords.

disobedience, ending up in in a 7 ft × 5 ft cell in a Nanking prison to await his fate. Chiang eventually had to free Fang owing to pressure from some of his influential friends and supporters. He next turned up in Shanghai during the 1932 Incident, where he urged the commanders of the 19th Route Army to resist the Japanese. Like most patriotic Chinese officers, General Fang was incandescent with rage over the Japanese invasion of Jehol in 1933. He felt humiliated by the Government's lack of resolve in fighting the Japanese and was determined to do something by himself if necessary. He wanted to form an independent army raised specifically to fight the Japanese but he knew this would be without Chiang Kai-shek's support.

Fang travelled to Shansi province to the town of Chaihsiu where some of his former soldiers were stationed. To form his army he sold all his private property and began to recruit a mix of loyal former soldiers and patriotic volunteers. With little more than patriotism to motivate them and with no prospect of any payment it was amazing that he managed to recruit 20,000 men into this shoestring army. On the 1st of March 1933 he began to move his so-called 'Resist-Japan-Save-China Expeditionary Army' northwards. Fang was elected Commander-in-Chief and he issued a number of edicts as they marched.

These denounced Chiang's failure to resist the Japanese and at the same time proclaimed his army's determination to resist. On the 18th Fang sent an open letter to the Chinese people in which he explained his motivation for forming his army. His objective was to 'recover Manchuria, to fight for the independence of Korea, to free China from the terrorist policy of Nanking, and to bring about the freedom and independence of China'. As the Expeditionary Army advanced westwards across the southern part of Shansi province it was cheered on by the population. Fang's aim was to get to the Peking–Hankow Railway in Hopei province and transport his army along it to the northern frontier in Chahar province. When they finally reached the railway they were told that Chiang had sent orders to stop them using his trains to get to Chahar. Instead of forcing the railway workers to take his army northwards, Fang told his men that they would have to march to the front. They found that the main road north had been blocked by Chiang's troops and not wanting to fight fellow Chinese, they took the mountain road. Nothing was going to stop Fang and his men and on the 22nd of May they reached the city of Hsuanhua in Chahar province.

## Fang's Army in Chahar

When Fang's army arrived in Chahar they roused the fighting spirit of the poorly organised anti-Japanese forces already there. Many of these smaller military forces approached Fang and asked to be incorporated into his 'Resist-Japan-Save-China' army. Fang also made contact with his former commander, Feng Yu-hsiang, whose own anti-Japanese Army was encamped at Kalgan not far from Hsuanhua. The two maverick generals met at the town of Changchiak'ou on the 26th of May and they agreed to unite their armies. This new army was to be named the 'The People's Anti-Japanese Allied Army' with Feng as the Commander-in-Chief. With two popular leaders at the helm and with a much larger army, the anti-Japanese cause was at its height by early June. Chiang Kai-shek was keeping a close check on this new force in China and became alarmed by Feng and Fang's popularity throughout the country. Japanese intelligence also kept track of their new opponents and both they and Chiang had a similar objective. For different reasons they both sought the crushing of the People's Anti-Japanese Allied Army. On the 31st of May Chiang Kai-shek's government had signed the Tangku Treaty with the Japanese and this further infuriated Feng and Fang. This treaty assured the Japanese that any move they made against the two anti-Japanese Generals would not provoke intervention by the Chinese Government. On the 7th of June the Japanese began an attack against Fang's troops at Tushihkow Pass on the Chahar-Jehol border. The nearest Nationalist Army to the fighting was under the command of General Ho Ying-ching. He did not go to the aid of Fang's army and instead simply predicted their destruction by the Japanese. The Kwangtung Army's commander, General Honjo, justified the attacks on Fang by saying it was covered under 'unpublished provisions in the Tangku Treaty'.

    As the fighting continued a congress was organised in Kalgan on the 14th of June to discuss the future of the Anti-Japanese campaign. This congress was attended by 70 officials from every patriotic association in the region who talked for days but never published its conclusions. It appeared that by mid-June the leadership of the Anti-Japanese cause was beginning to unravel as they came under pressure from the enemy.

The propaganda aspect of the anti-Japanese crusade was neglected at this vital time and the chance to recruit more support for their cause was lost. The Japanese and their Manchukuoan puppet allies were meanwhile advancing rapidly through Chahar, taking the towns of Paochang, Kangpo and Kuyan in quick succession. Chiang tried to solve the problem of the Anti-Japanese Army by approaching Feng through General Sung Che-yuan. He offered to let Feng remove his army to Peking so that they would not come under Japanese attack. Feng Yu-hsiang was wavering but his ally Fang Chen-wu was not and insisted that they continue their campaign. Fang now took the lead and with his command of the Northern Route Army began to retake territory and towns lost to the recent Japanese offensive. He appointed the famous Chinese General Chi Hung-chang as a frontline commander, thus raising the morale of his troops. Fang's offensive began on the 25th of June and within a few days the three towns which had fallen to the Japanese were liberated.

## Liu Kuei-tang's Army and the First Battle for Dolonor

General Liu Kuei-tang was another of those former bandit leaders in northern China who had risen to lead a unit of Chinese irregular volunteers. He had been a bandit since the age of 10 and served in a number of armies in the early 1930s on the Chinese Manchukuaon border. He joined the Chinese in 1931 and had led his men against the Japanese in Jehol in early 1933. The swift victory of the Japanese in Jehol saw the pragmatic Liu switch sides and join the Manchukuoan Army. He took his undisciplined irregulars with him and was stationed in the western part of Jehol. There was no way that Liu was going to settle into a conventional army career and he promptly led his cavalry into eastern Chahar. His target was the important city of Dolonor in northern Chahar, which his wild horsemen took in early May. In support of Liu's cavalry force was a small unit of Japanese disguised as Mongols, who operated a few field guns in his support. According to reports the turncoat General had 30,000 men under his command but this number was almost certainly an exaggeration. Dolonor was defended by a Nationalist garrison under the command of General Chao Sheng-shao. His troops had to withdraw to a new defence line at Sanchialing, where they dug in. His defence of the city had been disrupted by the setting of fires by a group of Mongols sympathetic to the attacking army. Chao's troops had only just managed to dig entrenchments at Sanchialing when they came under heavy Japanese artillery fire. The city was captured with the usual looting and raping by the undisciplined troops of Liu. He let them run amok for a few days before preparing to move out. Within a few days Liu and the bulk of his army were marching out of Dolonor looking for new conquests. Liu left a small garrison behind to hold the city with a handful of the Japanese to give them support. His men captured the strategic town of Kayuan before continuing their southward advance. General Liu was a law unto himself and his loyalty was always an issue for his Manchukuoan superiors. He did proclaim his continued opposition to Feng Yu-hsiang and taunted him by saying his army would continue to 'plant the flag of Manchukuo' in the province.

## Feng's Army and the March of the Manchurian Troops

Feng threw all his crack troops into the fighting in Chahar in August 1933, along with what little artillery he had. He had the 1st Army under General Luan Hsien-wu, the 2nd Army under General Tung Ling-ko and the 3rd Army under General Kao Shu-hsun. In addition, there was the Defence Army a three-division force formed from recent volunteers. Although this totalled a reasonable 45,000 men they were poorly armed and equipped compared to their enemies. Many of them were, however, tough veterans of many campaigns and were extremely loyal to Feng. General Feng Yu-hsiang's army was reported in late May to be 50,000-strong: the troops of General Sung Che-yuan and General Pang Ping-hsin – 20,000 – his bodyguard of 2,000 men, new recruits – 8,000 men – General Sun Tien-ying's Army – 6,000 – General Fang Chen-wu's Army – 8,000 – and 5,000 of General Feng Chan-hai's volunteers, refugees from Manchuria.

In September 1933 a story came out in the press which made little impact then and remains largely unknown today, about the 3,000-mile march of the Manchurian army. The men who undertook this march were the remnants of the armies of two Manchurian commanders. Their Generals were the famous Ma Chan-shan and Su Ping-wen, who had continued the fight against the Japanese in Manchuria until November 1932. When their armies broke up no one appears to have speculated as to what happened to the Generals' soldiers. They were said to number 75,000 men, mostly cavalry, and it was assumed they had scattered into the Manchurian countryside to become farm labourers or bandits. Instead, it was reported that the two armies gathered together at Manchouli on the Siberian-Manchukuoan border. Deserted by their Generals, the men formed a soldiers' council and decided to ride 800 miles towards the Mongolian city of Urga, where they would seek employment. Because of the arid and inhospitable terrain they were to cross they broke up into smaller units agreeing to meet in Urga. When they arrived in Mongolia three months later the survivors were swiftly moved on under threat of attack by the Mongolian army. A third had either died by this time or simply drifted away but the remaining 50,000 decided to offer their services to Feng Yu-hsiang by telegraph. He gladly accepted and they moved on again for the second, much longer leg of the journey. This time the men had to survive by hunting wild game and taking any food they could from the few farmsteads they came across. The cavalry did not ride their horses for this leg of the journey, using them instead to carry kit and food. As they had to constantly search for food, the length of their straight-line journey was doubled as they meandered towards Chahar. Finally, in June 1933, after seven months on the road and in the desert the first 15,000 cavalry rode into Kalgan. A few days later the second 4,000-strong unit followed them into the city and immediately into service with Feng's Army. Although there is no information as to what became of the other marchers, it can be assumed that some died of starvation, some became bandits and others simply disappeared off the face of the earth.

## Feng's Offensive

Feng and his army had to now go on to the offensive in June to justify their existence in the eyes of the Chinese people. Without any support from the Nationalist Government Feng's anti-Japanese crusade was doomed from the beginning. The only chance of any success was to persuade the Chahar Military Governor General Sung Che-yuan and his 29th Army to join his campaign. The 29th Army was a formidable force and if united with the Anti-Japanese Army would have created a real threat to the Japanese. Sung was a former Kuominchun general and did owe a certain amount of loyalty to Feng; but he was not prepared to bring his army into Chahar in support of his former commander. Sung contacted Chiang Kai-shek to assure him that he was not part of Feng's plans – but he refused to go to Kalgan to take up his new command as long as he was there. There was still plenty of good feeling behind Feng, with 150,000 Chahar farmers pledging their support for him in May. Thousands of the farmer volunteers turned up at his camp, some bringing their own arms and ammunition. Feng could not arm the remainder of them and 5,000 of them were sent to the frontline to dig trenches.

The Japanese meanwhile accused Feng of receiving Soviet aid for his campaign, falsely claiming the arrival of a 16-strong Russian Air Force at his HQ at Kalgan. When the Japanese did capture Soviet Moisin-Nagant rifles from Feng's troops, they told the world press about it. What they forgot to mention was that these rifles had been supplied to Feng's Kuominchun in the mid-1920s. Feng was now desperate for arms and even applied to Chiang Kai-shek for help but was rebuffed in no uncertain terms. He was informed that he had a reputation for using armaments against the people who supplied him.

A large part of the Anti Japanese Army now advanced towards Dolonor, which was still held in July by General Liu's Army. The city was to become the main focus of much of the backwards and forwards campaigning in Chahar. In command of Feng's troops was General Fang Chen-wu, who had joined his forces with the Anti-Japanese Army. General Liu Kuei-tang's garrison was a mix of former Chinese bandits, Mongol volunteers and Manchukuoan irregulars. Fighting for Dolonor began on the night of the 10th of July when Feng's troops tried to scale the city's walls. This first attack was beaten back by the Manchukoan defenders with the attackers suffering 540 casualties. Another night assault was launched on the 11th with both sides suffering heavy casualties in the hand-to-hand fighting. During this attack Feng's troops succeeded in capturing two lines of Manchukuoan trenches along with 290 troops. Other much needed war booty captured in this attack were 120 rifles, 3 heavy machine guns and 157 horses. The next morning the defenders finally broke when the attackers succeeded in scaling the walls on three sides. After some street fighting most of the Manchukuoan garrison chose to flee the city. The withdrawal of the majority of Japanese troops and advisors from Chahar had weakened the Manchukuoans' resolve. Fang Chen-wu took the city on the 12th of July after a two-day battle fiercely fought by two poorly armed masses.

The capture of Dolonor was never going to go unchallenged by the Japanese who began to build up their forces to take it back. They sent 20,000 Manchukuoan troops with Japanese officers towards Dolonor in mid July. At the end of the month another two brigades of Manchukuoan troops had arrived near to the city in preparation for an attack. General Liu Kuei-tang's troops were added to the force encircling Dolonor so that they could make amends for losing the city a few weeks before. Liu was still in league with the Manchukuoans.

## The Nationalist 29th Army in Chahar

A three-sided conflict now developed in Chahar with the Nationalist Army moving back into the province. Now there was Feng's Anti-Japanese Army, the Manchukuoan Army and the Nationalist 29th Army in Chahar. As Feng's Army and the Manchukuoan-Japanese forces fought it out over Chahar, the Nationalist Army began to build up its forces in the province. Four armoured trains were brought up to the Chahar border and troop trains were constantly on the move towards the border in late July 1933. In addition, Yen Hsi-shan was ordered to move troops from his Shansi Army up to the border with Chahar. These included the 35th Army under General Fu Tso-yi, the 3rd Army under P'ang Ping-hsin and the 17th Army under Hsu T'ing-yao. By the end of July Feng had established a defence line between the town of Hsuanhua and the provincial capital. In the last days of July Hsuanhua fell to the Nationalists, who then moved to envelop Kalgan from three sides. Feng's attitude throughout these setbacks remained defiant but his lack of heavy weaponry was a major problem. Facing him in Chahar was a force estimated at 45,000 organised into the 5th, 25th, 39th and 42nd Divisions. There were also in reserve 20,000 men in the 105th and 130th Divisions of the North-Eastern Army. Meanwhile, Chiang Kai-shek was using his tried and trusted tactic of buying off some of Feng's commanders. These included Generals Feng Chan-hai, Kang Pao, Li Chung-yi and T'an Tsu-i. Feng was nothing if not a survivor. He now realised that his position in Chahar was untenable.

## Feng's Retirement

Even as his Army continued its struggle, Feng Yu-hsiang decided that he was defeated and announced his retirement on the 5th of August. In typical Feng style he did not inform any of his subordinates and sent a telegram to Chiang Kai-shek announcing his decision.

He had been under pressure for a few weeks from Chiang to abandon his campaign and take his 'rebel' army out of Chahar. To Feng, his defeat in Chahar was just another of his failed ventures that he could escape from because of his high profile in China. For his abandoned men however, the future looked bleak as the

General Fang Chen-wu and his staff at the start of their march to Chahar in 1933. General Fang in the centre of the photo spent most of that year with his army fighting in Northern China. He was a patriot who thought that China should be fighting the Japanese aggression, in opposition to Chiang Kai-shek's appeasement policy.

cold weather began to bite and they shivered in their inadequate summer uniforms. Feng found his way to Shantung province with his bodyguard, where he was met by an armoured train sent by one of his old commanders, General Han Fu-chu. The press reported that Feng was very optimistic after his retreat from Chahar while his men continued to fight. On the 10th of August General Fang Chen-wu announced that he was determined to keep up the fight against the Japanese. He telegrammed the Canton Government, who were sympathetic to Fang's cause, to say that his fight would go on. Fang accepted the role of Acting Commander of the Allied Anti-Japanese Army and formulated his plans. He was now up against the Japanese and their proxy forces and the Nationalists, who just wanted him out of the way. General Ho Ying-ching, the Chinese War Minister, had sent the Japanese secret messages indicating he would be delighted if they recaptured Dolonor.

## The Second Battle for Dolonor, August 1933

The Manchukuoan Army, their Mongol allies and the Japanese advisors totalling 6,000 men had been besieging Dolonor since the first days of August. The city was defended by a strong garrison under the command of General Chang Ling-yin. Most of the garrison was dug-in in well prepared entrenchments a few miles outside the city but had little artillery or machine guns. To soften up the city's defences nine Japanese light bombers dropped hundreds of bombs, which largely destroyed its defences. On the 10th of August the besieging force began an assault supported by Japanese artillery and a small force of Japanese Type 92 'combat cars', or tankettes.

One of the more dramatic stories to come out of the fighting for Dolonor concerned the exploits of Feng's elite 'Big Sword' Corps. According to the press the strong force of Japanese tankettes attacking the city was 'set upon' by Feng's sword-wielding soldiers. With a combination of rocks thrust into tracks and swords thrust through the drivers' viewing slits they managed to disable eight of the vehicles. The first assault on Dolonor was surprisingly repulsed by the sheer bravery of Feng's troops. The Japanese did manage to capture the eastern suburbs of the town before being thrown out again by suicidal charges by Feng's 'Dare-to-Die' Corps with their swords. This defeat outraged the Japanese commanders, who asked their command to send strong reinforcements from Chengteh in Jehol. They were very disappointed by the performance of their Manchukuoan allies during the attack on Dolonor. They surely should have known the limitations of the poorly motivated puppet troops.

Having brought up more troops the Manchukuoan, Mongol and Japanese force launched another attack on the 15th of August, which after a day's fighting succeeded in taking Dolonor. This second assault was supported by Japanese light bombers who bombed the defenders from low level. Casualties were rising on both sides but the defenders were unable to bring in fresh troops and began to fall back into the town. The morale of some of Feng's troops was not helped when news leaked out that their leader was not at his headquarters as they thought but had fled. Before he ran away Feng had had the temerity to order his commanders to defend Dolonor at all costs! The Japanese military authorities said that the taking of Dolonor by their Manchukuoan allies was simply a return to the status quo, that there should be no cause for alarm for anyone in Chahar and that they had no further territorial ambitions there.

Elsewhere in Chahar the Japanese-led Manchukuoans had continued their advance with their first objective being the town of Kuyuan. This town was half-way towards Feng's headquarters at Kalgan but of course he was long gone. It appears that not many people were aware that Feng had resigned, few of his own troops still fighting in his name or the Japanese-led Manchukuoans. The town was defended by a Chinese force under the joint command of Generals Chi Hung-chang and Chang Li-sen. As the Manchukuoans approached the town on the 9th of August its population was fleeing in panic. They were heading to the nearest town, Changpei, and were joined by the people of Paochang, which had fallen on the same day. The Japanese aircraft were bombing the lines of communication from eastern Chahar to the capital Kalgan. The garrison put up a strong defence but when they were outflanked they retreated across the desert under attack from the air.

The war in Chahar was still a secret one, with denials issued constantly by the Japanese despite the constant press reports about the fighting. On the 17th of August Japanese reports suggested that the fighting in Chahar would not continue much longer. At the same time they said that the war had been between Feng, without Chinese Government support, and Mongols friendly to Manchukuo. No regular Manchukoan forces had taken part they insisted, and the Mongols with irregular Manchukuoan troops had taken Dolonor. According to the Japanese the city was defended by Chinese troops with 'Communist tendencies'.

## Peace in Chahar; Chi and Fang's War

Even while the battle for Dolonor went on, a peaceful settlement had been reached in the overall Chahar problem on the 7th of August. By telegram in exile Feng agreed to hand back control of the military and civil affairs of Chahar to the Nationalist Government. Military control would go to General Sung Che-yuan, commander of the 29th Army, whose units started to move into the province immediately. The Nationalist Army moved an 11-division army to Hsiahuayuan supported by several armoured trains sent from Peking. The 'People's Allied Forces', as the settlement described Feng's army, were to evacuate Kalgan with Sung's 29th Army taking over the garrison. A few days later General Fang Chen-wu was instructed to 'quit the military arena in Chahar' and resign the command of his army in favour of Sung Che-yuan. He and another rebel, General Chi Hung-chang, told General Sung they would not obey.

General Fang Chen-wu was ready to continue the struggle and was willing to build a new alliance in Chahar. He was prepared to ally himself with anyone who was willing to continue the fight against the Japanese. As well as General Chi Hung-chang he found a rather untrustworthy pair willing to join his new campaign. These were the nefarious General Liu Kuei-tang of Dolonor fame and Jehol's ex-Governor Tang Yu-lin. General Tang Yu-lin had fled his province with his 200-strong bodyguard and had managed to remove part of his dishonestly accrued treasure from Jehol. Many of Tang's troops had also crossed from Jehol into Chahar and ended up serving in the Nationalist Army. Some of his troops had fought as part of the defence force on the Great Wall in March 1933 before retreating in May. Other troops, however, were willing to rejoin their former leader Tang, who after all paid them on time. For some reason the inept Tang was now named as Deputy Commander of the reformed Anti-Japanese Army. It is suspected that Tang bought his position within Fang's army using some of his fortune from Jehol as a bribe. Fang was desperate for money and Tang was the only one offering to help him to finance the army. In late August 1933 the armies of Fang and Chi left their headquarters at Changpei and headed north. Sung Che-yuan, the 29th Army commander, had already left for Changpei to confer with the two generals. He wanted to try and bring a peaceful end to the situation and arrange for the demobilisation of their troops. The two Generals hoped to meet up with some of Tang Yu-lin's troops fighting in northern Chahar. When Sung arrived at Changpei on the 31st of August their absence made him determined to meet them on the battlefield and defeat them. He issued orders that General Chi's army be stopped from entering Suiyuan province and two Shansi divisions were sent to the border with Chahar. The Military Governor of Suiyuan, General Fu Tso-yi, sent a large Shansi army to block any advance by Chi into his province. One of General Chi's supporters, General Chang Mo-tu, was preparing a 'revolutionary' base in north-west Chahar. It was reported that a number of Soviet advisors had turned up in this fortified camp but it was never confirmed.

By the start of September it seems that Chi and Fang were ready to split their forces and operate independently. By the 4th they had broken up their alliance temporarily although both were still fighting against the Nationalists. Chi's army was on the march near Dolonor while Fang's army was at his HQ at Changpei. It soon became clear that General Chi was the more aggressive of the two and he moved to attack Shansi troops forming up to attack him. He was soon fighting a large force of Shansi troops under the command of General Chao Cheng-shau. After three hours fighting Chi's outnumbered troops had to retreat into the forests near to the town of Shangtu. Although the Nationalist Shansi force tried to surround the sheltering rebels, they managed to slip away and spent most of the month avoiding the encircling Nationalist armies. Both Fang and Chi now began to prepare fortified encampments that they could use as boltholes when under attack. General Fang had established a new camp at Niulangshan with a defence line built a few miles in front of it. Chi built a particularly strong encampment with three lines of trenches, protected by machine guns and artillery. From these camps units of both armies moved manoeuvred in the region around Peking with one unit getting to within a few miles of the city. They were operating in an area

Three officers of the Nationalist Army outside a Mongolian desert outpost during the mid-1930s. These three tough looking officers are typical of the type of troops defending Inner Mongolia in 1936. The fighting in Chahar and Suiyuan province between 1934 and 1937 mainly involved irregular, poorly trained troops. With little support from the Nanking Government, officers like this had to gather resources from wherever they could.

a little too close to the Japanese garrison at Tungchow, 13 miles from Peking, which resulted in a four- plane air raid on Chi's troops.

On the 30th of September Chi's 9,000-strong army was fighting against a large Nationalist force at Tangshan, 30 miles from Peking. Some of Chi's troops advanced too far ahead of the main force and were captured by the Nationalist soldiers. Chi's soldiers then made three desperate charges to penetrate Tangshan's defences but were repulsed with heavy losses. Fang's and Chi's armies now received news that their supposed allies had switched sides and joined the Nationalists. Without the support of the other two generals, Fang and Chi were marching their armies into oblivion. Despite this blow, the two men were as stubborn as each other and decided to continue their campaign.

On the 4th of October the Armies of Fang and Chi found their march blocked by the armies of their former allies, Generals Tang Yu-lin and Liu Kuei-tang. They switched direction and tried to advance into west Hopei by attacking the town of Changping on the Peking–Suiyuan Railway. Fang's army was badly defeated and he was nearly captured by the Nationalist troops during a skirmish. When his men were offered the chance to surrender they defiantly refused and Fang managed to lead his troops out of the trap laid for them and they melted away to fight another day.

By mid October it finally became apparent to the Nationalist authorities that Chi and Fang had no intention of surrendering. The Nationalist Army's general headquarters in Peking ordered an offensive against the rebel bases at Tangshan and Kaoliying. This time Chi and Fang's armies stood and fought but on the 13th, after a five-hour battle, they were soundly beaten. The remnants of both armies headed in the direction of the eastern border of Chahar, where they planned to create as much havoc as possible. By the end of October, with no prospect of victory, both armies had resorted to looting and attacking trains in the Peking area. Fang Chen-wu was trying to disrupt the Peking–Tientsin Railway with the help of his bandit leader ally, 'Old Rat'. Fang's old bandit friend and his men were busy pulling up the track after receiving payment from the Generals fast-shrinking war chest. At the same time General Chi's Army was trying to damage the track along the Peking–Hankow Railway to goad the Government garrisons into attacking. The grandiose plan of the two Generals was to organise a so-called 'East Asian Allied Army' designed to 'disturb the peace and order in North China'.

The rebels somehow survived into November but it was now obvious that with so many against them it was only a matter of time before they were defeated. Just as the noose closed around them Fang and Chi had a final meeting, where they fell out over strategy.

The two allies Fang and Chi fell out on the eve of their defeat over whether to try and enlist Japanese aid. Fang was totally against asking for help while Chi was happy to; the meeting broke up without a decision. Next morning the foces split, with Fang going eastwards and Chi's troops trying to move into Chahar. Neither army got very far and on the 15th of November the half-starved troops dressed in rags surrendered to Nationalist troops. The pitiful fragments of Fang's and Chi's armies were disarmed; of the 6,558 men who surrendered, only 2,000 had a rifle. Most of the defeated troops were sent to Paotingfu for retraining in order to be allowed back into Nationalist ranks. Both Generals were allowed by Sung Che-yuan to travel to Tientsin, the favourite destination for defeated Chinese military leaders.

In the aftermath of their role in the defeat of Generals Fang and Chi, the two disloyal Generals, Tang Yu-lin and Liu Kwei-tang, clashed. Beginning on the 19th of December their respective armies fought for four days and four nights as each tried to take control of the other's armaments. In what the Government decided was a strictly private affair, Liu came off best. His troops then chased Tang's defeated army back to its headquarters at Fengning. Tang's troops left a large number of rifles and four field guns behind them, which probably temporarily satisfied Liu's lust for more firepower.

## The War in Chahar, 1934–1935

The Japanese moved troops southwards towards the city of Dolonor in early January 1934 to take territory in eastern Chahar. At the same time they began to prepare to build up the infrastructure which would be needed to establish themselves in the province. They completed an airfield at Hataling near Kuyuan, half-way between Dolonor and the provincial capital Kalgan. A large force of 24 Japanese aircraft was established there. They also began to build several military highways linking Dolonor, Hataling and Yenching. Looking to the future, these new roads would mean that they would be within striking distance of the main road between Kalgan and Urga. The latter was the capital of the People's Republic of Mongolia and could be a potential target for the Japanese Imperial Army. By mid-March the situation in Chahar had settled down but the Japanese had sent additional troops to the Kuyuan district. They had also moved large amounts of military supplies into the province from their arms dumps in Jehol. Despite all the Japanese covert operations in Chahar, by the end of the year they still only controlled parts of the east of the province.

The first half of 1935 saw Lieutenant-General Umezu Yoshijiro, commander of the Japanese China Garrison Army, started a new campaign to occupy Chahar. In late January 1935 the Japanese increased the pressure in Chahar by sending a large mechanised force into the province. This force was made up of 600 Japanese troops with a 24-vehicle armoured unit made up of a mix of tanks and armoured cars. They advanced swiftly on the town of Tunghantze in eastern Chahar and met with little resistance. The only Chinese force in the area was a body of mounted irregulars soon routed by the overwhelming Japanese armour. As the Chinese withdrew towards the provincial capital at Kalgan, another Japanese-Manchukuoan force occupied more territory in eastern Chahar. As part of their plans to consolidate their hold on east Chahar the Japanese sent a construction force of several hundred to build a military aerodrome. They worked day and night to finish its construction and the airfield at Taitan soon received its first Japanese aircraft. A Squadron of eight planes arrived, a mix of light bombers, transports and fighters. One transport plane was earmarked for a regular flight from eastern Chahar to Jehol. Some of the other aircraft at the base were sent on regular reconnaissance flights over the whole of Chahar province. These were to establish the exact position of any Chinese provincial forces in preparation for their next advance. Telephone connections were established between the Japanese Imperial Army's secret headquarters in east Chahar with their army HQ in Jehol.

Japanese spies and secret agents were spending their time trying to foment trouble all over the province. The presence of Manchukuoan, Mongol, Chinese and Japanese troops in Chahar made the province a hotbed of conflict. In June 1935 for example, the Japanese plotted to set up a mini-state in several hsiens, or 'counties', in the Dolonor region. This small puppet state was defended by its own tiny army, which was given a distinctive uniform by its Japanese sponsors. Within a month the Japanese had decided to broaden their ambitions when they formed a 3,000 strong Peace Preservation Corps in Chahar. This force was under the command of General Chang Yun-jung but its role was strictly limited; just 150 bullets per soldier were issued.

## Sung's Che-yuan's Phoney War in Chahar

The continued attempts by the Japanese in the mid-1930s to establish total control of Chahar was still being challenged by the presence of the 29th Army. General Sung Che-Yuan's troops were disciplined and well trained and were not

Manchukuoan soldiers parade for their officer during the early 1930s wearing their padded cotton winter uniforms. These troops did much of the fighting during the Chahar Campaign with the support of some Japanese advisors and specialists. The performance of these soldiers varied from unit to unit and depended on the quality of the opposing army.

easily intimidated by the Japanese and their allies. Japanese military planners hoped that enough provocations by their troops would force a reaction by the Chinese that could be exploited. In mid-June the Japanese increased the pressure on the Chinese by claiming that 500 of General Sung's troops had crossed the Chahar-Manchukuo border. According to the Japanese, his soldiers had fired on a Manchukoan border guard post and wounded a number of troops. Press reports said that the Japanese felt justified in expelling all of Sung's troops from Chahar because of repeated incursions into Manchukuoan territory. These claims were accompanied by another declaration that the Japanese Imperial Army had no territorial ambitions in North China! The fighting between the border guards and Sung's force, now reinforced to 700 men, continued for 10 days. During the battle it became apparent that the border guards were not Manchukuoan troops but 150 tough Japanese veterans. On the 18th of June it was announced that General Sung had been dismissed from his role as Chairman of Chahar province. This was of course a humiliating climb-down by the Nationalist Government and a victory for the Japanese. The Japanese had wanted Sung out of the picture largely because of his army's brave performance against their troops in fighting on the Great Wall in 1933. They had long memories.

## The North Chahar Incident

On the 13th of June 1935 four Japanese civilians were arrested in the Changpei District of Chahar having strayed into Chinese-controlled territory without permission. They were taken to the headquarters of the local 29th Army divisional commander, who asked his superior for instructions. He was told to let the Japanese to go on their way with a warning not to travel without the necessary documents in future. As expected the Japanese tried to blow this incident out of all proportion and complained about the treatment their people had received. It was said that the four men had been intimidated and had been threatened with bayonets by their captors and held in cells for 24 hours. These four 'civilians' turned out to be members of the Kwangtung Army Special Corps at Changpei.

The Japanese immediately demanded the release of their innocent citizens and waited for the Chinese response. Colonel Doihara was called into negotiate with the Chinese and of course he used this non-incident to its full potential. Doihara held talks with General Ch'in Te-ch'un, the Deputy Commander of the 29th Army, and demanded the withdrawal of all Chinese troops from Chahar. He argued that there could be no peace in the province while the Chinese kept provoking the Japanese. Doihara pressured General Chin into signing the so-called 'Chin-Doihara Agreement', which called for the withdrawal of the 29th Army from Chahar north of the city of Changpei and the maintenance of peace in Chahar by a neutral Peace Preservation Corps. Under the terms of the agreement, General Ch'in was to be made head of the provincial government in place of Sung Che-yuan.

The withdrawal of the 29th Army left the Manchukuoan and Japanese troops in control of Chahar. They could now bring their plans forward to take their covert war with China into Suiyuan province using western Chahar as the jumping-off point. General Sung did not agree to this humiliation but did withdraw his forces from the east of the province. For the next few months the number of skirmishes between Chinese and Japanese forces increased. Sung tried to hold his positions in western Chahar but he received little support from Chiang Kai-shek. He and his forces were taunted by the behaviour of the Japanese on several occasions in an attempt to force a reaction. Sung knew full well that any retaliation would be used as an excuse by the Japanese for more aggression.

The situation in Chahar was further complicated by the short-lived campaign of some Mongol cavalry under the command of a hereditary banner chief. His Mongol name was Jodpajak but he was commonly known by his Chinese name, Tso Shih-hai. Tso had raised a small army in eastern Chahar and had convinced the Japanese to supply him with arms and ammunition. Tso's army captured six hsiens. He then demanded that he be made the ruler of the 'Chahar League'. With his newly acquired fiefdom of a few small villages and a few thousand people, his claim was uncontested and he was duly elected as chief.

## Chahar in 1936

At the start of 1936 Manchukuoan troops had occupied six border districts of eastern Chahar province. This was to be used as a base for the next westward expansion by the Japanese and their Manchukuoan allies into Suiyuan province. Suiyuan was strategically important to the Japanese because of its railway links to the People's Republic of Mongolia. This Japanese aggression did not go unchallenged by the Chinese Army in the province. General Chang Tse-chung, one of the commanders in the province, proclaimed 'We are determined to defend Chahar at all costs.' He stated that there was no intention to allow the Japanese and their Manchukuoan allies to take Kalgan. Chang went further: 'I would rather die in the defence of the city' than give it up. He demanded help from the Nationalist Government. A meeting was held chaired by Chiang Kai-shek where it was agreed troops would be from Nanking to defend Chahar, neighbouring Suiyuan and Shansi provinces. The Japanese continued to increase the pressure on the Chinese in Chahar in late February by sending a reinforcement of six aircraft. With limited resources in the region, the number of Japanese planes in eastern Chahar left them with only nine planes in Tientsin.

# 14

# 'IRON DETERMINATION':
# THE SUIYUAN CAMPAIGN, 1936–37

During the 1910s and 1920s the various Chinese Republican governments allowed unlimited immigration to Inner Mongolia by Han Chinese settlers. This immigration threatened to swamp the small existing population of ethnic Mongolians and led to great resentment amongst them. There was also resentment against the poor rule of Chinese Republican officials before 1928 and Nationalist officials after. A movement developed during the late 1920s early 1930s amongst the Inner Mongolian princes, many of whom were young men with ambitions for more power. Over the years one particular prince called Teh Wang in Chinese, or Demchukdonggrub in Mongolian, the leader of the West Sunid Banner, gradually rose to prominence. He had been active in Inner Mongolian politics since the mid-1920s and was the most westernised of all the princes. In 1928 Prince Teh Wang had visited the Young Marshal, Chang Hsueh-liang, in Manchuria and had come away with a gift of a thousand rifles and two mountain guns. With these arms the prince could establish a small army, which Chang hoped would remain loyal to him. Chang had to offer the other princes who visited him similar gifts in an attempt to keep a balance of power in Inner Mongolia. For the time being Teh Wang was happy to keep his power base within the Nationalist fold. As long as his claims for greater autonomy progressed, the prince would present himself as outwardly loyal to Chiang Kai-shek.

From the early 1930s however, the Japanese began to try and gain influence in Inner Mongolia. The Imperial Kwangtung Army even appointed its Chief of Staff, General Koiso Kunaiki, to try and make a deal with Prince Teh Wang in 1933. Unfortunately for the Japanese, the prince was a wily customer who did not want to become their puppet unless absolutely necessary. He tried instead to get greater recognition from the Nationalist Government for some kind of semi-autonomy. The Government did agree to establish a Mongolian Local Autonomous Political Council. This body was supposed to give the Inner Mongolians a level of self-government but soon turned out to be a straw dog. Pragmatically, Prince Teh Wang continued to hold talks with Chiang Kai-shek's representatives. But he was also secretly negotiating with the Japanese. Tehh Wang eventually realised that any alliance he made with the Japanese could be dangerous for Inner Mongolia and for himself.

## Tanaka's Scheming

Tanaka Ryukichi, known as the Japanese 'master spy' in China, had been scheming for several years to foment an Inner Mongolian independence movement. Tanaka had previously been involved in engineering the Shanghai Incident in 1932 but had moved his operations to northern China. His plan to sponsor the takeover of Suiyuan province had met with opposition from Tokyo as it could undermine the formation of the Chahar-Hopei Autonomous Council. Tanaka found an ally in Tokyo for his plan in Tojo, the future war leader of Japan, who was then Chief of Secret Police in Manchuria. The worries about the Chahar-Hopei Council were forgotten and full support was given to the Inner Mongolian scheme. This support included the formal acknowledgement of the title of Prince for Teh-Wang, which he had previously used anyway. Tanaka made sure that funds for his various schemes came from the Kwangtung Army directly or from a special fund raised from smuggling and the narcotics trade. He also arranged for a complete ban on tourists, journalists and missionaries from entering Inner Mongolia as they attempted to keep their secret war there secret. The Japanese press were also banned from writing a single word on the war in Inner Mongolia. This attempt at a news blackout failed and the outside world received regular reports on the war throughout 1936.

## Li Shou-hsin's Invasion of Northern Chahar in 1935

Even as the fighting continued in Chahar province, the Kwangtung Army intended to use their bases in the west of the province to gain control of neighbouring Suiyuan. They used the services of one of those shadowy figures who operated in northern China and Mongolia, Li Shou-hsin, to help them in their plans. Li Shou-hsin (1892–1970) was an opportunist former officer in the Jehol provincial armies who joined the Manchukuoan Army having served in the defence of his home province. Born in Jehol province, Li was part of the defence forces in his homeland in 1933 and then joined the Manchukuoan Army. He was a shadowy character well suited to the secret war in which he fought, first in Chahar and then in Suiyan provinces. (After July 1937 he was given command of the puppet Inner Mongolian Army and served in that role until the end of World War Two.)

Li was given a relatively high rank in the Manchukuoan Army in 1933 and was encouraged to recruit a large irregular force by the Japanese. He set about his task trying to recruit troops from whatever source he could; but the sparse population in Inner Mongolia made it difficult. Eventually he put together a small army made up of a few Mongolians and a large number of Manchukuoans. As he could not be choosy, the ranks of his army were filled with ex-bandits and former convicts. He was also driven to recruit ex-Manchukuoan troops who had been thrown out of their army by the Japanese.

His 3,000–5,000-strong army invaded northern Chahar on the 24th of December 1935. The renegade General was given limited support by the Kwangtung Army, which included the loan of a few Japanese-flown aircraft.

He also had the support of a few artillery pieces which were most likely ex-warlord mountain guns and a handful of armoured cars. The artillery and the armoured cars, probably British made Crossleys, were manned by covert Japanese crews. North Chahar was made up of six hsiens and was defended by about 2,000 men of the Peace Preservation Corps. Li's force was poorly trained and badly disciplined but was more than a match for the local Nationalist militia. The Mongolian-Manchukuoan army soon occupied Kuyuan, Paochang, Kangpo, Huateh, Shangtu and Changpei hsiens. Li and his army established themselves in their newly won territory, which became a base for future ventures by the Kwangtung Army. This military base could now become the conduit for all secret supplies and the starting point for clandestine operations by the Japanese.

Li Shou-hsin's invasion was supported according to the press by a few Japanese aircraft flying incognito. These were from the so-called 1st Kawaida Squadron, which had been formed by the Kwangtung Army to support its 'adventures' in Inner Mongolia. Its commander Kawaida Yoshimasa had joined the Manchurian Aviation Company, or MKKK. He was given the task of creating a small air unit with a mix of fighters, light bombers and transports. This flying circus was designed to provide air support in an environment where little or no air opposition was expected. It was equipped at first with several Fokker Super Universal transports and Fokker 3m transports. During the early campaigns in Inner Mongolia at the end of 1935 the transports doubled as bombers and reconnaissance planes

## Li and Tso's Army, January–October 1936

Generals Li Shou-hsin and Tso Shah-hai had ambitions to expand the territory under their control. The six hsiens they already controlled covered an area of 40,000 miles but they wanted to add another five hsiens to it. At the same time the two Generals decided that Tso should be the official head of the East Chahar Government while Li would be Defence Minister They set their sights on the neighbouring province of Suiyuan and rumours spread in January 1936 that they would be invading it soon. In early February 1936 reports on the build-up of an Inner Mongolian army appeared in Chinese newspapers. Li had entered Chahar at the head of an army estimated at 5,000 men but this force could not be kept in the field constantly.

In January 1936 Tso Shih-hai had a 3,000-strong army made up exclusively of Mongolians, with the majority cavalry. This force was stationed at the town of Paochang where Tso had established a headquarters. In June Li Shou-hsin's army was made up mainly of Manchukuoans although other reports say that he recruited soldiers from Shantung province. Li was often described as a 'freebooter' and it is hard to find any flattering comments about him. His army in early 1936 had a strength of several thousand men and they were growing restless having had no loot for a while. General Li Shou-hsin advanced to the Chahar-Suiyuan border with his force from his headquarters at Changpei. Li's army was said to be secretly under the command of Matsumuro Takayoshi, the

The personal bodyguard of Prince Teh-Wang rides past his desert headquarters in late 1935. Cavalry formed the majority of the Inner Mongolian Army in 1935–36 with most being poorly disciplined irregulars. This elite unit is part of the small personal army raised by the prince in the early 1930s who were loyal to their hereditary leader.

director of the intelligence bureau in Chengte, the capital of Jehol. In response, General Fu Tso-yi, the Chairman of the Suiyuan Provincial Administration, ordered the border defences to be bolstered. The two brigades that were stationed on the border were reinforced by two regiments and a large quantity of arms and ammunition was sent to them. News reports for some reason made great play of the despatch of hand grenades to the troops. There was no mention of much needed artillery and machine guns. Although poorly armed, Li and Tso's troops all had a rifle at least. A phoney war developed on the border as both sides dug in and awaited further instructions from their respective commanders. All four of the Mongol tribes or banners in Suiyuan were quick to pledge their support to Fu and his provincial government.

In early August General Li Shou-hsin finally decided to try and expand his territory as he had planned. He attacked the Nationalist garrisons around the town of Taoling in West Suiyuan on two occasions. His small army was repulsed on each occasion losing 100 killed and 200 wounded, which was a large proportion of his force. He was now approached by the Japanese to support Teh Wang in his coming campaign to invade Suiyuan province. Presumably money changed hands and Li and Tso agreed to add their forces to the polyglot army being put together by Tanaka and his Intelligence Agency. In late August the two future allies Li and Tso clashed over the control of a garrison they both coveted. They continued fighting until the Japanese stepped in, banged their heads together and demanded they prepare for the coming campaign in Suiyuan.

The commander of Prince Teh-Wang's bodyguard cavalry unit salutes his leader during a parade in 1935. His uniform is made up of a good quality fur lined coat and hat, provided to a small number of troops by the prince. Around his waist he wears a brand-new leather ammunition belt with pockets for his C-96 semi-automatic pistol. Some of the Inner Mongolian troops were seen with sub-machine guns bought in small numbers by the prince.

## The Armies in the Suiyuan Campaign

Like all of the Banner Princes of Inner Mongolia, Prince Teh Wang had his own army, which was really just a large bodyguard. In 1929 the prince organised a small army with the 1,000 rifles given to him by Chang Hsueh-liang on a visit to the Mukden Arsenal. With a strength of 900 men it was not a large army but compared to those of the rival princes it was adequate. Even in these early days it became obvious that the shortage of manpower in Inner Mongolia was going to be a problem. It meant he could not even recruit as many men as he had rifles. The town of Shangteh was to be used as the base for the Inner Mongolian invasion and in early 1936 a Military School was organised to try and supply them with their own officer class. It had an intake of 500 cadets, which was probably every even remotely suitable youth in Inner Mongolia. In early 1936, Prince Teh Wang established an official Inner Mongolian Army, which was divided into two separate units. The 1st Army was made up of Li Shou-sin's Manchukoan troops and the 2nd most made up of the prince's personal army of Mongolians. It was said that in the whole Chahar–Suiyuan region there were only about 60,000 able-bodied males fit to serve.

The overall defence of Suiyuan was in the hands of Marshal Yen Hsi-shan, who was Director of the Taiyuan Pacification Headquarters from 1931. Yen knew he needed to have a reliable commander to represent him in Suiyuan and picked General Fu Tso-yi. General Fu Tso-yi was the most able of Yen Hsi-shan's subordinates and had served in his Shansi army for many years. The General was a native of Shansi province and served in the army of the Shansi warlord Yen. Fu had risen swiftly through the ranks in the late 1920s. He took part in the Northern Expedition and the Central Plains War with the Shansi army and later developed a good working relationship with Chang Hsueh-liang. (His later service in the Sino-Japanese War and in the Civil War of 1946–49 confirmed his military and political abilities.)

In this Japanese propaganda postcard of the 1930s
Prince Teh Wang is seen in the formal traditional
dress he wore throughout his career. He was
occasionally seen in military uniform but this
was usually after the regularisation of the Inner
Mongolian Army after 1937. Teh Wang used the
Japanese while at the same time being used by
them; he soon lived to regret his collaboration.

When Fu arrived in Suiyuan to take up his new command in 1931, it was with
the promise of as much support as he needed to defend the province. Fu's troops
were involved in a number of clashes with the Japanese-sponsored forces in the
early 1930s in Chahar. By the time fighting began in Suiyuan in 1936, Fu and
his officers were well established in Suiyuan and were ready for the Mongolian
invaders. Fu had also developed a good working relationship with Chang
Hsueh-liang in case he needed help from the North-Eastern Army. Yen had sent
most of his better troops to fight in Suiyuan and had also sent two of his most
able officers to help Fu. These were his son-in-law, General Wang Ching-kuo,
and General Chou Ch'eng-chou. Fu also had the services of a German military
advisor recruited in 1933 to help in the campaign against the Inner Mongolians.
The Japanese support for the Inner Mongolians was seen as a direct threat to his
authority by the Shansi General Yen Hsi-shan. He suspected the Japanese would
not be content with the conquest of the three provinces of Inner Mongolia. He
feared that his province would be the next on the list. With this in mind, he was
prepared to commit his best troops and ablest commanders to the campaign. The
majority of the Nationalist Army in Suiyuan was well trained and well armed
with rifles and machine guns. Shansi troops who made up the vast majority of
the army were also quite liberally armed with copies of the Thompson M1921
sub-machine gun. These were produced in the Taiyuan Arsenal.

General Fu Tso-yi had supplied 37,000 rifles to Suiyuan provincial militia in
August. Nationalist reinforcements for the defenders on the Eastern Suiyuan
Front arrived in the form of the 13th Army Corps under General Tang En-peh,
the 7th Cavalry Division under General Men Ping-yo and the 25th Army Corps
under General Wang Yao-huang. In preparation for the expected Inner Mongolian
offensive against Suiyuan, Fu Tso-yi appealed to the Central Government for

support. He also called for aid from the Shansi Governor Yen Hsi-shan, whose forces had been reinforced by Central Government units. These units had been sent into Shansi as part of Chiang Kai-shek's plan to trap the survivors of the Long March. Yen responded to Fu in August by sending the 19th Army under General Wang Ching-kuo to neighbouring Suiyuan. The 19th was made up of the 68th Division, the 7th and 8th Independent Brigades, four artillery regiments and a small anti-aircraft unit. Chiang Kai-shek also responded to Fu's request for help by sending General Tang Enbo's two-division 13th Army and General Men Ping-yueh's 7th Cavalry Division to the front.

To try and co-ordinate the defence of Suiyuan, a meeting was held on the 30th of October with Chiang Kai-shek, Yen Hsi-shan and Fu Tso-yi in attendance. At the meeting the troops' dispositions for the coming campaign were agreed and Chiang expressed his confidence in Yen and Fu's ability to handle the fighting. As a result of the meeting Yen reorganised his forces into three Route Armies, a large cavalry force and reserve force. Final deployments were to be made as soon as the 13th Army arrived at the front. Before this could be achieved however, the Japanese-supported offensive began on the 15th of November.

Five hundred men of the Central Government's Anti-Aircraft Corps also arrived at the front. This unit was supposed to have a number of 'large calibre guns' and were stationed at Pingtichuan. The war is well documented in photographs and there is no evidence of these weapons; it was probably 20mm light anti-aircraft guns that they had. The shortage of weaponry on both sides was highlighted by the detailed list of rewards offered to anyone who brought men, or more

This Inner Mongolian bodyguard stands guard over the yurt of Teh Wang's headquarters at Pailingmiao in July 1936. He is one of the better and more loyal troops in the Inner Mongolian army who fought alongside less reliable irregulars. His padded cotton uniform carries the blue and yellow cap badge of his army and his armband proclaims his allegiance to the prince.

Scruffy-looking Inner Mongolian infantry take a smoke break during the fighting with Nationalist troops in late 1936. These soldiers of Prince Teh Wang have been recruited from all over Inner Mongolia and many are ex-bandits. Their uniforms are ill-fitting and not all the men seem to have been issued padded cotton winter hats. The lucky ones have the yellow and blue badge of the Inner Mongolian Army on the headwear and on their upper sleeves some have armbands. These presumably carry the name of their commander, their unit number and the name of the army they serve in. They have not yet been trusted with rifles, which they might have run off with if they were given them before the battle.

importantly, weapons, to the Nationalist Army. These rewards were offered by the Nationalist Government to any 'irregular' who came over to the Suiyuan army. A sum of $500,000 was offered to any army or divisional commander who brought all his men over to the government side. Lower sums were offered to a brigade commander ($30,000), regimental commander ($10,000) and $5,000 to a battalion commander. Any soldier who deserted to the Nationalist Army got $10 and a pilot who flew his plane over to them got $20,000. An anti-aircraft gun was worth $10,000 and a field gun or anti-aircraft machine gun was worth $5,000. An armoured car was valued at $2,000 and a heavy machine gun was $1,000, with a light machine gun worth $500. A radio was valued at $500, a rifle $30 and a revolver $20.

The Nationalist Army in Suiyuan in December 1936 was made up of 12 divisions. There were 80,000 Shansi troops and 30,000 troops from Nanking. In eastern Suiyuan there were the 68th, 73rd and 191st Infantry Divisions as well as three cavalry divisions and one regiment of artillery. In northern Shansi province there were four divisions and in north-west Shansi another four. The

This parade of a mixed infantry and mounted unit of the Inner Mongolian Army is taking place just before the Battle of Pailingmiao. The infantry to the left of the photograph may well be seconded soldiers of the Manchukuoan Army and appear to have uniforms. In contrast, the cavalry mounted on hardy Mongolian ponies are wearing their own clothing. The man stood in front of the infantry may even be one of the elusive Japanese advisors who usually kept well away from the camera.

Chinese in Suiyuan also received support from a Mongol Volunteer Force led by Prince Yun, whose troops fought at the battle of Pailingmiao.

## Prince Teh Wang Joins the Japanese

Prince Teh Wang had been flirting with the idea of throwing in his lot with the Japanese for several years. He had tried working with the Nationalist Government for a long time as he sought at least partial autonomy for Inner Mongolia. He had joined the Inner Mongolian Political Council set up by Nanking in April 1934 but this was a body with no power. In 1934 his trust in Chiang Kai-shek largely disappeared when his trusted advisor and second-in-command was arrested and then murdered in Nanking. The Japanese charm offensive to get the prince to accept their sponsorship continued with a visit in October 1935 to his headquarters. Two Kwangtung Army officers, Nakajima Manzo and Nakazawa Oyoshi, persuaded Teh-Wang to attend a meeting in Changchun in Manchukuo. There the prince met the then Kwangtung Army commander, General Minami Jiro and discussed Mongol-Japanese co-operation. The meeting was not a total success as the prince refused to agree to Japanese plans to hand four of the Eastern Leagues of Inner Mongolia to Manchukuo. The prince asked nevertheless if the Japanese would still help him in his quest to establish an independent Inner Mongolia and they agreed. As a sign of their good will the Japanese gave the prince 500,000 Yen for his war chest as well as 5,000 Arisaka rifles for his own personal army. Bribes and gifts kept coming the prince's way; the Manchukuoan government presented him with his own

A Nationalist sentry patrols around his unit's camp wearing a padded winter uniform along with a long fur-lined coat, also made from padded cotton. The Suiyuan Campaign in November and December 1936 was fought in the bitter cold of a desert winter. This soldier has wrapped the breech of his rifle with rags to stop the trigger mechanism from freezing up in the cold.

transport plane in January 1936. At the same time they guaranteed him 'ample' arms and ammunition for his proposed military campaign.

From the beginning of 1936 pressure began to build on the Inner Mongolians and Prince Teh Wang to declare independence. It appeared that the Mongolian population was in favour of this move and in mid March, 59 of the 77 Inner Mongolian Banners agreed to accept Japanese support. In late April Prince Teh Wang and his military commander Li Shou-hsin had a meeting with Captain Takayoshi Tanaka. Tanaka was the head of the Japanese Special Service and was responsible for organising the Inner Mongolians' military operations. Tanaka and his agents now put heavy pressure on Prince Teh Wang to declare independence. The prince was quite isolated in his palace surrounded by guards who had formally served in the pro-Japanese east Chahar army. Although he was not happy under Nationalist rule, he was aware that he could easily be exchanging one master for a worse one. In the press it was reported that he spent a few days in early June consulting with General Li Shou-hsin and General Tso Shih-hai, the east Chahar leaders. Both men were in fact firmly in the Japanese camp.

The Inner Mongolians had some justification for wanting to break away from the rest of China. Fu Tso-yi's governorship of Suiyuan had been oppressive with heavy taxes imposed on the Mongol population. Funds which had been allocated to the Mongol people had been given to the Han Chinese immigrant population.

## The OOB of the Inner Mongolian Army in 1936

The Inner Mongolian Army was recruited from a variety of sources and was never a united force. Its exact strength is open to debate as different sources give conflicting figures. It was somewhere between 11,000 and 25,000, which of course is a big difference but it has to be remembered that only 50% of the troops had rifles. The first order of battle has Wang Ying with only 300 cavalry under his command while the second says he had 7,000! General Chin Chia-shan has 3,000 in one order of battle but only 2,000 in another; these were mainly ex-Nationalist troops from Sun Tien-yang's army (see chapter 11). General Li Shou-hsian's contingent made up mainly of Manchukuoans has a strength of 3,000–5,000 in the first instance and 6,000 in the second. Li was said to have a large number of mercenary troops raised in Shantung province in this total. General Pao Yueh-ching's 3,000 men listed in the second order of battle are attributed to another unknown commander, Chang Fu-t'ang, in the first list. Pao's troops were mainly ex-east Chahar troops who had seen action for several years against the Nationalist Army. In the second order of battle 3,000 Mongolian militia men of General Tso Shih-hai are listed, whereas in the first they are not mentioned. Wang Ying's force is almost certainly exaggerated in the second order of battle, so 2,000 which is mentioned in yet another order of battle would be realistic. Just to confuse the issue, a press report from the time gives Wang's army's strength at 5,000 men. His men were said to have received training from Japanese advisors for longer than any other contingent in the army. Wang's contingent was given the grand title of 'The Great Han Righteous Army' and had been recruited mainly in south Chahar. Wang had persuaded the Japanese that if they funded him he could recruit an army from disgruntled Nationalist soldiers. He was successful and the several thousand men he raised were sent into Jehol for training, which was not a success. Despite this training an eyewitness said that his 'bandits' were amongst the worse disciplined in the army. Taking all the variants into account it would appear that the 15,000 mentioned in other sources for the total number of troops is probably more or less correct. And with the shortage of rifles a frontline strength of between 7,000 and 8,000 men is probable. The rest of the army was kept in reserve and anyway, few these soldiers had any combat value. There was also a 200-strong artillery force which was reported to crew the few artillery pieces that the Inner Mongolians had. The Inner Mongolians probably only had three field guns, although they still probably had a few 75mm mountain guns. Arms used by the Inner Mongolians included 10,000 Model 13 rifles produced in the Fengtien Arsenal in Manchuria and supplied by the Japanese. Other small arms came from the war booty captured by the Japanese in Manchuria in 1931 and Jehol in 1933. These included Czechoslovakian ZB-26 light machine guns as the main type. The Japanese advisors who had helped train this composite force were highly doubtful as to its capabilities. They had spent a number of months trying to whip these troops into shape and were not confident about them. Some appealed to their superiors in the Kwangtung Army to cancel the coming offensive but their opinions were ignored.

The Chinese provincial troops defending Suiyuan in 1936 had little heavy weaponry and this Swedish Bofors M1930 75mm field gun was one of the few in use. A few light anti-aircraft guns were sent from Nanking to help combat the Japanese aircraft in Suiyuan. On the other side, the Inner Mongolians had a handful of field and mountain guns supplied by their Japanese sponsors. Even machine guns were rarely seen and it was usually rifle against rifle in the skirmishes and battles in the Mongolian desert.

## The Build-up to War and Japan's Covert Air Support

In early October large shipments of arms and ammunition arrived in Eastern Chahar province for the Inner Mongolians. On the other side Nationalist General Liu Ju-ming, the acting governor of Chahar, sent the 142nd Division to assist Fu Tso-yi. Scores of lorries carried ammunition to Suiyuan from Jehol while 5,000 of Wang Ying's irregular Manchukuoans proceeded to the Suiyuan border. On the 22nd of October the vanguard of the Inner Mongolian invasion force clashed with the 'elite' Shansi Cavalry Division under the command of General Chao Cheng-shao. General Pao Yueh-hsing, who had just joined the Inner Mongolians, began to recruit and train troops at Kapotze in Eastern Suiyuan.

The Japanese phantom air force supporting the Inner Mongolians was made up of 28 planes of various types flown by 80 pilots under the command of Colonel Kawaida Yoshiaki. His 1st Kawaida Squadron which had been used in Chahar in 1935 was now re-formed as the 2nd Kawaida Squadron. The 2nd Squadron had an official strength of four Nakajima Type 91 fighters, two Kawasaki Type 88 light bombers, six Super Universal transports and a single De Havilland DH80 of the Manchukuoan Airline MKKK to perform a transport role. This small air force operated throughout the Suiyuan campaign losing a number of planes to Nationalist anti-aircraft fire. The official strength of the Kawaida Squadron was unofficially boosted according to press reports by more aircraft during the campaign. There were reportedly three light bombers, eight fighters and five scout planes stationed at Changpei, 40 miles north of

Kalgan. There was also a small five-plane mixed squadron at Shangtu and a similarly sized unit at Pailingmiao. Even though this secret force was supposed to be fighting incognito, all its aircraft carried Japanese markings. In the press the Japanese air support for the Inner Mongolians was described as coming from 'a certain quarter' and unexploded bombs were said to have worn the markings of 'a certain foreign country'. Although the Japanese launched a large number of bombing raids in support of the Inner Mongolians, they were not always effective. One report said that instead of dropping conventional bombs the crews of the light bombers were throwing grenades as they flew at low level over Chinese lines.

## Chinese Preparations and Japanese 'Privatisation'

All over China but especially in the North, patriotic school girls sewed padded cotton uniforms to send to the troops in Suiyuan. Students at the Medical College in Shantung province organised an Ambulance Corps to go to Suiyuan. Teenage girls from high schools began training as nurses to go to the frontline with it. Middle school students from Nanking and Shanghai asked their education authorities to change the dates of their holidays. This was so they would be able to help the Suiyuan troops in any way they could during their extended holidays. Students in the chemistry department of the Peking Medical College were working around the clock to try and produce medicines. Supplies donated by civilian groups were sent to the province in columns of horses and carts when trucks were unavailable. Students in Peking showed their support for the troops on the

This unit of Citizen Volunteers parade with their new flag before going off to the frontline. The volunteers have been issued with basic winter uniforms from the provincial army stores. Many of these items of winter clothing were donated by patriotic Chinese associations across the country. Although most of the men have been issued with Gew-88 rifles, they may not have much ammunition in the canvas bandoliers around their waists.

Suiyuan front by fasting and working in unheated classrooms. The savings they made on food and heat were then spent on warm clothing and comforts for the troops. Another group, the émigré 'Suiyuanese Civil Society of Nanking' asked its members to donate a percentage of their salaries to the defence of their homeland. By early December the daily amount being raised from all the various support groups throughout China had reached a staggering high point of $500,000 per day. It had reached a total of $1,200,000 by the end of the month, which the authorities decided should be shared out amongst the Suiyuan Army. In an attempt to raise morale, each soldier was to receive $3. Officers under the rank of 2nd Lieutenant were to get $5, and any under the rank of Captain were to get $10 each. Unusually for Chinese armies of the period, compensation was paid to the families of wounded and killed soldiers. Wounded other ranks were to get $70 to send to their families and officers above the rank of captain were to receive $100. For soldiers killed in action or who died from wounds the family received $700, a huge sum for an ordinary soldier. Officers' families received $1,000, which caused problems as it was not that much higher than that received by the ordinary soldier. Marshal Yen Hsi-shan beginning during the November fighting received regular deputations from all parts of China. These brought messages of support and more importantly large sums of money to finance his war effort. Money had been raised for the Suiyuan campaign under the slogan 'Donate One Day's Wages for the Boys at the Front!' Other messages of support came from the majority of his fellow military governors, who told him he was fighting on behalf of all Chinese. Chiang Kai-shek himself flew into the Shansi capital Taiyuan on the 18th of November to meet with Yen and Fu Tso-yi. He praised them for their efforts in Suiyuan and assured them their fight was not a local but a national effort. The visit

Fresh Chinese troops march up to front to relieve their comrades who are going back for a rest from the fighting. The flag bearer at the front of the column has rolled his standard up and carries it in a sleeve for protection. Both armies were fighting the bitter winter conditions as much as each other in the November-December campaigns. Goggles worn by the troops helped protect the eyes against the wind and the sand.

from Chiang did not, however, bring any material support, although he assured the two generals that he had plans for dealing with the Japanese. In reality, Yen and his commanders were more or less on their own throughout the campaign. Requests sent from the commanders of remnants of the pre-1931 North-Eastern Army asking for permission to go to the aid of Yen were vetoed by Chiang. He insisted that they remain where they were, fighting the Communists, whom he still regarded as the main foe. During Chiang's visit Yen and Fu emphasised that theirs was a national fight but this did not change their leader's mind.

On both sides, preparations for the inevitable war continued throughout 1936, with the intensity building during the summer. These included the production of gas masks for the Nationalist troops, who had reason to worry after Japan's use of the banned chemical weapon in Chahar. A gas mask factory in China was put into full production with 200 workers working at full capacity to produce 500,000 masks per month at $15 each. At the same time 10,000 copies of an anti-gas instruction manual were printed and were handed out to officials and village elders in the war zone. Fu Tso-yi recruited a large number of labourers to start building extensive defence systems around the main towns. These were described by eyewitnesses as 'elaborate' but many of them were to be destroyed by the Inner Mongolians' air support. Fu also tried to use economic warfare against the Inner Mongolian Army by blocking coal supplies from reaching their bases.

In early October large shipments of arms and ammunition had arrived at bases in eastern Chahar. The Japanese used the Peking–Suiyuan Railway to secretly move arms and other supplies to the front. This covert arms supply route was organised by the so-called 'International Transportation Company', a Japanese private company working for the government. The improvised nature of the Inner Mongolian expedition was illustrated by the loan of 150 trucks seconded to their army by the South Manchuria Railway. Some of the Inner Mongolian's radio personnel were on temporary secondment from the Manchuria Electrical Company. Enough small arms had been stockpiled for the Inner Mongolian Army and a few field guns had been donated by the Japanese. Other weaponry was theoretically on loan to the Mongolians including tanks and armoured cars but these were never handed over to them.

## The Inner Mongolian Offensive

Sporadic clashes began to build up in early November. In one three-day period there 17 identifiable skirmishes between the Nationalist defenders and the Inner Mongolians. The serious fighting began on the 14th of November with the Mongolians initiating it by surrounding and then assaulting the town of Hungkeherhtu on the eastern border of Suiyuan. Several desperate frontal attacks were launched on the town defences but were all beaten off with heavy losses to the Mongolians. Hungkerehertu's garrison received a timely reinforcement from advance elements of the Nationalists' 35th Army on the 17th. The final Inner Mongolian attack was launched on the 18th and was followed up by a strong Chinese counter-attack. After a three-hour battle the attacking Chinese force chased the Mongolians eastwards with the defeated force leaving 300 dead on the field. Amongst another 300 captured Mongolians were two Japanese advisors, Reikichi Wamu and Toshio Matsumura. These two had been part of the team operating the radio equipment for the Inner Mongolians. They had been issued with the radio codes for all stations in Inner Mongolia as part of their equipment. Although the fate of these two Japanese is unsure, Fu Tso-yi was known to have some prisoners executed as 'illegal combatants'. Wang Ying, one of the Mongolian commanders, only just managed to escape by horseback from the battle to rejoin his retreating army. On the day of Fu Tso-yi's victory his superior Yen Hsi-shan made a rousing speech to his troops. He proclaimed his 'iron determination' to defeat the Mongolian invaders and their Japanese sponsors. Yen saw the defence of Suiyuan as part of a greater war against the Japanese and their proxy allies. 'The least I can do to assist in the task of National Rejuvenation is to preserve the territorial integrity of Suiyuan and whatever sacrifices have to be made will not be regretted.'

Aspects of the clandestine nature of Japan's support for the Inner Mongolians were often comical. One report from the 21st of November stated that 100 foreign military officers had arrived in Tulun and joined the Manchukuoan troops there. They had been sent from Jehol and were kitted out with 'Mongolian type clothing'. The report does not state that these men were Japanese, only that they were 'ready to take part in fighting in Suiyuan'.

## The Battle of Pailingmiao

The Inner Mongolians withdrew from their unsuccessful attack on Hungkeherhtu and retired in disorder back to their base at the town of Pailingmiao. Pailingmiao was an important town in Inner Mongolia, strategically and culturally. It was situated 300 miles north-west of Kalgan close to the Mongolian border in the north of Suiyuan. As well as being a communications centre the town was also the headquarters of the Mongolian branch of the Buddhist religion. It was full of Buddhist temples and monasteries and had one of the largest communities of priests in Inner and Outer Mongolia. Pailingmiao had been selected by Prince Teh as the future capital of his independent state, so the Chinese wanted to recapture it as soon as possible. On the 23rd of November Fu Tso-yi rushed all the troops he could to the town to capture it before the Inner Mongolians could fortify it. Fu discovered that the Inner Mongolians were moving 5,000 reinforcements to the town so had to attack before they arrived. Using what the world press called 'brilliant strategy', a two-pronged attack was launched with a large Chinese cavalry force making a flanking movement. They came up behind an Inner Mongolian force advancing to the nearby town of Wuchuan and destroyed it. At the same time another cavalry unit surprised a mixed Manchukuoan-Mongol force close to Wuchuan. Having largely destroyed the Inner Mongolian main formations around Pailingmiao, Fu's troops moved into the town. Again operating in two separate groups, one force attacked the town centre. The second force attacked the Inner Mongolian stronghold at Shiramuren on the outskirts. These battles attracted worldwide attention, as for once a Chinese Army was coming out on top against a Japanese force. The Inner Mongolians were pushed back and their rearguard, their 'elite' 7th Division, was destroyed bravely defending the Shiramuren Temple. Prince Teh Wang's army was definitely a case of too many chiefs and not enough Indians, with a total of 26 commanders killed during the fighting. Total Inner Mongolian losses were 900 killed and 300 taken prisoner including one Japanese advisor, Wujokoshi Kohama, whose fate was unknown. By the 2nd of December the last of the Inner Mongolians were withdrawing from the battle and their campaign had received a near fatal blow.

When Fu's troops occupied the town they found a lot of damning evidence of Japan's involvement in the fighting. Amongst the secret Japanese documents was one describing a harebrained scheme for the formation of a Pan-Mongol Empire. This so-called 'Great Yuan Empire' or 'Ta-Yuan Ti-Kuo' was supposed to encompass Inner Mongolia and several western Chinese provinces. This ambitious plan called for Inner Mongolia to be joined with Jehol and Sinkiang provinces. The fact that Jehol province had been 'reunited' with Manchukuo in 1933 was not mentioned in the captured documents. Presumably the Manchkuoan Emperor Pu-Yi would be persuaded that he didn't really want Jehol after all! Given that Manchukuo's claim on Jehol was the reason for Japan's invasion, this showed the lack of joined-up thinking at times in the various Imperial Army Headquarters in China in the 1930s. Another document was found which claimed that the Kwangtung Army had offered the Mongolians $1,000,000 if they captured the city!

Of more practical use to Fu's Army were the munitions and other military equipment captured at Pailingmiao, which included several Japanese field guns. There were also 10 machine guns, 1,000 rifles, 10,000 cases of small arms ammunition and several short wave radios. Other supplies captured included 20,000 bags of flour and 500 tins of petrol. The food and ammunition captured was enough to last the Nationalist Army in Suiyuan for several months. Japanese officers were captured in fighting outside Pailingmiao and these were moved to Kweihua for interrogation.

Away from the main battle for Pailingmiao the Japanese kept up their air campaign to try and subdue other parts of the province. One of their biggest attacks involved 17 aircraft, which flew over the town of Hsingho in Eastern Suiyuan on the 24th of November. According to the locals this large squadron only dropped a total of 12 bombs on the town (so that's fewer than one each) but did manage to inflict a lot of material damage. They killed seven civilians before flying off after what appears to have been a half-hearted raid. On the same day nine unidentified planes dropped bombs on the town of Yenmenkwan in Northern Shansi province. The intention of this raid, which was beaten off by anti-aircraft fire, was to destroy the main highway from Shansi into Suiyuan to cut off supplies to Fu's troops.

On the 30th of November Japanese aircraft dropped gas bombs on the town of Pinghichtuan on the Peking–Suiyuan Railway. The 40 dead were seen as a warning from the Japanese to the Chinese military in northern China to stay out of the war in Suiyuan.

# Winter Fighting

### December

Prince Teh Wang and his Japanese advisors knew that the morale of his ad hoc army would not survive any more reverses. It was therefore planned to try and take back the initiative by recapturing Pailingmaio before Fu Tso-yi's troops could react. The only available Inner Mongolian force was Wang Ying's 'Grand Han Righteous Army'. This force was taken by Japanese trucks on the 2nd of December to the outskirts of the city and told to attack it with predictable results. Without the artillery and air support they had grown accustomed to, this attack was bound to end in disaster. Wang's army was slaughtered in a frontal assault with most of the irregulars killed and the remainder taken prisoner. Prince Teh's Army was now reduced according to some reports to 2,000 Mongol cavalry from Jehol province, 3,000 Manchukuoan infantry under the command of General Chang Hai-peng and a 3,000-strong force of irregular troops with a few pieces of artillery. The loyalty of this new force was now doubtful and it was estimated that only 2,000 of them could be relied upon to support the prince.

After the failure of the Inner Mongolian attack on Pailingmiao the Nationalists began preparations for an attack against the town of Pangkiang. The Nationalist Army had concentrated several divisions in Pailingmiao to attack Teh Wang's new headquarters. In the meantime, one officer of the Inner Mongolian Army was being dealt with for his incompetence. General Chin Chia-shan was in command of a force of irregulars who mutinied at Shangtu during the fighting for Pailingmiao. He was taken back to the Kwangtung Headquarters in Jehol and after interrogation he was taken out and shot.

During early December Pailingmiao came under heavy air attack by the 2nd Kawaida Air Group. By the 5th of December four Japanese aircraft had been shot down by the anti-aircraft gun crews sent from Nanking. These were having to counter regular raids by the Japanese light bombers on Pailingmiao and according to Chinese propaganda were crack shots. It was claimed that in one raid by eight bombers two were shot down. When the bodies of the four dead crewmen were recovered it was found that all were Japanese.

More than 30 armoured vehicles and numerous machine guns had been transported to Shangteh from stores in Manchukuo via Jehol. Reports of 46 planes arriving in crates to be assembled in Suiyuan were, however, exaggerated. This would have been too much of a commitment by the Japanese. On the 9th, Nationalist forces captured the hills surrounding the town of Tamiao and took the surrender of large numbers of Inner Mongolian troops. For the first time the Chinese had the support of a few homemade armoured cars that had been sent to the front. During this heavy fighting the Nationalist commanders accused the Mongolians of using gas bullets supplied to them by the Japanese.

The Japanese continued to support the Inner Mongolians until the end of the year despite their failures in the November fighting. Four Japanese planes began bombing the Nationalist positions at Taolin in North Suiyuan on the 27th. Their positions were almost completely destroyed by the air raid with heavy casualties suffered by the Chinese. There were reports that a supply column of 18 lorries was carrying ammunition and some new rifles for Manchukuoan troops stationed at Kapotze in Western Chahar. There was also supposed to be 20 light tanks stationed on the border. In addition, the Kwangtung Army had sent a 30-strong air element to support an offensive against the towns of Hsingho and Taolin. The advance force for this new offensive was made up of 3,000 Manchukuoan troops, who were proving to be totally unreliable. This new offensive to recapture the city of Pailingmiao was planned to take advantage of Chiang Kai-shek's kidnap at Sian (see page ***). On this occasion Teh Wang was told that by the Japanese that they would not support him and he had to abandon it. In the preparations for the offensive a number of Japanese military advisors got too close to the frontline. They were captured wearing a mixture of Mongolian and Manchukuoan uniforms and, following Fu Tso-yi's directive, were shot.

## Unreliable Manchukuoans

After the defeat of the Inner Mongolians in November and early December thye Manchukuoan contingent was blamed. Now they had been defeated in a series of battles, the Manchukuoan rank and file and their officers began looking for a way out. On the 21st of December forty Japanese advisors were killed by their Chahar troops, who deserted to the Nationalist Army. Seven days later a Brigade of Manchukuoans mutinied at Patai in west Chahar and looted the town they were garrisoning. They escaped across the border into west Hopei province. The Japanese estimates of the number of Manchukuoan soldiers who had deserted or gone over to the Nationalist Army since the start of the fighting had reached 7,000. Amongst units that had gone over to the Chinese en masse was the 14th Manchukuoan Battalion, who killed their Japanese advisors before crossing the lines. In the wake of the Inner Mongolian defeat a number of officers, mainly from the Manchukuoan army, tried to ingratiate themselves with the Nationalists. On the 30th of December General Pao Yueh-ching begged Fu Tso-yi to pardon him and let him serve the Nationalists. A day later two more Manchukuoan Generals, Ching Sen-chang and Shi Yun-san, offered their services to Chiang Kai-shek. The Japanese were swift to punish any 'traitors' they captured and when a large group of Manchukuoan and Mongolian troops mutinied at Pangkiang and looted the town, as well as Shangtu and Tehina, a number of them were captured and sent to Jehol to be court-martialled and executed in early December.

## Japanese Public Opinion

The Japanese population knew little about what was going on in Inner Mongolia but Japanese language newspapers in China had their opinion. One paper in Tientsin was bold enough to state that the Inner Mongolians and their Manchukuoan allies were not worth supporting. The Japanese military attaché in Shanghai, Major-General Kita, had a lot to say about the campaign in Suiyuan and was quite candid. In November 1936 Kita said the Japanese had established a large military school in Chahar province to instruct the Inner Mongolian troops and Japanese instructors were being paid for by Prince Teh Wang and were not officially allowed to go to the frontline. 'In order to offset Outer Mongolia's highly mechanised army, which is equipped by Russia, we have assisted Inner

Mongolia by selling them airplanes … Reports that these Mongols are too poor to buy tanks, armoured cars and munitions are untrue, for they have assets such as a vast opium harvest. We have been paid in kind'.

## The Results of the 1936 Fighting

Documents captured in Pailingmiao in December 1936 showed that the Japanese had invested close to $50 million in their Suiyuan adventure. The Kwangtung Army did have plans to spend a total of $400 million if necessary! The victory of their army in Suiyuan was a real boost to the morale of the Chinese public, who had endured years of humiliation at the hands of the Japanese. It also gave a false sense of confidence to the Chinese that they could now face the Japanese on an equal footing. In reality, although it was a great victory, it was a local victory, which was won against a proxy army merely supported by the Japanese. This overconfidence led them to dream of further victories that were not achievable. Chinese newspapers called for the re-conquest of northern Chahar and the pushing back of the Japanese into Manchukuo. Some even called for the liberation of Manchukuo, which would mean full-scale war with the Japanese, something Chiang Kai-shek was determined to avoid.

# 1937

By January 1937 both sides were regrouping and preparing for a probable resumption of fighting. The drop in temperature in Suiyuan to 20 degrees below stopped any Japanese flights and the fighting ground to a halt. On the 4th of January General FuTso-yi announced: 'The enemy's forecast that they would celebrate the New Year as masters of Suiyuan has proved to be wrong, but our victory has been won at a heavy cost.' In the Inner Mongolian camp there were many disagreements about the future of their independence campaign. Some of Pao Yueh-hsiang's army rebelled against their commander and went on a looting spree in north-eastern Suiyuan. Teh Wang's army retreated back to northern Chahar while his Japanese supporters denied any connection with his 1936 campaign. Japanese military advisors from the Kwangtung Army met with the prince and gave him a detailed appraisal of the failure of the campaign. They told him his army needed complete reorganisation with a limit of 11,000 men set. From then on troops were to be recruited exclusively from the Inner Mongolian population, which was too small to support a larger army. No Manchukuoan troops were to be used and ex-bandits were to be purged. Training was to be improved, smarter uniforms to be introduced and better weaponry was to be supplied.

In late January, Manchukuoan reinforcements arrived in the district of Shangtu ready to join in an attack on the Nationalist lines in north and east Suiyuan. As soon as the Inner Mongolian Army had purged some of its undesirable elements, Prince Teh Wang wanted to take advantage of fighting going on in Shensi province. His intention was to launch a big attack on Hsingho and Taolin in north Suiyuan while a small force engaged the rear of the Chinese defenders near

Shangtu. The prince's plans did not get off the ground and the Inner Mongolian Army continued with its reorganisation.

In March, rumours surfaced of the possible raising of a White Russian army in Manchukuo to go into Inner Mongolia. This mercenary army was intended to replace the Manchukuoan army in Chahar and Suiyuan provinces. It was to be led by Ataman Gregori Semenov, the former White Russian warlord who had ruled over the Trans Baikal in Siberia in the early 1920s. After going into exile in Manchuria he had spent over 10 years plotting with his Japanese sponsors against the Soviet Union. His plan was briefly discussed by the Kwangtung Army command – but the last thing the Japanese wanted was to upset the Soviet Union.

In April, the threat of a new invasion of eastern Suiyuan was reported, this time by an army of Manchukuoan irregulars led by General Pao Yueh-ching. His army did make a few advances reaching the towns of Changpei and Paoyuan by the 16th. At the same time the Inner Mongolian army's newly organised 9th and 10th Divisions advanced to Shangtu. Any renewed invasion of Suiyuan would be met with a Nationalist army of 100,000 men. This force included 40,000 well trained Shansi troops including the elite Shansi cavalry division. On the political front, Prince Teh Wang was pushed by the Japanese in April 1937 into declaring a new state, to be called 'Mongokuo'. This puppet state was to incorporate most of northern Chahar province with its six hsiens. The border of the new state was only 20 miles to the north of the Chahar provincial capital, Kalgan. It was intended to create a buffer state between Manchukuo and Suiyuan and bordered Jehol province to the east. Covering an area the size of of Ohio, it may have looked insignificant on a map of China but was still vast.

Preparations for the further defence of Suiyuan by the Nationalists included the building of a defence line from the Great Wall to northern Chahar province. This huge undertaking was to be done by hiring a 200,000-strong labour force to dig a line of trenches and embankments. At the same time Prince Teh-wang was being supplied by the Japanese with large amounts of arms and ammunition. He was also given substantial sums of money to fill his war chest. His army was being reinforced by 20,000 regulars and irregulars from Manchukuo. They were take their part in the successful Japanese offensive launched after the outbreak of the Sino-Japanese War in July 1937. Teh Wang's cavalry were to play an important part in the northern front of the Imperial Army's conquest of China.

# 15

# 'FIGHT THE JAPANESE OR WE FIGHT YOU': CHINESE PUPPETS AND REBELLIONS, 1935–37

The Tangku Treaty signed in May 1933 left a large tract of land which officially was neither under Chinese Nationalist nor Japanese Imperial Army control. During the mid-1930s this territory was to see a number of attempts by the Japanese to try and split the northern provinces of China from the rest of the country. Japanese claims to have the best interests of northern China at heart were of course ridiculous but this did not stop them from making them. At the same time, the Japanese were exploiting their control of the Jehol poppy harvest to introduce more drugs into the Chinese market. The poppies were sent to Tientsin and were processed there and then distributed to China's addicts using a new chain of drug dealers. North China was seen by the Japanese as an open market for drugs and anything else that they decided to sell there. In April 1934 the Japanese Foreign Minister said that his government would not be happy if any foreign powers were to get involved in northern China. As far as the Japanese were concerned, the only power that Chiang and his government should be getting involved with was them. The pressure was kept on the Nationalist Government with Colonel Doihara in early 1935 making a tour of northern China. Doihara was still head of the Special Services Agency and was constantly plotting to cause problems in the north. He had run several short-lived 'mini-states' which hardly even got into the papers and usually consisted of a renegade Chinese officer and his men. A few hundred men would ride into some northern Chinese town and raise the five-barred Republican flag over the town hall. When the public did not support the new state the officer and his men would ride off to be used by Doihara in another futile plot later. Doihara's attempts to bribe northern Nationalist Generals like Sung Che-yuan into co-operating with Japan were also usually unsuccessful. One attempt to gather all the northern Generals at a meeting described as a 'State Building Conference' was a failure. Doihara's plan was to force a breakaway of Hopei, Shansi, Shantung and the Inner Mongolian provinces of Chahar and Suiyuan. On the day of the meeting a highly embarrassed Doihara found himself sat at an empty table. Doihara was nothing if not persistent and continued talking to a number of old and 'unemployed' warlords. These included General Wu Pei-fu, the former leader of the Chihli warlord clique, who had been in contact with the Japanese since 1933. Doihara had a grandiose plan to build an alliance to run his five-province breakaway with Generals Yen Hsi-shan of Shansi, Han Fu-chu of Shantung and Sung Che-yuan, the commander of the 29th Army. Ruling over these generals would be Wu Pei-fu, who would act as the highest ranking official in the new state to be known as

Hua-pei Kuo or 'North China Land'. The plans were cancelled when a meeting between Wu and Doihara in September 1935 ended with the old general's refusal to join the scheme. The Japanese finally decided to get something for the money they had invested in Doihara's schemes in northern China. The solution was to use the demilitarised zone as the base for their new puppet state, naming it the 'East Hopei Anti-Communist Autonomous Council'.

One Japanese attempt to force the breakaway of the five northern provinces ended in high farce. A Japanese-organised autonomous movement was launched in the northern city of Tientsin in November 1935. Local volunteers took over a number of public buildings armed with nothing more lethal than batons and wooden swords. These volunteers were raised from amongst the ranks of the local unemployed labourers who were promised to be paid a few pence a day. Although the volunteers did manage to take over a few official buildings they were immediately faced by fierce resistance from Tientsin citizens. They did attempt under orders from the organisers of the plot to enlist more volunteers. Parading through the streets they tried to hand out special armbands to anyone willing to join the movement. Hardly anyone joined the movement and any that did wanted the money. Japanese Gendarmes who were allowed to patrol the city were ordered to try and instil some enthusiasm amongst the volunteers. This met with little response as the volunteers realised that they were being led like lambs to the slaughter. When the city's Chinese police confronted the rebels, they threw away their recently issued uniforms. They protested that they weren't willing to fight for a pittance and complained that they had not even received the little money they had been promised.

## The East Hopei Regime, 1935–1937

The proclamation of the bogus 'Autonomous Government of Eastern Hopei' on the 25th of November 1935 was not exactly met with delirious acclamation. A crowd of peasants or coolies were paid to wave the regime's five-barred flags enthusiastically. During the ceremony a flight of Japanese planes flew overhead and dropped some leaflets proclaiming the government. It was led by a former Nationalist official, General Yin Ju-keng, who had previously served as commissioner of the Luantung demilitarised zone. Yin may have been easily persuaded by the Japanese to lead the puppet government but it was more difficult to find other Chinese officials to join him. In the end the Japanese had to staff the government with a sorry group of four forgotten and aged Chinese officials. This 'phantom' government with its capital at Tungchow was padded out with five military commanders. The new 'state', which was not even officially recognised by its Japanese sponsors, covered 10,000 square miles and had a population of 4 million. East Hopei's importance to Japan was its coastline, which allowed them to bring in goods without having to pay taxes or duties. It was estimated that during the period of East Hopei's existence the Nationalist Government lost $50 million in taxes. When the invading Japanese Imperial Army took the region in July 1937 Yin and his puppet state were ceased to

General Yin Ju-keng (right), the puppet leader of the state of East Hopei, reviews his troops during a parade in 1935. Yin had previously served in the local government in Hopei province but had been persuaded by the Japanese to lead this mini-state. East Hopei was proclaimed as the 'Autonomous Government of Eastern Hopei' on the 25th of November 1935. The former neutral Peace Preservation Corps was converted overnight into the pro-Japanese Army of East Hopei.

exist. The East Hopei regime was absorbed into a larger puppet 'Provisional Government of China' based in Peking.

### 'The Grey Clad Army'

Every new state needs an armed force to defend it and this was the case with East Hopei, which was protected by a 20,000-strong army. This had been raised by the reorganisation of the Peace Preservation Corps or Pao-an-tui, which had previously served the local political council. Dressed in brand new grey uniforms the East Hopei Army was organised into five new divisions commanded by the officers of the Pao-an-Tui's five companies. Armament was limited to ex-Nationalist Mauser rifles and despite pleas by Yin they were not even allowed a machine gun. Each division was divided into two regiments, and each regiment had three battalions of 480 men. Yin was constantly worried about attacks on his puppet government and tried to recruit more soldiers. This was not as success as service in the East Hopei Army marked men as traitors in the eyes of most Chinese. He did however reorganise his local militia into a mixed brigade to reinforce the regular army when necessary. Japanese military advisors were sent by the Imperial Army to train the East Hopei troop. A senior Japanese advisor was on the staff of every division and these men had much of the responsibility for the running of their unit.

## General Sung Cheh-yuan and his 29th Army, 1935–1937

During all the machinations in northern China the Nationalist 29th Army and its leader General Sung Che-yuan led a precarious existence. Sung Che-yuan was a former Kuominchun officer who first came to the public's attention during the fighting for the Great Wall in 1933. As commander of the 29th Army in

1935 he was stationed in Hopei province when the Japanese issued their latest demand: the withdrawal of all Nationalist troops from Hopei to create another demilitarised zone. Chiang Kai-shek rejected the demand but proposed instead the setting up of a Hopei-Chahar Political Council. It was proposed that General Sung should be given the role of chairman of the council as a compromise candidate. The 29th Army was seen as an almost independent force by the Japanese, as it had never fully assimilated with the Nationalist establishment. Chiang Kai-shek did not trust Sung but the General had to perform the ultimate fence-sitting exercise or be swallowed up by the Japanese in northern China. Sung was a loyal patriot who had to be pragmatic in the circumstances. Although ultimately loyal to the Nationalist Government he had to deal with the Japanese and the situation as it was. Sung had been isolated from the government in Nanking since the signing of the Tangku Treaty in May 1933. After the treaty was enacted he decided to make his own agreements with the Japanese rather than awaiting instructions from Chiang Kai-shek that never came. In the spring of 1935 Sung and his army were pressured by the Japanese into moving out of Chahar into Hopei province. Because Sung acted without consultations with Nanking, he was able to avoid the military clash that the Imperial Army was pushing for. Without support from far-off Nanking, Sung knew that if he didn't withdraw from Chahar he would be attacked by the full might of the Japanese. He also calculated that no military support would come from the Nationalist Army and his 29th Army would be sacrificed. Sung became more independent not through choice but through circumstances and knew that he could only rely on his own resources. To emphasise his independent political stance, he removed all the political advisors sent to him from Nanking. The die was now cast for Sung when the Japanese came out with their scheme to split the five northern provinces from the rest of China. This was brought up in discussions in the autumn of 1935 and Sung had little choice but to enter into the discussions. The Japanese said that North China was receiving no positive governance from Nanking and the region should look for its own leaders. General Sung, top of the Japanese list of possible collaborators, was trapped between loyalty to China and fear of the Imperial Army. He did go through the pretence of discussing the formation of this so-called 'North China Autonomy Movement' but was looking for an excuse to break off talks. This came when the Japanese organised the Autonomous Government of Eastern Hopei in late 1935. When too much power was given to this strictly local government, Sung now had reason to say that any talk of an autonomous North China was pointless. For the next 20 months Sung tried to perform a balancing act between loyalty to China and obedience to the Japanese. In 1936 he was faced by two challenges to his position, firstly during the Kwangsi Rebellion and then during the Japanese invasion of Suiyuan province. On both occasions he neither condemned nor supported either side. He did give in to some of the Japanese demands but was careful to pick the less onerous ones to obey. By the summer of 1937 Sung could no longer tolerate either Japanese demands or Chinese accusations of disloyalty. He chose to make his peace with Chiang Kai-shek, even though neither of them had any great trust in each other. What they both men shared was their love of China and now they were both prepared to fight to defend it. When the Japanese launched their attack on North China in July 1937, it was Sung's 29th Army which bore the brunt of the first attacks.

## Trouble in the South

### The Kwangtung Warlord, 1936

In the early 1930s a southern general described by one writer as a 'picturesque little warlord' rose to prominence. He was General Chen Chia-t'ang, the military governor of Kwangtung province, in charge there from 1931. He was described as being 'avaricious, ambitious, scheming and deceitful' by his detractors. Like most governors of the period, Chen had his idiosyncrasies when it came to law making. One of his most famous laws was that no one under the age of 60 could celebrate their birthday and even then, any present should not cost more than $2! Any expenditure on an engagement ceremony could not exceed $50. Chen may have been mean but he certainly knew how to make money. In 1933 he stopped the import of foreign refined oil into Kwangtung. It transpired that he owned his own oil refineries and did not want British and US oil damaging the lucrative trade.

On the military front Chen was also well organised and had built himself a powerful base in the south. During the 5th Anti-Communist Encirclement campaign in 1934 Chen had been given command, at least on paper, of 300,000 Nationalist southern troops. He was supposed to use all these troops to block any escape southwards from the Kiangsi Soviet. Chen was however wary of Chiang Kai-shek's motives and did not want to give up his province by default. His worry that was if Chiang decided to move into Kwangtung, the troops under his command would switch sides and fight for the Government. So in

A soldier of the Peace Preservation Corps of the demilitarised zone in Northern China gives directions to a western journalist. These men went from being the police force of the demilitarised zone in 1933 to the army of the puppet state of East Hopei in 1935. Whoever commanded them, these troops tried to stay out of any fighting that might break out in the region. This man's rifle is the heaviest weaponry that the PPC were allowed, even when they converted to the East Hopei Army.

anticipation of a possible takeover of Kwangtung by Chiang he only used 180,000 of his troops against the Communists. A secret deal was made with the Communists to allow them to pass through Kwangtung, so that there was no excuse for Chiang to move troops there. Chen lived to fight another day by his scheming and left Chiang stewing as he could not afford to move against the troublesome southern general at that time.

Chen spent the next few years building up his armed forces into one of the most formidable in China. By spring 1936 his army was four times the size it needed to be to defend Kwangtung. It was armed with the latest weaponry, including tanks. The Kwangtung leader had followed his own weapons acquisition policy, buying all the paraphernalia of war, such as searchlights, anti-aircraft guns and modern artillery from Europe. In 1936 he had 12 Carden-Loyd M1931 amphibious light tanks, bought in 1933, and 15 Thorneycroft six-wheel armoured cars. Chen had also bought 12 Vickers M1931 75mm anti-aircraft gun along with the Vickers tracked tractors to pull them. Like his neighbours and sometime allies in Kwangsi, he spent a large amount of money on Japanese armaments. By 1936 he had already spent $20 million and owed another $10 million to Japanese small arms companies. He bought a couple of small cruisers for the Kwangtung Navy along with a large number of fast patrol craft. His pride and joy was his air force, which by 1936 had six squadrons of modern fighters and light bombers. There was one squadron of ten US Boeing 281 fighters and two Squadrons of nine Curtiss Hawk Is, a squadron of nine British Armstrong Whitworth AW-16 fighters and five US Douglas O2C light bombers. Trainers were nine German Focke-Wulf FW44Fs and six British DH60 gypsy moths. This air arm could challenge the Nationalist force. Chen's impressive ground, air and naval forces were not just for show.

## The Kwangsi Army in 1936

The other strong southern military force in China alongside the Kwangtung Army was the army of the Kwangsi clique. It was only a matter of time before Kwangsi and Kwangtung with so much politically in common would combine militarily against Chiang Kai-shek. As the Kwangsi army prepared for a possible war in 1936 it tried to improve and expand its forces. One of its major problems was the shortage of officers and it had been forced to employ about 100 Japanese advisors as an affordable alternative to European advisors. This strange situation where the very people that they wanted to fight were serving in their ranks is difficult to understand; but it must be remembered that in the south of China Japanese aggression had not yet had the impact it had in the north. One possible source of officers was the large number of redundant former 19th Route Army officers who were out of favour with Nanking. When approached, the Chinese officers refused to serve alongside the hated Japanese and so the 100 or so foreigners were duly dismissed.

The militia system was very important to the defence of Kwangsi with huge numbers of men and some women in its ranks. With a total strength of 300,000, the militia was difficult to arm properly and some would have been armed with spears until rifles were available. With 700 miles of frontier to defend, a two-line system was introduced with the first line stretching along the Kwangsi-Hunnan

These rather pathetic looking characters belong to the newly raised paramilitary force that tried to foment rebellion in Tientsin in November 1935. Armed with nothing more lethal than staves, they were recruited from the flotsam and jetsam of Tientsin's streets. This Japanese-organised revolt ended almost as soon as it had begun when the supposed support for a breakaway Northern China failed to materialise.

border and defended by 100,000 militia. A seconnd line stretched in an arc in front of the provincial capital Nanning, protected by another 150,000 militia. The proportion of women recruited into the Militia is not known but a 200-strong unit was formed with the intention of fighting. This Special Volunteer Corps was given the same grounding as the men, what its chief instructor called 'stiff military training'.

## Japanese Arms to Kwangsi

From 1934 onwards a strange situation developed in Kwangsi province; one of its army and air force's biggest suppliers was Japan. In 1934 the Kwangsi leadership arranged a deal with a Hong Kong company to buy four Japanese aircraft, two Nakajima Type 91 fighters and two Mitsubishi Type 92 light bombers. In addition the deal involved the sale of 12,000 barrels of cement, with which to build Kwangsi's defences. The provincial leadership looked around for more arms from its sworn enemy! In late June 1936 a deal was reached with the Japanese to supply 10,000 modern rifles, 20 aircraft and another 10,000 barrels of cement. Between them, Kwangtung and Kwangsi were spending $50 million on arms for their joint army; Kwangsi was paying $20 million in instalments. Kwangsi tried to settle a large portion of its debt by exporting $15 million worth of silver to what the press described as 'a certain country'. One of Kwangsi's biggest arms deals from Japan arrived in Hong Kong on the 19th of June. This shipment included 2,000 machine guns with 2 million rounds of rifle and machine gun ammunition. Amongst the other equipment on board the ship were 200 trucks for civilian or military use. Also aboard this huge ship were reportedly 500 tons of barbed wire and 30,000 barrels of cement for the ever growing fortifications. To add to the debt being built up by Kwangsi, in August 1936 eight new aircraft from Japan arrived just as war in the region intensified. Kwangsi had been buying weaponry independently of Nanking for many years and before 1934 had purchased rifles from Sweden, as had Kwangtung. In June 1936 a large German arms shipment arrived in Kwangsi including rifles, machine guns, anti-aircraft guns and intriguingly, so-called 'small tanks'.

## The Southern Rebellion, 1936

Ever since the Kwangsi clique's participation in the Central Plains War of 1929–1930 the loyalty of the province's leaders had been suspected by Chiang and his government. No matter how many times the Kwangsi leadership expressed their loyalty to Chiang Kai-shek, he did not trust them. Their independent defence policy was one sign of their attitude to the Nanking Government. In a few years before the outbreak of war in 1936 they had spent about $10 million in arms deals, which included the buying of a large number of military aircraft. In another sign of their independent attitude they had purchased these English fighters and fighter bombers not used by the Central Government.

The Kwangsi Army in 1936 was still powerful, with between 270,000–300,000 men but they were hemmed in by Nationalist armies. These armies totalling 600,000 men were stationed in the provinces of Kweichow, Fukien, Kiangsi and Hunan. They had been stationed there during the campaigns against the Communists in the early to mid 1930s. The four provinces stretched in a great arc around Kwangsi and Kwangtung threatening the 'rebellious' generals' territories. The large number of potentially hostile troops on their doorsteps made the Kwangsi and Kwangtung leadership cautious. In 1935 they showed every sign of loyalty to Chiang but with the death of the prominent southern politician Hu Han-min in May 1936, the situation changed. As the most fervent opponent of Chiang Kai-shek in the south of China, Hu was a figurehead for the various southern generals, including Chen. Hu had been a friend of Sun Yat-sen and his support gave the southern leaders prestige and political credibility.

Instead of proposing an anti-Chiang campaign, the Kwangsi generals instead launched an anti-Japanese one. It was intended to show Chiang as a weak defender of China in comparison to the Kwangsi clique. It was now expected that Chiang would try to dismantle the clique's autonomy. The southern leaders'

General Sung Cheh-yuan, the commander of the Nationalist 29th Army held important political and military posts in Northern China. Sung had to perform a precarious balancing act between the Japanese Imperial Army and Chiang Kai-shek. As head of the Hopei-Chahar Political Council he was effectively under the orders of the Japanese. At the same time as a Nationalist General he had, as he said, to 'look to Chiang Kai-shek for supreme authority'.

reaction was to conspire with each other to overthrow Chiang once and for all. With a combined military strength almost equal to Chiang's, it was the best opportunity that the southern alliance would have to defeat him. In May the joint Kwangsi and Kwangtung armies were reorganised as the 'Anti-Japanese National Salvation Army' with four commanding generals: Li Tsung-jen and Pai Ch'ung-hsi of Kwangsi, General Ch'en Chi-t'ang of Kwangtung and General Tsai T'ing-k'ai. Tsai was of course famous for his command of the 19th Route Army at Shanghai in 1932 and as one of the leaders of the Fukien Rebellion in 1933–34. As a true Chinese patriot. Tsai had reluctantly come out of exile in Hong Kong to add legitimacy to the National Salvation Army. By late June an alarmed Chiang Kai-shek was sending messages to the southern generals demanding that they evacuate Hunan. They answered with threats against Chiang and the Nationalist Government and with demands that he change his attitude to the Japanese. The headline in a newspaper of the time summed up their attitude in five simple words: 'Fight Japan or We Fight You!'

Nationalist troops were concentrating in southern Hunan province in preparation for an offensive against Kwangsi. The two provincial armies were always going to operate separately and the first of the allies to move was the Kwangtung General. In June Chen began to move his large, well armed army

A truck-full of Nationalist soldiers waits for the order to go into action against some of their mutinous comrades during a local rebellion in Peking in July 1935. This mutiny was triggered by the transfer of some northern Chinese troops to the west of China against their wishes. The soldiers involved in the mutiny were also unhappy that they were not going to be fighting the Japanese and instead were expected to fight Communists.

northwards, 'to fight the Japanese as Chiang would not'. At its head were the elite 10,000 Salt Guards of General Chen Wei-chou, the 'best trained and equipped troops in Kwangtung'. It was intended that the Kwangtung Army would join up with the Kwangsi armies in Hunan before moving towards Nanking. In mid-July the 1st and 4th Group Armies of the Anti-Japanese Salvation Army combined their strength to make a force of 200,000. To arm this expanded force, two arsenals in Kwangtung province and one in Kwangsi were working day and night, seven days a week. In Kwangsi the communications system was augmented by 14 new radio stations making a total of 80 throughout the province. The Kwangsi military began work on a large aerodrome at Yungchow giving more modern facilities for its air force. On the Kwangtung side, a new 4th Infantry Division was formed to join the 1st, 2nd and 3rd Divisions already in the field. General Miao Pei-nam was given command of the 4th Kwangtung Division. In overall command of the joint army was General Pai Chung-hai. At the end of July Kwangtung troop movements took place as several divisions moved up to the Kwangsi border. Many troops were moved by commandeered small boats up the Sikang River towards the border town of Wuchow. Chen's advance took him into Hunan province and just when it looked like he might be a threat to Chiang, the wily old leader outfoxed him.

First, he engineered the defection of the whole of the Canton Air Force, 136 pilots, planes and all, to the Nationalists. Then he arranged the defection of Chen's right-hand man General Yu Han-mou, naming him the new governor of Kwangtung. The first blow was probably enough to crush Chen as he had spent so much time and money building his precious air force. Chen was at least wise enough to know when he was beaten, not in this case on the battlefield but by the age-old Chinese tradition of of 'Silver Bullets'. He wisely took himself off to Hong Kong in a British ship leaving his erstwhile allies, the Kwangsi clique, to face Chiang alone.

Chiang was to pay for putting the incompetent Yu Han-mou in charge at Canton when he gave up the city to the Japanese in 1938. Chen was to come back from exile a few years later having paid a part of his large fortune into the Nationalist coffers. With Chen out of the picture and with his usurper Yu Han-mou now opposed to them, the odds were stacked against the Kwangsi clique.

## Kwangsi Fights Kwangtung

In early August the Kwangsi army invaded south-western Kwangtung province, now controlled by Chiang's ally General Yu Han-mou. They advanced into the province occupying the town of Lingshan. Their intention was to move into the coastal province in force and take one of the ports along its coastline. To counter this threat, strong pro-Chiang Kwangtung provincial forces were mobilised and martial law was declared in the threatened region. Twelve Government pilots were transferred to Canton from their air base in southern Hunan to bolster the Kwangtung air force. As the threat of all out-war grew, the Nationalist Government sent 12 divisions to the northern Kwangsi border. They were held back by Chiang for a few days in the hope that war could be avoided. Chiang was determined to crush the rebels if necessary and began preparations to send more troops from Yunnan, Kweichow and Hunan, as well as from Kwangtung.

Reports of Japanese interference in Kwangsi were dismissed at the time although three military attaches were sent to the province to 'watch the situation'. It was also claimed that the Japanese had loaned Kwangsi the money to buy 10,000 rifles and several aircraft to help in the war with Chiang. On the 5th of August fighting took place on the south Hunan border between Kwangsi and Government forces. The Kwangsi armies had suffered a major problem with the cutting of their communications after a Nationalist bombing raid. Chiang issued the rebel generals with yet another warning telling them not to issue their expected independence declaration. The military build-up continued on the government side with more troops moving towards the Kwangsi border. The navy gathered off the Kwangtung coast as Chiang tried to show his superiority over the rebels by land, sea and air. Although the loss of Ch'en's armies ended the anti-Japanese campaign, it did not necessarily stop the Kwangsi generals from pursuing their anti-Chiang campaigns.

Kwangsi armies were withdrawn back into their home province as the rebels prepared to resist any moves by the Nationalist Army against them. On the 12th of September the Kwangsi generals announced the demobilisation of their armies, officially ending the war. A reconciliation between Chiang and the Kwangsi leadership took place on the 18th of September at a meeting in Canton. The Kwangsi generals were represented by General Li Tsung-jen, who had flown into the Canton from his headquarters at Nanning. Chiang was nothing if not pragmatic and knew that the Kwangsi armies were important to the make-up of the Nationalist army. Although 300,000 Kwangsi troops were to be 'disbanded' this was basically a re-branding of them into the Nationalist 5th Route Army. This army was to be financed partly by the Central Government with $2 million and another $1 million came from the province.

The anti-Japanese stance of Kwangsi had not gone unnoticed by the Japanese and as they always did, they looked for an excuse to punish the province. When

General Chen Chia-t'ang, the Kwangtung warlord, in the early 1930s, a few years before his rebellion against Chiang Kai-shek. Chen was a highly ambitious military leader who believed he could use his support in the southern provinces to challenge Chiang. Like many rebels before him, he was to find that the Nationalist leader was a past master at outmanoeuvring men like him.

the only Japanese in the port of Pakhoi in South-Western Kwangsi was killed by soldiers of the 19th Route Army, they acted. Several Japanese gunboats moved into Pakhoi harbour waiting for a reaction from the Kwangsi authorities. Although the incident was settled by September its significance was not lost on the Kwangsi leaders. Realising that China had to be united to face up to Japan, Li and Pai came to a settlement with Chiang. This brought the two rebellious generals back into the Nationalist fold and both served loyally during the 1937–45 Sino-Japanese War.

## The Communist Invasion of Shansi: The East Campaign, 1936

After a period of settling in to their new base in Shensi province the Communists decided in early 1936 to take the war to the Japanese and Nationalists. A large army of 34,000 men crossed the Yellow River in February into the northern part of neighbouring Shansi province. Officially, this large-scale raid was aimed at Japanese-held positions but in reality the Red Army avoided them whenever possible. Instead they attacked the troops of the Shansi Military Governor Yen Hsi-shan, who had returned from exile in 1931. Mao's policy was to avoid any military confrontation if possible and to spread the propaganda message amongst the Shansi population. To gain popularity the Communists targeted hated landlords and local government officials, especially tax collectors. They took advantage of their new-found popularity in parts of Shansi to recruit about 8,000 new volunteers who returned with them to Yenan. Supplies and donations from the peasants were also collected before they returned to Shensi in late 1936. Yen, ever the pragmatist, did not want Communists or Nationalists interfering in his fiefdom and made a secret peace deal with Mao Tse-tung. He had already fallen

Cadets from the Kwangsi provincial training academy on a route march around their barracks. The Kwangsi leaders tried to improve their army with a number of measures including training more officers. Even though the Kwangsi Army was in some cases superior to other Nationalist formations, it was outnumbered in the 1936 fighting.

A company of women soldiers march through the streets of a Kwangsi town during the rebellion against Chiang Kai-shek in 1936. The Kwangsi leadership was promoted at the time as being progressive in all matters and the recruitment of women was part of this policy. It is doubtful that any of these young women would get near the frontline but could be used in support roles. They are mostly armed with rifles, which may be being carried purely for propaganda purposes.

out with Chaing Kai-shek owing to the increasing presence of Nationalist troops in Shansi in the mid-1930s.

There were ambitious plans for the Red Army to continue their march to the border of the Mongolian People's Republic. This was so that the Communists could get aid direct from the Mongols' sponsors, the Soviet Union. Chiang sent his loyalist General, Chen Cheng, with 150,000 troops to discourage the Red Army from this plan. The Red Army eventually returned to their Shensi base taking their new volunteers and supplies with them.

## Delay of the 6th Encirclement Campaign

Chiang kai shek had no intention of leaving the Red Army in Shensi unmolested and would continue his extermination policy until the last Communist was dead. He knew he had not defeated the Communists, they had simply removed themselves to a new base from which they could torment him. After the Red

Army's destructive raid into Shansi he was even more determined to crush them for good. He began to assemble his troops in the region, with 150,000 initially earmarked for the renewed campaign. These men were gathered in central Shensi and across the Yellow River forming a loose blockade around Yenan. Most of these troops were under the command of Marshal Chang Hsueh-liang's North-Eastern Army. The rest belonged to General Yang Hu-ch'eng's North-West Army, so nearly all were stationed away from their home provinces. This was never a good idea as it upset the local population and the homesick soldiers equally. Chang was now made commander and Yang vice-commander of the new 'Bandit Suppression Headquarters' at Sian.

Instructions from Chiang for Chang Hsueh-liang to begin his operation against Yenan were issued in early 1936 but nothing happened. Chiang waited through the spring and early summer for Chang's offensive to begin and then ordered him to begin his operation immediately. A series of telegrams went backwards and forwards as Chang reasoned with Chiang to forget about the Communists for the time being and fight the ever more aggressive Japanese. Chang's homeland of Manchuria was still occupied by the Japanese and he was loath to fight his fellow Chinese when this was the case. Chang begged Chiang to form a United Front with the Communists to jointly fight the Japanese. It now began to emerge that Chang had been in contact with Mao's representatives for months. Chang and Yang's armies did begin rather cautious moves in the autumn of 1936 but it was obvious to anyone that they were stalling for time. It was difficult for Chiang to judge from a distance what was really going on and if this long-delayed offensive was a sham. Chiang Kai-shek realised that he could not trust anyone else to face up the powerful Chang. He was not 100% certain that Chang had betrayed him but decided to fly to Sian to confront him. With luck, Chang would soon get back in line and begin his offensive against the Communists in earnest.

Red Army troops march over mountainous terrain during an operation in the mid-1930s carrying all their equipment on their backs. The survivors of the Long March were joined by new recruits to expand the Red Army ready to face the Nationalists in 1936 and 1937. These same men would be expected to serve in units that were officially part of the Nationalist Army after the formation of the United Front in 1937.

Chiang Kai-shek and his 'ally' Chang Hsueh-liang are photographed in the period of the Sian Incident in 1936. Chang was in turmoil about his betrayal of Chiang and his kidnapping by his North-Eastern Army. He was driven by his patriotism and his wish eventually to liberate his homeland in Manchuria, now under Japanese occupation.

## The Sian Incident, 1936

When Chiang arrived at Sian on the 7th of December his plan was to work out what was happening and then if necessary take command personally. He and his entourage were greeted warmly by Chang and Yang and after a period of rest, talks began. Chiang explained his programme and reiterated his policy of destroying the Communists before dealing with the Japanese. As he was not used to criticism he was shocked when not only the two commanders but also lower ranking officers argued with him. By the 11th he was beginning to lose patience with Chang after telling him repeatedly what he expected of him and his troops. For one final time he ordered Chang, Yang and their armies to begin a serious attack on the Communists. The talks broke up that night and Chiang went to bed early, as he always liked to rise at about 5.00 am. Early next morning Chiang awoke to do his usual half an hour of exercise to the sound of gunfire outside his guesthouse at 5.30 am. There was a firefight going on between his bodyguards and troops of Chang Hsueh-liang. Chiang got out of the house with a few bodyguards and took refuge in the woods around the guesthouse after climbing over a wall. When Chang's men found him three hours later he was wearing his dressing gown and had lost his false teeth. He was taken into 'protective custody' and treated with respect but was moved under guard to Chang's HQ in Sian city centre. Chiang now showed the stubborn courage for which he was known and refused to recognise the authority of Chang and Yang. Surrounded by enemies who still called him Generalissimo or leader but who could have shot him at any time, he kept his dignity. He refused to enter discussions with Chang. The younger officers of the North-East Army wanted to kill him. Chang Hsueh-liang behaved in an honourable way and continued to treat Chiang as his superior even if he was his respected prisoner. After nearly two weeks of stalemate, Chiang was still refusing to talk and challenged Chang to do what he must do. He said 'I cannot sacrifice my integrity even to save my life' and was quite prepared to die for what he believed in.

Around this time a meeting took place at a Catholic Mission in Sian between Chang and a Communist negotiator, Chou En-lai. Chou had been sent by

General Niaz Abdul Kamal was one of the last of a line of Muslim warlords who tried to defeat the Sinkiang warlord Sheng Shi-tsai. His rebellion was initially successful but Sheng still had the backing of the Soviet Union. Niaz was to die, like many before him, in front of a firing squad of NKVD soldiers in the summer of 1937.

Mao Tse-tung as he knew that Chiang would never speak to him directly. Chang Hsueh-liang was no friend of the Communists but he knew that the only way to defeat the Japanese was with the support of all the Chinese. The two men talked about the Chiang situation and Chou conceded that the Nationalist leader was the only man who could lead the country, at least for the time being. Chang now put a proposal to Chiang, the main points of which called for the formation of a united front and the committed prosecution of war against the Japanese. On the 22nd of December, Chiang's wife bravely flew into Sian and three days later she flew out with her husband. During those three days a series of shadowy talks took place involving Chou in some way or another before an agreement was reached. Chiang in theory accepted the need to fight the Japanese and the formation of a united front after further discussions were held. Although Chiang never accepted all aspects of the original proposal, he did feel honour-bound to change his policy towards the Communists. The 6th Encirclement campaign was called off and for the foreseeable future the Communists and Nationalists agreed to fight the Japanese. Chang Hsueh-liang – who had never been an enthusiastic rebel – flew back to Nanking as Chiang's prisoner. He was to remain under comfortable house arrest for the rest of his life as the price for his 'betrayal' of Chiang.

## Continued Rebellions

In mid January another local rebellion broke out in Shensi province with hostilities taking place in the depths of winter. General Yang Hu-cheng rebelled against Chiang Kai-shek, as so many had done before, with little chance of success. Much of the fighting took place on the Lunghai Railway 50 miles to the east of the city of Sianfu. It was just one of those regular rebellions led by an unhappy general who thought he might gain by fighting the Government. By early February the rebellion had fizzled out with most of General Yang's troops deserting to the Nationalist army. Yang's garrison at Sianfu surrendered and

Soldiers of the 29th Army parade in Peking in the weeks before the outbreak of the 2nd Sino-Japanese War in July 1937. They are armed with Type 38 heavy machine guns which were a copy of the French Hotchkiss of 1900. This type of machine gun was made by Japan and in the Taiyuan Arsenal of Yen His-shan who may have supplied a few to the 29th. Under the command of General Sung Che-yuan, these troops had been under Japanese pressure in North China since 1935. When the fighting began the 29th Army was to face the first Japanese attacks alone. They were overwhelmed by the Imperial Army.

the Shensi army and their leader retreated to the town of Sanyuan 30 miles to the north. In Sinkiang province there were problems for the military governor, General Sheng Shi-kai. A local Muslim leader, General Niaz Abdul Kamal, raised a rebellion against the unpopular government of Sheng. He had 10,000 men and on the 30th of May 1,500 of them captured Kashgar under the command of Kiahik Akund. The Muslim troops wore armbands which read 'In the Way of Allah' and some fought with scimitars. At the same time there was a rising in Kumul by Kyghiz tribesmen, which was defeated at a battle in the town of Aksu. Sheng's army was led by a 5,000-strong Soviet expeditionary force supported by T-26 tanks, armoured cars, heavy artillery and R5 light bombers. The bombers, according to the rebels, dropped gas, which completed their rout. Former troops of the Muslim warlord Ma Chung-ying fought alongside the rebels but they were totally outgunned by Sheng's troops and their Soviet allies. They retreated to the city of Yarkand where they were defeated on the 9th of September. General Abdul Niaz was captured. He was dragged out a few days later and shot by a Soviet NKVD firing squad. This left Sinkiang still in the hands of the brutal Sheng, who unleashed a terrible bloodletting amidst his long-suffering population over the next few years.

## Divided China and Divided Nationalist Army, 1937

The nine years of broken peace covered by this book was to end in July 1937 with the outbreak of full-scale war between China and Japan. All the internal conflicts – civil wars, revolts, coup-d'etats and guerrilla warfare – had ravaged the country. External attacks by Tibet and the Soviet Union had added to the many Japanese incursions into Chinese territory. China had already fought the Japanese during several incidents between 1928 and 1936 as well as in proxy wars in Suiyuan and other outlying provinces. The constant Japanese provocations had become too much for even Chiang Kai-shek and his fearful Government to take. Although the majority of conflicts with Japan were fought on the outer fringes of Nationalist Chinese territory, they tore at the heart and pride of China. It was obvious that Imperial Japan was not going to be satisfied with what it had already gained and its next project was the taking of all of northern China. When the next violation, incident or outright attack came from the Japanese, Chiang knew he would have to fight.

Even on the eve of war with Imperial Japan in the summer of 1937 there were still divisions within Nationalist China. Chiang Kai-shek had been successful in controlling rebellious generals in the 1930s but several of these had regained their positions after a period of exile. Yen Hsi-shan was still the incumbent in Shansi province, with a powerful army behind him. The Kwangsi clique had been severely weakened by their defeats in 1929 and 1936 but still

Pictured in 1936, these Nationalist troops are from one of the better trained, armed and uniformed divisions stationed in North China. Few soldiers outside the central heartland of Nationalist China were as well drilled as these men, who belong to the 29th Army. Their commander General Sung Che-yuan had a delicate balancing act to perform in the 1930s. His army was stationed in North China surrounded by Japanese troops who were stationed there following treaties made by the Nationalists from 1933.

had powerful armies under the command. Their loyalty to Chiang would be dependent on his changing his policy of resistance to the Japanese. Shantung province was firmly in the hands of General Han Fu-chu but he was to prove less than reliable. Szechwan was still under the control of independently minded generals who had split the province between them. Liu Hsiang was the dominant commander in the south-western province but was ill and was losing his grip on the troublesome region. Yunnan in western China was ruled by General Lung Yun, another independent warlord who would remain reluctant to give his full support to Chiang. Sinkiang in far western China was still under the control of General Sheng Shih-ts'ai who had 'mortgaged' his province to the Soviet Union. The Ma clique who ruled the remote western provinces of Ninghsia, Chinghai and Kansu would try to keep out of the war if humanly possible.

The Nationalist Army on the eve of the war with Japan was also deeply divided as it neared its titanic struggle. Just before the war broke out a US analyst gave a breakdown of the loyalties of the various armies. He divided the Nationalist Army into six categories with the most loyal being in the first category. Category 1 was made up of 380,000 men he deemed to be almost 100% loyal to Chiang Kai-shek. Units listed within this category were the 1st, 2nd, 5th, 6th, 13th, 16th and 25th Armies as well as the 1st–4th and 9th Divisions. Category 2 was the bulk of the Army: 520,000 men who were described by analyst Field as 'traditionally loyal to Chiang Kai-shek'. This category included the 4th, 7th, 11th, 15th, 17th and 26th Armies. The third category were described as 'semi-autonomous' but were still capable of serving Chiang loyally when the going was good. These troops were made up of Yen Hsi-shan's 120,000 men in the 19th, 33rd, 34th and 35th Shansi armies. The 80,000 troops from Shantung province and the 100,000 soldiers from Kwangtung province were also in Category 3. In Category 4 were divisions described by Field as 'practically autonomous provincial troops which can only be controlled by Chiang for the duration of an anti-Japanese campaign'. This category included the 29th, 32nd, 33rd, 53rd and 63rd Divisions from Hopei province and the former North-Eastern Army. The Manchurian divisions of the North-East Army were, after the Sian Incident, no longer under the command of Chang Hsueh-liang. Because of Chang's house arrest the 16 divisions were at best ambivalent toward Chiang. The 5th category was a job lot of useless or totally disloyal armies from Kwangsi, Yunnan and Szechwan provinces. The 150,000 regular and irregular Kwangsi troops were deemed to be potentially rebellious, and the Yunnan 10th Army were totally indifferent. As for the 250,000 Szechwanese soldiers (category 6) they were almost disregarded as 'China's worst troops'.

Thus the stage was set for the largest Asian war of the 20th century: a stage initially crowded with too many Chinese actors. In November 1946, the Japanese would lose Manchuria, Formosa and the Pescadores, all returned to the Republic of China, which would be be acknowledged as one of the Big Four. The cost? No one can be sure. Certainly more than 3 million combatant casualties and an estimated 17–22 million civilian deaths. What would follow this catastrophe, of course, was civil war. Millions more would die.

# SELECT BIBLIOGRAPHY

Aitchen. K. Wu, *Turkistan Tumult*, Methuen & Co Ltd 1940

Andersson, Lennart, *A History of Chinese Aviation: Encyclopedia of Aircraft and Aviation in China until 1949*, AHC of ROC 2008

Benton, Gregor, *Mountain Fires: The Red Army's Three-Year War in South China, 1934–1938*, University of California Press 1992

Braun, Otto, *A Comitern Agent in China 1932–1939*, Stanford University Press 1982

Chaurasia, R.S., *History of Modern China*, Atlantic Publishers 2004

Chong-Sik Lee, *Revolutionary Struggle in Manchuria: Chinese Communism and Soviet Interest, 1922–1945*, University of California Press 1983

Chubb, O. Edmund, *China and Russia: The Great Game*, Columbia University Press 1971

Dreyer. Edward. L, *China at War 1901–1949*, Longman 1995

Dupuy, Trevor Nevitt, *The Military History of the Chinese Civil War*, Franklin Watts Inc 1969

Duus Peter, Myers Ramon. H, Peattie Mark. R. editors, *The Japanese Informal Empire in China, 1895–1937*, Princeton University Press 2014

Fleming, Peter, *A Forgotten Journey*, Rupert Hart Davis, London 1952

Forbes, Andrew. D. W, *Warlord and Muslims in Chinese Central Asia: A Political History of Republican Sinkiang 1911–1949*, Cambridge University Press 1986

Gillan, Donald. G, *Warlord Yen Hsi-shan in Shansi Province 1911–1949*, Princeton University Press 1967

Goldstein, Melvyn. C & Rimpoche, Gelek, *A History of Modern Tibet 1913–1951: The Demise of the Lamaist State*, University of California Press 1989

Goldstein, Melvyn. C & Dawei Sherap, William. R., *A Tibetan Revolutionary: The Political Life and Times of Bapa Phuntso Wangye*, University of California Press 2004

Gray, Jack, *Rebellions and Revolutions: China from the 1800s to the 1980s*, Oxford University Press 1990

Gunther, John, *Inside Asia*, Harper & Brothers 1939

Hallet, Abend, *Tortured China*, Ives Washburn, New York 1930

Harries Meirion & Susie, *Soldiers of the Sun: The Rise and Fall of the Imperial Japanese Army*, Random House 1991

Hedin, Sven, *Big Horses Flight*, The Macmillan Company 1936

Hsiao-Ting, Lin, *Tibet and Nationalist China's Frontier: Intrigues and Ethnopolitics, 1928–49*, University of British Columbia Press 2007

Hsiao-Ting, Lin, *Modern China's Ethnic Frontiers: A Journey to the West*, Routledge 2011

Hung-mao Tien, *Government and Politics in Kuomintang China, 1927–1937*, Stanford University Press 1972

James, William Christopher, *Conflict in the Far East*, Brill Archive 1932

Jarman, Robert. L, *China Political Reports 1911–1960, Volume 5*, Archive Editions 2001

Jocelyn Ed, McEwen Andrew, *The Long March: The True Story Behind the Legendary Journey that Made Mao's China*, Constable 2006

Jowett Philip, *Rays of the Rising Sun: Armed Forces of Japan's Asian Allies 1931–45, Volume 1, China & Manchukuo*, Helion 2004

Jowett Philip, *China's Wars: Rousing the Dragon 1894–1949*, Osprey 2013

Kapp, Robert. A, *Szechwan and the Chinese Republic 1911–1938*, Yale University Press 1973

Kamal Ahmad, *Land Without Laughter*, Charles Scribners Sons 1940

Lary, Diana, *Region and Nation: The Kwangsi Clique in Chinese Politics, 1925–1937*, Cambridge University Press 1974

Levich, Eugene William, *The Kwangsi Way in Kuomintang China, 1931–1939*, Bme, Sharpe 1993

Lindt, A.R, *Special Correspondent: With Bandit & General in Manchuria*, 1933

Mitter, Rana, *The Manchurian Myth: Nationalism, Resistance and Collaboration in Modern China*, University of California Press 2000

Montgomery, Michael, *Imperialist Japan: The Yen to Dominate*, St Martins Press 1987

Morgan Young, A, *Imperial Japan 1926–1938*, George Allen & Unwin Ltd 1938

Newman, Major Harry. T., *Henry L. Stimson and the Japanese Dilemma, 1931–1932*, Pickle Partners Publishing 2014

Nish, Ian Hill, *Japan's Struggle with Internationalism: Japan, China and the League of Nations 1931–1933*, Routledge 1993

Nish, Ian Hill, *Japanese Foreign Policy in the Interwar Period*, Praeger 2002

Paine. S.C.M, *The Wars For Asia 1911–1949*, Cambridge University Press 2012

Powell, John. B, *My Twenty Five Years in China*, The Macmillan Company 1942

See Heng Teow, *Japan's Cultural Policy toward China, 1918–1931; A Comparative Perspective*, Harvard University Asia Center 1999

Sheridan, James. E, *Chinese Warlord: The Career of Feng Yu-Hsiang*, Stanford University Press 1966

Sheridan, James. E, *China in Disintegration*, The Free Press 1975

Snow, Edgar, *Far Eastern Front*, H.Smith & R.Haas 1933

Snow, Edgar, *Red Star Over China*, Victor Gollancz Ltd 1968

Starr, Frederick. S, *Xikiang: China's Muslim Borderland*, M.E.Sharpe 2004

Tatsuji Takeuchi, *War and Diplomacy in the Japanese Empire*, Routledge 2010

Teichman, Sir Eric, *Journey to Turkistan*, Hodder & Stoughton Ltd 1940

Van de Ven, Hans, *War and Nationalism in China: 1925–1945*, Routledge 2003

Vespa, Amleto, *Secret Agent of Japan*, Garden City Publishing Company Ltd 1938

Woodhead, H.G.W., *The China Year Book, 1934, The North China Daily News & Herald* 1934


## Articles and Papers

Boyd, James, 'In Pursuit of an Obsession: Japan in Inner Mongolia in the 1930s', Japanese Studies, Vol 22, No 3, 2002

Coogan, Anthony, 'The Volunteer Armies of North-East China', *History Today*, July 1993.

Hearn, Lawrence, 'Suiyuan: Heart of Eastern Asia', *China Today*, December 1936

Rossinger, Lawrence. K, 'Six Years of Revolt in Manchuria', *Amerasia,* December 1937

Walsh, Billie. K., 'The German Military Mission in China 1928–38', *Journal of Modern History* # 46, September 1974.

*North China Daily News*, December 2nd 1936

*The China Weekly Review*, February 15th 1936, November 21st 1936, November 28th 1936, December 5th 1936

# INDEX